Dreaming the New Woman

Dreaming the New Woman

An Oral History of Missionary Schoolgirls in Republican China

JENNIFER BOND

OXFORD
UNIVERSITY PRESS

Oxford University Press is a department of the University of Oxford. It furthers
the University's objective of excellence in research, scholarship, and education
by publishing worldwide. Oxford is a registered trade mark of Oxford University
Press in the UK and certain other countries.

Published in the United States of America by Oxford University Press
198 Madison Avenue, New York, NY 10016, United States of America.

© Oxford University Press 2024

All rights reserved. No part of this publication may be reproduced, stored in
a retrieval system, or transmitted, in any form or by any means, without the
prior permission in writing of Oxford University Press, or as expressly permitted
by law, by license, or under terms agreed with the appropriate reproduction
rights organization. Inquiries concerning reproduction outside the scope of the
above should be sent to the Rights Department, Oxford University Press, at the
address above.

You must not circulate this work in any other form
and you must impose this same condition on any acquirer.

CIP data is on file at the Library of Congress

ISBN 978-0-19-765479-8

DOI: 10.1093/oso/9780197654798.001.0001

Printed by Integrated Books International, United States of America

In memory of Rosalyn Koo (Chen Jinming 陳晉明*)*
McTyeire class of 1947
1926–2021

Contents

Acknowledgments ix
Note on Chinese Sources xiii

Introduction: Finding Students' Own Voices 1

1. Establishing Missionary Schools for Girls in East China 20
2. Envisioning a Gendered Christian Republic 52
3. Dreaming the New Woman 83
4. Awakening: The War, 1937–1945 119
5. Negotiating Christian and Communist Identities 152
6. Reimagining Missionary Schools for Girls 186

Appendix: List of Interviewees 211
Notes 217
Bibliography 251
Index 273

Acknowledgments

I am deeply grateful to many people and institutions that have provided support and encouragement as this book took shape. The book is based on research I carried out in pursuit of my PhD degree at the School of Oriental and African Studies (SOAS), University of London. I would like to thank my doctoral supervisor, Andrea Janku, who generously read many versions of my thesis and was unfailingly encouraging throughout the project. I would also like to thank my other doctoral supervisors, who gave me invaluable feedback and advice, including Lars Laamann and Eleanor Newbigin at SOAS and Jiang Jin at East China Normal University (ECNU), Shanghai, where I undertook my fieldwork.

This book would not have been possible without the help of seventy-five alumnae who generously shared memories of their schooldays with me. I am indebted to every one of my interviewees, and a complete list of their names can be found in the appendix. I am particularly grateful to Zhang Long and Rosalyn Koo (1926–2021), who invited me to attend the McTyeire alumnae reunions in San Mateo, California, in 2016 and 2017. Rosalyn kindly hosted me in San Francisco and introduced me to many of the McTyeire alumnae living in California. I will always remember her generosity, energy, and good humor. I am also grateful to Xu Meizhen and Xiao Jiaxun for putting me in touch with the Shanghai Number Three Girls' School. They shared with me many of the photographs that appear in this book and reminisced about their schooldays while walking around their school campus with me. Yu Huigeng and Wu Yan of the Beijing branch of the St. Mary's Alumnae Association were instrumental in helping me to contact alumnae in Beijing. Family members of alumnae, especially Debbie Soon and Robert Wu, provided me with access to invaluable sources and practical assistance. Other interviewees to whom I owe my sincerest thanks include Zhang Luoluo, Zhu Lizhong, Pastor Cao Shengjie, and Lucy Hong, who not only kindly shared their memories with me but also became good friends.

Between 2015 and 2019 I undertook research for this book in the United Kingdom, China, and the United States. I am grateful to the following people and institutions for their help in connecting me to alumnae and accessing archival collections. At the Sicheng Church in Hangzhou, Pastor Chen Wei shared with me his deep knowledge of Christianity in Zhejiang Province and helped me to contact Hangzhou Union Girls' School alumnae. At the Shanghai Number Three Girls' School, I am indebted to Chen Jinyu, He Yanan, and Xu Yongchu, who introduced me to many alumnae and helped me to access the archives at the Shanghai Number Three Girls' School. I am also very grateful to the following librarians and archivists who provided generous assistance with my research: Ms. Pan and Qian Yiguo at the Ningbo City Archives, Mr. Sun and his team at Ningbo Education History Museum, Joan Duffy and Kevin Crawford at Yale Divinity School, Lisa Jacobson at the Presbyterian Archives and History Centre, Frances Lyon-Bristol at the Methodist Archives and History Centre, Deborah Bingham Van Broekhoven at the Baptist Historical Archives, Tim Horning at the University of Pennsylvania, and Lance Martin at SOAS Archives.

Several scholars and friends in China and the United States provided me with vital advice and practical assistance during my fieldwork. In particular, I would like to thank Sun Bowen at Nottingham University, Ningbo, who accompanied me on several trips to the Ningbo City Archives, and Lu Hui, who helped me to access the Zhejiang Provincial Archives. Bill Lee, who I first met when researching one of his ancestors in China in 2015, hosted me in San Francisco and drove me to interview several alumnae in the Bay Area. Gail Hershatter introduced me to Joseph Wampler and Betty Bar, who spoke to me about their parents' careers in China and provided me with access to invaluable primary sources. I am also very grateful to Tao Feiya and Xiao Qinghe of Shanghai University, Yuan Jin at Fudan University, University Gong Yingyan of Ningbo University, Zhou Donghua of Hangzhou Normal University, Li Xueping at Zhejiang University, and Ying Yin at ECNU, Shanghai.

This book was completed with the support of several scholarships and research grants. These include a three-year Arts and Humanities Research Council Doctoral Award (1353062). I was able to undertake my doctoral fieldwork in China with funding from the Confucius Institute, SOAS Elizabeth Croll, and Doctoral Fieldwork Awards. My thanks also go to the University of San Francisco Ricci Institute for a Travel Grant Award which enabled me to carry out fieldwork in San Francisco. I thank Wu Xiaoxin and Mark Mir for their kind assistance when I visited the Ricci Institute and for putting me in touch with many of the scholars mentioned above.

My current and former colleagues at Durham University, University College Dublin, and University College London gave me much-appreciated advice on the publishing process and provided great moral support as I completed the manuscript. Thanks, in particular, to Georgina Brewis, Chris Courtney, Lily Chang, Catherine Cox, Mark Freeman, Robert Gerwarth, Jennifer Keating, William Mulligan, and Fionnuala Walsh. I am also grateful to the following people whose scholarly advice, friendship, and pastoral support have been invaluable: Ryan Dunch, Harriet Evans, Gail Hershatter, Henrietta Harrison, Isabella Jackson, Joan Judge, Jennifer Lin, Rosemary Seaton, Francis Slater, Gary Tiedemann, Kailing Xie, Lara Yang, Wang Zheng and Harriet Zurndorfer. I would like to say a special thank-you to friends and colleagues who kindly read early drafts of chapters and made suggestions, including Mark Baker, Paul Bailey, Chris Courtney, Louise Edwards, Elisabeth Forster, Natascha Gentz, Shiamin Kwa, Helena Lopes, Coraline Jortay, Chang Liu, Helen Schneider, Fionnuala Walsh, and Shi Xia.

At Oxford University Press, I would like to thank Nancy Toff and Rada Radojicic for steering this book through publication with great kindness and thoughtfulness. My thanks also go to Bala Subramanian and Debra Ruel as well as the two anonymous peer reviewers.

I am extremely grateful to Judy Bloomfield, who proofread the whole manuscript for me at several stages and provided invaluable editorial support during the publication process.

Finally, I would like to thank all my family in the United Kingdom and China for their unfailing love and support. In particular, I would like to thank my parents, parents-in-law, grandma, and siblings, who have always encouraged and believed in me. My deepest thanks and love go to my husband, Yitao, for his tireless support and care of me and our daughter, Sophia, who arrived as this book was going to print.

Some material from Chapter 2 has been published previously in Jennifer Bond, "'How I Am Brought into the Light': Representations of Childhood by Missionary Schoolgirls in East China," *Twentieth Century China* 48, no. 3 (October 2023): 250–269. Material from Chapter 4 of this book will appear in a chapter entitled: "'At the Centre of a Tornado': Missionary Schoolgirls' Experiences of the Second-Sino Japanese War in Shanghai," in *Rethinking Childhood in Modern Chinese History*, ed. Isabella Jackson and Yushu Geng (London: Routledge, forthcoming).

Note on Chinese Sources

Chinese names and place names are Romanized using the standard Hanyu Pinyin in most cases throughout the book with the exception of names which are well known in Wade Giles, such as Chiang Kai-shek. I refer to alumnae by their English names when they introduced themselves to me by those names. When citing students' contemporary English language writings, I have used their own Romanization of their names, adding the modern Hanyu Pinyin spelling and Chinese characters where possible in the main text for clarity. The traditional form of Chinese characters is used throughout the book except when citing texts published in simplified characters.

Introduction

Finding Students' Own Voices

On a sunny day in February 1992 a group of alumnae, dressed in blue to represent their class color, posed for a photo in front of their old school dormitory, Lambuth-Clopton Hall, today known as May First Hall (Wuyi tang 五一堂), on the campus of the Number Three Girls' School in Shanghai (Shanghai shi di san nüzi zhongxue 上海市第三女子中學). This was an immensely special day for the alumnae, who had traveled to the school from across the globe to celebrate the centenary of one of its missionary school forerunners, McTyeire (Zhongxi nüzhong 中西女中), founded in 1892 by the American Methodist Episcopal Mission.[1] Earlier in the day they had once again assembled in Richardson Hall, now May Fourth Hall (Wusi tang 五四堂), to remember their school history. A baby grand piano, procured by the alumnae for the occasion, acted as a reminder of the school's excellent reputation for music. Their old headmistress, Xue Zheng 薛正, now ninety-three years old and the honorary principal of Number Three Girls' School, beamed proudly at the achievements of her old pupils.

After the ceremony they filed outside through the entrance hall, where the stained-glass windows pooled yellow and orange light onto their whitening hair, out onto the immaculate lawns for the photo shoot. Alumnae clutched at the green and gold gas-filled balloons emblazoned with the McTyeire emblem and motto, "Live, Love and Grow," while current pupils of the Number Three Girls' School stood around, shyly watching and offering help to the alumnae who were their counterparts of a different age: honored bearers of the school's newly prestigious missionary past. Rosalyn Koo (Chen Jinming 陳晉明, McTyeire, class of 1947) remembered: "It was an all-day affair and at night we had glow sticks. And we walked around, singing music. Xue Zheng was so happy."[2]

Two decades earlier, such an event to celebrate the history of their school would have been impossible. In Mao's China, missionary schools were branded as "tools of cultural imperialism" and their pupils labeled "foreign

2   DREAMING THE NEW WOMAN

A group of McTyeire alumnae from the class of 1946 gather at the school's centennial anniversary in 1992. Alumnae wear their class color (blue) and sweaters emblazoned with the school motto "Live, Love and Grow." *Courtesy of Xu Meizhen.*

Lambuth-Clopton Hall, built in 1922, was the dormitory building on the McTyeire school campus, located on Edinburgh Road, Shanghai. These luxurious Western-style buildings were funded by the high tuition fees that McTyeire, as an elite missionary school for girls, could charge. In 1952 McTyeire and St. Mary's were merged to become the Shanghai Number Three Girls' School. *Courtesy of United Methodist Church Archives—GCAH, Madison, New Jersey.*

lackeys" who had aided Western powers' encroachment of China. Indeed, by the 1940s the students who could afford to attend missionary schools for girls were from China's social and political elite, including the Soong sisters and the daughters of the Yong'an Department Store owners. On the eve of the Communist Revolution in 1949, many students whose family members worked for or were well connected to the Nationalist Party (Guomindang) left China for Taiwan, Hong Kong, and the United States. For alumnae still living in the twenty-first century, who had left China in their late teens and early twenties, their memories of their schooldays, which occupied six days of the week, constitute the most salient memories of their life in China and thus form an important part of their identities as Chinese. This is why for many alumnae like Rosalyn Koo, who visited China after Deng's reform and opening policies of 1978 for the first time in over three decades, finding out what had happened to their schools, teachers, and classmates was so important.

In an age where fluency in English and a foreign-style education once again confer social and cultural capital, alumnae saw an opportunity to restore their school and former headmistress to their former glory. They decided to recapture its history and direct its future development through their financial investment in the school. Koo explained that the first step was to "restore English and music, and get rid of the boys."[3] She mobilized the alumnae to donate to the school, with one alumna living in Taiwan donating US$100,000. According to Koo, the alumnae bought the school instruments to form a brass band, a new computer laboratory, and a revamped gymnasium.[4] Today, the Number Three Girls' School is the only government-run, all-girls school in Shanghai, and it is renowned for producing girls who are both academically and musically outstanding, much like the *guixiu* 閨秀, or accomplished upper-class young ladies who graduated from the school before 1949.

The reunion of 1992 marked the start of a new era in the history of missionary schools in China and the culmination of the work of the alumnae, who after all these years had not forgotten their almae matres. Now, at last, they were able to formally celebrate the illustrious history of their school and their own elite status in Republican China. The alumnae included not only famous political wives and the daughters of business magnates, but also writers, scientists, educators, doctors, bankers, lawyers, diplomats, pastors, feminists, and revolutionaries. Among them was Lucy Hong (Hong Lüming 洪侶明, McTyeire class of 1948), daughter of pastor Hong Deying 洪德應

and wife of the Episcopal bishop of China, Shen Yifan 沈以藩. After graduation Lucy Hong had entered St. John's University and devoted her life to helping establish an independent Chinese church through her contributions to Chinese church music and work for the Chinese YWCA. Rosalyn Koo, the main instigator of the reunion, had been a tomboy at school and had almost been expelled for rebelling against an English language teacher. Her parents had had her shipped off to an elite women's college on the West Coast of the United States in 1948 to prevent her from becoming a Communist. Another rebel, who wanted to run away to Yan'an to join the Communist Party, was Ellen Cao (Cao Baozhen 曹寶貞, McTyeire class of 1939). Rejecting the superficiality and extravagance of her dormitory-mates, Ellen was awakened to the inequalities in Chinese society through participating in social service activities organized by the YWCA during the Second Sino-Japanese War. She did succeed in becoming a Chinese Communist Party (CCP) member and worked to influence other students at the school to join the Communist Party. This history of missionary schools for girls in China is by no means a straightforward one, and many different versions of their story could be told. It is also a highly political and personal one, as each member of the school had different experiences and took a different path upon graduation. Collectively, the alumnae's memories allow us a unique insight into how girls experienced mission education at the beginning of the twentieth century and how these experiences influenced their lives and later careers.

This book explores the history of missionary schools for girls in East China from the perspective of alumnae themselves. Within much historiography of the Republican period, Christian women are subject to a threefold process of exclusion. For many historians, particularly those of the Maoist era, their elite status marked them as the wrong class. Moreover, their status as Christians marked them as being of questionable loyalty to the nation—they were seen as subjects of a process of Western cultural imperialism. And their status as women meant that they were considered to have little agency in the politics of the Republican era. Yet the way that history has viewed these women is in marked contrast to the way these women perceived themselves. In their experiments with gender, Christianity, and nationalism, girls advanced a form of gendered Christian modernity—that is, a vision of how highly educated Christian Chinese women, such as themselves, could transform and strengthen the nation, allowing China to stand up to and eventually overtake encroaching imperialist powers, such as Japan. By virtue of their Christian education, missionary-educated women saw themselves as uniquely positioned to minister to the needs and transform the lives of their downtrodden female compatriots.

In the process of positioning themselves as China's elite, missionary-educated Chinese women adapted and assimilated different aspects of their Sino-foreign school experience to create new ways of being an elite woman in modern China. They took on board missionaries' exhortations for them to be models of Chinese womanhood but created their own version of that model: She was not only the perfect Christian housewife but also a politically active national citizen. She adopted certain elements of Western gentility—how to appear in public, raise her children, and keep house—but rejected faulting displays of commodified modernity (such as too much makeup and overly tight *qipao* 旗袍) as gauche.[5] She could even, in aspiration if not in reality, work for the benefit of China in a fulfilling career as well as having a happy marriage and family life. By creating this model of Christian womanhood, missionary-educated girls positioned themselves as trailblazers: They were the ones who could represent China to the Western world, restore her national pride, and even become the leaders of the international women's movement. Alumnae memories also testify to the paradoxes of being a missionary-educated woman in this period: The school offered girls a space where they could dream new roles for themselves and experiment with new gendered subject positions. Upon graduation, however, girls woke up to the reality of a society in which traditional ideas about women's homemaking roles were firmly entrenched.

Telling Stories about Mission Schools for Girls

The story of missionary schools in China has been reinvented many times with the momentous political and social changes that have marked China's twentieth century. In much of the early literature, missionaries themselves took center stage and Chinese women were presented as the passive recipients of a modernizing "Western-style" education, unbinding their feet and freeing them from arranged marriages. Apart from a few studies of well-known Christian women who received a missionary school education and became pioneers in the fields of medicine and education and missionary work, such as Ida Khan (Kang Aide 康愛德), Mary Stone (Shi Meiyu 石美玉), Yang Buwei 楊步偉, Zeng Baosun 曾寶蓀, and Christiana Tsai (Cai Sujuan 蔡蘇娟), who left biographies, we know very little about how Chinese women experienced the education they received at school.[6] As Kwok Pui-lan has observed, it is much harder to find Chinese women's voices in the missionary archive.[7]

Within the field of Chinese women's studies, which has blossomed since the 1980s, very little systematic attention has been played to the role of Christianity in the emergence of the Chinese New Woman. Wang Zheng's case studies of May Fourth women provide tantalizing evidence of the important role that Christianity played in the lives and careers of educators Chen Yongshen and Lu Lihua.[8] In histories of the Chinese women's movement, missionary schools are usually briefly mentioned by scholars as the start of public education for women but are then largely ignored. In the writings of early CCP feminists such as Xiang Jingyu 向警予, the Christian women's movement was dismissed as a bourgeois, foreign-inspired form of feminism, one that could not provide a foundation for a true Chinese women's movement.[9] In anglophone historiography since the 1980s, calls from scholars such as Paul Cohen to shift our focus away from foreigners and foreign institutions in China in favor of a more Chinese-centered approach have resulted in an aversion to giving too much attention to the role of Christianity in China.[10]

Unfortunately, this has resulted in the mislabeling and dismissal of missionary schools for girls as essentially foreign institutions, enclaves that were rather closed off from the rest of Chinese society. This perspective denies the agency of the generations of Chinese women who passed through their doors and created unique cultures within their schools. It also fails to recognize the substantial shift in the composition and governance of missionary schools over the course of the modern era. After 1927, missionary schools had to register with the Guomindang (GMD) government, which required them to have a Chinese headmistress and for a majority of board members to be Chinese. Indeed, by the 1930s missionaries were rather marginal actors in the life and running of missionary schools in treaty-port China, which were essentially Chinese-run institutions. However, the image of these schools as "foreign" has been a persistent one, to the extent that recent studies of modern Chinese education, nationalism, and citizenship often leave out the missionary schools on the grounds of their supposedly non-Chinese status.[11] By doing so, scholars have missed an important conception of citizenship that developed in the Republican period: a gendered Christian notion of citizenship.

Over the last three decades, scholars have sought to address this imbalance, examining how Christianity became a Chinese religion through the efforts of male and female Christians to apply their faith to the problems faced by Chinese society in the early twentieth century.[12] Much of this scholarship on the Sinicization of Christianity has focused on leading male Chinese Protestant reformers. A few studies on protestant women have looked at their pioneering roles in medicine, education, and social service. These include studies of Shi Meiyu and Kang Cheng, early female Chinese Christian doctors whose service was a result of the medical training they received in the United States.[13] The careers of Christian women educators and the social service contributions of women who worked for the Young Women's Christian Association (YWCA) have also been uncovered.[14] Still, the contours of how Chinese protestant women framed their nation-building contributions and their visions for a new gendered Christian Republic, remain unclear. According to Ryan Dunch, the heyday for Chinese protestants' nation-building activities, which were founded on visions of a liberal democratic Christian China, ended with the rise of authoritarian state actors, first the Nationalist (GMD), and then the Chinese Communist Party (CCP).[15]

The writings and memories of missionary schoolgirls provide crucial evidence of Chinese women's agency in creating a vision of a Protestant modernity for China, which was distinct in many ways from a male vision. Indeed, the 1930s can be seen as a period where many Christian ideas about women's gendered roles in society came to fruition. Unlike their male counterparts, Christian women never tied their vision of a Chinese Christian Republic so strongly to democratic politics. Instead, they believed an alliance of Christian womanhood would have the power to transform the nation via the home. The New Life Movement launched by Chiang Kai-shek's government in 1934, which called on women to rejuvenate the nation via their homemaking roles, was therefore by no means contradictory to the protestant vision of a model gendered modernity for Chinese women but, in fact, reinforced it. This rather conservative version of the Christian New Woman as moral homemaker thus became part of an officially endorsed gender ideology in Republican China.[16]

This book explores how missionary schoolgirls developed new ideas about how to be a modern Chinese woman in their writings and experiences at school. In thinking about how students combined aspects of their school experience with nationalism and feminism in this period, the book is less concerned with the theological contributions of Chinese women leaders to the Church, which have already been the focus of much excellent work.[17] By focusing on how girls experienced missionary education and what girls did with this education, rather than on whether or not they defined themselves as Christian, we can gain a broader perspective on the influence of Christianity in early twentieth-century China. This book builds on Hyaeweol Choi's conception of "Protestant modernity" that she developed for colonial Korea.[18] Choi points out that in Koreans' own vision of Protestant modernity (as distinct from the missionary one), sometimes the spiritual may have been secondary to more material and mundane advantages to women who had some affiliation to Christian institutions: "Christian affiliation tended to provide opportunities for education, employment, leadership, and even lifestyle. It is in this coalescing dynamic between the sacred and the secular, and between discourse and experience, that the concept of Protestant modernity can be fruitfully understood."[19] By the 1930s most girls at elite missionary schools such as McTyeire did not define themselves as Christian. However, by virtue of their elite status by the 1920s, these schools served as transmitters of new performances of female gentility which were being created, enacted, and policed by several generations of elite Chinese women who passed through their doors.

Middle (Wo)men: Networks and Agency

In the Sino-foreign treaty-port world of Republican Shanghai, missionary schoolgirls helped to shape new ideas about how an elite modern Chinese woman should behave. A fluency in English, Western social graces, membership in Christian churches, and sometimes a foreign degree admitted them as members of a new Western-educated Chinese elite. The cultural hybridity of their school experience equipped them with the skills to successfully navigate and become fluent interpreters or mediators of a cosmopolitan world, which they were simultaneously the participants in and creators of. Chen Hengzhe 陳衡哲, the only non–missionary school graduate to win the first round of Chinese government scholarships for women to study in the United States in 1914, recalled how she felt socially awkward and ill equipped for life in America compared to her missionary-educated classmates: "I was an absolute 'green-horn' in the whole procedure, for I was the only girl amongst the candidates that had not attended a missionary school, where examples of American ways of living were not lacking, and the American mentality was not an entirely strange phenomenon."[20] There have been myriad studies of the formation of "cosmopolitanism" in Republican-era Shanghai.[21] While Hanchao Lu has suggested that this cosmopolitanism was not experienced by ordinary Chinese residents, Isabella Jackson, although cautioning against the positive connotations of the word "cosmopolitanism," shows that the transnational Shanghai Municipal Council did have a dramatic impact on the lives of poor Chinese living in the international settlement via their public works and health initiatives.[22]

In contrast, for the elite upper classes (my interviewees) this cosmopolitan modernity was a lived reality. Girls spent their free time shopping in the commercial district on Nanjing Road or attending theaters and cinemas showing the latest American films. They appeared on the front covers of fashionable magazines in Western-style dresses. Girls communicated to each other within the school in three languages (English, Shanghainese, and later Mandarin) and made jokes based on their reading of English literature and Chinese cultural habits. They acquired a dual set of knowledge about how to run their households and switched between polite Chinese and American manners and social graces effortlessly. They equipped themselves for their studies abroad by polishing their Western-style table manners, posture, and deportment. They lived and worked alongside missionary teachers and then in the company of American and British peers when they went to school overseas. They were the interpreters of a hybrid social world of the treaty ports. It was very much a city with multiple racial, class, dialect, and religious boundaries, which by virtue of their class, gender, religion, and education they were uniquely positioned—and, in their view, entitled—to traverse.[23]

Christian-educated Chinese women were therefore just as much, if not more so, the "middlemen" or compradors of treaty-port cities as their counterparts who dealt with foreigners on a daily basis in their business transactions.[24] Jeffrey N. Wasserstrom has hinted that Chinese women were active "nodes of contact" in the networks which linked foreign and Chinese Shanghai which have largely been treated as separate entities in the literature on treaty-port cities. Wasserstrom has used the example of Song Meiling 宋美齡, who was perhaps the most well-known example of a Christian-educated Chinese woman.[25] Others quickly spring to mind: Yang Buwei, the first Chinese woman to co-open her own maternity hospital in Beijing; and Wu Yifang 吳貽芳, president of Ginling Women's College, to name two well-known examples. However, the lives and experience of many other Chinese Christian-educated women who were the creators of Shanghai's cosmopolitanism, remain unknown. Missionary schoolgirls were such effective middle-women precisely because they grew up at the boundaries of a hybrid cultural world, and any understanding of Shanghai's cosmopolitanism is incomplete if we ignore the important role they played in its creation.

That is not to say that tensions did not exist. Chinese women found the overbearing cultural superiority of their Western teachers, who were in fact often their social inferiors in terms of class, irritating.[26] They could not accompany their missionary teachers to Western-only summer resorts or enter the exclusive public parks in Shanghai's international concession. These exclusions and boundaries all fed into Chinese women's conceptualization of a distinctly independent Chinese Christianity. However, while post-colonial perspectives have provided a very necessary corrective to our understanding of missionary education in China, focusing too much on boundaries and resistance obscures what was created by native elites in the process of adaptive, two-way transfer. Henrietta Harrison and Ryan Dunch have both explored how homogenization and differentiation are mutually constitutive processes in the globalization of Christianity.[27] Dunch explains how focusing on indigenous agency in the missionary encounter is key to this.[28]

In thinking about how to re-center our focus on Chinese Christian women's agency within the story of Chinese Christianity and the Chinese women's movement, the insights posed by Xia Shi are particularly helpful. Xia puts forward the concept of "collective agency" to describe how married women who did not receive a modern education were, through the support of male relatives and family and lineage networks, active in transforming public philanthropy in the early twentieth century.[29] Similarly, while elite Chinese women who had received a missionary school education undoubtably had the resources to act more independently than their home-based counterparts, in fact it is only by studying these elite Chinese women's networks and family contacts that we can understand their career trajectories. Family, missionary, alumnae, and other Christian networks for women, such as the YWCA, provided girls with crucial stepping stones into careers outside the home. Christian-educated Zeng Baosun, for instance, was able to start her own Christian school for girls in Changsha partly because she had access to powerful family and government connections which enabled her to use the Zeng Guofan ancestral temple in Changsha as her campus.[30] We cannot, therefore, understand the life choices and careers of Chinese Christian women out of their social context, family ties, and new Christian networks which they created for themselves.

Case Studies

In this book I focus on girls who attended missionary school in five cities across East China. In Shanghai: St. Mary's Hall (Shengmaliya nüxiao 聖瑪利亞女校), founded by the American Episcopal Church in 1881; and McTyeire (Zhongxi nüzhong 中西女中), an American Methodist Episcopal school founded in 1892. In Ningbo and Hangzhou I concentrate on two union schools for girls: Riverside Academy (Yongjiang nüzhong 甬江女中), established in Ningbo in 1923 by the Northern Presbyterians and Northern Baptists (and in 1934 joined by the English Methodists); and Hangzhou Union Girls' School (Hongdao nüzhong 弘道女中), established by a merger of the Northern Presbyterian and Northern Baptist girls' schools in Hangzhou in 1912. In Suzhou I examine the Laura Haygood Normal School (Jinghai shifan nüzhong 景海師範女中), established by the American Methodist Episcopal Church in 1902.

All of these schools were Protestant missionary middle schools for girls. Although Catholic schools for girls did exist in substantial numbers, they tended to remain smaller, less elite institutions, with the exception of Catholic schools for girls in Shanghai's French concession, such as Aurora Women's College (Zhendan nüzi wenli xueyuan 震旦女子文理學院) and its associated girls' high school (Zhendan nüzi zhongxue 震旦女子中學). This is because the treaty-port business world was dominated by Anglo-American business interests, which resulted in a demand for English language education for the new treaty-port commercial elite. New avenues for Chinese women's college education in the US or UK also demanded fluency in English from the middle school level on. Schools established by the Shanghai Municipal Council, which employed foreign teachers, and Christian schools established by Chinese women themselves represent a fascinating avenue for future research, but are, regrettably, outside the scope of this study.

This book focuses on middle school–level education which, with the exception of a few case studies, has attracted much less attention than the study of Christian universities.[31] This lack of attention is partly because missionary middle schools are much harder to trace in both Chinese and foreign missionary archives than the universities, which left more records. Many records were lost or destroyed when the schools were merged in the People's Republic of China (PRC) reorganization of the national education system in 1952. Schools that did not register with the GMD government after 1927 are even more difficult to find traces of in Chinese archives. One might ask: Why go to the trouble of looking at missionary middle schools for girls when the documentary evidence is much harder to trace? What remains gives us a fragmentary insight into what was a formative period in students' lives. The writings of daydreaming teenagers, aged between eleven and eighteen on average, provide an important perspective into how girls imaginatively harnessed Christianity to nationalism and feminism at an impressionable and often idealistic age. They also provide us with an insight into what remained throughout the Republican period an all-female environment. By the 1930s most primary schools and universities (Christian, government, and private) had become co-educational.[32] However, middle school–level education was (and still is) regarded as a period where girls do better academically in a single-sex environment, and many Christian girls' middle schools resisted becoming co-educational during this period. This all-female environment was crucial to the gendered experiments that daydreaming girls performed within their school.

Apart from an all-female environment, missionary middle schools for girls maintained other selling points which distinguished them from government and Chinese private schools. They were the main providers of higher-level middle school education for girls (outside the teacher training system) well into the 1920s. This meant that for the tiny minority of elite women who aspired to go to university in the first few decades of the twentieth century, missionary middle schools often offered the best academic training that could prepare them for higher education. They also maintained unique Sino-foreign campus cultures and strengths in English, Music, Dance, and Drama. Rather than civics classes, missionary schools utilized different religious aspects of school life, from daily prayer and chapel services to songs, hymns, and literature as the main means by which they attempted to mold moral citizens.

Focusing on five schools across four cities in East China also helps us to put the modernity that was developing in Shanghai into perspective. Scholars have rightly stressed the uniqueness of Shanghai in contrast to other Chinese cities the early twentieth century. By the 1920s it was the commercial and cultural capital, which Chinese visitors from other cities and provinces often felt to be a rather different place from their home towns with the presence of its large foreign concessions, coffee shops, dance halls, shopping and amusement centers. In some ways the missionary schools that developed in Shanghai reflect the city's unusual status. Due to the extraordinary concentration of merchant wealth in the city, they were generally larger, better equipped, and more expensive than the average missionary middle school for girls across the region.³³ With their elite reputations and status as pioneers, their catchment areas reached to provinces as distant as Guangdong, Shandong, and Sichuan. In contrast, missionary schools in Ningbo, Hangzhou, and Suzhou tended to have a more local catchment, but still attracted the new merchant-gentry and politician families of these wealthy lower Yangzi cities. These cities had long histories as centers of commerce, and like Shanghai were also newly, if less rapidly, industrializing.³⁴

In other ways, the Christian modernity that missionary schoolgirls envisioned was surprisingly similar across this region. Anti-foreign and anti-Christian nationalism that engulfed China at particular flashpoints during the 1920s was driving girls at missionary schools across China to consider how to be Christian, female, and a patriotic Chinese citizen. During this period, girls used an overlapping gendered, Christian, and patriotic language of "service" to describe their social work with poor women and children and defend their contributions to society. How far this vision of a gendered Christian modernity for China was limited to the treaty ports and other urban centers is much harder to determine. We have some second-hand evidence in girls' writings about their activities and interactions with their rural counterparts that show how girls were trying to spread these ideals of Christian womanhood via their own networks. Concrete evidence for how prevalent and influential these new Christian modes of being a modern woman was outside of the treaty ports and China's major urban areas which had missionary schools for girls, remains elusive however.

Oral and Archival Sources

In order to understand Chinese women's own experience of missionary education, I have drawn on two main types of sources: writings by girls in their annual school magazines and oral history interviews with former pupils. The annual school magazines produced by missionary schools are rich, bilingual, and multivocal sources that give us a fascinating insight into the hopes, fears, and daydreams of teenaged schoolgirls.³⁵ Like other school magazines of this era, missionary school yearbooks contain girls' essays, poetry, short stories, and plays, as well as artwork, cartoons, and doodles. At McTyeire and St. Mary's these yearbooks were also produced by the graduating class as a memento of their schooldays, with class histories and a yearbook page dedicated to each pupil. The yearbooks were started as part of the trend toward student self-governance in the May Fourth period. For girls, they were also conceived as important pedagogical spaces where they could hone their writing and argument skills, preparing them to step into the world of male public political debate upon graduation.[36] Yearbooks are imaginative spaces where students formed their own ideas, literary skills, and reading habits.[37] Alumnae recalled with pride their involvement in the yearbook editorial teams, and their experience as yearbook editors helped some secure jobs upon graduation. Renee Kwang Ming Nieh (Nie Guangming 聶光明, McTyeire class of 1933) recalled how being the business manager of the *McTyeirean* "changed my life." Through her experience in getting advertisements to sponsor the magazine, Kwang was able to get a job in an advertising company which paid her a high salary upon graduation.[38] Similarly, Laura Haygood Normal School graduate Hu Binxia 胡彬夏 went on to become editor-in-chief of an early and influential women's magazine of the period, *The Ladies Journal* (*Funü zazhi* 婦女雜誌).[39]

These magazines were produced for a specific audience of pupils, teachers, missionaries, and parents and thus reflect an officially approved version of the school's daily life. They were also designed to showcase the school and the girls' musical, sporting, and academic achievements to the wider public. The result is a rather rose-tinted image of the school and there was thus little space for negative reflections in these magazines. Indeed, one alumna recalled that their more critical literary compositions in the years immediately prior to the 1949 Communist Revolution would not have been considered appropriate for the school magazines.[40] Each yearbook also had a missionary teacher as an "advisor" sitting on the editorial board, who undoubtably helped with the girls' English-language compositions. While girls certainly self-censored and missionary teachers no doubt helped to edit girls' writings, we should not dismiss these publications as purely top-down productions. Instead, we should view students' writings in this period as a two-way dialectic between pupils and parental and teachers' authority.[41]

The magazines served as important devices for transmitting school and class culture to the next generation of graduates. Today they also act as devices which can transmit and trigger memory. For alumnae they are rare and fragmentary physical reminders of their schooldays. Many personal documents, photographs, or items of clothing from the Republican period did not survive the iconoclasm of the Cultural Revolution. Indeed, although a relatively complete run of the *McTyeirean* and *Phoenix* are preserved in the Shanghai Municipal Archives and Shanghai Library, very few yearbooks for

St. Mary's students who were responsible for editing the English language contributions to the *Phoenix* school magazine in 1932 pose for a photo. The editor-in-chief, Ouyang Airong, sits in the center next to Miss Catherine Barnaby, who was the faculty advisor. The positioning of the students suggests that girls were supposed to take the lead in the production of the magazine. Being an editor on the school magazine board also provided important vocational work experience for students, some of whom worked as editors and journalists upon graduation. *Photo from The Phoenix (1932), Shanghai Number Three Girls' School.*

other missionary schools in this region survive. Most schools also halted production of their yearbooks during the war years. McTyeire published a retrospective volume for the years 1940–1945, but St. Mary's ceased publication of its yearbook in 1941. We are thus left with gaps in our understanding of how girls weathered the Civil War years or experienced the 1949 Revolution.

I therefore turned to an even richer and more complicated source of information for girls' experience of their missionary education: oral history interviews with alumnae themselves. I interviewed seventy-five alumnae from the five schools under study. I contacted interviewees via the school alumnae associations, using a snowball sampling technique. As a result, my interviewees tended to cluster in groups of classmates or friendship groups who have remained in contact with each other. For example, I interviewed ten alumnae from the class of 1947. Contacting alumnae via the alumnae associations also meant that I was mainly getting a positive image of their schools, from graduates who had made the effort to stay in touch with their almae matres. St. Mary's and McTyeire as two of the most prestigious schools for girls in the Republican era had larger and much more active alumnae networks than smaller schools for girls outside of Shanghai. St. Mary's also benefited from its institutional ties to St. John's University, which was run by the same mission and has an alumni association that functions globally. As a result, I was able to collect many more interviews with St. Mary's and McTyeire graduates than those from smaller schools such as Riverside Academy in Ningbo and the Hangzhou Union School for Girls.

Rather than having a script with a set of questions for each interview, I learned to let the interviewees direct the flow of conversation, adapting myself to their own interests and storytelling style as much as possible. This sometimes resulted in hours-long conversations that spanned their whole lives from their family background, schooldays, experience in Mao's China, and later careers. Interviewing alumnae who had remained in China after 1949 and those who had left to live in the United States revealed important differences in how they wanted their schools to be remembered. Were missionary schools elite or down to earth? Open or closed-off to society? Foreign or Chinese? Religious or rather secular in their environment? In the course of my research, I realized such binary framings were more a product of the alumnae's experiences since graduation and modern-day preoccupations to combat the pervasiveness of the political narratives about their schools than reflective of their school experience at the time.

Having suffered in Mao's China from the label that they had attended a "foreign," "closed-off," and "elite" school for girls, many alumnae living in China were at pains to explain how their schools were by no means ivory towers, but were in fact politically engaged, secular, Chinese institutions. In contrast, some of the alumnae who left China before 1949 prided themselves for attending an elite, American missionary school. They were also more likely to talk to me about the religious aspects of their school experience. This fracturing of memory was particularly apparent in alumnae recollections of the Second Sino-Japanese War and Civil War years. Alumnae living in the PRC were keen to stress how they patriotically resisted their Japanese language teacher and to tell me about how they had become interested in communism, whereas alumnae living overseas were much more ambivalent about whether they felt patriotic at school. While we must bear in mind the different political and personal circumstances under which these narratives were recalled, alumnae's complicated and contradictory experiences of their education challenge standard tropes of women's wartime roles and provide further nuances to our conventional chronologies of the war and the 1949 Revolution.

Differences in how alumnae wanted to retell their school's history were also emphasized by Rosalyn Koo, who explained that during the process of editing the official three-volume history of McTyeire, recently published in China, alumnae agreed not to talk about politics or religion, such were the ideological differences which underlay the task.[42] Koo also gave me access to an earlier, unpublished collection of oral history interviews, "Telling Women's Lives," undertaken by her and Heidi Ross in 1992 to celebrate the school's centenary.[43] This volume represents a much more balanced and, at times, critical approach to the school's history, including tensions between staff and pupils, foreigners and Chinese that have largely been smoothed out of the official volumes.[44]

Language affected the course of the interviews, which were sometimes conducted in English, other times in Mandarin, and many times in a mixture of the two languages. At times, my interviewees broke into Shanghainese, which I could only partially understand. This was particularly the case in group interviews, where alumnae would often switch into Shanghainese to address each other. Though focus group interviews presented an excellent opportunity for me to gain an understanding of the school culture as it was performed at reunions, and sometimes prompted further memories than would have been forthcoming individually, at other times I encountered drawbacks in talking to alumnae in a group setting. Some members of the group had less of a chance to speak than others, and negative recollections were largely impossible in such settings. I made the effort to try to interview alumnae individually after I had spoken to them in a group setting, which sometimes yielded different, subversive, or more subtle interpretations of their school experiences. Most alumnae were happy for me to record them and use their real names; a few preferred that I took handwritten notes and preferred to remain anonymous.

Finally, a word must be said about my own relationship to the interviewees. As a young female foreign researcher, I was treated with great kindness and hospitality by many of my interviewees. Some alumnae were keen to talk to me in English, using a language that they had mastered at school but had not used in years. Using a mixture of English and Mandarin sometimes aided their recollections of their schooldays when they were used to switching between several languages. Another condition that encouraged openness was the age differential between me and the interviewee. Because I was a young female graduate student who had an introduction from the university in China that now runs their alumnae association (East China Normal University), some alumnae treated me as a junior *tongxue* 同學—a classmate from the same school. Many of the alumnae whom I interviewed had become teachers, and their desire to impart knowledge and help a younger student, who was more than half a century their junior, was clear in their manner and narratives. They spoke slowly, as to a younger person and foreigner, and explained political events in Chinese history, often assuming I did not know what these were. I was thus able to gain an insight into their understanding of these events. Although there was clearly a didactic and student–teacher relationship dynamic in the interviews, my foreign status may have allowed me to ask more probing and personal questions that may have been considered impertinent if I were a Chinese student.[45] At other times, my foreign status and accented Mandarin proved a drawback when contacting potential interviewees by phone. Having suffered because of their elite status during the Cultural Revolution, I was aware that some memories could be difficult and painful for alumnae to recall.

I have had the great privilege to get to know and interview many remarkable alumnae who attended missionary schools. At the St. John's biannual world reunion in 2016 I was immediately impressed by the grace, eloquence, and talent of these women, some of whom were in their early nineties but were still formidably sharp, both physically and mentally. Rosalyn Koo told me she could always identify a McTyeire girl when she entered the room, and the more I got to know the alumnae, the more I started to appreciate what she had said.[46] As Zhang Luoluo 張羅羅 (McTyeire class of 1947) put it, there was something different about McTyeire and St. Mary's girls, something in the way they carried themselves and spoke, and with many, a great force of personality underlay their polished manners.[47] The extent to which this was a result of the training they received at school will be unpicked in this book, but although trying to maintain the cool, detached eye of a researcher, I myself could not but succumb to their charm, wit, and generosity. I felt myself under great obligation to do justice to the rich memories they had shared with me, while knowing that, trained as a historian, I must unpick their narratives and be critical of the ways in which they presented themselves and their schools. As Antoinette Burton reminds us, we must always be aware of the political and historical situatedness of our own narratives and the power dynamic and potential for violence that claiming authority to "speak for" or authentically "represent" the other engenders.[48] I have endeavored to honor the trust the alumnae placed in me, situating their memories within the social and political changes happening around them. I do not claim to "speak for" the alumnae, for they have already done so eloquently in their own volumes of oral histories. Nevertheless, I hope that the story I tell will be both sensitive to my interviewees' desire for self-representation, while drawing attention to the social, political, personal, and historical circumstances that lie behind their narratives.

As I attempt to analyze the wealth of narratives, both oral and archival, collected for this project, I am keeping in mind Hershatter's advice: "Oral narratives, then, are called forth under particular circumstances, unevenly recorded, selectively remembered, and artfully deployed . . . as indirect commentary on a troubled present. Oral narratives told in the present about the past need to be valued as history of the present precisely for the ways they slip older moorings of meaning and re-lodge to engage new situations. The challenge is not to fix meaning and interpretation, but to keep track of what accounts for changing meanings and interpretations."[49] There are many different contradictory and overlapping narratives which lend themselves to telling many different versions of the schools' histories and the stories of girls who went there. Historical writing, like oral histories and archival sources, is subject to the same silences and distortions by both the teller and the listener. Using oral narratives critically, and in conjunction with documentary sources, paying attention to the weaknesses and exclusions of both, this book aims to glean a more complicated, nuanced, and multifaceted history of the schools, shedding light on what it meant to be a young female student attending a missionary school in early twentieth-century East China, what it means to those individuals today, and how their experiences at school have influenced these alumnae's subjective identities throughout their lives.

1
Establishing Missionary Schools for Girls in East China

On the afternoon of June 3, 1922, the sun shone down on a group of Chinese students, teachers, churchmen, and foreign missionaries from the American Northern Presbyterian and Northern Baptist missions who had gathered to celebrate the laying of the foundation stone of Riverside Female Middle School.[1] The school building that was taking shape represented the merging of the Baptist (Shengmo nüxiao 聖莫女校) and Presbyterian (Chongde nüxiao 崇德女校) schools for girls in Ningbo. The school's earliest forerunner, established by British missionary Mary Ann Aldersey in 1844, is widely regarded as the earliest public school for girls in China. The architects had designed a three-story, grey-brick building with large wooden sash windows, a long balcony, and arched doorways.[2] The elegant building that would eventually emerge backed onto the fast-flowing waters of the Yongjiang River from which the school derived its name: Riverside Academy, or Yongjiang Female School (Yongjiang nüzhong 甬江女中).

The school was a product of the trend toward cooperation between missions of different denominations in China. Although at first they competed fiercely for territory and converts since their entry into China in the mid-nineteenth century, by the early decades of the twentieth century a "cultural revolution" had taken place in the sphere of women's education, and missionary schools now needed to combine forces to compete with the growing educational options, including Chinese private and government schools, available to girls. Representatives of the two different missions were seated in a specially constructed pavilion, shading them from the heat of the Ningbo summer sun. Presiding over the meeting was Francis White, the president of Shanghai Baptist College and director of the Riverside Academy School Board. Presbyterian missionary Robert Fitch, the newly appointed principal of Hangzhou Christian College, acted as Chinese–English interpreter.[3]

All attention, however, was directed toward six Chinese women, each of whom made a speech representing a different phase of the school's history. The first to speak was eighty-two-year-old Mrs. Sing, a graduate of Mary Ann Aldersey's first school for girls in China. After graduating from the school, Mrs. Sing had returned to teach under Aldersey. Although she spoke steadily and clearly, her son, Shen Zaichen 沈載琛, the first Chinese bishop of Zhejiang, repeated her carefully prepared speech word for word for the gathered audience so that none might miss her message, which celebrated the ecumenical history of the school since its foundation.[4] The second and third speakers, Mrs. Dzing and Mrs. Alexander Ting, represented the Baptist and Presbyterian girls' school history from the 1880s, respectively. Mrs. Ting, who had entered the Presbyterian school in 1889, had upon graduation from the junior high school studied at the Joshi Gakuin in Tokyo, Japan. She later married a judge in Shanghai and became the mother of four boys. The fourth speaker, Miss Tong, a graduate and teacher of the Baptist school, represented the alumnae of that school who had helped to raise 1,000 Mexican silver dollars toward the cost of building of the new Riverside Academy. The last two speakers were students of the two schools who were about enter the new Riverside Academy: a junior high school student, who represented the first class of girls who would graduate from the school the following June, and a Baptist primary school student. Dr. Fitch carefully lifted the primary school child onto a table so she could address the assembly about how she looked forward to attending the new high school. According to Presbyterian missionary teacher Esther Gauss, who watched from the pavilion, "She talked with much decision, as though what she was saying about the future of the Union School would certainly come to pass. The audience was quite captivated."[5]

The speeches reflected the developments in women's education over the past half-century, from a time when missionaries struggled to attract the poorest of girls to their schools to a period in the mid-1920s, when widespread recognition of the importance of women's education as a cornerstone of Chinese national strengthening enabled missionaries to educate elite daughters. Indeed, a new Christian-educated Republican elite had emerged from the schools and were now leaders of civic and philanthropic organizations in Ningbo.

Just before the foundation stone was laid, the catalogues of the two present schools, a list of the American donors who had given money for the new school building, the program of the day's exercises, the day's newspaper, and, "as a happy afterthought," the manuscript of the address given by Mrs. Sing were put into a copper box. Esther Gauss reported: "Then Miss Hodge took the trowel and laid the stone in cement mortar, thus typifying in a beautiful way the spirit of union between the two missions in the united efforts for the Christian education of young women in China." The ceremony ended with the new Riverside pupils singing a school song written for this occasion by one of the Chinese teachers.[6]

More than two and a half decades later, on March 24, 1949, at the cusp of the Communist Revolution, another group of missionaries, Chinese clergy, teachers, and female pupils again gathered in front of the school to celebrate the re-laying of the foundation stone. The small copper box, or time capsule, was opened and Esther Gauss examined its contents.[7] Much had changed in the previous quarter-century. The school building stood in ruins, having been badly damaged by a fire during the Japanese bombing of Ningbo in 1937.[8] By 1949, a Chinese female principal, Esther Sing (Shen Yixiang 沈贻緗), rather than a foreign male missionary, presided over the ceremony. The Chinese female alumnae who gathered to remember the school history were not only teachers and housewives but also headmistresses, doctors, pastors, and revolutionaries. Women's place in society had also undergone a profound transformation, wrought by the war. Demonstrating their ability to fight and organize in the national effort to resist Japan, many educated women were unwilling to go back to the domestic roles still expected of their class in prewar China. Some had even taken the radical step to run away from home, joining Mao Zedong's Communist Revolution and participating in fighting for a New China from Yan'an.

Some things had not changed however; the ceremony closed with the singing of the school song. Alumnae and teachers themselves also proved a vital link between past and present. Presbyterian missionary Esther Gauss was still there, this time helping to translate and read the speech given by Mrs. Sing, Aldersey's old pupil, who had died several years before. In 1922 Gauss had commented on the timeless and universal spirit of the alumnae who had gathered to celebrate the opening of the new school: "The former students, older as well as younger, proved themselves no different from students the world over with their school songs, jokes and reminiscences."[9]

They could not have known that this "re-laying ceremony" was also a decisive turning point. Less than one year later the new school building would be once again destroyed, this time by a Nationalist bomb during the struggle for the liberation of Ningbo in the traumatic Chinese Civil War.[10] Far from

ESTABLISHING MISSIONARY SCHOOLS FOR GIRLS 23

A group of missionaries, Chinese teachers, and pupils celebrate the re-laying of Riverside Academy's foundation stone in 1949, after its destruction during a fire during the Second Sino-Japanese War in 1937. *Courtesy of David Chen.*

being the start of a new chapter in their history, this was actually the beginning of the end for missionary schools in China. Two years later, by 1952, foreign missionaries would be forced to leave China, and the schools they had founded were merged, reorganized, or disbanded into the new education system established by the PRC government.

These snapshots of the school's history through the lens of missionary observers highlight the key changes that took place in the one-hundred-year history of female missionary schools in China. These include the transfer of missionary-run schools to Chinese control, changes in the student body—from poor church families to a new Republican elite—and the changing position of women—from housewives and helpers to principals and pastors.

During this period, rapid changes took place in the sphere of women's education as private, and then government-run, schools also became available to girls. What made missionary schools different from the other types of female education on offer in this period? Missionary schools were distinguished from other educational options available to girls by the high level of English required, and the music, drama, and dance training offered. Religious education, rather than civics classes, was the main method by which the schools attempted to mold students' moral characters. Through their student societies, traditions, and signs and symbols of class loyalty, missionary schoolgirls created unique campus cultures and school identities which became a marker of elite identity in Republican-era East China.

Difficult Beginnings: 1844–1898

Despite the jubilation of missionaries, Chinese students, and teachers in these vignettes, missionary schools for girls in China endured a tenuous early period of existence, with failure and closure the norm, rather than exception to the rule. Education itself was regarded as a rather dubious "secular" enterprise by the earliest missionaries to China, who preferred to concentrate their energies on direct evangelism, and only a small proportion of mission resources were devoted to schooling. However, widespread indifference to Christianity soon forced missionaries to change their tactics. When British Church Missionary Society (CMS) missionary Matilda Laurence arrived in Ningbo in 1869 to start a girls' boarding school, Protestant converts in China only numbered 5,753 and missionary tracts were being sold as waste paper or being made into shoes.[11] Her efforts were also hampered by the embarrassing but unavoidable fact that missionaries had been allowed into China by a series of unequal treaties that foreign powers had forced China to sign in the aftermath of the Opium Wars. The continuing British-dominated trade in opium was having a debilitating and financially ruinous effect on many of the families who she was trying to convert.[12] Faced with such difficulties, missionaries changed tactics and increasingly recognized that their fledgling schools and hospitals were the most effective way to secure an audience for their message, capitalizing on Chinese demand for education and Western medicine.

The educational effort was furthered by the need to train Chinese Christians as preachers, teachers, and bible women (female evangelists) for church work. Moreover, by capitalizing on Chinese respect for education and popular desire for literacy, missionaries sought to combat widespread hostility to the "foreign" religion.[13] Education was thus gradually accepted as a legitimate tool of evangelizing within the missionary enterprise. Although at the Shanghai Missionary conference of 1877 education was barely discussed and had to be vigorously defended by a few missionary educators, by the conference of 1890 almost all agreed upon the value of mission education, and much time was spent on discussing methods, curriculum, and textbooks.[14] However, despite the growing popularity and acceptance of mission schools, their primary purpose in the late nineteenth century remained to evangelize.

Historians have stressed the importance of "women's work"—both in terms of statistical strength (by 1890 more than 50 percent of the mission force in China was female) and in terms of the unique access female missionaries could gain to the inner, exclusively female sphere of Chinese homes.[15] Female medical missionaries were especially useful in this function and could even gain access to the upper-class homes from which all other missionaries were barred.[16] The importance of "women's work" was founded on the theory that by evangelizing women, Christianity would be spread to the rest of her family, producing self-perpetuating generations of Chinese converts.[17] However, this theory, based upon Western cultural misconceptions about the position of women in Chinese society, was problematic.[18] Matilda Laurence reported on the frequent failure of this larger scheme. While she continued to try to reach individual souls for their own sake, she was skeptical about the supposed power of Chinese women to convert their male family members. Indeed, she reports one horrific incidence of abuse of a woman whose son persecuted her ceaselessly for refusing to worship the ancestors and converting to the foreign religion.[19]

With the growing number of male Chinese Christian graduates from missionary schools, missionary societies began to recognize the need to produce Christian-educated women to be their wives. Indeed, some missionaries, such as Laurence and Aldersey, went as far as to usurp the role of matchmaker in local society, acting as go-betweens for girls and potential husbands and asking parents to sign contracts giving up betrothal rights for their daughters, to ensure that they married Christian men upon leaving their schools.[20] Laurence believed that only "one in ten" pupils at missionary schools should be trained to "become useful teachers for their own sex" and that the "vast majority" should become "intelligent and exemplary wives and mothers."[21] Mission education for women was thus founded not for the sake of raising Chinese women's position in society but to produce Christian wives and mothers who were trained in the latest principles of Western domestic education, health, and hygiene. They would rear healthy Christian sons and thus create self-propagating generations of Chinese Christian families. This conservative tendency remained a characteristic of missionary education well into the twentieth century.

While mission schools for boys took off relatively quickly, fueled by Chinese desires for educated sons, girls' missionary schools developed more slowly and encountered numerous difficulties in attracting students.[22] Female missionary educators not only had to persuade the Chinese parents that public schooling for girls was of value, they also had to overcome widespread anti-foreign sentiment and fears of the nefarious purposes of missionary designs for girls.[23] For example, Aldersey had to dispel rumors that she had murdered all of her own children and was now attempting to kill Chinese girls.[24] Although there were many avenues for literary and vocational learning for women in late imperial China, female missionaries faced great challenges in persuading parents that it was a good idea to send their daughters to mission schools alongside their sons.[25] As girls were barred from the official examination system, Chinese parents simply did not see the point of public schooling for girls, who would never be able to bring the family honor as officials. Moreover, as girls would soon leave home to become the property of their husbands' families, education for girls was regarded as a waste of families' resources. Girls' time was thus better spent in helping contribute to the family finances through spinning and needlework at home or manual labor in the field. It was also widely feared that schooling would spoil girls for their future roles as wives and mothers. Missionaries in the early period could recruit girls only from the very poorest families, who were eager to ease themselves of the burden of having to support their daughters. Not only did Laurence and other missionary educators have to feed, clothe, and provide all school material for these girls, they were also impelled to pay the girls to attend their schools in the 1860s to 1880s.[26] Overall, therefore, mission education for girls in the late nineteenth century remained a difficult and marginal enterprise.

Expansion, Consolidation, and Competition: 1898–1925

Although missionary schools were the earliest public educational options available to girls in China, it was not until late nineteenth-century Chinese reformers started to advocate women's education as a key to national strengthening that missionary schools were able to attract higher class pupils and start charging tuition fees. Drawing on ideas about Chinese fetal education and social Darwinist principles, Liang Qichao 梁啟超 directly related the position of women's education with the strength and vitality of the nation: "Education for women will enable them to assist their husbands on the one hand and instruct their sons on the other; in the short-term it will benefit the household, in the long term it will benefit the race."[27] In what became known as the Hundred Days' Reform, Chinese reformers persuaded the Guangxu Emperor to adopt a series of sweeping reforms of the military, economic, and education systems. Although swiftly crushed by the reactionary faction led by Empress Dowager Cixi, many of these reforms were implemented by the Qing Government in the aftermath of the Boxer Rebellion during the Xinzheng reform period of 1901 to 1911.

These reforming ideas about female education also stemmed from Meiji Japan, which attracted increasing numbers of Chinese male and female students at the turn of the twentieth century.[28] Japan, having undergone rapid military and industrial modernization since the 1860s, had inflicted a humiliating defeat on China in the Sino-Japanese War of 1895, and was regarded as a model which could provide a shortcut to Western learning by Chinese reformers in the Late Qing period. Chinese reformers directly drew upon Japanese ideas about the importance of women's education, which was leading the way in reforming female education in Asia.[29] Women in Meiji Japan were expected to contribute to national prosperity through the efficient and skilled running of the household. This new kind of domesticity, based upon the ideal of *ryôsai kenbo* ("good wife and worthy mother"), was very influential in China at the turn of the century, translated as *xianqi liangmu* 賢妻良母. Shimoda Utako, who founded the Jissen School for Chinese overseas students in 1899, aimed to inculcate traditional feminine virtues and domestic education from a strongly social Darwinian perspective.[30] In order to strengthen the race, Shimoda placed great emphasis on domestic and physical education for girls in her school curriculum. Many of Shimoda's pupils, such as Kawahara Misako and Hattori Shigeko, became teachers in China and thus played an important role in popularizing the idea of education for women as essential training to become "mothers of citizens."[31] Female students studying in Japan after the 1898 reform period also expressed their views on female education in student journals such as Chen Xiefen's 陳擷芬 *Nü xuebao* 女學報.[32]

Although formal provision for female education within the new school system was not made until 1907, prior to this a number of private schools for girls were set up by Chinese reformers. In 1898 the Chinese School for Girls (Jingzheng nüshu 經正女塾) was formally opened by a group of like-minded reformers in Shanghai, and in 1902 the Patriotic Girls' School (Aiguo nüxiao 愛國女校) in Shanghai was established "to cultivate model mothers" so that they would be able to "train future citizens."[33] By 1906 there were 245 private Chinese girls' schools nationwide with a total enrollment of 6,791 students.[34]

Because of fears about the propriety of female education, the beginnings of public education for women in China faced many difficulties and, similar to missionary schools, private and government schools for girls were justified on the grounds of the need to train "good wives and wise mothers." Some of the earliest schools for girls were established as family or lineage schools to give elite girls a higher-level education within the safe confines of the family circle. For example, Wu Huaijiu 吳懷久 established Wuben Girls' School 務本女塾 on the site of his family home at Xicang Bridge 西倉橋 in Shanghai in 1902 in order to educate his own daughters.[35] Such schools were seen as a "safe option" for other prospective parents from the reform-minded elite.[36] The establishment of private, non-missionary schools for girls varied greatly from region to region, as did the level of tuition, funding, and number of students. In some areas in East China, private schools for girls predated the founding of missionary middle schools and spurred them to compete in terms of facilities and resources. For example, in Hangzhou, Manchu noblewoman Hui Xing 惠興女士 established a school for girls, Zhenwen nüxue 貞文女學 (which later became known as the Huixing Girls' School 惠興女子中學), as early as 1904.[37]

Missionaries' schools were quick to capitalize on the opportunity that this new demand for female education offered. Rather than taking a cautious approach in the aftermath of the 1901 Boxer Rebellion, missionary efforts were redoubled in the first two decades of the twentieth century. A wave of support for British and American missions at home saw the rapid expansion of mission activity in China, as 6,890 schools were founded across twenty-one provinces by 1922.[38] This was the peak of the American women's mission movement. The Student Volunteer Movement encouraged women across campuses in the United States to sign up for missionary work, and by 1916 female missionaries in China outnumbered their male counterparts.[39]

Missionary schools also sought to reassure this new clientele of elite parents that their daughters would be protected and cloistered away from prying male eyes at their schools. When McTyeire formally opened on

March 15, 1892, Chinese parents who had enrolled their daughters were relieved that the headmistress, Laura Haygood, chose not to appear in public in the presence of the male patrons of the school, but hosted a separate welcome event for new students and their female relatives the following day.[40] Haygood thus made it clear that she respected Chinese traditional segregation of the sexes and reassured this first cohort that their daughters would be protected. Similarly, Louise Barnes, headmistress of the CMS Mary Vaughan High School in Hangzhou, was keen to emphasize that "no man should live on the premises."[41] Barnes was delighted when several members of the Chinese upper classes enrolled their daughters in her school, including Zeng Baosun 曾寶蓀, the great-granddaughter of Zeng Guofan 曾國藩, who is noted for his role in suppressing the Taiping Rebellion.[42]

As Shanghai grew to become China's most important treaty-port city, merchants and reform-minded gentry flocked to the city to exploit the commercial opportunities it offered. It was this class of gentry-merchant elite that most desired missionary education for their daughters. Zhang Long 張瓏 (McTyeire class of 1947) explained that her grandfather Zhang Yuanji 張元濟, former president of Jiaotong University and a co-founder of the Commercial Press in Shanghai, was a late Qing official, Hanlin scholar, and supporter of Liang Qichao. He shared Liang's progressive ideas about women's education, so he hired a private tutor for his daughter and sent his granddaughter to McTyeire.[43]

During the political, social, and cultural awakening of the May Fourth Period, the modern, Western-educated Chinese man desired a companionate marriage to a modern, educated woman.[44] A Western-educated daughter-in-law, schooled in perfect American or British English, therefore became increasingly desirable in the urban marriage market. By the 1920s, going to an elite missionary school for girls, such as St. Mary's or McTyeire, had become an essential status marker for the social elite or those aspiring to this status. The Soong Sisters all briefly attended McTyeire (before they left for the United States), and seven of the eight daughters of the Guo 郭 family, who owned the Yong'an department store in Shanghai (Shanghai Yong'an baihuo gongsi 上海永安百貨公司), sent their daughters to St. Mary's.[45] These schools had also become vehicles for upward social mobility in the urban-elite marriage market. Mae Yih (McTyeire class of 1946) remembered that her parents sent her to McTyeire because of its elite reputation, in the hope that she would make a good marriage within the new Western-educated elite upon graduation.[46]

The Qing government belatedly sanctioned female education in 1907, but only to primary level. After the establishment of the Republic in 1912, a new educational system was introduced that provided for women's public secondary education.[47] The government school system in 1912 provided three types of schools for boys and girls: middle schools, normal schools (teacher training), and industrial schools. This can be compared to the missionary system, which included middle schools, normal schools, and vocational schools, as well as seminaries and bible schools which were dedicated to training future church workers. In 1922 the Provincial Educational Associations adopted a new education system which theoretically put girls' education on an equal footing with that of boys. This system consisted of six years of elementary education, three years of junior middle education, three years of senior middle education, and four years of college.[48]

During the 1920 and 1930s, many government universities and middle schools eventually became co-educational. However, missionary schools tended to resist the trend toward co-education at the middle and higher education levels.[49] For example, Ginling College in Nanjing fiercely resisted merger with Nanjing University. Fearing that female staff and pupils would lose out in such a merger, Ginling faculty pointed to the unique educational needs of women students.[50] This all-girls' environment became one of the hallmarks of missionary middle schools in the Republican period. Interviews with pupils who had the experience of attending both single-sex and co-educational schools suggest that girls did better in a single-sex environment due to the gender discrimination still widely prevalent in society. For example, Lucy Hong (Hong Lüming 洪侶明), after attending McTyeire from 1943 to 1946, transferred to government-run, co-educational Datong Middle School (Datong zhongxue 大同中學) for the last two years of senior high school, where her father worked as a teacher. Lucy found it a daunting experience to be one of only a handful of girls in each class and she remembered that girls and boys sat separately.[51]

Increasing competition from private and government schools appears to have damaged enrollment figures at missionary schools. Fearing to lose out on pupils, the CMS Mary Vaughan High School in Hangzhou, which opened in 1909, was consciously trying to compete academically and in terms of facilities with other schools in the province for upper class pupils.[52] Similarly, CMS missionary Annie Wolfe, who ran a day school for girls at the north gate of Fuzhou, wrote in 1918: "The day school for girls still exists but does not flourish as I would like it to. One simply cannot compete with all the government schools. There is one about five minutes' walk from here in this direction and then about ten minutes' walk in another direction."[53] The fact that missionary schools were responding to a growing Chinese demand and competing for a limited pool of female students in the early decades of the twentieth century challenges the conventional image of missionary schools as leading the way in female education in this period.[54]

The need to compete for enrollment of daughters from elite families with emerging private and government school counterparts led to an unprecedented level of cooperation between missionary societies. Missionary societies realized that they could achieve stronger schools by pooling their resources and working together, rather than competing for female students at smaller and more poorly resourced schools. Moreover, with pressures of limited funds on mission societies after the end of the First World War, mission schools were merged to make them more efficient.[55] Pooling resources into larger schools that could accommodate more students, many missionary schools bought new land and expanded their campus buildings and facilities in this period.[56] In Shanghai, however, high demand for English-language education meant that missionary societies could afford to maintain their own schools and expand them independently. As a result, Shanghai maintained a much higher number of mission schools for girls and boys throughout the late Qing and Republican period than its neighboring centers of missionary activity in Ningbo, Hangzhou, and Suzhou.[57]

In response to continued conservative anxieties about the appropriateness of women's education, the government focused its energies on founding normal schools for girls in the early Republic.[58] As teaching was one of the few career options available to women in this period, this focus on teacher training was successful from a vocational point of view. Indeed, statistics from the Hangzhou Union Girls' School reveal that the majority of female graduates became either teachers (36 percent) or homemakers (36 percent) in the period 1912–1932, with a significant and increasing minority going to college (11 percent).[59] In contrast, missionary schools lagged behind their government counterparts in the provision of teacher training throughout the 1920s.[60] This fact was noted with some alarm by Protestant mission boards, who feared that they could not compete with the government normal schools and were thus not producing enough Christian-educated teachers to staff their schools.[61] Government normal and middle schools were also more evenly distributed across China's provinces, whereas missionary schools tended to be clustered in centers of missionary activity in treaty-port cities along the east coast.[62]

While the government schools were outstripping the missionary schools in terms of teacher training provision and geographical coverage, missionary schools were providing proportionally more opportunities for women to go on to study at university in the early 1920s. Table 1.1 reveals this continued lack of provision of government middle-school-level education for girls.

In a 1923 survey of women's education in China, Chindon Yiu Tang remarks on this problem in the government school system:

> If we pay attention only to girls' elementary education and co-educational college, and neglect girls' secondary education, it is just like expecting a person to go to the top floor of a building without providing a stairway. Girls' secondary education will be the key to our new educational system. If it is properly promoted elementary education will become more prosperous, and college education more successful.[63]

As a result, from the late nineteenth century into the early decades of the twentieth, elite Chinese families in inner Chinese provinces often had to send their daughters to missionary middle schools on the east coast as the only educational options that would equip them academically to apply for university.[64] Although missionary schools were providing a higher proportion of places to girls at the middle-school level, the fact remains that in the

Table 1.1 Number of Middle School Pupils in China

	Missionary (1921–1922)	Government and Private (1922–1923)	Normal (1922–1923)
Boys	12,644	100,136	31,553
Girls	2,569	3,249	6,724
Total	15,213	103,385	38,277
% Girls	16.89	3.14	17.56

Source: Chindon Yiu Tang, "Women's Education in China," Bulletin 9 in *Bulletins on Chinese Education issued by the Chinese National Association for the Advancement of Education*, Vol. 2 (Shanghai: Commercial Press, 1923), 14–19. Note: Tang cites statistics from the 1921–1922 academic year for missionary schools and 1922–1923 academic year statistics for other types of secondary schools.

1920s the provision for boys' education was still far outstripping that for girls in the missionary, private, and government school systems at all levels.

At the tertiary level, provision for girls' education was even worse. Up until 1919 there were only three institutions offering university courses open to women: North China Union Women's College in Beijing (Huabei xiehe nüzi daxue 華北協和女子大學), Ginling College in Nanjing (Jinling nüzi wenli xueyuan 金陵女子文理學院), and Huanan College in Fuzhou (Huanan nüzi daxue 華南女子大學). All of these universities were missionary institutions, and it was not until 1919 that Beijing Women's Normal University (Beijing nüzi shifan daxue 北京女子師範大學) was established, following which government universities began to accept female students, starting with Peking University (Beijing daxue 北京大學) in 1920.[65] As a result, out of the ten female students who won the first round of Boxer Indemnity scholarships open for women to study in the United States in 1914, nine were graduates from missionary schools.[66] China, however, was not far behind global trends in provision of girls' tertiary education. The United States led the way, establishing the first women's colleges in the 1830s. In Great Britain, although day and boarding middle schools for girls became common in the mid-nineteenth century, the University of London did not admit women for examination until 1868, and it was not until 1920 that Oxford and Cambridge allowed women to be awarded degrees. Japan, although leading the way in Asia by providing state-sponsored middle schools for girls during the Meiji reforms of the 1880s, did not sanction women to obtain university degrees until the postwar period.[67]

Period of Chinese Control: 1925–1937

After the establishment of the Nationalist government in Nanjing in 1927, all missionary and private schools were required to register with the government. Registration required missionary schools to conform to minimum government standards in facilities, academic levels, and staff pay. More importantly, the principal of the school had to be Chinese, as did over half of the school board members. Bible classes and worship services became noncompulsory activities. The issue of registration was hotly debated by missionary societies, and while many schools chose to eventually register, others opted to close, fearing they would struggle to meet the new requirements or would have to abandon their original evangelical purpose.

The debate about registration was closely linked to the issue of "indigenization" of the church that many missions were facing in response to the rising tide of Chinese nationalism in the 1920s. While some missionaries took a progressive stance, stressing the need for Chinese leadership of Christian institutions in China from an early period, other missionaries were unwilling to relinquish control of the institutions that they had carefully nurtured. This proved a particularly contentious issue at union institutions for girls such as Riverside Academy and Hangzhou Union Girls' School, where different cooperating missions took opposing stances toward the issue.[68] Eventually both schools did register, recognizing, in the words of the Presbyterian teacher at Riverside, Esther Guass, that the choice was "to comply or to close."[69]

Some schools managed to dodge the issue of registration completely. St. Mary's Hall in Shanghai, run by the American Episcopal church, did not register with the government until 1947.[70] Consequently, St. Mary's graduates' high school diplomas were not recognized by the government and girls could not take the entrance exams for government-run universities. The majority of its graduates went on to study in the missionary universities or abroad, and in the 1930s and 1940s top students were guaranteed automatic entry to St. John's University in Shanghai, which was run by the same mission.[71] Not registering with the government was not an option for smaller and independent missionary schools of other missions outside of Shanghai. St. Mary's, linked with prestigious St. John's University, could run the risk of not registering, knowing it had the resources, infrastructure, and reputation necessary to survive and, crucially, that its graduates were guaranteed a place to study at St. John's. As a result, St. Mary's and St. John's became favorite options for students with church and commercial family backgrounds who did not desire to place a son in the government bureaucracy. The commercial families were drawn to the school, for its elite reputation, links to St. John's, and the English language and musical training it provided.[72] As a result of its non-registered status, St. Mary's (like St. John's) retained a much higher number of foreign teachers on staff, kept English as the main language of instruction, and did not elect a Chinese principal (with the exception of Huang Su'e 黃素娥, who served as principal from 1881 to 1890) until forced to do so in 1942 due to the internment of American missionary teachers during the Second World War.

As a result of registration, missionary schools became more secular and more Chinese in the 1930s. Riverside saw a drop in the number of pupils from Christian family backgrounds from 42 percent in 1929 to just 14 percent in 1937.[73] Despite having to conform to new government regulations that made the teaching of religion and chapel attendance optional, missionary schools found ways to retain their religious atmosphere by appointing Christian teachers. Florence Webster, a Baptist missionary stationed at Hangzhou Union Girls' High School, wrote: "Personally I feel that even with only electing courses in Bible and voluntary church and chapel attendance the Christian character of the school would not necessarily be lost if we could maintain a staff of Christians who were thoroughly evangelistic and willing to be used of God."[74] Missionary teachers often got around the regulations by using bible extracts to teach English classes, and the schools often chose to elect their first Chinese principals from among their own graduates, ensuring continued loyalty to the school and mission.[75]

After registration, the Nanjing government had much more control over missionary schools than before. The government mandated certain standards of equipment, teachers' pay, and facilities, which some smaller schools could not hope to meet. It also required missionary schools to follow the same core curriculum, using government-approved textbooks, and required pupils to compete with their government counterparts in provincial examinations. For the first few years after registration, this put missionary schools at a distinct disadvantage. From 1931 to 1937, chronic problems of limited finances meant that Riverside Academy in Ningbo was struggling to keep up with rising national standards in terms of facilities and funding. In 1935 headmistress Shen Yixiang reported that, after a government inspection of the school, it was deemed deficient in library books and laboratory and physical education equipment, and teachers' salaries were too low.[76] More worryingly, the senior high school girls were not able to pass the Zhejiang provincial examinations because of a lack of time to learn the material in the new textbooks required by the government.[77] Missionary schools were thus often trying to catch up and respond to government standards in this period. The schools that survived registration, after a period of some disruption, eventually caught up and continued to perform well academically, often sending their students to prestigious universities in China and abroad.[78] Indeed, McTyeire and St. Mary's maintained their reputations as top girls' schools in Shanghai, and Laura Haygood was designated as the provincial provider of kindergarten teacher training for Jiangsu Province in the postwar period.[79]

Fees, Student Backgrounds, and Catchment

Both missionary and non-missionary schools for girls in this period tended to draw their pupils from merchant, government, and teaching family backgrounds.[80] This reflects the fact that education for girls in this period remained the preserve of the elite. During the Nanjing decade the average annual tuition and boarding fees for government middle schools in East China ranged widely from 52 yuan to more than 130 yuan (Chinese silver dollars), not dissimilar to their missionary school counterparts, which ranged from 48 yuan to 156 yuan.[81] Therefore, only a tiny section of the urban professional classes or rural elite could have afforded to send their children to missionary, private, or government-run middle schools in this period.[82] The exception to this trend was normal schools, which often offered free tuition and board.[83] Girls from more humble family backgrounds were more likely to train to be primary and secondary school teachers in this period if they could access any school education beyond the primary level.

As well as merchants, educationalists, and government official families, Christian families, particularly those who worked for the church, tended to send their daughters to missionary schools. Some schools, such as St. Mary's in Shanghai, offered scholarships based on financial need to students who were from Christian backgrounds, aware that poorly paid church workers would otherwise struggle to send their daughters to these schools.[84] Shanghai, with its concentration of merchant wealth, became an outlier in regard to tuition fees. McTyeire and St. Mary's Hall were by far the most expensive missionary schools for girls in East China, charging 156 and 120 dollars per year, respectively. This was well above the average tuition fee of 85 dollars that more representative missionary schools for girls, such as Riverside (75 dollars) and Hangzhou Union Girls' School (90 dollars) charged.[85]

Some Chinese clergy could not afford to send their daughters to the expensive missionary schools in Shanghai even if they worked as pastors for churches run by the same mission. Mary Jean Dai (Dai Lizhen 戴麗貞, Laura Haygood class of 1937) remembered that her father was a Methodist pastor whose salary would not allow him to send his daughters to McTyeire. She was sent instead to Laura Haygood, where her tuition fees were discounted on the condition that she worked as a kindergarten teacher at the Methodist Moore Memorial Church in Shanghai (Mu En Tang 沐恩堂) upon graduation.[86]

Girls from more ordinary church family backgrounds were likely to go on to teach in the missionary school system or to become church workers. In contrast, merchant and government families tended to see Western-style missionary education as a social adornment to make their daughters more attractive in the urban marriage market or as a stepping stone to enter missionary universities or study abroad.

That church workers were struggling to afford the costs of elite mission education for their daughters indicates a particular dilemma that the missions in China were facing: on one hand, the high fees charged at missionary schools for girls could help finance the mission endeavor as a whole. On the other, missionaries were concerned that their education would be used by graduates simply to gain lucrative employment via their English language skills upon graduation, or be used as a social adornment by women, rather than to advance the cause of the church in China. Ultimately, more pragmatic concerns won the day. Missions were increasingly aware of the need to capitalize on the elite image of their schools and to shore up their reputations by continuing to charge high fees. The creation of a Republican elite, who had been impressed with Christian ideals during their formative years, was aligned with the original strategy of early missionaries: to convert Chinese society via the upper classes. This was certainly the goal of Young John Allen, who founded McTyeire in 1892 specifically to provide a Christian education for the daughters of the reform-minded elite. The school consequently charged high tuition fees from its foundation.[87]

The catchment area from which missionary and non-missionary schools drew their pupils also, to a large extent, depended on the reputation of the schools. Well-known and academically outstanding schools, such as McTyeire, St. Mary's, and Hangzhou Union School for Girls, attracted girls from provinces as far away as Sichuan, Guizhou, Shandong, and Guangdong.[88] In the first two decades of the twentieth century this wide catchment area was also due to the continued lack of government middle school provision for girls across China. Many families also sought to place their daughters in the "feeder schools" for prestigious missionary universities concentrated in eastern coastal cities. Many St. Mary's alumnae reported that their families had chosen St. Mary's for them because it was the easiest route to get into the prestigious St. John's University in Shanghai. In contrast, smaller, less well-known schools for girls did not have such a large catchment area.[89]

English and Religious Education

After registration with the Nationalist government in 1927, missionary schools' curriculum and textbooks increasingly came into line with the government system. This typically included English, Chinese, Mathematics, Science, Civics, Hygiene, Home Economics, Physical Education, Art, and Music. The curriculum for missionary boys' and girls' schools was broadly the same, with the exception that the boys' curriculum included Bookkeeping and Typewriting, and the girls' curriculum Music, Art, and Home Economics.[90] However, missionary schools continued to distinguish themselves from government schools by their high-level provision of English, Music, Dance and Drama, and religious education.

American and British missionary schools in East China became well known for the high level of English-language instruction they could provide.[91] At particularly elite schools for girls, English was the main language of instruction. With the exception of Chinese language, Chinese history, and Chinese geography, all classes at McTyeire and St. Mary's were delivered in English. Despite early missionary reservations about the teaching of English, this became one of the missionary schools' strongest selling points. English language instruction was becoming an indicator of class status for girls, and many mission teachers who sought to attract upper class students consequently emphasized English language in their curriculum. For example, when McTyeire opened its doors in 1892 it highlighted its multi-lingual curriculum (which included English, Latin, and music) as a means of attracting upper-class students.[92]

Alumnae remembered their schools' excellence in English with great pride as one of the defining features of their schools. However, entrance into the foreign language environment of missionary school could be a daunting and humiliating experience for girls. Many students failed to pass the entrance requirements in English at McTyeire, and St. Mary's had two years of preparatory classes for students to get their English up to scratch if they could not pass the language requirement.[93] New entrants from non-mission primary schools found themselves totally at sea and reliant on the kindness of their more fluent classmates. Lydia Zhu (Zhu Wenqian 朱文倩, St. Mary's class of 1953) remembered:

I was at St. Mary's from age thirteen to eighteen. The biggest influence going to St. Mary's had on me was just that, apart from Chinese language which was taught by a Chinese teacher, all the other classes, Maths, Home Economics, all were taught in English and I did not understand one bit! But there were some classmates who already understood.... Even "Stand up" I couldn't understand. So, when my classmates stood up, I quickly followed them and stood up, when they all sat down, I also quickly sat down. But my classmates were very caring, they did not tease or bully me, but helped me. When I started the classes I didn't even understand ten per cent of what the teacher was saying, I couldn't remember any of the vocabulary... it was really pitiful. You could say I was the worst in the class![94]

Other students, whose parents or elder siblings had been to missionary schools, studied abroad, or worked for foreign firms or universities in China, had an advantage because they were exposed to English at home from an early age. Zhao Fengfeng's 趙鳳鳳 (St. Mary's class of 1948) father, Zhao Shen 趙深, was a graduate of Tsinghua University and then obtained a scholarship to study at the University of Pennsylvania in Philadelphia for two years. Her aunts were all McTyeire graduates. With exposure to English at home and having attended Juemin Primary 覺民小學 (a privately run Christian primary feeder school for St. Mary's), Zhao Fengfeng had no problem with her English upon entering St. Mary's.[95]

While St. Mary's and McTyeire alumnae recalled that the English classroom environment was one of the defining features of their schools, that does not mean that English was better taught by foreign than Chinese teachers. Missionary teachers, chosen for their evangelical zeal, were not always equipped with the skills of teaching English as a foreign language. Ling Yourong 凌又融 (McTyeire student from 1947–1949) remembered that her Chinese teachers were better at explaining the intricacies of English grammar than the missionary teachers.[96] Similarly, Zhu Yonglin 朱永琳 (McTyeire class of 1951) thought that grammar was not well taught at McTyeire, as she came across a book which explained it more clearly than her missionary teacher, who taught the girls English by simply perching on the front of her desk and reading Shakespeare to them.[97]

Missionary schools were often criticized for focusing too much on English and not paying enough attention to Chinese language and literature. Many alumnae felt that their Chinese was weak compared to girls who studied at government schools. Although they were well versed in American history and geography, they were comparatively weak in Chinese history. Ruth Lea Tsai (McTyeire class of 1924) admitted:

> When we went to McTyeire everything was in English except the Chinese lesson. We had one Chinese teacher and one Chinese course every day. I never entered a Chinese government school. From the beginning I went to American missionary school; I really had the foreign interest in English. And for me it was easier to write in English than Chinese. I am sorry to say that. But some of my friends who went to Chinese government schools, they had a better chance.[98]

Similarly, one McTyeire alumna in the class of 1947 remembered that English was much more desirable than Chinese Language as a subject of study at school:

> We were awful to every teacher who taught Chinese—we bullied them. It was terrible in retrospect. Almost cruel, and the way we treated them, they had to leave. Thinking back, it was cruel. Primarily the Chinese language teachers. Nobody did any work, just acted up, and Principal Xue Zheng had to come. I think because of the environment we didn't pay any attention to Chinese language. We were daughters of Westernized families.[99]

High-level training in Western music, dance, and theatrical arts became a selling point for missionary schools in the Republican period. Kuan Yu Chen (Chen Guanyu 陳觀裕 McTyeire class of 1936) explained that despite missionary efforts, girls at McTyeire were more interested in learning English and Western music than Chinese music and culture:

> Musically, we were very good in Chorus, in all kinds of Western music. We had a traveling Chorus. We were very famous, gave very sophisticated piano concerts, but we never learned anything Chinese. An American missionary teacher who came about one year before liberation thought that she should be appreciating Chinese culture and teaching Chinese students about Chinese culture. So she tried to teach the students Chinese folk songs and the students refused to learn. At that time, ever since the overthrow of

the Manchu Dynasty, anything old was bad ... so we absolutely criticized our own culture. Modern things, you know. We wanted Western music; we never played Chinese instruments at all.[100]

Articles about and photographs of Chinese music clubs which appear in early editions of Laura Haygood's school magazine, *The Laura Haygood Star*, as well as *The McTyeirean* suggest that some missionary schools did pay attention to Chinese music in the early 1920s.[101] However, it is clear that learning Western musical instruments was more popular by the 1930s. Music recitals in which senior girls displayed their talents in violin, piano, and organ, playing to an audience of proud parents, teachers, and local notables, were a highlight of the schools' academic calendars.[102]

Skills such as playing the piano and ballroom dancing became essential accomplishments for brides in the elite marriage market of treaty-port Shanghai. Xu Meizhen 徐美貞 (McTyeire class of 1946) remembered that McTyeire had a whole corridor of pianos in individual rooms where pupils could practice their skills during their leisure period. According to Gwendolin Lee (Li kui 李葵, St. Mary's class of 1952), St. Mary's was famous for its dance training, and her mother sent her to the school so she could

McTyeire school had a whole corridor of rooms where students could practice piano in their spare time. *Photo courtesy of Xu Meizhen.*

learn ballet, which Gwendolin later taught after graduation.[103] The McTyeire senior play, performed by the graduating class, also became an occasion in the social calendar of the Shanghai elite, with professional theater companies called in to train girls to perform their parts, and to provide the costumes, props, lighting, and scenery.[104]

Religious education was another distinctive feature of the missionary curriculum and the means by which the school attempted to cultivate moral and model Chinese Christian citizens.[105] In government schools students were molded into moral and patriotic citizens via the civics curriculum, which became increasing politicized after 1927. Based on the Three People's Principles (*Sanmin zhuyi* 三民主義) of Sun Yat-sen, students listened to lectures on nationalism, political organization, and the management of modern socioeconomic systems.[106]

Although missionary schools were also required to teach civics after 1927, the GMD had less control than in government-run schools over content and delivery of these classes. And despite new requirements that made chapel attendance and religious education elective rather than compulsory, missionary middle schools used many tactics to retain a "Christian" atmosphere. From a missionary perspective, at least, bible study classes, daily church services, prayers, and music remained vital tools for cultivating students' morality.[107]

Alumnae memories conflict over the extent to which their schools had a religious atmosphere. Unsurprisingly, alumnae who remained in China during the Cultural Revolution or had renounced Christianity to join the Communist Party tended to downplay the formal religious elements of their school's history. Alumnae who fled with their families to the United States after 1949 were much more interested in highlighting the Christian history of their schools. Indeed, some had become more religious after moving to the United States. Zhang Long, who remained in China after 1949, believed that the religious atmosphere at McTyeire had weakened over time:

> The Christian atmosphere of the school was not strong. I think all of the articles written here [referring to the McTyeire Alumnae history volumes] all had the same feeling, that the religious atmosphere was not strong in McTyeire. . . . I think maybe during the early days of McTyeire, that the

Christian influence was stronger, but by our time it was not so obvious anymore.[108]

Despite the increasing secularization of the schools over time, other evidence suggests that the Christian message was inculcated in students in more subtle ways. Although chapel attendance was voluntary, the culture of some missionary schools meant that all students attended chapel as a matter of course, to the extent that students remembered it as compulsory, even after the schools had registered with the government. Zhang Long acknowledged that, although students were not obliged to attend chapel at McTyeire, the school culture was for everyone to attend chapel, so all the girls went:

> We were not forced to attend, but actually we all went. And we were happy to have those services, because we learned a lot of things even if we were not baptized, but I think we were quite influenced. . . . Nothing was forced on us, we were left to choose our own way of living, but actually I think we were deeply influenced by Christian doctrines, such as all men are born equal, and we should love our neighbors, etc. I think that has given us a life-long influence, although we were not Christians.[109]

Theresa Chen (Chen Zongci 陳宗慈, McTyeire class of 1951), who left school early in 1948 to move with her family to Taiwan and eventually the United States, remembered that although McTyeire was not a very religious school, Christian moral values were inculcated in girls in various ways, through a system which encompassed moral, academic, and physical aspects (de zhi ti 德智體). According to Chen, Christian values were conveyed through music, hymns, plays, and stories and through contact with their teachers:

> My own Christianity from McTyeire, that really depends on the teacher. . . . My second-grade teacher, she was amazing. She would pray at the beginning of the day, and would get the children to do spontaneous prayer, so that was how I learned to pray. Junior 2, she would cry if the kids were not behaving, and her image is still deeply imprinted in [my] mind, I can still see her all red and upset, she was very emotional, but the emotion that was passed on to us was amazing. . . . On Friday we would gather and . . . one teacher would take a whole school assembly and give an inspiring story.

So it was method teaching, so that was the moral and Christian value part, there was no bible study or anything. Maybe at the gathering there may have been some prayer, but the story, that's the bit I can remember.[110]

Other, more subtle ways Christian life was continued at missionary schools included the Christmas and Easter plays and pageants performed by students. At St. Mary's the best parts in the Christmas and Easter plays and pageants went to the Christian students, and those who wanted to join the chapel choir or church committee had to be baptized.[111]

Sometimes girls' choice to receive baptism was a pragmatic rather than spiritual choice. Scholarships for Christian missionary school graduates to study abroad or enter Christian universities undoubtably provided motivation for some to convert. Other alumnae were motivated by wanting to cultivate a good relationship with their missionary teachers. Zhang Luoluo 張羅羅 (McTyeire class of 1947), from an official family background in Beijing, was good at speaking Mandarin Chinese, the standard Chinese language. One of her teachers, Miss Butler, asked her to help the pastor translate and practice giving the sermon in Mandarin. She was baptized in order to become a member of the chapel committee. She remembered this rather ironically, as she did not really believe in Christianity at this time, but was willing to be baptized more out of loyalty to help her teacher:

> She was a Christian, and I liked her, she was such a good teacher, so when she appointed me to do this thing, I thought I should take this responsibility, I didn't want to let her down in her hopes towards me. Actually, my knowledge of religion at that time was not really sufficient, it really wasn't because I wanted to get closer to Christianity that I received baptism.... So if you ask me am I very religious, I can say not very devoutly. I wanted to repay her teaching. I needed to stand in for her, to do a job for her, so that is why I received baptism, so I could fill that position. So later, I helped in the church. In Senior Three I was the head of the Haygood Church worship committee. I liked this work because I got to see Miss Butler about once a week. Miss Butler would write the bible stories and then I and the teacher would translate them, I would teach my classmates and the pastor how to read them properly. I would correct his pronunciation.[112]

Other mission school students were converted to Christianity, not through overt efforts by teachers but via more subtle and intangible means, such as the Christian environment in the schools, and by the Christian teachers' examples. Lian Shu Tsao (Shu Lian 舒麗安, McTyeire class of 1937) remembered:

> When students went into McTyeire maybe they were not Christians, but most McTyeire students left being Christians. Because we had a very strong Christian education. It's not forced upon us. You [don't] have to go to the prayer meetings. And for the religions we learned all of them, we studied comparative religion. And the teachers' examples, they were so well-liked by everybody. All of the teachers went to worship. Whenever we went, there they were. They never forced anything on you. That's the good part. They just lived Christian lives.[113]

Similarly, Zhang Luoluo remembered that these Christian values were slowly inculcated day by day, year by year, in the school environment and by the Christian behaviors modeled to them by teachers and classmates:

> So what I want to say about Christianity at McTyeire is that, you didn't have to be Christian, you just learned to be a good student and good person. This was just a gradual process that you came to a realization inside this big family you should act in a certain way, this wasn't forced on you, but you were in an environment where you slowly realized how to act. This is my own feeling. There really was not anyone telling me how to act. This was an influence of the school environment and the classmates. For example, in the first year when I didn't understand, a classmate came and taught me the set text, Heidi, so I wouldn't fall behind, and I could move up with everyone else. She wasn't a friend or family member, but she came to help me. So of course you learn that you should help other people. So slowly, slowly you grew up inside of this big family. She saw me, this little girl who couldn't speak English or Shanghainese and decided to help me.[114]

Therefore, although by the 1940s many students did not define themselves as Christian, they embraced the Christian atmosphere of the school as part of its unique identity within the educational milieu of treaty-port East China. Receiving a Christian education, even if it did not mean converting to Christianity, became an important identity marker for the Western-educated elite in treaty-port East China during the Republican period.

Student Societies and School Identities

During the 1920s, both missionary and government schools developed thriving student associational life, with a profusion of student-led societies and extracurricular activities. In China, as in the United States, student unions or student self-government associations (*xuesheng zizhi hui* 學生自治會) were first conceived as a means to improve student behavior via peer-to-peer monitoring and to give students a practical lesson in democracy and leadership.[115] The trend toward student self-government in China took off in the May Fourth period. McTyeire, like many schools across the country, founded its student union in 1918 with the aim of "the better organization of the school, the higher development of the students in the ideals of womanhood and the creation of a spirit of democracy. From these purposes we hope to attain self-respect, self-control, and also a liberal spirit for our later lives."[116]

Missionary school student associational life was distinguished by the emphasis placed on Christian social service. In America, although these student-run societies were initially designed to promote school-sponsored values, as time went by these autonomous student bodies grew into powerful student-led organizations. They provided an important forum where students developed their own campus cultures and school identities which were sometimes radically different from the founder's original visions and intentions for women's education.[117] This was also the case at missionary schools for girls in East China. Although founded with quite conservative aims in mind, students developed their own distinctive campus culture around their student-organized activities. By 1920, St. Mary's students ran a Student Union, Patriotic Club (Guoguanghui 國光會), Christian Fellowship Association (Qingxinhui 清心會), Girls Guides Association, Athletic Clubs, and four Music Clubs (including Senior, Junior, Choir, and Glee Club).[118] These student-led organizations provided girls with a space where they could test and hone their skills as leaders, develop their own distinctive campus cultures and school identities, and put their Christian, patriotic, and feminist ideals into action.

Rituals, signs, symbols, and ceremonies were all important in inculcating citizenship in the early Republic. These included national flags, portraits of Sun Yat-sen, national anthems and patriotic songs, military drills, and ceremonies.[119] At government schools the GMD made use of student clubs and organizations such as scouting to foster students' patriotism.[120] Government schools also tightly monitored students' self-governing associations, which they feared were becoming a hotbed for communism, as the CCP's influence among students grew in the 1930s. In 1933 Chiang Kai-shek's notorious "Blue Jacket" secret police entered the Wuben Girls' School in Shanghai to violently suppress a protest led by the Wuben student union over its promotion of their unpopular Civics teacher to school dean.[121] Throughout the 1930s the GMD tightened its control on student-led activities at government schools, and introduced the wearing of military-style uniforms and martial drills as the country geared up to fight Japan.[122]

In contrast, missionary-school student societies remained comparatively free of GMD government monitoring in the 1930s. Daughters of leading GMD politicians attended these schools, making them less likely targets for political monitoring, and missionaries sought to protect girls within their own bubble of extra-territoriality. School library books went uncensored and girls continued to have more freedom in their dress and hairstyles than their government-school counterparts.[123]

In addition to government-sponsored symbols of national loyalty, missionary schools in East China also developed strong traditions and symbols of school loyalty and class identity, based on their long histories and Sino-foreign roots. Students drew heavily on traditions and rites of passage derived from American women's colleges, where their teachers had been educated. At private schools around the world, school traditions and rites of passage often comprise an important aspect of an elite school identity. It is also through their long history and transmission that such traditions and symbolic markers of school identity derive legitimacy. These school identities were inculcated in several ways: via school and class songs, rites of passage such as graduation ceremonies, and symbols of class loyalty.

At both St. Mary's and McTyeire, a *jiemei* 姐妹 (big-sister/little-sister) scheme functioned, whereby new girls were paired with more senior students to help them settle into school life. This system also helped to transmit school traditions from one generation of students to the next. Privileges afforded to the senior class of girls were also important rites of passage at missionary schools. McTyeire seniors had exclusive use of the Senior Parlor, where they could socialize with each other and host guests. Graduation ceremonies were also important rites of passage in which school identity could be inculcated.[124] At St. Mary's these graduation ceremonies included a tradition directly drawn from American women's colleges known as "step singing," where the graduating class sang the school and class songs on the steps outside the main hall. The graduating class of girls gave a shield with the school motto "Justice

48 DREAMING THE NEW WOMAN

and Wisdom" written upon it to the Senior 2 class of girls, symbolizing that it was now their turn to take the responsibility to lead the school.[125]

Following the traditions of American women's colleges, each graduating class at McTyeire had its own colors, flower, motto, and sometimes a class ring. *Image from* The McTyeirean *(1930), courtesy of United Methodist Church Archives—GCAH, Madison, New Jersey.*

The school yearbooks also served as important means of transmitting school traditions, and it was here that girls put their own stamps on these rites of passage. The yearbooks abound with the symbols of class loyalty which were developed by the graduating class, including a class color, flower, motto, song, and sometimes a class ring. It was these symbols and traditions which also served as markers of difference, imbuing students with an exclusive identity as a graduate of an elite missionary school. These markers of class identity (rings, mottos, colors, and songs) feature strongly in alumnae memories of their schooldays. Gong Zhengguan 龔正冠 (McTyeire class of 1952) remembered nostalgically being able to wear her class colors and flowers upon graduation from junior high:

ESTABLISHING MISSIONARY SCHOOLS FOR GIRLS   49

This is my junior graduation photograph.... You see at that time, we were wearing a white dress with a violet flower, when we graduated from (senior) high school, it was a violet dress with a white flower. You see every class has their special color—green, blue, red, or violet. Four different colors, and our color was violet. This was 1949. So this was the last time we could wear this. When I graduated from senior high it was white shoes and blue trousers.[126]

Many alumnae expressed their disappointment that these specific symbols of class and school identity were abolished after 1949. Today alumnae try to relive these traditions, wearing their class colors, flowers, and rings to their annual reunions as important markers of class loyalty and identity. At their 2002 class reunion, Gong Zhengguan and her classmates all wore purple shawls symbolizing their continued class loyalty and sisterhood. Annual and semi-annual reunions for the schools are usually opened and closed by alumnae singing the school and class songs. Alumnae networks thus serve to reinforce and keep alive these class and school traditions, which were once markers of their status as students of famous missionary schools in Republican China.

Gong Zhengguan (third from left) and five classmates pose for a photo at the McTyeire Junior High graduation of 1949. This was the last junior high class to follow the McTyeire tradition of wearing white shoes and *qipao*, the latter adorned with the class flower and color (purple). *Courtesy of Gong Zhengguan.*

At the 2002 McTyeire reunion, Gong Zhengguan and her classmates all wore purple shawls symbolizing their continued loyalty to the class of 1952. The friends are standing in the same formation as in their junior high graduation photo, with Gong Zhengguan third from left. *Courtesy of Gong Zhengguan.*

Creating a Christian Elite

The missionary schools for girls that developed across East China in the period 1844–1949 varied greatly in terms of students' family backgrounds, fees, enrollment, curriculum, funding, and campus culture. Although by the mid-1920s they were being outstripped by government schools in terms of number, geographical distribution, and resources, missionary schools retained some unique selling points throughout this period. They offered girls advanced training in English, Western music, dance, and drama. Despite becoming more secular after registering with the government in 1927, missionary schools found ways to maintain the religious atmosphere of their schools through the appointment of Chinese Christian teachers. Therefore, although by the 1930s many students did not actively identify as Christian, missionary schools imbued students with an exposure to a Christian education designed to "promote social welfare, high ideals of citizenship and develop Christian character."[127] By catering for the growing demand for an English-language education, the schools contributed to the creation of a Christian-educated elite that was emerging in treaty-port East China.

Missionary schools for girls in the Republican era also fostered strong school identities and class loyalties in addition to a national identity as Chinese citizens. Within their Sino-foreign school environments, students were active agents in developing school identities and campus cultures, drawing inspiration from the traditions and rites of passage of American women's colleges. In doing so they created unique school identities, which became important markers of their status as the elite of Republican-era treaty-port society. These identities did not always sit in harmony with each other, especially during the 1920s when the rising tide of nationalism forced students to staunchly defend their position as both Christians and patriotic Chinese citizens.

2
Envisioning a Gendered Christian Republic

In 1925, Riverside student Margaret Fan (Fan Boli 範博理) wrote in her school magazine that Christianity could strengthen China by providing things that the country lacked, including "knowledge of hygiene," "knowledge of agriculture," and "deep spirituality."[1] Fan was a strong believer in the social gospel and was deeply concerned about the condition of China's laboring classes. In a description of her school's visit to a local match factory on Christmas Day 1924, she wrote: "If we want people to have equal treatment and social standing, then we must emphasise what Jesus said, that He came for all the world and take steps to realise it. Therefore, we are anxious to seek a way to come close to the labourers in order that we may get acquainted with their condition." She and her fellow students gave a short program of "singing, reciting bible verses, telling stories, and giving short speeches about salvation through Jesus Christ."[2]

After the program, girls distributed gifts of soap to women and towels to men and boys along with pennies for their wages and snacks. She reported happily: "If you had been there, you would have been surprised to see the sudden change on the anxious faces of more than two hundred people. I found they needed Christ so much."[3] Born into a Christian family of three generations, Margaret was a devout Christian student who combined her Christian faith with the patriotic imperative of saving China via uplifting her downtrodden masses, teaching them how to be hygienic, moral, and productive citizens. A few months later, however, Margaret left Riverside Academy under a cloud, after getting into trouble with her principal for attending a patriotic rally in Ningbo, which criticized missionary schools as aiding foreign imperialism in China.[4]

Margaret's story illustrates the tensions in their identities as both patriotic Chinese citizens and Christian students that missionary schoolgirls had to negotiate during the 1920s. As highly visible symbols of foreign involvement in China, missionary schools came under attack during the waves of anti-foreign and anti-Christian nationalism that rocked China in this decade. In 1922, left-wing students and intellectuals launched an anti-Christian movement in response to the meeting of the World Student Federation in Beijing. Chinese students and intellectuals were increasingly concerned by the level of penetration of Christian churches, schools, and hospitals into the fabric of Chinese society. This was not helped by the strident and sometimes openly militaristic language that foreign missionaries used to describe their efforts to evangelize in China. In 1922 a survey of Protestant missions and their affiliated institutions was published under the inflammatory title *The Christian Occupation of China*.[5] In 1924 these left-wing students and intellectuals started the Movement to Restore Educational Rights (Shouhui jiaoyu quanli yundong 收回教育權利運動), an agenda that gathered pace after the shooting of unarmed protestors by British police in Shanghai on May 30, 1925, and reached its apex during the anti-foreign violence that accompanied the Northern Expedition of 1926–1927.[6]

Being a pupil at a missionary school in this period was an ambiguous experience. How did female missionary school students in East China respond to and participate in the patriotic movements of the 1920s? How did students reconcile the anti-imperial, anti-foreign, and anti-Christian sentiment sweeping the country in the 1920s with their own identity as students at a foreign-run missionary school? Pushing back against the charge leveled at Chinese Christians both at the time and in subsequent historiography, that they were unpatriotic bystanders at best, or active "tools" of foreign imperialism at worst, there has been a wealth of studies to show how Chinese Christians developed mutually reinforcing patriotic and Christian identities in this period.[7] Scholars have shown how Chinese male Protestant reformers used their philanthropic enterprises to position themselves as leaders of a new Christian Republic.[8] Female students' responses to these patriotic movements can reveal how these formulations of Christian citizenship in the 1920s were gendered.

During the May Fourth period students argued that Christianity could help China to become a leading nation and that Christian-educated women were the necessary agents who could bring this about. Far from being cut off from society, they were active participants in the student protests of 1919. Missionary schoolgirls eagerly responded to the nationwide movement to uplift the masses through education, and they employed a complementary gendered, Christian, and patriotic language of "service" to position themselves at the vanguard of this movement. They expounded a utopian vision of a Chinese Christian Republic in which Chinese Christian women, by virtue of their Christian education, would play important leadership roles. In doing so, they helped to widen the sphere of accepted female activity in China, justifying their own ambitions for higher education and work outside of the home. In formulating these arguments, missionary schoolgirls were forging new identities as female Chinese Christian citizens, identities that they would negotiate, defend, or reject as anti-Christian nationalism swept the country in the latter half of the 1920s.

During the second half of the 1920s, missionary schoolgirls sought to use their social service activities to defend their schools from the anti-Christian movement, along with their own positions as Christian citizens. Although some missionary educators sought to curb girls' patriotic activities for fears about the safety of their pupils and their schools, this did not stop missionary schoolgirls from defying their teachers and becoming active participants and leaders in patriotic movements. Indeed, spurred by external pressure from anti-Christian groups in society, missionary schoolgirls were at pains to point out how a Chinese-controlled and Chinese-run church could be of great benefit to Chinese society.

Harnessing Christianity to Nationalism in the May Fourth Period

In 1920, Chu I Shiu (Zhu Yixuan 朱懿宣, McTyeire Class of 1927) wrote a fictional story for her school magazine. In her story, the protagonist, Woo Sien, travels forward through time by one hundred years to the year 2020, where she discovers to her shock and amazement that China has become one of the most powerful countries in the world and, more surprisingly, has even become an imperial power, celebrating the twentieth anniversary of its victory over Japan:

> She could not recognize one person. The houses were different and people were dressed in a strange way, which she had never seen before.... Soon she came to a place where there were many people. She asked why they gathered together. One of them laughed. "You silly girl, don't you know that today is the twentieth anniversary of our having got control over Japan? You must be dreaming if you do not know this." Woo Sien was amazed. She

thought she was in a fairy land. She was told that China now was one of the leading nations.⁹

In this uncannily accurate prophecy, Chu is able to envision a future where China is one of the leading nations of the world and had even conquered Japan, which just a few years earlier, in 1915, had forced China to sign a humiliating treaty known as the Twenty-One Demands, giving Japan territorial and economic concessions in Northeast China. In 1919, students across China protested against the further disintegration of China's territorial sovereignty, when the Treaty of Versailles handed German concessions in Shandong to the Japanese. In this period of national humiliation, the confidence with which missionary schoolgirls write about their visions for a future strong Chinese society is remarkable. Girls actively participated in debates about national strengthening and suffrage in this period. They argued that China could only achieve this position of international strength through women's education. As the first generation of Christian-educated women, missionary schoolgirls saw themselves as the vanguard who, by educating and awakening other women, would lead the way in helping to prepare Chinese women to participate in politics.

The 1920s was a period of crisis and anxiety, as well as hope and excitement, for China's students and intellectuals, studying and working in a plethora of recently founded missionary, private, and government educational institutions. It was also a time of great fluidity and openness to new ideas and possibilities. Students and intellectuals, many who had recently returned from studying abroad, debated how to strengthen China. This "New Culture Movement," which had started a few years previously, was aimed at radically transforming China, and was characterized by new forms of literature, as well as an attack on Confucian norms which governed Chinese society and family life. They discussed in new journals how a myriad of ideas, including socialism and feminism, might be applied to China.¹⁰ American YWCA secretary Eleanor MacNeil, writing in a supplement to the Shanghai YWCA *Green Year* magazine in 1925, captures this sense of flux and great change sweeping through Chinese society: "Education, family life, religious ideals, economic life, personal freedom are all being revised and in many cases radically changed. There is nothing stable and visible above the horizon; everything is in flux. Every new theory, every new educational experiment, every lately developed conception of sociology, every radical criticism of the established order is making its way to China, and this heady mixture is the daily diet of a great many students."[11] Girls at missionary schools made sense of these myriad ideas circulating in society during this period in specific ways that were inflected by their gendered, Christian, and class identities.

The May Fourth student protest started in Beijing on May 4, 1919, when students and intellectuals violently protested the handing of former German concessions in Shandong province to Japan in the Treaty of Versailles. The students marched to Tiananmen Square, where they made impassioned patriotic speeches and then ransacked the home of the minister of communications, Cao Rulin 曹汝霖, who was seen as politically close to the Japanese.[12] The protest quickly spread to other urban centers in China via newspapers and telegraph systems. When news of the political unrest in Beijing broke in Shanghai on May 7, 1919, St. Mary's students were still hard at work in the classrooms all morning and, despite hearing the commotion taking place on the neighboring St. John's campus, it was not until that afternoon, when somebody threw a newspaper over the wall dividing the schools, that they received the news. Strictly guarded by their missionary teachers, it was thus only by these covert means that St. Mary's students were able to communicate with their male counterparts and find out about the student movement.[13]

Girls' responses to May Fourth were also gendered in particular ways. They sent two representatives from their school to the Shanghai Students' Union, and they also formed their own St. Mary's Student Association to coordinate patriotic activities within their school. Girls at St. Mary's eagerly joined in the anti-Japanese boycott that was taking place across the country. Their representatives returned from the meeting of the Shanghai Students' Union with lengths of cloth, and girls undertook to make at least five hundred cotton cloth hats to replace the Japanese straw hats universally worn in the summer.[14] They also put their needlework skills to good use in making handkerchiefs, moneybags, and lace to be sold in order to raise money for the Shanghai Students' Union. They took several days off from their studies in order to participate in these patriotic activities.[15]

May Fourth was a turning point in women's public political participation. Whereas a few female students had participated in the 1911 revolution, the student protest in 1919 was the first time large numbers of female students protested publicly on the streets alongside their male classmates.[16] The excitement felt by St. Mary's girls at stepping into the public world of political protest is tangible in their writings. Tsang Kyi-ying (Zhang Jiying 張繼英, class of 1920), described attending a rally at the Shanghai Public Recreation

St. Mary's girls in their self-made cotton tennis hats (*bottom right*) wait to demonstrate outside the public recreation ground in Shanghai, June 1919. The demonstration commemorated Guo Qingguan, a Peking University student who died after being wounded by police during the May Fourth demonstrations. Girls hold banners with slogans protesting the terms of the Treaty of Versailles, which handed former German concessions in Shandong province to Japan. *Image from The Phoenix (1920), Shanghai Number Three Girls' School.*

Ground in June 1919 to commemorate Guo Qingguang 郭欽光, a Peking University student who died after being wounded by police during the May Fourth demonstrations:

> In the Public Recreation Ground, Shanghai, eighty-two bodies of students, both boys and girls, were standing solemnly in lines of exquisite order before an elevated platform on which was hung the portrait of a gallant youth, amid wreaths and memorial writings. National flags, school flags, and memorial couplets from each student's body waved in the air. Tennis hats, used by every student in place of Japanese hats or parasols, formed a wave of white. This was a memorial meeting in honor of a brave patriot.[17]

It was through participating in such public ceremonies and parades that St. Mary's schoolgirls felt deeply connected to other schools in Shanghai society in their patriotic concern for the nation. Tsang's narrative is filled with such symbols of loyalty to school and country, including flags and songs.[18] Missionary schoolgirls were thus far from being unpatriotic bystanders in this period.

Missionary teachers' responses to the girls' patriotic activities varied. The granting of suffrage to certain groups of women in Britain and the United States meant that many missionary educators recognized that the May Fourth protests represented a significant step for women's public political participation. Over time, however, they became wary of where these protests might lead and frustrated with the disruption to schoolwork the strikes and boycott movements represented. At St. Mary's, teachers were initially willing to grant holidays to give girls time to make their tennis hats and raise money for the Shanghai Students' Union. However, they soon began to fear that the strike would not end, and following the example of many other missionary schools across China they decided to close the school early for the summer. This meant that students had to disperse to their home towns and that their safety was no longer the responsibility of their missionary teachers. St. Mary's students were dismayed by the early closure of the school.[19] They were not unaware of the fact that foreign forces were preventing them from showing their patriotism. In her description of National Day Celebrations in October 1919, Eur Yang-Sih (Ouyang Xue 歐陽雪, St. Mary's Class of 1920) mentions that the students were prevented from processing through the international concessions. However, rather than resort to violent protest, St. Mary's girls pursued a more pragmatic stance, explaining that they had decided to go back to the public recreation ground to carry on with the protest there.[20]

Missionary schoolgirls' pragmatic approach to demonstrating their patriotism departs from a more radical stance taken by an early generation of Chinese feminists, such as Tang Qunying 唐群英, who in the course of their suffragette activities in 1912 disrupted parliamentary sessions and verbally abused and physically assaulted male politicians who had betrayed their cause.[21] While missionary school students believed in male-female equality, they critiqued the female suffragettes who resorted to violence in order to obtain their political rights. They were more sympathetic to the moderate Chinese suffragists, such as Zhang Zhaohan 張昭漢, who believed that Chinese women must first receive an education before they would be qualified to vote.[22] Yen Wei Tsing (Yan Wanqing 顏婉清, McTyeire class of 1921) declared that Chinese women must seek the right for equality with men like their American counterparts. However, she did not believe Chinese women were ready for the fight for suffrage due to their lack of education: "I say American women fought for their rights, but I do not mean that we Chinese women must raise a rebellion and fight for our rights, for we have not yet reached their standard. If we do, we may receive the same fate as the inexperienced women revolutionists. Therefore, the first thing a woman should do is to get an education which will prepare her to share the responsibility of society and government."[23]

The importance of education as a pre-requisite for female suffrage is highlighted by McTyeire student Tsu Tsung Kyung (Zhu Chunjing 朱春景, class of 1923). In her 1922 article, "The Present Situation of Popular Democracy in China," Tsu linked the patriotic student movement to the women's movement by suggesting that China can only become strong by allowing women to participate in politics:

> The students' movement in 1919 against the signing away of Shantung, and the boycott of Japanese goods are the reaction produced by this genuine nationalism and patriotism. Now her people are busy with the redemption of the Kiaochow-Tsinan Railway. The right of suffrage has not been extended yet for the majority of her people have not been educated. The women of Canton are demanding the right of suffrage but it has not been granted. I do hope that the day will soon come when Chinese women can vote.[24]

Girls were therefore by no means radical suffragettes who were prepared to use violent methods in order to fight for Chinese women's political rights. Instead, by stressing the need for education as a prerequisite for female suffrage, girls were effectively empowering themselves as the harbingers of a true patriotic women's movement in China. Indeed, they used their qualifications as the first generation of women to have received public schooling in China to position themselves at forefront of the patriotic student movement in this period.

Not to be deterred by the early closure of their school, St. Mary's girls used the long summer break of 1919 to carry the patriotic message to their sisters in inner Chinese provinces. Kyung Ming-Ge (Jin Mingqi 金鳴歧, St. Mary's class of 1920) described how, in her home town of Shasi (Shashi 沙市) in Hubei province, girls had been ridiculed for publicly appearing alongside their male counterparts in the May Fourth student protest, riding in sedan chairs because of their bound feet. The movement had lost its impetus, until the arrival of several well-educated missionary school students from east-coast China effectively galvanized the people of Shashi into a realization of true patriotism:

> Having obtained help from the ladies who came back to Shasi from other places, the students again held meetings regularly. People in Shasi again stopped buying Japanese goods. These ladies not only aroused patriotism by making speeches, but by making jokes as well. As there were many people who still wore the straw hats made in Japan, Miss Kyung [the author] one of these six ladies, put one of the same straw hats on the head of a dog and walked through all the streets with this dog in order to scorn all those who wore Japanese straw hats. Wherever this dog went, crowd after crowd came to find out what was the matter. After seeing this, many people burned up their hats made in Japan because they thought that they were dogs if they put on that kind of hat again. Indeed, this joke helped the students' movement a great deal. It awakened the dull minds of the ignorant people of Shasi.[25]

The tone of Kyung's article is strikingly reminiscent of the sense of mission and conviction of their own cultural, educational, and social superiority, held by many female missionary educators. According to Kyung, the people of Shasi were pitied for their lack of patriotic zeal and backward attitude toward women. It was the "responsibility" of missionary-educated elite women to awaken and uplift their foot-bound sisters into a position of political activism and independence, much as their missionary teachers were aiming to inculcate in their students a Christian zeal for reform. Missionary-educated girls thus positioned themselves at the forefront of the patriotic women's movement in this period: "After the six well-educated ladies came from other schools, patriotism was once more developed among the people of different classes in Shasi. Everyone wished to be a true citizen and was willing to promote the welfare of China."[26]

Girls believed that their Christian education qualified them to be the leaders of the patriotic women's movement and helped them to discern how to be truly patriotic. Some students critiqued a type of "rash" and "unthinking" patriotism that was sweeping the country. For example, in her short story written in 1919, McTyeire student Tsiang Ku Ying (Jiang Ruying 蔣如英, class of 1923) recounts the tale of a "young scholar and brave knight,"

Earnest, who is filled with a burning desire to do patriotic deeds but does not know which country he belongs to as he is an orphan living on a deserted island. In the story, Earnest is forced to choose between joining a patriotic crowd of youths on a steamship who can reveal to him his nationality and saving an old man from drowning. Earnest finally decides to "sacrifice" his own "selfish" desire to be patriotic in order to save the old man's life. He is rewarded by the old man, who explains to him how Christianity can transcend patriotism to any one nation by gaining entry to a heavenly kingdom:

> The old man slowly took out a small bible, still wet and said: "Now my friend! Your kind deed in saving me is no obstruction. It cannot be isolated from patriotism. For when God created man He made him the incarnation of kindness, bravery, and love. Child, you need not seek your kingdom, and try and do patriotic deeds beyond your home. If you know yourself well, you should know God, and the source of all kingdoms and patriotism.". . . "Ah," said the youth, "I failed to find my earthly kingdom; I have secured the better one, God's Kingdom, the home of my soul."[27]

For some missionary school students Christianity was deeply embedded in their views on how to be a truly patriotic citizen. They formulated a self-consciously Christian version of patriotism that subsumed loyalty to any one country to the fidelity owed to a higher power. This belief that Christianity was no obstruction to patriotism would become a sore point for missionary school pupils as they were forced to defend their identities as both Christians and patriotic citizens in the latter half of the 1920s.

Female missionary students' responses to the May Fourth Movement ranged from participation in political protest to critical reflection, but their desire to help their country comes through strongly. As Christian-educated Chinese women, they believed that they were the key agents who could provide solutions to China's problems. Tsao Ming Zok (Zhao Minshu 趙敏淑, McTyeire class of 1922) wrote:

> It is not too much to say that China's future is in the hands of present-day women. . . . The call for women leadership of the highest order is a call for advanced learning, a call for betterment of the home and society, then a call for social service. The need in all spheres of life is a challenge to every trained woman to-day. But those who have received special training will better meet the opportunity.[28]

Christian-educated Chinese women saw themselves as a chosen group whose, in Tsao's terms, "special training" conferred both power and responsibility. By virtue of their Christian education, it was their moral and patriotic duty to uplift their backward and uneducated counterparts and bring them to a realization of their patriotic duty and rights as women in the cause of strengthening the nation and resisting imperialism. This "special training" also empowered and equipped them with the skills, knowledge, and experience to experimentally apply Christianity to the needs of Chinese society. This rather paternalistic power dynamic can clearly be seen in the social service activities that girls pursued in the May Fourth era.

"Sent on Service": Experimenting with Gendered Christian Citizenship

Writing in the McTyeire school magazine of 1921, pupil Tsu Tsung Kyung describes how she felt "desolate" and "powerless" in her former life before entering missionary school. She describes her internal transformation after becoming a Christian at McTyeire: "When I came to the mission school, I became familiar with Christ. I found I was greatly mistaken in my attitude toward the problems of life. A new spirit within me glowed and now I feel that the world is a pregnant laboratory in which to make experiments."[29] Responding to the imperative of "saving China" that the May Fourth movement engendered, patriotic urban students across the country eagerly experimented with new ways to uplift the downtrodden "masses" in the 1920s.[30] Missionary schoolgirls also took part in these experiments, drawing on the social gospel and their responsibilities as Christian women to envision new ways of being a modern Chinese citizen.

In the 1910s and 1920s, a craze for social service swept college campuses in Britain and the United States as the social gospel was expounded by inspirational speakers including Sherwood Eddy, John Mott, and John Dewey. The global spread of student social service was facilitated by international Christian student conferences, missionary educators, and traveling YWCA/YMCA secretaries. This Christian concept of student social service also became fused with longstanding indigenous ideas about charity and service around the world.[31] Students who returned from the United States played a big part in the spread of social service, resulting in new modes of student activism. Perhaps most famously, Chinese Christian James Yen (Yan Yangchu

晏陽初), having graduated from Yale and Princeton and after teaching literacy to Chinese laborers digging trenches in France during the First World War, returned to China in 1921 to help start the Mass Education Movement (Pingmin jiaoyu yundong 平民教育運動), which developed into the Rural Reconstruction Movement (Xiangcun jianshe yundong 鄉村建設運動).[32] Students saw themselves as the leaders in the movement to improve the lives of their impoverished rural counterparts, and social service work, including mass education, was a feature of almost all Christian, private, and government schools in the early 1920s.[33]

Christian girls at missionary schools in eastern China responded enthusiastically to the call to social service. During the 1920s and 1930s they undertook a range of social service activities, including setting up Sunday Schools for poor children in the local vicinity, teaching children working in local factories, visiting and studying the conditions of people in the surrounding rural areas, distributing food and medical aid, and collecting donations for flood and famine relief.[34] At Riverside Academy in Ningbo, Li Rongmei 李榮美 explained that her classmates were making a "great contribution to society" through their Sunday School for street children. By teaching children bible stories and hymns they were cultivating "moral" and "vivacious" future citizens.[35] In Suzhou, Laura Haygood Normal School student Zhang Hanchu 張菡初 documented how she and her classmates were inspired by the visit of Yan Yangchu to Suzhou to join together with other middle-school students to set up mass-education schools. Large group classes (one hundred to two hundred students) were delivered by projecting glass lantern slides with characters and pictures onto a cotton screen as well as smaller classes of twenty to thirty students being divided by ability. Her report on the school's numbers reveal that female mass education was taken as seriously as male, with a total of 586 female compared to 457 male students across the thirteen mass education schools established in the city.[36] This was perhaps thanks to the presence of several female missionary and government teacher training schools in Suzhou, which could train women. Indeed, the majority of student teachers who took part in the movement were female (eighty-five female teachers compared to forty-two male).[37]

Missionaries and YWCA student secretaries were keen to convey to their Chinese pupils how such social work was, by its very nature, a Christian enterprise. A YWCA student handbook published in 1924 emphasized: "Our best evangelistic work is often done not by preaching or teaching but by living. . . . Social service work can therefore be a very strong and appealing piece of evangelistic work."[38] Girls understood their social service work as not just a patriotic but also a Christian project. The entry of Christian organizations such as the YWCA resulted in new modes of elite female-led philanthropy of which there was a long tradition in China.[39] Missionary schoolgirls in East China helped to shape this new type of "social service" that was emerging. Riverside pupil Tu Fengyun 屠鳳韻, in her description of her schoolmates' charitable social service work, wrote: "Mencius said: 'everyman possesses a sympathetic heart,' my schoolmates have a charitable project for everything, such as disaster relief, helping at orphanages, all have the spirit of self-sacrifice, fearlessly go out to collect contributions, these in short, are carrying the foundation of Jesus Christ's spirit, ah!"[40] By combining Christianity with longstanding Chinese ideas about philanthropy, missionary schoolgirls were active agents in formulating a distinctively Chinese Christian mode of social service.

Girls at missionary schools in East China also believed that they were uniquely qualified to carry out such social service activities by virtue of their Christian education. Consciously influenced by the village studies being produced by intellectuals to document the conditions of China's rural masses, Chang E. Tsung (Zhang Aizhen 張藹真, McTyeire class of 1920) published her own "Study of the Village Life around McTyeire High School" in her school magazine in 1921. Chang describes her mission to study and improve the living conditions of poor families in villages in the environs of McTyeire based on her superior training as a missionary-educated student:

> It has always been the desire of the Missionary Society of our school to do something for the betterment of the villages during our leisure time.... Through the casual talks and visits to the villages and observations of the need of reforms we are all inspired to apply our ethical convictions to the social needs and home life in these villages where life has become hard and uninteresting. It is our sincerest desire to take these villages as our laboratory where we can make an experiment in different reforms by investigating, assimilating and adopting certain phases of western civilization to our Chinese village life.... Let us do the work and make these villages the model villages of China.[41]

As missionary schools had been the experiment of their missionary teachers, missionary schoolgirls now defined themselves as the agents in continuing this experiment, using the village school as a "laboratory" for "investigating," testing, and creating new forms of Christian-inspired social modernity for women in China.

Chang's proposed solutions for how to remedy the problems that she documented in the village (including "Lack of real homes," "Superstition," "Lack of sanitation," "Child Labor," and "The absence of social gatherings") reveal not only the influence of the social gospel in her education but also how girls' conception of social service was highly gendered. Chang and her classmates were convinced that China's weaknesses were rooted in the "lack of real homes" in which children could be properly reared or nurtured. According to missionary schoolgirls, "degenerating" influences including drinking, smoking, and superstition surrounded Chinese children, who were often forced to work all day in factories, harming them "bodily, mentally and spiritually."[42] Worst of all, husbands and wives did not know "what real love is, or how to enjoy real life. They do not help each other in the best spirit."[43] Chang and her classmates believed they could remedy this situation with their advanced training in Christian homemaking and childrearing.

There is a certain amount of self-Orientalizing going on here as missionary schoolgirls internalized overlapping missionary and May Fourth reformers' critiques about the backwardness of Chinese family life. The Chinese family system became a target for reformers in this period, who placed the blame for China's backwardness on loveless and hierarchical families who could not rear healthy, happy, and productive future citizens.[44] This self-Orientalizing tendency can clearly be seen in Chang's patronizing critique of her compatriots for failing to have an innate grasp of ideas of Western childrearing habits and domestic hygiene: "Dogs, cats, chickens and babies seem to play in the same yard.... That the parents should take part with their children or even engage with them in any game whatever, is, so far as I can see, a thing wholly outside their wildest imagination."[45]

We might question why girls undertook social service activities in this period. Were they motivated by true patriotic and religious zeal, or just "joining in" an activity expected of them, perhaps trying to curry favor with their teachers? An article in the 1922 *McTyeirean* entitled "Is the Village School Worthwhile?" reveals that sometimes girls needed a little "push" or reminder about the value of undertaking such activities. In the article, two students debate the point of the village school. While pupil Wong Yoeh Wo (Huang Yuehua 黃月華, McTyeire class of 1925) believed her time would be better spent on studying so she could go to university, and thus later in life make more of an impact on society, her classmate Tsu Tsung Ling (Zhu Zengling

朱增齡, McTyeire class of 1925) eventually convinces her that these schools are worthwhile:

> Tsung Ling: Is there a better way of getting our minds clear than to walk over there, and at the same time doing a little service in starting the education of our less fortunate future citizens? . . . Moreover, experience is part of our training. Before we can take part in social work, we must know the conditions of society. To teach in a village is a good chance to inspect these conditions, therefore it is the first step for our future success.
> Yoeh Wo: Then, if it is trying doing them this much good, why should I not also do my part in helping them? I will go with you to render my service, for I am willing to sacrifice some of my pleasure and time if I can save somebody out of darkness.[46]

Yoeh Wo consciously borrowed from her missionary teachers' language, deploying the overlapping Christian, patriotic, and gendered rhetoric of "service" and "sacrifice" while adapting it to her own understanding of China's needs and her role in society. This conversation also highlights one of the key motivations for girls' participation in social service: justification for personal power and ambition. As Helen Schneider has explored for women who attended Ginling College, in the 1920s girls at missionary middle schools were constructing a "benighted" female "other" who it was their "responsibility" to "serve" and "save."[47] This process of representing uneducated Chinese women who needed their help was essential for missionary school students' own empowerment. For some of the rural reformers who undertook mass education work on the outskirts of Nanjing, the aim was to "get closer" to the masses and be "commonerized" by them.[48] In contrast, elite missionary schoolgirls in Shanghai drew a clear line between themselves and the poor women and children who were the objects of their social service work. A good example of this power dynamic is provided by a McTyeire student's fictional story in which the heroine convinces her father, who is opposed to the higher education of women, that she should go to university. She is inspired by the words of her teacher and reasons that it is her "duty" to help her less fortunate "sisters" who have not had the privilege to receive an education as she has had:

> "It's not fair," she cried, "not fair. I ought to have that chance. It is my duty to society. I owe it something which I must repay, but, I'm not ready for that

work yet. College will prepare me for it and then I can truly be useful for society. I ought to have this chance. I must. I hear the women of China calling to me, calling for freedom, for equality, for life, while I sit here and do nothing. It is impossible! What am I made for if not to serve? No, no, I must work for women, for their freedom, against men's bondage. These poor women are buried in their homes, buried in the lives of their husbands."[49]

In her writing we can clearly see that the author, Tsong Tuh wei (Zhang Dewei 章德衛, McTyeire class of 1930), employs the same rhetorical devices that missionaries used to describe and justify "women's work" and their own calling to be female missionaries. Tsong uses the rhetoric of her "calling," "duty," and "service" to help her less fortunate sisters in China in the same way that missionary women justified women's work as a natural extension of their caring roles.[50] Missionaries were keen to instill in their pupils a sense of their own privilege for having the rare opportunity to receive an education and, consequently, their duty to extend this privilege to their less fortunate sisters in China. In her article, Tsong takes the argument a step further, arguing that she must have access to a college-level education in order to fulfill her duty. Missionary school pupils used the same rhetorical devices as their missionary teachers to justify their own ambitions and widen their sphere of operation within society. In Tsong's case, it is poor, uneducated Chinese women who become the downtrodden "other" who must be "saved," and the vehicle to justify the fulfillment of her personal ambitions for higher education.

This was not just a rhetorical device. Chinese women used the sectioned sphere of homemaking to professionalize these domestic roles and ultimately expand the range of career options open to Chinese women into the realms of nutrition, Home Economics, and social work.[51] Indeed, several missionary school graduates, including Chang E. Tsung (Zhang Aizhen 張藹真, who studied village life around McTyeire) used such social service activities as stepping stones to professional roles as social workers and child welfare experts upon graduation. Chang worked for the YWCA, and during the Second Sino-Japanese War she helped to coordinate wartime relief work for women and children as founding members of the National Association for Refugee Children (NARC).[52]

Although missionary school students might have drawn on the rhetorical tactics of their missionary teachers in order to justify their ambitions, they were far from passively imbibing and reproducing these ideas. Girls stressed that it was only through a Chinese controlled and financed church that Christianity could fulfill its potential to transform Chinese society and the position of Chinese women within it. In 1921 Laura Haygood student T'sao Ai Fang (Cao Aifang 曹愛芳) argued for the adoption of Christianity as the state religion of China. She reasoned that if Christianity were sanctioned and financed by the state it could be spread more easily and thus "be independent from the contributions of foreigners."[53] Girls were unequivocal about the fact that it was they, as Chinese Christian-educated women, rather than foreigners, who were best placed to know and minister to the needs of their less fortunate counterparts.

McTyeire student, Mo Sih Tsung (Ma Xuezhen 馬雪珍), also argued that it was only through the "adaptation" of Christianity to Chinese society that the religion would become acceptable to Chinese people. According to Tsung, missionary schoolgirls could transform Chinese homes and, by extension, Chinese society by adapting the "uplifting" elements of Western Christian music to suit Chinese musical instruments and produce new forms of Chinese Christian music. She believed that uniting families around this wholesome pastime would produce love in families, which would "expand to include country love, it can also be perfected by being extended to all our brothers and sisters all over the world."[54] Girls thus believed themselves to be the crucial agents who were uniquely placed to interpret the knowledge they have learned from their missionary education and adapt it to the pressing needs they encountered in Chinese society. By positioning themselves as the leaders of a self-consciously Chinese Christian Church, they also sought to defend their schools during the waves of anti-foreign nationalism that engulfed China during the latter half of the 1920s.

Negotiating and Defending Christian Identities: 1925–1927

During the patriotic student activities of May Fourth, anti-foreign hostility was directed mainly toward Japan and foreign imperial aggression against China in general, rather than at missionary schools and churches in particular. Girls at missionary schools expressed their patriotism by contributing to the student rallies organized by their local student unions, writing articles to express their patriotic sentiments, participating in social service activities, and by boycotting Japanese goods. This situation was to change a few years later as anti-foreign and anti-Christian sentiments circulating in society came to a head in the aftermath of the May Thirtieth Incident in 1925 in

Shanghai. The shooting of a Chinese factory worker at a Japanese-run cotton mill led to student protests and demonstrations in the city. When a group of students was arrested, others marched on the police station just off the Nanjing Road in support of their classmates. The Shanghai Municipal Police force, following orders of the British inspector in charge of the station, opened fire on the unarmed protesters, killing several outright and wounding dozens more.[55] News of the shooting sent shockwaves throughout the country, stirring up of old grievances about the extra-territorial privileges that foreigners enjoyed in China under the system of unequal treaties. Students in cities across China began to stage their own protests and demonstrations.

Anger at foreign imperialism and the continued unequal treatment of foreigners under the system of extraterritoriality made missionary schools and churches very visible targets of attack. In Ningbo, news of the massacre dominated the papers for several months after the shooting. The public comments section of the Ningbo newspaper *Shishi gongbao* 時事公報 was filled with debates about the extent to which Christianity could be divorced from imperialism.[56] On August 8, 1925, a certain Zhang Chuanshen 張傳申 critiqued the hypocrisy of missionaries for preaching about universal love, freedom, and equality while their governments bullied other countries, murdered his compatriots, and suppressed freedom of speech:

> Christian truth includes equality, universal love, and freedom. Today the British Empire and Japan use their strength to bully the weak. Not only have they killed our students, workers, and merchants, but they have also gathered a fleet of battleships for war. Is this universal love? No matter how our government has resisted, not only have they never compromised, they even blame our government for not protecting the foreigners who live here. Is this equality? Moreover, they obstruct our people from speaking in public, and prohibit our people to strike. Is this freedom? You, Christian States, always talk about peace and human rights. Such liars![57]

Chinese Christians in Ningbo also wrote to the paper to defend themselves from the accusations that they were the unpatriotic "running dogs of foreigners" in the aftermath of the May Thirtieth shooting. On September 4, 1925, Lin Wentian 林聞天 attempted to divorce Christianity from imperialism, and he defended Chinese Christians as patriotic citizens. Lin complained that his compatriots "take all of the evils in society and blame them on Christianity. . . . Actually, every country's government has imperialistic tendencies, industry is also imperialistic, however only Christianity completely lacks the taint of imperialism. The bravest of those who resist imperialism, we Christians are also Chinese citizens, we were never unpatriotic."[58] Lin critiqued the rash and unthinking nationalism that some of his countrymen advocated. To his detractors' scorn and annoyance, no doubt, he urged Chinese Christians to use Jesus' teaching, "Love your enemies," to bring others to a realization of the Christian truth and thus neutralize those who were currently attacking them.[59]

May Thirtieth also fueled the Movement to Restore Educational Rights, which had started with student protests at Trinity College in Guangzhou the previous year and had quickly spread to missionary schools across China.[60] Christian education came under sharp attack as a means of indoctrinating and denationalizing students, and pupils were exhorted to leave missionary schools. One father who sent his son to the Presbyterian boys' school in Ningbo, Riverbend (Siming zhongxue 四明中學), complained that his son only learned English and bible stories and was "completely westernized."[61] Missionary schools were thus branded the tools of foreign imperialism whose graduates were unpatriotically aiding in the economic and cultural invasion of China. Another contributor to the Shishi gongbao, Fu Lüe 傅掠, explained how missionary education was deeply embedded in the imperial invasion of China by capitalist countries, by creating a class of English-educated "lackeys" who willingly did foreigners' bidding:

> Missionary schools are not only a form of cultural invasion; they are also a tool of economic invasion. Here is an example: Missionary schools focus on English. Because of the principals' recommendation to foreign companies and foreign services, after graduation, under the false name of spreading religion, they actually cultivate workers for economic invasion. In this way, missionary schools and economic invasion actually have a very close relationship.... My countrymen, after this massacre, how can we still allow missionary schools to exist? What is the remedy to this situation? It is to call on those students who are at schools under the control of foreigners to leave.[62]

Such sentiments reveal the extent to which a new Christian-educated, English-speaking elite was unsettling the status quo in treaty-port East China. Missionaries' promotion of their schools via their English-language curriculum was backfiring in this period of anti-foreign feeling. There is also evidence that missionaries' worst fears—that their schools would become used by Chinese for purely commercial advantage, generating a class of English speakers who had no interest in or were even actively opposed to Christianity—were coming to pass. Zhang Ruiyun 張瑞雲 (St. Mary's class of 1952) remembered that her grandfather had sent her father to the American Episcopal missionary school in Suzhou (Taowu zhongxue 桃塢中學) because of the English-language education offered, but had expressly forbidden him to imbibe the foreign religion, fearing that his son might desert a commercial career to work for the Church.[63]

The most damning indictment against missionary schools came from former pupils themselves. At a time when all forms of religion were being dismissed as superstitious, missionary school pupils objected to having to study the bible, which, according to Lin Shiguang 林時光, was "boring" and "dry," and the missionaries who taught it had "outmoded" and "unscientific" thinking. Lin complained that missionary school teachers were unwilling to compromise on the point of teaching the bible, and for this reason he had decided to leave his school.[64] Similarly, former missionary school pupil Gan Mengxiong 幹孟雄 felt that missionary schools had "become an outdated phrase", and no matter the nationality of the missionaries running their school, students must not return to them or they would be "cursed as running dogs of the imperialists, and traitors of your countrymen."[65] Perhaps most grievously, missionary school teachers were prohibiting students from demonstrating their patriotic feelings freely. Gan Mengxiong's report goes as far as to claim that the headmaster at one missionary school had threatened students with a gun.[66]

Across East China, many students walked out of their schools after the May Thirtieth Shooting, causing several missionary schools to close, some of which did not reopen. The best known walk-out took place at St. John's University. President Francis Lister Hawks Pott refused to admit outside representatives of the student movement to speak on campus or allow the national flag to be flown at half-mast when classes were not in session. As a result, more than half of the college students and three-quarters of the middle-school students chose to leave the university.[67] They formed their own rival institution, Guanghua University (Guanghua daxue 光華大學).[68] The walk-out included nearly all of the Chinese faculty.[69] St. Mary's and McTyeire also suffered a severe drop in their student numbers after the May Thirtieth shooting. Student enrollment fell from 360 in 1925 to 280 in 1926 at St. Mary's.[70] In Ningbo, pupils at English Methodist Feidi middle school

(Feidi zhongxue, 斐迪中學), CMS Trinity boys' school (Sanyi zhongxue 三一中學), Riverside Academy (Yongjiang nüzhong 甬江女中), Presbyterian Junior middle girls' school (Chongjing nüxiao 崇敬女校), and Baptist Junior middle girls' school (Chongde nüxiao 崇德女校) all walked out of their classrooms in the summer of 1925.[71]

Baptist missionary teacher Florence Webster, who was stationed at the Union Girls' High School in Hangzhou, allows us an insight into missionary reactions to the patriotic feeling among pupils at the school during the May Thirtieth protests. According to Webster, teachers felt that they were "on a volcano which might break forth at any time." She detailed the student protests in her letter to the missionary board:

> Their first mass meeting was held the day the other students in Hangchow were parading as a protest against the shooting in Shanghai and as they were meeting other students were marching around the compound yelling such things as "foreign slaves," "Down with the Mission Schools," and it was no wonder the girls got almost frantic. One girl got up and made a very impassioned speech whereat the other girls with one accord bowed their heads and wept, and some stamped their feet. I felt sorry for the poor things and was glad when it was decided to let them go out to parade. Marching in the hot sun for three hours may not be the best way of showing one's patriotism, but to me it seemed a pretty good way of letting off steam, and if they had been forced to hold in their seething feelings I think their reaction later might have been more serious. As it was, they came back at noon, hot and tired but too good sports to admit it, and went to afternoon classes as usual. The girls sent delegates daily to the students' union, had a campaign in school to raise funds for the strikers, and also went out on the streets between 4 and 6 for the same purpose, but all classes with the exception of singing, handwork and gym went on as usual.[72]

Despite Webster's somewhat patronizing tone in describing the student protests, her letter reveals the extent to which missionary schools were struggling to contain anti-foreign sentiment within the school. Webster was not without sympathy for her pupils and demonstrated an understanding of the tensions that girls who went to missionary schools had to negotiate in this period.

Student unrest did not quickly die down at Hangzhou Union Girls' School as Webster had hoped. She wrote on January 29, 1926, at the time when registration of the school was being discussed, that girls complained about having to attend bible study and religious services: "There is some unrest now amongst the non-Christian girls in the school. They ask, 'Why do we have to go to church when we are not Christians?' 'Why do we have to study the bible when we don't believe in it?' So we cannot tell when this may cause trouble and can only hope that our Bible classes and religious services may be made of real interest to them and that the issue may not come up."[73] Webster reported that she was worried about the "low ebb of Christianity" among the students and the fact that only one-quarter of the girls came from Christian backgrounds.[74]

Webster's letter reveals the uncertain and difficult conditions under which missionary schools tried to operate in the latter half of the 1920s. Some missionaries admitted that there had been a conflation between Western values and Christianity in many educators' minds. A general acknowledgment prevailed among liberal-minded missionaries that more must be done to end the system of extra-territoriality, encourage their students in their patriotic activities, and give over control of the schools and churches to their Chinese counterparts. For example, Rev. Harris E. Kirk of Baltimore, in his address to the Washington missionary convention, admitted the need for a "confession on our part that we have not fully understood Christianity, and furthermore that perhaps we have defiled it by allowing it to be too closely associated with something that is not essentially Christian at all—Western Civilization. . . . The time has happily gone, let us hope for ever, when we shall be sending out crowds of inexperienced enthusiasts, impregnated with the idea that our civilization is not only the best, but a normal expression of Christianity itself."[75]

Kirk was not a lone voice in urging missionaries to move away from the position that Christianity was synonymous with Western culture and civilization. Webster declared in the aftermath of May Thirtieth: "I want to go on record as against extraterritoriality and unequal treaties because they are a hindrance to the spread of the gospel and express the hope that the Christian forces of America will do all in their power to right the wrong and injustice. . . . Of course I realize the difficulties in the way because of the lack of a strong Central Government in China but hope my native country will find herself a real friend of my adopted country."[76] A few months later, in January 1926, she reiterated her feelings to the Baptist mission secretary: "I have already expressed myself as being very strongly for abolishing all the clauses which make missionary work dependent on armed force and as being willing to trust my life and safety to God. . . . Christianity has enough handicaps in China without the added inconsistence of trying to preach the gospel of peace and goodwill backed by the gun."[77]

Though they were quick to condemn the system of extra-territorial privileges and promote the idea of a Chinese-run and -supported church, missionaries' words and deeds sometimes failed to match up. Chinese Christians criticized missionaries for talking about equality and ending a system of foreign privilege but failing to carry this through in their actions.[78] They used the teachings of Christianity to shame foreign missionaries into a realization that their actions were against the true principles of their religion. For example, B. S. Siao of Hangzhou Christian College wrote in an appeal on June 6, 1925, which was published in a supplement to the quarterly YWCA magazine:

> The missionaries have been cursed as the tools of imperialism, and we, the co-workers with them, have been cursed as the tools of the tools. We cannot argue with them by words, we must show ourselves by deeds. To them I beg to offer the following suggestions: They should exchange their ideas with Chinese co-workers in a sportsman like spirit. . . . They should know they are Christians first and citizens second. If it is necessary to sacrifice nationalism in order to save Christianity they should do so.[79]

These sentiments reveal how the ideal of Christianity being able to overcome a narrow-minded patriotism that missionary schoolgirls envisioned in their writings in the May Fourth era were easier to talk about than to achieve in reality.

The response of many missionary educators to patriotic protests of May Thirtieth was cautious and ambivalent. At Hangzhou Union Girls' School the students were initially allowed to join in a patriotic rally with other schools in Hangzhou. However, students were subsequently prevented by their teachers from going on a three-day strike, with the threat that the school would close if they did so. Despite her sympathy for the students' anxiety and willingness for them to demonstrate their patriotism, Florence Webster was ultimately not in favor of allowing students to go on strike, because of the risks and responsibility it represented for the teachers. She had no qualms about telling students that the school would close if they chose to strike:

The Students' Union tried to get them to declare a three-days strike to go out to the smaller villages to tell the story and collect money but they were not in favour of it themselves and we just couldn't take the responsibility either for their health or conduct. They were just wrecks as it was with the worry and extra work. Then again, the faculty had made it plain that if school didn't go on as usual, we would just declare school closed and send them home. They knew that would mean scattering and that the movement would lose its impetus so they were anxious to stay. So they reviewed, took final exams and had graduation as planned. By that time they were ready and willing to go home and we drew a sigh of relief when the responsibility was off our shoulders.[80]

Webster presented herself as having the girls' best interests at heart, but she was unequivocal about the fact that the school forced girls to curtail their patriotic activities with the threat of closure. There was also a palpable sense of relief in her writing that the school had survived this turbulent period. Her stance highlights the wariness missionary schoolteachers felt about letting girls participate in such patriotic activities for fear that the tide would turn against their own schools. Webster's relief was somewhat premature, however, as in the summer of 1927 missionary schools were to face an even greater challenge to their survival in the aftermath of the Northern Expedition.

Crisis Point: The Northern Expedition

Hostility toward foreign missionary establishments, which gained momentum in the aftermath of May 30, 1925, peaked in the wake of the Northern Expedition of 1926–1928. The Expedition, a military campaign led by Chiang Kai-shek brought about the partial reunification of China under Nationalist rule, with a new capital established in Nanjing. The campaign saw a temporary alliance between the CCP and GMD, which ended in April 1927 when the CCP were purged from within the Nationalist ranks.[81]

During the military conquest, foreigners and foreign institutions, including Christian missions, were again targeted as symbols of imperialism in China and were attacked by anti-foreign and anti-Christian groups.[82] Violence against foreigners in the wake of the expedition was widespread, most notoriously during the Nanjing Incident on March 24, 1927. As Nationalist forces entered the city, the British, American, and Japanese consulates were looted, the British Consul was wounded, and several foreigners were killed, including the president of the University of Nanjing, John Williams.[83]

At Riverside Academy in Ningbo, the crisis point came in July 1927, when a group calling itself the "Committee for the quick taking back of educational rights," composed of Ningbo middle-school teachers and students, occupied the ground floor of the school's main building and opened a rival summer school called Yongguang 甬光.[84] To prevent the school from being taken over by the anti-Christian group, several Riverside Academy missionaries, missionary school students, and Chinese teachers decided to remain at the school over the summer, occupying the third floor and conducting their own summer school.[85] Both sides appealed to the government for support, and the school was sealed by the local authorities.[86]

Debates about the legality of the takeover raged in the pages of the Ningbo newspapers; both sides used the concept of "educational rights" (*jiaoyu quanli* 教育權力) to convince the public and government authorities that they were acting legitimately.[87] Although Principal Shen claimed that the school was already under the control of the Chinese and the matter had been placed in the hands of the local government, the rival Yongguang summer school complained that Principal Shen was trying to mislead the public and in fact power was "in the hands of missionaries and foreigners so that they can poison the young people."[88]

Frank Millican, who was stationed at the Ningbo Presbyterian boys' school, Riverbend, appealed to the Provincial Commissioner of Education in Hangzhou, Jiang Menglin 蔣夢麟, but his visit proved fruitless and the school remained closed.[89] During the winter of 1926 and spring of 1927 Ningbo had fallen in and out of Nationalist control several times.[90] The provincial government was in flux, and during the fighting missionary schools very narrowly escaped closure at the hands of anti-Christian forces within the United Front.[91] From April 1927, the purge of the Communists from within the GMD ranks began, starting with the infamous massacre of Communists in Shanghai in what has become known as the "White Terror."[92] This purge of the "left," according to Riverside teacher Esther Gauss, stabilized the situation and secured the future of missionary schools in China.[93]

Eventually, it was the newly appointed principal of Riverside Academy, Shen Yixiang 沈貽瓛, who managed to effect the release of the school by paying a personal call to Chiang Kai-shek, who was resting in his villa near Ningbo. Shen Yixiang was an old family friend of Chiang, and they were both natives of Fenghua 奉化 in Zhejiang province.[94] Chiang converted to Christianity upon his marriage to his wife Song Meiling, who was from a devout Christian family and had been educated at McTyeire and at Wellesley College in the United States. Given his wife's Christian educational and family background, it is unsurprising that Chiang was sympathetic to the plight of Riverside. The Generalissimo donated more than 1,000 Chinese silver dollars to the school, and his calligraphic inscription prefaces the 1931 *Riverside Echo* yearbook.[95]

The troubles experienced by missionary schools during this turbulent period cemented the importance of Chinese leadership for missionary schools and sped up the appointment of Chinese principals. The Ningbo Presbyterian boys' middle school, Riverbend, which had recently appointed a Chinese principal, J. M. Wong, suffered comparatively less disruption than Riverside, although it still faced anti-Christian hostility. Similarly, according to the missions' annual report, schools which were already transitioning to Chinese leadership, such as Northern Presbyterian Mary Farnham Girls' School (Qingxin nüzi zhongxue 清心女子中學) in Shanghai, "weathered the storm" comparatively well, mainly thanks to the "tact, wisdom and patience" of the Chinese leadership of the school.[96]

How did missionary schoolgirls themselves respond to this period of vehement attack and reconcile their identities as Christians and national citizens? The stories of three Riverside pupils, Margaret Fan, Chen Aizhen 陳愛貞, and Yang Yinsui 楊音綏, offer us an understanding of the tensions that existed in missionary schoolgirls' identities in the period from 1925 to 1927 and the different strategies that Christian-educated women used to display their patriotism.

For some students, rejection of their missionary schools was the only option left open to them. Margaret Fan was a rather unlikely rebel. A third-generation Christian, she was the daughter of a Chinese Methodist pastor, Fan Mianqing 範冕卿. Her mother, Gu Xiuzhen 顧秀貞, was missionary-educated and founded the first school for girls in Zhenhai 鎮海, Zhejiang province at the end of the Qing dynasty.[97] Fan's writings in the school's magazines reveal her to be a devout Christian and patriotic student, who was strongly influenced by the social gospel. However, she was forced to choose between loyalty to her missionary school and her patriotic sensibilities by the heavy-handed actions of Riverside principal Dora Zimmerman, who denied Margaret her graduation diploma when she refused to publicly deny her attendance at a patriotic rally in 1925 when her name appeared in the newspaper. According to a report in the Shanghai *Shenbao* in June 1925, Fan, along with approximately twenty other Riverside girls, took part in a student protest after an incident in Ningbo when five Chinese civilians were stabbed by a Japanese civilian. Riverside girls were aggrieved that their school was forbidding them to take part in patriotic activities organized by the Ningbo Student Union. They denounced their missionary school as part of a system of foreign imperialism that was oppressing China and declared their intention to leave, never to return. Accounts of what happened to Margaret differ, and we cannot know if this was the rally for which Margaret was punished, whether she left the school of her own accord, or if she had already been excluded and was now publicly declaring her intention to leave.[98] According to her brother, Fan Aisi 範愛寺, Zimmerman later admitted to him that she regretted her decision to punish his sister.[99]

Margaret Fan went on to teach in a school in Shanghai and became a member of the GMD as well as a secretary for the Chinese Christian Women's Temperance Union (CWTU).[100] During the Northern Expedition, she took part in relief work distributing food, clothing, and medical aid to wounded soldiers along with other leaders of women's organizations.[101] Her family was alarmed by her participation in the Northern Expedition. Her father pursued her from Suzhou, to Shanghai, to Nanjing. When he finally caught up with her, he was shocked by her appearance: she wore a torn military uniform and she was ill.[102] Fan was clearly a patriotic and progressive student, and like several other women such as Xie Bingying 謝冰瑩, she took a radical step by daring to get involved in military activities in this period.[103] Although we do not know Fan's exact motivation for joining the Northern Expedition or the extent of her participation in military activities, her story illustrates how this period was a catalyst, pushing some patriotic Chinese Christians to take a stand against their schools, when circumstances forced them to take sides. It is possible that the experience of being punished for wanting to show her patriotism at Riverside cemented her determination to display her patriotism even more openly, leading her to support the GMD's efforts to unite the country and be rid of foreign imperialism in China.

Though Margaret Fan's decision to rebel against her school principal is one example of how students reacted when compelled to choose between their patriotism and loyalty to their schools in this period, it does not tell the whole story. In contrast, other students found that in the face of anti-Christian and anti-foreign hostilities their identities as missionary school students and patriotic citizens could be mutually reinforcing. Yang Yinsui and Chen Aizhen were part of a group of more than twenty Riverside students and five teachers who voluntarily remained over the summer vacation in 1927, occupying the third floor to ensure that the school would not fall into the hands of the anti-Christian group.[104] Although we know little about their family backgrounds, their writings reveal them to be, like Margaret Fan, both very patriotic and Christian students. In the spring of 1927 Yang Yinsui also attended a patriotic rally for students in Ningbo, but in this case she went with the goal to defend her school.[105] Yang cleverly invoked the incontrovertible spirit of Sun Yat-sen (the father of the Chinese Republic and figurehead of the 1911 Revolution) and his "Three People's Principles"[106] to disarm those who wanted to denounce Christianity:

> This Monday they wanted to hold a meeting against Christ (anti-Christian). Then I stood up and said, "Freedom of religious belief is in the Three People's Principles. I confess I am a Christian. I cannot oppose Christ!" They heard it. They couldn't speak any word for five minutes. Later they changed the name of the (proposed) meeting.[107]

Another Riverside student, Chen Aizhen, found in the gospel of "social service" a means by which to defend her school's patriotic and Christian contributions to society. In 1927 she wrote to the Ningbo newspaper *Shishi gongbao* to defend her school as a Chinese-controlled institution and complain about its illegal occupation by the anti-Christian group.[108] Her writings allow us an insight into how patriotic students effectively combined their patriotism with Christianity in this period. In her article in the 1931 *Riverside Echo* entitled "The Smallest Contribution of Mission Schools for Girls to Modern China," Chen wrote:

> Lately the outside world's opposition to mission schools for girls has been extremely strong. Their attack of us is truly very harmful, we know that they want to blot out in one stroke our mission schools for girls, to sweep them away. In the summer of 1927, this school also suffered this kind of intimidation. In Ningbo prefecture (Zhejiang province) there were several schools, in a similar situation to us. . . . Was their interference in the

end correct or incorrect? . . . What value did our missionary school still have? . . . I fear that they wrongly blamed us, now I will tell you about our special contribution.[109]

Chen listed three ways in which missionary schools for girls have made a great contribution to China: by educating women who would previously be denied an education, cultivating girls who could create happy Christian homes or become primary school teachers for poor village children.[110] Chen explained how missionary schoolgirls, with their advanced American training in household management, could transform the nation by creating "happy" and "good" families: "At female mission schools housewives can receive foreign education and accomplishments. She can properly manage the household, determine artistic and religious thinking, can protect and raise children. She can use American education to cultivate children in sleep, play, eating, and study, all have equivalent lengths of time." Moreover, the Christian-educated wife knew how to love and care for her (preferably Christian-educated) husband. They could mutually help each other, uniting the family at dinnertimes where they would talk and laugh around the table.[111] Christian language and imagery suffuses the essay, and Chen borrows from her Christian teachers the language of "service" and "self-sacrifice": "There are many female students who after graduation, based on the principle of self-sacrifice, wish to serve society, for the happiness of mankind, go to the rural villages to instruct children, becoming primary school teachers."[112]

Chen's case reveals a little-told part of the story of Chinese Christianity: faced with increasing hostility, Christian women were forced to justify their contributions to society, forging as they did so a unique gendered vision of protestant Christianity for China. In troubled times, teachers and students at Riverside were concerned not to present the school as cut off from, but as intimately connected to, local Ningbo society. By highlighting their local contribution to nation-building efforts, students and staff at Riverside sought to defend themselves from attack as an American missionary establishment. The anti-foreign nationalism, which peaked after May 30, 1925, and during the Northern Expedition in 1926 and 1927, had the effect of speeding the indigenization process of the Christian Church in China. Girls at missionary schools were essential participants in this process. While some left their schools, forcing missionaries to recognize that the days of a foreign-dominated church were numbered, others found in the rhetoric of social service a means to reconcile their identities as both Christian and patriotic citizens, and took their places as leaders of the schools after 1927.

Serving Women, Saving China

During the 1920s Chinese women formulated new identities as both patriotic female citizens and Christians. Taking part in the May Fourth Movement, missionary schoolgirls harnessed their patriotic ideals to the tenets of their Christian education which exhorted them to serve and love their fellow countrymen. Impressed with their responsibility to serve their less fortunate counterparts, Christian-educated Chinese women positioned themselves as the vanguard of the women's movement in this period. As missionary-educated Chinese women it was up to them to strengthen China, by "uplifting" their less fortunate counterparts, who had not had the benefit of a Christian education. This process of uplift was twofold. First, by giving Chinese women an education and teaching them how to be patriotic, missionary schools were preparing Chinese women to participate in politics. Second, by applying their knowledge of Christian homemaking and child-rearing to the conditions that they found in Chinese society, missionary schoolgirls claimed to be able to help create the happy, healthy, and productive families that could strengthen the nation. Chinese women, like their missionary educators before them, constructed a downtrodden female "other," in this case poor Chinese women and children, to justify widening their sphere of operation in society and fulfillment of their personal ambitions. Missionary school students went further than their missionary teachers, however, by insisting that only a Chinese-controlled church could build a strong and prosperous Chinese society.

These patriotic Christian identities that girls built for themselves in the May Fourth period were tested and honed during the waves of anti-foreign and anti-Christian hostility that rocked Chinese society in the succeeding years. While individual students' reactions to this hostility varied, ranging from defense to distancing, and sometimes even attack of their own schools, Christian pupils were far from the passive tools of foreign imperialism that their critics labeled them as. Students continued to stress how a Chinese-controlled Christian church could benefit China. Former missionary school pupil Gan Mengxiong suggested to his classmates that the way forward for patriotic Chinese Christians would be to establish their own church, free from foreign control: "Dear reader, if you want to be a true Christian, you can yourself found a Chinese Christian church, all you need to do is to put into practice Jesus' teachings."[113] In an environment of mounting hostility, girls used their social service activities to defend their identities as patriotic citizens and demonstrate their unique contributions to society as female Christians. In doing so, they helped to build a self-consciously Chinese and gendered vision of a Christian church for China.

3
Dreaming the New Woman

In 1923 Deu Miao Kung (Dou Miaogen 竇妙根, McTyeire class of 1923) wrote a fictional story for her school magazine in which she falls asleep and in her dream is shown a vision of what she and her classmates will achieve after graduation:

> "This is the Lilly of the Valley where all your classmates live. Sit on this rock and you shall see their different occupations." . . . Zung Sieu was the chief manager of the international banking corporation, with an annual income of $10,000. After looking over the various documents lying on her desk, she began to read the day's newspaper. While reading, her eyes gleamed and her face flushed with delight. "It is astonishing that Vung Sung has found out that star which for many years the astronomers were uncertain of. . . . I declare, here is some more surprising news! 'Tsung Kyung has been made minister of foreign affairs and will soon begin negotiations with Japan about the rehabilitation of Chinese property in Shantung and other places. Chong Ming has won the prize in a World Lawyers' debate and is now Chief Justice of the Supreme Court of China.' . . . A wise judge! A second Portia! What they have accomplished is astonishing and I must say this is a great day for the class of 1923!" . . . Amidst all the excitement and ecstasy, I felt some one patting my shoulder and saying: "Hey, go in, you little dreamer. The dew is falling heavily and you will surely catch cold here." I opened my eyes and saw that it was Li Faung. I asked her delightfully, "Oh, wasn't it funny?" She went off laughing at me and told me not to talk any more nonsense because it was long after the light bell.[1]

This and other "Class Prophesies" that are included in St. Mary's and McTyeire's annual yearbooks provide insight into how missionary schoolgirls playfully drew on different influences in their education—Christian, patriotic, and feminist—to "dream" new visions of what Christian-educated Chinese women might achieve in the future. Apart from becoming pioneering female scientists, lawyers, judges, bank managers, politicians, newspaper editors, and university professors, they also pictured themselves in more conventional roles: enlightened Christian housewives, social workers, and missionaries to inland Chinese provinces.[2] We can clearly see influences of McTyeire's English curriculum, which included several of Shakespeare's plays, in the girls' writing. Deu Miao Kung, for instance, references Portia from Shakespeare's *Merchant of Venice*. Many of the McTyeire class prophesies have a utopian tone, reminding the reader of Gonzalo's "If I had planation of this Isle," and most end on a bittersweet and nostalgic note of longing to continue dreaming after Caliban's "I cried to dream again" speeches from *The Tempest*. Indeed, senior girls' writings are tinged with a sense of sadness and nostalgia, which came from an awareness that they would soon leave the safe environment of their school and enter society. Throughout the magazines, girls display a gratefulness for the "refuge" that their school provides. Sheltered from the realities of a society where gendered assumptions of men's and women's roles were still deeply entrenched, girls found in their schools a free space in which to dream or experiment, forging their own vision of what a modern, Christian-educated woman could be.

Missionary educators, the Chinese government, and schoolgirls themselves had overlapping and competing visions of how to be a modern Chinese woman. Missionary and Chinese government educators agreed that the purpose of women's education was to create the model wife and mother, whose healthy body and knowledge of hygienic homemaking could produce strong (Christian) citizens for China. Missionary schoolgirls drew on these patriotic and Christian influences in their education in their visions of New Chinese Women's roles. As the first generation of Chinese women to receive an education in China and overseas, they were highly aware that they represented modern Chinese women on the world stage. They rejected the unpatriotic and frivolous "modern girl" figure who used her education as a social adornment, and policed their classmates and teachers according to their patrician ideas of how an elite Chinese woman should dress and behave. Girls thus participated in the creation of a rather conservative vision of modern Chinese womanhood.

At the same time, missionary schoolgirls found in their all-female school life a refuge from the gender norms and expectations still so prevalent in Chinese society. Within this all-female space, they experimented with new roles by adopting stereotypically "masculine" behavior in their dress, extracurricular activities, and relationships with each other. The school afforded girls the space to "dream" new roles for women which were a blend of "old" and "new" ideas. Girls at missionary schools in East China dreamed of a Chinese New Woman who was both genteelly feminine and fought for women's rights, was equally devoted to serving her family and society. She could be simultaneously a perfect Christian mother, social activist, and professional woman. She could both enjoy a companionate marriage to a husband who supported her ambitions and have a fulfilling professional career beyond the home. In short, she could "do it all."[3] However, upon leaving school girls were forced to wake up to the reality of a society which was not yet ready for their heady ambitions.

Making Christian Homes for China

Although Chinese reformers gradually accepted the need for women's education as key to national strengthening at the turn of the century, debates raged about what the goal for female education should be. Early conservative statesmen such as Zhang Zhidong 張之洞 and Zhang Baixi 張百熙 urged that women be educated in order to become better mothers to future Chinese male citizens.[4] Radical Anarcho-feminist He Zhen 何震 believed that educated women would help bring about male–female equality and their participation in politics and economics.[5] Conservative government officials continued to be fearful about where public education for women might lead well into the 1920s and 1930s.[6] Girls traveling to school on the streets, no longer cloistered in their family homes, were subjected to public scrutiny and were seen as susceptible to temptation and moral corruption.[7] Despite her increasing prevalence on the front covers of fashionable women's magazines, the figure of the female student who too obviously flaunted her sexuality and adopted the trappings of Western modernity, such as high heels, permed hair, and lipstick, was a source of public discussion and consternation.[8] The economic depression of the 1930s witnessed a retrenchment of conservative gender values toward women, with calls for women to return to their traditional roles as homemakers, trained in the latest Western ideas about hygienic housekeeping and childrearing.[9] Thus a conservative rationale, that education would make women better prepared for their future roles as wives and mothers, remained surprisingly stable throughout the Republican period.

Missionary educators also clung to their belief that Christian-educated women were key to producing self-propagating Chinese Christian families, and continued to emphasize the importance of women's homemaking roles throughout this period. Domestic education had always been a central component of missionary education for women, and during the 1920s and 1930s this developed into the academic discipline of Home Economics or Domestic Science.[10] The Home Economics curriculum was developed over time and differentiated according to the class background of girls who attended their schools. Early missionaries who could only attract girls from poor families attempted to allay fears that education would unfit girls for their domestic duties by highlighting the prominent role of domestic education in the curriculum. Both boys and girls were expected to perform a variety of chores and technical skills that were designed to educate them about their future roles in life. Chores for girls included washing, sewing, and mending their clothes, cooking, cleaning, and gardening.[11] Girls at mission schools also received advanced training in sewing, embroidery, and other forms of needlework.[12] Such activities were designed to equip students with skills that would make them more attractive brides and enable them to contribute to the family income.[13] Needlework had long served as a form of non-literate education for Chinese women and was compatible with the conventional virtues of "womanly work."[14] Missionary education in many ways conformed to Chinese values about the appropriate forms of education for women.

As missionary education took off with new elite interest in women's education at the turn of the twentieth century, schools were able to expand their domestic training curriculum, introducing the latest scientific equipment and methods. Riverside Academy invested a significant amount of money in its domestic education facilities. In 1923 the school spent 2,000 dollars on a "model Chinese home," and in 1931 it built a new domestic science hall.[15] According to a Presbyterian missionary stationed at Riverside, Esther Gauss, the model home was of vital importance to fulfilling the aims of the school, by giving girls a chance to practice their skills as homemakers:

> I have only just mentioned the model Chinese home that appears on the plans. We have as yet no estimate as to its cost. In money outlay it will be a very small item compared to the cost of the other buildings, but we plan for it to play a very large part in sending out girls fitted to make Christian homes in China. And that after all is the big thing we are here to do. Our plan is to make this model home in style of architecture and appointments not above the means of the average girl in the school; and that every girl before she leaves the school shall have had the opportunity of living in the

house for several months, a member of a group not too large to suggest the family group. And that while in the same house each girl by actual experience in every branch of homemaking shall have learnt the different ways in which she can make her own and other humble homes in China sanitary, pure, and lovely, as Christ would have them. . . . It is our hope and prayer that the graduates of the Riverside Girls Academy may be filled with the love of Christ and go out eager and well-equipped to do much for Christ and their country in establishing Christian homes.[16]

As Gauss's letter hints, domestic science was differentiated in different schools across the region according to girls' class backgrounds. Girls from middle-class backgrounds who attended more typical missionary middle schools, such as Riverside and Hangzhou Union School, were expected to learn vital domestic skills by undertaking chores such as washing and mending their own clothes and cleaning their dormitories and classrooms. The formal domestic education curriculum at Riverside in the 1930s also included hygiene, sewing, nursing, and cooking.[17] At elite schools such as St. Mary's and McTyeire in Shanghai, girls lived privileged lives and expected to marry into a class where domestic tasks such as sewing, cooking, and cleaning were performed for them by an army of servants. Thus girls' Home Economics courses at these schools consisted of learning skills which were more suited to their position in society. They learned to bake cakes and other delicacies, how to set a table for a Western-style dinner party, how to master American table manners, and how to match their clothes according to which colors best suited them. Domestic education was therefore founded on gendered, cultural, and class-specific ideas of how a modern Christian-educated woman should comport herself. That women could best serve China by making hygienic and well-ordered homes and nurturing children to become happy, healthy, and strong future citizens became an important part of government-backed gender ideology in the 1930s, particularly during the New Life Movement.

The New Life Movement and Building a Healthy Body

The New Life Movement (NLM) (Xin shenghuo yundong 新生活運動) was launched by Chiang Kai-shek in Nanchang in 1934.[18] Drawing on elements of Confucianism, Christianity, and anti-communism, the NLM was a political campaign aimed at the rejuvenation of Chinese society via moral values such as filial piety and personal habits of cleanliness, discipline, and temperance.[19] The movement reinforced women's roles as household managers who were responsible for improving the moral fiber of the family and, by extension, the nation, through their modern domestic training in hygiene, cleanliness, and citizenship.[20]

Some Christian groups welcomed the movement as complementary to the practices of hygienic homemaking; abstinence from gambling, smoking, and drinking; clean dress; and disciplined personal conduct, which they had long sought to inculcate in Chinese society. The Chinese Christian Women's Temperance Union (Zhonghua jidujiao funü jiezhihui 中華基督教婦女節制會) even claimed to be the "Grandmother of the New Life Movement" in an article published in its quarterly magazine in 1934.[21] Chiang Kai-shek relied upon Christian groups such as the YMCA and YWCA to implement the movement at a local level.[22] Despite some missionaries' distaste for the nationalistic, martial, and what they characterized as increasingly fascist elements of the movement, we can see the NLM as an example of a Christian-influenced form of modernity that became part of mainstream political life in China during the 1930s. In fact, one of its main proponents, Madame Chiang Kai-shek, Song Meiling 宋美齡, was a McTyeire and Wellesley College alumna. The gendered and class-based personal habits which were drummed into girls at missionary schools from a young age, including personal hygiene, cleanliness, and discipline, are evident in the core tenets of the NLM.[23]

Riverside Academy in Ningbo provides a good example of how the NLM was implemented at a local level. Riverside's first Chinese principal, Shen Yixiang 沈貽薌, was a personal friend of Chiang Kai-shek, and it is therefore unsurprising that Riverside enthusiastically adopted the tenets of the NLM after 1934.[24] Principal Shen explained how the NLM was implemented at Riverside in two-week periods. Rather than being imposed from a top-down perspective, as the movement is conventionally depicted, Riverside took a more inclusive and democratic method by asking each class, in consultation with its teachers, to decide which aspects of the movement the students would give their attention to during each two-week period. It was hoped that this way the movement would become practical enough that girls would follow it as a natural part of boarding school life.[25] Girls' dormitory rooms were subjected to daily inspections, and prizes, including a banner to hang on the wall, were given out to girls who kept their classroom most clean and orderly.[26] Regardless of Shen Yixiang's personal connection to Chiang Kai-shek, it is easy to understand how the NLM, with its focus on cleanliness and discipline, was seen as complementary to the orderly running of boarding school life.

Martial discipline and the drilling of the body through physical exercise were also promoted during the NLM. The creation of strong, physically fit citizens who could become soldiers was increasingly important as China geared up to fight the Japanese as they encroached in the northeast. Scouting and military drill became compulsory subjects at girls' and boys' schools in this period.[27] Military-style discipline was implemented at Riverside during the 1930s as a core tenet of the NLM. There was a Dean of Discipline for each class, and the school paid particular attention to punctuality and absences.[28] Girls' lives at school were ordered around the ringing of the school bell. Students were expected to line up in perfect silence at meal times and conduct themselves with decorum, walking slowly in the corridor between classes.[29] There was also an annual deportment prize.[30]

The active and efficient housewife needed to be strong and able-bodied in order to carry out her domestic duties effectively. Both government and missionary educators had long held physical education for women (including the elimination of footbinding) as important for strengthening China. While Chinese reformers had framed this in social-Darwinian terms of strengthening the race, missionary educators also saw this as important to enlivening girls both physically and mentally.[31] At Riverside, physical education formed an essential part of the curriculum in the 1920s and 1930s. Principal Shen reported in 1936: "Physical education has always been an important course in this school . . . the students are becoming more interested in physical education."[32] The chiming of the bell told students to exercise two times each day: before breakfast and after lunch.[33] Riverside spent a large amount of money on sports equipment; in 1930 it built a new gymnasium and in 1935 it added new basketball and volleyball courts.[34] In 1948 the sports offered at Riverside included basketball, ping pong, volleyball, and athletics.[35] The school had winning basketball and volleyball teams that competed in tournaments hosted by the YWCA against other missionary schools for girls across Zhejiang Province.[36]

The NLM's emphasis on the importance of health, hygiene, and exercise for building a healthy body resonated with the concerns of Riverside students. In 1931, student Ke Hailun 可海倫 wrote: "We are already Modern

本校奪得一九三〇年
寧波市公開排球競賽錦標之排球隊

The Riverside Academy volleyball team won the Ningbo City championship in 1930. Physical exercise was a longstanding, important feature of the missionary school curriculum and, in the 1930s, was complementary to the Nationalist government's efforts to strengthen its citizens' bodies in preparation for war against Japan. *Image from* Riverside Echo *(1931), Ningbo Municipal Archives.*

Women. A rich young girl who resides all day long cloistered in a stuffy dwelling, is averse to the needs of modern society. For this reason we must do all we can to protect our most treasured possession, our health."[37] One of the principal movements of the Riverside Student Union was a "health movement" (*weisheng yundong* 衛生運動).[38] In her article "Military Preparation and the Drilling of the Body," Lin Mixuan 林米軒 reveals the extent to which Riverside girls imbibed this rhetoric of the crucial link between healthy bodies and a healthy nation that was being propounded by the Nationalist government at this time: "My China seems to need to revitalize its national strength, firstly it needs to implement physical training of the body for its citizens, to make every one of our citizens healthy, only then can we prepare our military forces."[39]

There was therefore a neat alliance between Christian missionaries' emphasis on homemaking and the goals of the New Life Movement, which similarly placed women's domestic responsibilities as the foundation for a rejuvenated national culture. Knowledge of hygienic childcare and homemaking as well as physical fitness and rigorous habits of cleanliness and personal hygiene became essential markers of a government-sponsored elite womanhood in treaty-port China in the 1930s.[40]

Representing Modern Chinese Womanhood to the World

Missionary schoolgirls were highly conscious of their position as representatives of modern Chinese womanhood, not only inside China but also on the international stage. As the first generation of women to receive a public education, missionary school graduates were also the first Chinese women to venture overseas to receive higher education in Japan, the United States, and Europe.[41] This pioneer generation of Chinese women to attend university overseas included the adopted daughters of Episcopal missionary Gertrude Howe, Ida Khan (Kang Aide 康愛德), and Mary Stone (Shi Meiyu 石美玉), who were among the first Chinese women to earn medical degrees in the United States.[42]

Chinese women were made acutely aware that their own cultural habits were not considered "polite" in American society when they went to study abroad. In 1918, Ting Mei-Ying (Ding Maoying 丁懋英, McTyeire class of 1910), who was studying for a degree in medicine at the University of Michigan, gave her junior classmates some advice on "what a Chinese girl should know before going abroad for study." She devoted the first two sections of her article to "outfit" and "table manners." She cited the case of a pitiful Chinese girl who embarrassed herself at the dinner table because she had not yet mastered "polite" American table manners:

> I have seen our Chinese students eat salads with spoons, and cut meat with spreading arms. I never can forget the contrast that I saw at a college restaurant. There were six college girls seated at one table; among the six was a Chinese student. The five American girls were so straightly seated and seemed to possess unusually polished manners. Everything just magnified the awkwardness of that Chinese student's table manners. I know that girl personally; she is the equal in intelligence and character to any American girl. She is from a refined home, yet that little lack of gracefulness at table made her, to the superficial observer, appear unpolished and inferior.[43]

Keeping up Chinese national pride for elite Chinese women, who saw themselves as representatives of their country when they went to study abroad, involved the mastery of genteel American table manners, dress, and deportment. Being made to feel the social inferiors of their American counterparts for not having mastered Western norms of upper-class female gentility was particularly galling as Chinese women were aware that they were often the social superiors of their missionary educators, who usually came from middle- or even working-class backgrounds.[44]

In the semi-colonial environment of treaty-port China, where foreigners enjoyed extraterritoriality, race often trumped class. Chinese elites were particularly incensed that even the coarsest foreign sailors could enter the Shanghai Municipal Council's public parks, which were barred to all Chinese.[45] By mastering Western-style manners and social graces, Chinese women saved themselves the embarrassment of appearing inferior to Western women in terms of class in social settings where both Chinese and foreigners were present. This was a pressing task to restore China's national pride in the foreign-run treaty ports and Western educational institutions in which they lived and studied.

The missionary middle school was seen as an essential training ground where girls could learn these "polite" foreign forms of comportment: how to dress, how to eat, how to sit, and how to stand and walk. Alumnae saw these aspects of their education as a defining feature of their schools. Wu Qihui 吳其慧 (St. Mary's class of 1947) recalled: "They paid great attention to manners at our school; they told us, when you sit, you must sit very straight and upright, when walking, you mustn't walk in a casual way, that is to say, when you enter a particular society, naturally not in the company of working people, it's a formal occasion so you must act in a certain way. You could tell a St. Mary's girl by the way she carried herself. The girls who came out of this school were not the same, along with McTyeire girls, we were more polite."[46] St. Mary's student Yang Zhiling 楊之嶺 (St. Mary's class of 1951) related her memory of Deaconess Ashcroft reprimanding her for running in the corridor, telling her to come back and walk more slowly, to "walk like a lady."[47]

Missionary schools for girls thus inculcated very specific class-based notions of female gentility that drew heavily on American modes of polite comportment and manners. By the 1930s and 1940s, such etiquette had been internalized by many students as quotidian practices. In Kuan Yu Chen's (Chen Guanyu 陳觀裕, McTyeire class of 1936) memory of her schooldays, Western-style manners had become essential elements in her vision of how a "modern" elite Chinese woman should behave: "We learned how to be polite. We came from better families, some very wealthy. First of all, good family background, and then Westernized, and modernized in a way, and courtesy. You learned how to dress, pay attention to your appearance."[48]

While girls living in the hybrid Sino-foreign cultural world of treaty-port Shanghai internalized the idea that their training in Western-style table manners and comportment made them "more polite," they also mastered code-switching between foreign and Chinese modes of behavior depending on their social setting. In an article on domestic science at McTyeire, Zung Seu Ling (Cecilia S. L. Zung, Cheng Xiuling 程修齡, McTyeire class of 1920) described how girls were taught to "arrange and decorate a foreign table, and also table etiquette." Zung was conscious that she was learning an alternative mode of polite behavior but did not denigrate Chinese table manners, as Western missionaries might have done: "There is quite a contrast at table between our polite custom of stooping forward and the foreign custom of sitting straight."[49] Zung's somewhat defensive use of the word "polite" here suggests that she was aware of the extent to which Chinese girls' lifestyles and habits, particularly in the home, were targeted as needing to be reformed by Western missionaries.

Girls developed a dual cultural knowledge of manners and deportment, which they learned to use as easily and interchangeably as they slipped between Mandarin, English, and their home dialects. They regarded themselves as intermediaries or interpreters who could seamlessly move between Chinese and foreign social worlds by virtue of their education. Many alumnae felt that having a missionary school background gave them an advantage in the company of foreigners compared to their non-Western educated counterparts. Yang Zhiling 楊之嶺 (St. Mary's class of 1951), chosen as one of the first educational delegates to visit the United States after the Cultural Revolution, felt that the warm reception she received among American families and her ability to make friends with them was partly due to her familiarity with American cultural norms and "polite" manners learned from her days at St. Mary's.[50]

As elite Chinese women, with the cultural cachet of a Western-style education, girls positioned themselves as arbiters of how an upper-class Chinese woman should dress and behave. Missionary schoolgirls appeared on the front covers and in the pages of fashionable women's magazines of the era. They were often in the spotlight, either for their academic, athletic, musical, or dramatic accomplishments or as beautiful and eligible female graduates poised to enter society and the urban marriage market of Shanghai.[51] Students were aware that they were often in the public eye and thought of themselves as trendsetters in treaty-port society. In her article "Changing Styles," Tsih Zoen Shang (Qi Ruixin 戚瑞馨, McTyeire class of 1923) explained how fashions in Shanghai had changed since the 1911 Revolution and asserted female students' leading roles in setting the trend: "Schoolgirls are the most fashionable class in Shanghai and take the lead in determining new modes."[52] According to Tsih, schoolgirls acted as the arbiters between West and East in terms of evolving women's fashion, consciously interpreting Western fashions and redeploying them for Chinese women.[53]

While they touted their Western education, polite manners, and fashion sense to distinguish themselves as the elite, missionary schoolgirls rejected the overly commercialized "modern girl" figure, who immodestly wore too much makeup, a too-tightly fitting *qipao*, and just wanted to have fun.[54] In doing so, missionary schoolgirls policed the limits of upper-class female gentility for women in treaty-port Shanghai. A controversial figure in Republican-era print media, the "Modern Girl" was contrasted unfavorably to the patriotic "New Woman." Her wholehearted embrace of the seductions of Western modernity, in her dress, lifestyle, and behavior, would inevitably lead her into a dissolute life and national disgrace.[55] Elite Chinese women disparaged the public displays of affection and showing of too much skin by American women as a way to reassure themselves of their own superiority when it came to virtue in the 1930s.[56]

Missionaries were also alarmed at the speed of the changes they saw occurring in Chinese society and continued to impart rather conservative views on how men and women should dress and interact in public. Girls clearly picked up on some of their missionary educators' concerns. In their fictional short stories, unchaperoned girls who go to mixed-sex parties and fall into bad company inevitably come to a sticky end.[57] And while they denounced the "old fashioned" practices of footbinding, concubinage, and superstition, they also admired the virtues of chastity, thrift, hard work, and self-sacrifice that characterized the older generation.[58] Girls thus propounded a rather hybrid new/old model of Chinese womanhood.

At McTyeire, students critiqued their classmates and teachers whose immodest dress caused damage to their school's reputation. Rosalyn Koo (Chen Jinming 陳晉明, McTyeire class of 1947) recalled how she was almost expelled for leading a class rebellion against a new Chinese language teacher who did not conform to McTyeire girls' standards of how a high-class,

St. Mary's student Yang Ruiyun was featured on the front cover of the popular women's magazine *Linglong* in August 1931. With fashionably bobbed and waved hair, carefully shaped eyebrows, and immaculate makeup, Yang epitomized the upper-class educated woman in Shanghai's society. *Courtesy of the "Chinese Women's Magazines in the Late Qing and Early Republican Period (WoMag)" database, Heidelberg Research Architecture, https://kjc-sv034.kjc.uni-heidelberg.de/frauenzeitschriften/*

well-educated Chinese woman should comport herself.[59] Her classmate Zhang Long 張瓏 (McTyeire class of 1947) elaborated on how this teacher's appearance was doing harm to their school's reputation:

> Once there came a Chinese teacher, Miss Wang, to teach us Chinese. She dressed herself in a very unusual way, not the way a McTyeirean would do. She came with full high heels, lipstick, and we did not like her. She wore her *quipao* very tight, and very full high heels, we did not like that, because no teacher was dressed like that.... I think [Principal] Xue Zheng 薛正 understood that she was not actually a good teacher for us, so at the beginning of the next semester we did not see her.[60]

While images in Republican print media indicate that missionary schoolgirls certainly adorned themselves with the latest fashions, hairstyles, and makeup outside of school, alumnae highlighted the strict and rather conservative mode of dressing of girls when at school. After having suffered from the label that they were bourgeois *xiaojie* 小姐 (young ladies) during the Cultural Revolution, it is unsurprising that missionary school alumnae who remained in China after 1949 tended to emphasize how "down to earth" their schools were. Many of the alumnae in China explained how they dressed in a "toned down" way at school, with no makeup, expensive clothing, or jewelry allowed. Zhang Long recalled how her classmate was sent home from school one day for wearing red nail polish: "So it's rather strict. We never used makeup and we never dressed too fantastically. We were allowed to curl our hair but we didn't maybe until senior [high]."[61] Members of both St. Mary's and McTyeire, which were rival schools in Shanghai during the Republican era, told me that their school was more "down to earth" and less "aristocratic" than the other.[62] They were thus still competing, but this time to shed, rather than shore up, their reputations as the most exclusive schools for girls in China. Alumnae in the United States who had left China shortly before 1949, having not lived through the Cultural Revolution, were not so sensitive about this "aristocratic" label attached to their schools.

Girls' concerns with the vanity and frivolity of the "modern girl" were not simply a reflection of their Christian education and patrician gender identities but were also closely linked to students' patriotic concerns. The privileged Chinese woman who had the opportunity to study abroad saw herself as a representative of modern Chinese womanhood on the world stage, and thus must be highly patriotic. Girls therefore internalized conservative ideas which projected elite women as vessels for the preservation of cultural essence in the face of a rapidly modernizing and Westernizing society.[63] During the National Products Movement in the 1930s Chinese women were exhorted to buy Chinese goods rather than foreign imported products.[64] In 1931, Riverside student Tu Fengyun 屠鳳韻 explained how her classmates were enthusiastically following the national goods movement: "The national goods movement is to encourage our classmates to love to use national products, to do their utmost to boycott foreign commodities, for the purpose of establishing a patriotic and powerful national determination."[65] Like McTyeire girls, Riverside pupils did not approve of women who wore too much foreign makeup and high-heeled shoes.[66]

Positioning themselves as patriotic "New Women," whose educated status conferred the weighty responsibility of helping to strengthen China, missionary schoolgirls rejected the type of student who did not want to serve society but simply used her education as a social adornment.[67] In 1931 Riverside student Chen Xingying 陳杏英 expressed her disdain for this type of student who used her education to attract a husband and was of no use to society: "There are many upper-class students whose goal in entering school is not for the purpose of studying, merely to create a stir, for the purpose of making friends.... They cheat their way into this excellent position, or perhaps by getting to know a beautiful man or woman."[68] McTyeire girls were also quick to critique their classmates who just wanted to study abroad "with no definite aim" but just to get a "'society culture.' The latter consists of having a few popular songs, a number of piano pieces and a speaking knowledge of English." The author's suggestion is: "If you are coming to America, get something which will be of real value to our country ... seeing the need of our country, knowing the condition of our people, and appreciating the age in which we are living, every intelligent and patriotic daughter of China cannot fail to ask herself, 'How can I best prepare myself to serve my country?'"[69]

Missionary schoolgirls therefore had to perform a difficult balancing act. On one hand, they used their modern education and "polite" Western-style manners to position themselves as the leaders of a new elite, representing Chinese womanhood when studying abroad. On the other hand, girls had to make sure that they did not go too far in their consumption of Western fashions to avoid the label of being "unpatriotic" and "immodest." This careful, self-consciously patriotic performance of how to be a modern Chinese woman can perhaps most visibly be seen in the figure of Song Meiling, who was from a Christian family background and spoke flawless

English from her time spent at American schools and college. When Song gave a speech at the US House of Representatives in 1943 to win support for China's war effort against Japan, the US media were receptive to this upper-class Chinese woman who sounded and acted like one of them.[70] Her Chinese qipao served as a marker of national difference and helped hammer home her patriotic message of raising sympathy for China's war effort. The cultural cachet of mastering Western-style manners and polite modes of behavior has continued beyond the Republican era. Rosalyn Koo, who went to Mills College in Oakland and then remained in California after 1949 to pursue a career in an architectural firm, related how her mostly white male colleagues often found themselves wrong-footed by the presence at board meetings of a Western-educated Chinese lady with flawless American English and manners, dressed in an immaculate tailored qipao. Rosalyn recalled with glee the reversal of gendered and racial power dynamics that resulted from their confusion over how to treat her.[71]

Missionary schoolgirls were therefore surrounded by a complex mixture of images and ideas about the ideal Chinese New Woman which implored her to be modern, patriotic, and educated but also genteel, thrifty, hardworking, and chaste. Girls participated in the creation of these contradictory ideas about modern Chinese womanhood, based on their class status, patriotic feelings, and Christian education. This complex and contradictory image of the Christian-educated "New Chinese Woman" was summed up by Christian educator Zeng Baosun 曾寶蓀 in 1931: "For the modern Chinese woman, let her freedom be restrained by self-control, her self-realization be coupled with self-sacrifice, and her individualism be circumscribed with family duty."[72]

The School as a Refuge: Views on Marriage

While the goal of missionary educators was to produce the model Christian homemaker, paradoxically, the first generation of missionary school graduates used their education to escape marriage and pursue careers beyond homemaking. Female missionaries unintentionally role-modeled professional female single lifestyles.[73] Early missionary school graduates seized new opportunities to stay single in order to pursue careers as doctors, nurses, and teachers, which were sometimes highly desirable alternatives to an unwanted arranged marriage. Although missionaries encouraged filial obedience to parents, they were not above helping their students to avoid a match that they deemed spiritually harmful to their students. For example, Ding Maoying (the student who gave her classmates advice on American table manners) was engaged to a man who smoked opium. Her great-niece, Ding Yuming 丁毓明 (McTyeire class of 1941), recounted how, with the help of the headmistress of McTyeire, Helen Richardson, her aunt was able to escape this marriage and pursue a medical degree in the United States:

> Ding Maoying, my grand-aunt, went to McTyeire.... So she finished high school and my great-grandfather wanted her to get married to a young man that the family had fixed for her. This young man smoked opium... and my grand-aunt said, 'No. I am not going to marry this man, I don't want a husband who smokes opium.' So, with the help of a missionary teacher from McTyeire, a Methodist missionary from Mississippi, she was able to escape before the day she was going to get married. They helped her get out, and they financed her to apply and come to Mount Holyoke College in the United States.... Then she finished her studies at the University of Michigan medical school. At that time her father did not want to give her any money, so they gave her a Barbour Scholarship for Oriental Women.[74]

Although reform-minded Chinese literati, such as Ding Maoying's grandfather, had sanctioned women's education as key to national strengthening since the late nineteenth century, most girls did not yet have the freedom to choose who they married. After graduating from the University of Michigan, Ding Maoying returned to China to start the first obstetrics and gynecology hospital for Chinese women in Tianjin, which later developed a pediatrics department. She remained single throughout her life.[75]

In the May Fourth era, missionary schoolgirls subscribed to the ideal of a free-choice marriage even if this was still far from the reality for many elite girls in this period. They also dreamed of a society where women could pursue a career alongside marriage. In a fictional piece entitled "A Broken Engagement," which to some extent parallels Ding Maoying's story, pupil Tseu Mei Yuin (Zhou Meiyun 周湄雲, McTyeire class of 1921) creates a heroine who escapes from an unwanted arranged marriage to pursue a medical degree in America. Her choice, which struck her family as a "death blow," is justified when she returns several years later and "the prodigal daughter" is received with "tears and forgiveness." The fictional heroine works diligently for her countrymen, saving a village from an epidemic, and eventually marries a doctor who works alongside her.[76]

According to alumnae, the all-female environment of missionary middle schools offered girls a space where they could escape from the gender discrimination that was prevalent in Republican society. Students who were unhappy in their own family situations sometimes saw their schools as a "refuge" where they could just "be themselves." Rosalyn Koo saw her school as a haven, an escape from her home where her father ignored his wife, and sons were treated differently from daughters: "I was eager to get back to school after the weekend. To see my friends. Because it was no fun staying at home—I was alone.... I was also very disappointed. Disappointed in my parents for not recognizing me as a person. They put me in a category— you are a girl. It's alright if I made a mistake, you don't expect much from girls. Now, if my brothers should make a mistake like that, they would get reprimanded but not me."[77] Jean Koo Lea (McTyeire class of 1929) also regarded school as a sanctuary from her unhappy home life: "I am glad I went to school, because I did not like it at home. I was the only one who graduated from college. My parents did not love me."[78]

Considering the unhappy family situation of many students, with fathers who kept concubines, and with aunts and sisters in unhappy arranged marriages, it is perhaps unsurprising that they should have a negative view of marriage and regard their school as a refuge from a society which did not treat women as equals. Cecilia S. L. Zung (Cheng Xiuling 程修齡), a McTyeire graduate of 1920 who became a pioneering female lawyer, remembered:

> My Aunt killed herself because of a bad marriage. She died long before I was born. And her life-size picture is in my home, the castle. And one wing of the castle was her living quarters. So her life-size picture was hung on the wall. To a little girl walking into that room, you can see the impression on the girl. And then my sister married and her husband took all her money to keep three women on the side. My sister returned home after her husband spent all her money. My sister was eleven years older than I. So she was grown up when I was a child. My sister returned home because he had used all her money. So when the husband came, I said, "Don't talk to me, you are a beast. Don't talk to me you are a beast." I called him a beast. "You use my sister's money and you keep three women." I made up my mind I would have nothing to do with boys.[79]

Prevalent throughout alumnae memories is the concept of the alternative all-female "family" environment which their school provided. At school, girls could forge strong familial relationships in a safe, all-female environment that encouraged them to learn, grow, and develop without the overt discrimination which they witnessed at home and in society. Many alumnae described the close relationships they formed with classmates and teachers at school, invoking the rhetoric of a "family" to describe their campus environment. Newly arrived students were paired with a "big sister" from an older class who would help them to settle into this new family. Amy Siao Yen (McTyeire class of 1928) felt that "most of the teachers were graduates from the school so we were very friendly.... Just like friends, like family almost, I feel that way."[80] This idea of the school as a surrogate family was prevalent in many all-women's educational institutions in this era. According to Jin Feng, this familial environment not only helped forge close bonds between students and teachers at Ginling College, it also provided Chinese women with a safe environment in which they could form new relationships and identities removed from their place within the Chinese family hierarchy.[81] The need for a caring family environment was perhaps even more pressing at the middle-school level, as girls formed their ideas about life and took their peers and teachers as examples of what independent womanhood could be.

Inverting Gender Binaries: Playing Men's Roles

Within this "safe" all-female refuge of the school family, girls often experimented with new roles that both transgressed and reinforced traditional gender boundaries. Some educational research has suggested that, within an all-female school environment, girls have more scope to pursue "hard" science subjects and assume traditionally "male" leadership roles within the classroom.[82] Alumnae believed that this all-female environment was beneficial to their personal and academic development. Kuan Yu Chen (Chen Guanyu), a student of McTyeire and later principal of the Presbyterian True Light School for Girls in Hong Kong (Zhenguang nüshu yuan 真光女書院), approved of girls' schools as giving girls a forum to develop their leadership skills without the distraction of male classmates: "I approve of girls' schools. It avoids social and peer pressures. You don't have those distractions. At least you can spend your adolescence in a very free and healthy way. If your family encourages you, you can do it outside. Also, leadership. You have more chance to have leadership positions. You might say that it is not natural. Well McTyeire girls never had any trouble getting married. They can adjust very well in college."[83] Anita Li Chun (McTyeire class of 1943), growing up at home with ten siblings including six elder brothers, felt it a relief to escape from her male-dominated family environment to the companionship of her female friends at school: "I am glad I went to a girls' school. I did not want to be bothered by the boys, I had so many older brothers. And also, my brothers got so many friends coming in and out of the house. Enough is enough! I'd rather have peace and quiet."[84] Rosita Li Wang (McTyeire class of 1946) felt that an all-girls environment contributed to the sense of family or belonging experienced by many of the graduates. She remembered:

> I am glad I went to an all-girls' school.... If you have both boys and girls the feeling is very different. There is a lot of distraction. And here it was much more unified, you feel much more a sense of belonging. You can always have co-education in college. That makes college life more exciting, because now you are going to a different world.... A twelve-year-old girl does not need all that boyfriend business.[85]

Although the majority of alumnae felt that an all-girls environment was "freeing" for them, there were some who believed that it hindered them in later life as they felt uncomfortable and did not know how to interact with men. Mae Yih (McTyeire class of 1946) recalled: "I was very awkward with boys. In mixed company, for a long time, I didn't quite know what to do. Girls that went through mixed education knew how to joke, how to be very calm and natural. With me, I kind of froze in front of mixed company."[86] Zhang Luoluo 張羅羅 (McTyeire class of 1947), reminiscing about her schooldays with a group of alumnae at a reunion to celebrate the fiftieth anniversary of the school, could see both the advantages and the pitfalls of an all-girls education: "I think it is definitely an advantage to go to an all-girls school. You can concentrate on your study. The disadvantage is you don't know how to relate to boys. I didn't know what to talk to them about. But I don't have any regrets."[87]

In the absence of male classmates, some girls performed traditionally defined "male" roles at school in their dress, behavior, and relationships with each other. Some girls self-consciously styled themselves as "tomboys" at school, wearing male attire and performing according to stereotypically male behavior. For example, Rosalyn Koo went to the extent of dressing as a boy to school. She explained how she wanted to be treated as a boy and was disdainful of stereotypically feminine behavior: "I felt very restless. I'd ask myself, 'Why am I here with this bunch of girls?' I said I will never be like the stereotype of a girl which is gossip, gossip, and gossip, play mah-jongg, and talk to each other about their husbands having mistresses outside. I mean, all the stuff I saw going on in my house. Or go shopping. How to make demands on your husband who's not faithful. Because you can't leave. So what do you get? You get money. Because wives have no control. But all this gossiping."[88] Koo revealed that part of her disdain also came from witnessing the difficult position of women in society at that time and direct experience of gender discrimination at home by her father. Consequently, she felt she would rather be a man than a woman:

> I said, I don't want to be a girl, I never want to be a girl. I am very articulate. You use double standard. You treat my brothers one way and you treat me another way. I had a report card. I wanted to show him that I had good grades. He said, "Why do you need to study so hard? You don't need to. Girls don't need to study so hard." My brother got a C; he got chewed out. But my father did not care about me. He said, "We hire a music teacher to teach you music, a French teacher to teach you how to speak French. And maybe if you need, we will hire a dancing instructor to teach you how to do ballroom dancing. You don't need to study that hard." And I screamed at him. I went to my mother and said, "Look at him, he treats me like a second-class citizen." I would blow up.[89]

Rosalyn Koo styled herself as a rebel and tomboy at school. She recalled her extreme displeasure at having to switch into Home Economics when she flunked her math class: "I refused to sew, to cook, to knit. Anything attached to the feminine I refused. That's why I said to my high school principal, 'Why should I have to go into Home Economics? I have no use for that.'"[90] Koo was not only rebelling against the style of feminine behavior she witnessed at home and in society but also the highly feminine gender norms and expectations prevalent in the school. Koo's words reveal what was considered elite ladylike attributes for upper-class women in treaty-port Shanghai: domestic arts, music, a working knowledge of French and ballroom dancing—traditional accomplishments of upper-class young ladies in late nineteenth- and early twentieth-century Europe. These were also the gendered accomplishments that elite schools such as St. Mary's and McTyeire built a reputation for providing.

McTyeire principal Xue Zheng applied a "male" gender stereotype when describing "naughty" girls, such as Rosalyn Koo at school: "Rosalyn was very naughty. She was very, very naughty. When she was in school, she dressed as a boy, never in a girl's dress. Naughty girls were boys. I was quite serious with the girls, because I thought they were spoiled by their parents so tried to balance it."[91] The memories of alumnae and their teachers and pupils actually reinforce existing gendered stereotypes in their descriptions of being a "tomboy" or "girl." The crucial point here is that the school provided a space where girls could self-consciously don stereotypically defined "masculine" attributes to express themselves and thus find a relief from society's pressures of how a "woman" should perform her roles in society through behavior and dress.

Plays and pageants performed by students at Christmas and for graduation were another venue where girls had opportunities to play men's roles. The highlight of the McTyeire school calendar was the senior play, which was put on by girls of the graduating class. Teachers, parents, and other family members were invited to attend along with members of the school board, church, and other patrons of the school. No expense was spared in preparation for this event; professional lighting teams, set designers, and theater directors were recruited to coach the girls how to say their lines and ensure the event was a success. This event, which was covered in newspaper and magazine reports, showcased not only the school and its facilities but also the girls themselves, indirectly advertising them as eligible future brides.[92]

Dramatically talented girls eagerly auditioned and participated in the senior play.[93] However, in an all-girls environment, male roles were performed by female classmates. Gender stereotypes came to the fore as the prettiest girls in the school were often chosen to be the heroines. Taller girls, or those with deeper voices, were cast in male roles. Mae Yih (McTyeire class of 1946) explained: "And then we had plays, senior plays, all that, which helped us establish public speaking, performing in front of the public. You know, encourage leadership qualities which I think was very important. My role in the senior play was the prince. I was always a boy. All the queens and princesses went to the good-looking gals in the class."[94]

How did missionary schoolgirls feel when they donned men's clothes and assumed male roles in school plays? According to Jiang Jin, female Yue opera stars playing both male and female roles could experiment with new subject positions, pushing at the boundaries of what was considered permissible between sexes in terms of onstage intimacy, as the viewers were aware that both

DREAMING THE NEW WOMAN 105

Zhang Luoluo, tall and admired by her classmates for being good at sports, portrays the prince in the 1947 McTyeire senior play. According to alumnae, casting in the school play reinforced gender stereotypes, even as it afforded some girls new freedoms to play male roles and experiment with their gender identity in the environment of an all-girls school. *Courtesy of Zhang Luoluo.*

players were female.[95] Interviews suggest that missionary schoolgirls also enjoyed the freedom which this temporary gender inversion afforded them. Xu Meizhen 徐美貞 (McTyeire class of 1946) related the fun she had playing a male role in the 1946 McTyeire senior play, Guo Moruo's 郭沫若 (1892-1978) *The Peacock's Gallbladder* (*Kongque dan* 孔雀膽). She also played the part of courtly lover Essex in *Elizabeth and Essex*. She performed her male role so well that the audience thought she was a man:

> I was very naughty. The senior play was usually very professional. In our class there was a classmate who knew a film studio, and also knew some stage actors, very famous ones. She invited them to come to our school to act as directors. So it was extremely professional. She invited an extremely famous male actor to come and be our director, and he went to the Lyceum theater in Shanghai, to borrow their scenery. Also a professional advertising station, which had their own orchestra, someone also knew the conductor of this orchestra, and they invited the conductor to come to our school and help develop the music, and this conductor also composed the theme song for our play. And then there was also a professional who came to do the lighting, so this play was really very professional, all of it was borrowed from a film studio. . . . Have a look [showing me photographs], this is our play 'Elizabeth and Essex' and 'The Peacock's Gallbladder.' . . . Look, I bet you can't find me? . . . I was already dead . . . lying on the stage! [laughing]. Our makeup was all done by professionals. Look at this, in Chinese opera, men's shoes were very thick were they not? This was a type of stage drama. I am now quite short but previously I was quite tall, five centimeters taller! Because I was tall, I played a man's part in the play, I put on a deep voice. The audience found this very strange, they asked, which school did you go to to borrow male classmates? We said, "Hey! We are all girls" [laughing], they thought we were boys![96]

Her account, along with the photographs she showed to me, illustrated Xu Meizhen's enjoyment of playing these male roles and adopting male attire. Xu Meizhen's performance of male roles was also influenced by Western notions of courtly love, facilitated by her elaborate and expensive European-style costumes. Girls learned about traditions of courtly love in their study of Shakespeare's plays and had fun performing these ideas on stage, playing the roles of both sexes in their body language and poses. Xu Meizhen characterized herself as a "naughty" student in the same way that Rosalyn and Xue Zheng characterized the naughty students as playing boys' roles at school. Similar to Rosalyn Koo, Xu Meizhen preferred wearing more gender-neutral outfits to school. Xu Meizhen also took on leadership roles and was elected as class president. She was, according to the American college stereotype, the "all-round girl," who learned to take on stereotypically male attributes of directness, leadership, and assertive behavior in an all-female school.[97]

Xu Meizhen (McTyeire class of 1946) gets down on one knee as the courtly lover Essex in *Elizabeth and Essex*, the McTyeire school play. *Courtesy of Xu Meizhen.*

Xu Meizhen plays the dead male lead in the 1945 McTyeire senior play, *The Peacock's Gallbladder*. She enjoyed wearing male clothes for the play and recalled that she played the part so well the audience thought she was a man. *Photo courtesy of Xu Meizhen.*

Xu Meizhen relaxes with her classmates in their dormitory at McTyeire in 1946. This photo reveals her tomboy identity and leadership qualities. Xu Meizhen stands out for her dungarees and uncurled hair. She gazes directly at the camera, and with glass raised to her lips she commands the attention of the viewer and is the center of the group in a social as well as physical sense. *Courtesy of Xu Meizhen.*

Within the all-girls environment of a missionary school gender roles could become more fluid, and girls often pursued and flirted with each other, forming intimate same-sex relationships. The formation of close same-sex relationships (platonic and sexual) was a common feature within missionary, private, and government all-girls' schools in this period.[98] Early twentieth-century sexologists, such as Pan Guangdan 潘光旦, pathologized homosexuality in China and were concerned with the phenomenon of female relationships that seemed to be prevalent in all-girls schools.[99] Although Pan suggested that this phenomenon in China lacked the strength to be called a "tradition," evidence from missionary schools such as McTyeire and St. Mary's suggests that female same-sex relationships were institutionalized to the point that it became a rite of passage. At McTyeire, according to Theresa Chen (Chen Zongci 陳宗慈, McTyeire class of 1951), there existed a tradition called "*chao pengyou*" 炒朋友 or "*la pengyou*" 拉朋友, which can be translated as "getting friends together" or "making friendships," where students acted as matchmakers, encouraging the formation of "crushes" of girls on teachers or between students. She explained:

Miss Harris, she was one of the youngest ones, and boy how many girls go after her! Ow, ow ow! Well, infatuation, adolescent infatuation. I never had that because I was close to her. But then also in school, that was like girls together, *women jiao zuo chao pengyou*. . . . Let me explain to you what it is. One party would say, "Oh, she's cute," and so we say "*chao pengyou*" we get you to meet, and so then they go to have tea together, get them together, it's sort of like the same-gender romance. It's only in girls' school, but that was very strong, and they always say, somebody, kind of looks up to so and so, and so if they express that, so it's kind of a game too, and it's really fun. Well they just have some time together, and the other ones who get them together, they have fun teasing, like matchmaking. I remember when I was in Junior One, there was a Senior Three, and they thought, "Oh, that's a cute kid," about me! But there are some people who were well known as coupled together, usually younger and older ones, the younger one will look up to the older, and the elder one will say "She's kind of cute kid." It's a group thing, I had my friends and if we know someone, we gang up and try to get them together, and sometimes they get kind of embarrassed because you know . . . because your showing your, it's not exactly infatuation, but it's more a game, more teasing than anything else, but it's very prevalent, but I think that's a girls' school culture. And the other thing. We had softball, and if someone admired someone with ability, we were like "*chao pengyou la!*"[100]

Rosalyn Koo clarified that this phenomenon at McTyeire was quite an institutional tradition or rite of passage. According to Rosalyn, the end result of "*chao pengyou*" involved the elder student inviting the younger one to walk one round of the school grass field in front of Richardson Hall together, and then they were matched. It also appears that older students used such relationships to get younger girls to perform chores for them.[101]

It is unclear how their teachers viewed these relationships, and, while it is unlikely that they encouraged them, many missionaries had chosen to remain single to pursue their careers or escape pressures to marry. As graduates of women's colleges, many of their American and British missionary teachers would have been familiar with the phenomenon of women falling in love with each other in an all-girls educational environment. Evidence suggests that "smashing" or "crushing" in the American context or "piping," "pashing," "raves," or "spooning" in the British lexicon was common in all-girls schools of the era.[102] As a Smith College clipping explained, "this distinctly woman's college word" described a situation when "one girl . . . usually a freshman, becomes much attached to another girl, usually an upper-class girl. The young girl is 'crushed' on the other, sends her flowers, and tries in various ways to give expression to her admiration."[103] American women's college authorities tried to discourage "smashing" or "crushing." Rather than policing students' sexuality, however, college authorities were more concerned about the development of an independent college life, outside of its control.[104] Moreover, it became an accepted practice that unmarried faculty women would frequently pair off and set up their independent household outside of college grounds together.[105] In China, single missionary women often lived together.[106]

Girls in a single-sex environment consciously experimented with same-sex relationships, sometimes in anticipation of the traditional heterosexual relationships they would be expected to form later. In the pages of the school yearbooks we find images of girls practicing proposing to each other, cartoons depicting student "crushes," and writing about the answers they would give to potential suitors.[107]

Both written sources and alumnae's memories are very circumspect about whether girls' flirtations and crushes involved sex. What is clear is that the all-girls school environment of Republican China unintentionally provided new and relatively free spaces where girls had agency to experiment with new forms of same-sex companionship and more fluid expressions of gendered identity. As Tze-lan Sang points out: "Female same-sex bonding in school was not simply a matter of physical pleasure; more often than not it was about camaraderie and a creative search for the self."[108]

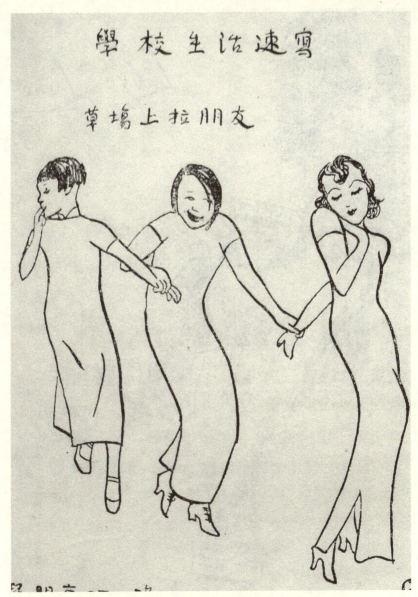

A cartoon from St. Mary's *Phoenix* depicts a stereotypically "feminine girl" with waved hair and curved figure being paired with a more masculine "tomboy" with shorter hair by a mischievous classmate acting as matchmaker. The cartoon encapsulates the culture of same-sex romantic teasing that was prevalent in all-girls schools of the period. The caption reads: "Sketches of school life: getting friends together on the school lawn." *Image from The Phoenix (1936), Shanghai Number Three Girls' School.*

A cartoon entitled "Love Lane," from *The McTyeirean* (1930), depicts girls walking arm in arm down "Love Lane," progressing from "class mates" and "table mates" to "room mates" and "friends," with the final destination of their relationship teasingly crossed out. The cartoon invited the viewer to join in the school culture of teasing and speculating where the boundaries of such relationships might be drawn.
Courtesy of United Methodist Church Archives—GCAH, Madison, New Jersey.

These female relationships forged in the context of an all-girls school perhaps provided a refuge from, and in some cases a viable alternative to, heterosexual marriage in an environment where the May Fourth ideal of a companionate, free-choice marriage was yet to become a reality for most women of this era. Indeed, with their mothers and sisters trapped in unhappy marriages to unfaithful husbands, and their independent female missionary teachers providing a new model of same-sex domesticity in China, it is unsurprising that many missionary schoolgirls sought refuge in the all-female society of their school and the intimate and fulfilling female relationships they made there. In some cases, these same-sex friendships lasted a lifetime, with girls pairing off and living together after graduation.

Waking Up: Dreams vs. Realities

In the 1930 edition of the *McTyeirean*, pupil Tsong Tuh Wei (Zhang Dewei 章德衛, McTyeire class of 1930) describes how a McTyeire graduate might feel at the cusp of leaving the safe environment of the school and about to enter society: "She stood for a moment before its open door like one who was afraid to enter some unknown abyss. In that brief moment she dreamed over all the dreams of her happiness on that peaceful campus, the deep green trees under those wide-spread branches she had lain on quiet Sunday afternoons, the dark winding pathway where she had waited for the moon, memories of the past surged up and captured her. She sighed in painful weariness."[109] Later that day, the words of her teacher, who encourages her to further her education so she will be better placed to help society, echo in her ears as she tries to convince her father to let her go on to university:

> She pictured herself in their palaces, labouring, bearing, and torn down by children, without freedom, will power of their own, but slaves of their ignorance. She saw them as the playthings of men and her soul rose up against the injustice of people. She saw them as dependents on men and her heart cried forth that she would undertake to teach them to work, help them to a better living and enable them to support themselves. She would help them to be economically independent.
>
> Then she thought of her teachers and words came back to her, words that aroused her ambition. "Miss Tsung, you're going to college after school?"
>
> She had expressed her doubts.

"Indeed you ought to. I'm sure your father will be proud to prepare you for work. Think how much China needs women, well educated women. I tell you have a big task before you."

These words had stirred her. She was needed and was glad to carry that burden. Her teacher trusted in her and she must do her best. But how was she to do it?[110]

While girls playfully daydreamed on the pages of their school magazines about being able to fulfill new roles, they were acutely aware that they were about to "wake up" from their school-day daydreams to face a very different reality upon entering society. Tsung's short story takes us to the heart of the paradox of missionary education for girls in this period: at school they were exhorted by their teachers that they should be of "service" to other women and were given the chance to test and hone their leadership and organizational abilities in their student-led activities. In the safe all-female environment of the school, they also found scope to experiment with their gendered identities, dreaming myriad new roles for themselves in China's future society. However, upon graduation they were forced to confront the realities of a society which offered women very few opportunities to work outside the home. This tension that an educated woman felt between her academic training to be "useful" and the demands on her to fulfill her traditional roles that society still expected of her was a paradox experienced by the first generations of college-educated women in the United States.[111]

While girls imagined being able to have fulfilling careers outside of the home, serving their country, building a Chinese Christianity and contributing to the international women's movement, alongside a companionate marriage in the pages of their magazines, the reality for most girls who graduated from missionary schools in the 1920 and 1930s was marriage and motherhood, rather than a career. Ling Van Chang Tang (Zhang Lingfan 張令範, McTyeire class of 1930) remembered: "I have two other sisters, I am the middle one. We all went to McTyeire. I married after I graduated. I had to marry. I didn't want to marry. I would like to go to school. My two sisters had arranged marriages too."[112] Although the opportunities for girls to continue their education to college level did increase over time, as women's education became more widely accepted and popular among the elite, pressure to marry early and well remained strong according to interviewees who attended school in the 1920s and 1930s. While women in this period did become the first group to have the opportunity to pursue a single lifestyle by pursuing a career, going to college, teaching, or charity work, this new "life phase" was normally regarded as a transitory period of singleness before they settled down and gave up work to get married.[113] In 1930s China, as in many Western nations, many professions had a marriage bar, which forced women to give up their work upon marriage. The view that women who married should give up work to devote themselves to the needs of their husbands and children was firmly supported by their missionary educators, who often left their posts to be married.

Alumnae pointed out that missionary schools did not always reflect the reality of the outside world. Rosalyn Koo recalls this paradox that girls who received an education in the 1920s and 1930s had to face:

> So my mother and my aunts went to college, ahead of time, so they came back, they were frustrated. Why? Because women cannot get good jobs could not work anyway, and if you divorce the children go to the father. So in a way, the women would not divorce. Because then what? They couldn't work and have no children. So women would get frustrated. But they got educated. See this is the unfortunate thing. You educate a woman, to think more of herself and then the society suppresses them, and said you're no good, you just get married, have kids, and in the meantime the husbands could have girlfriends and concubines, that's okay, the man is dominant throughout history of China, men! So growing up I felt very inferior being a girl, but the thing is I don't feel that I am inferior, why should I be inferior, you know, so I think, it is important that I went to McTyeire. It gives you a refuge. A refuge from the outside society, the outside pressure, the war. I felt safest at McTyeire, because it was a boarding school we were living in school five days and come home two days. I was grateful, see I would go home, and here would come the unequal treatment of men and women. The real world right?[114]

Rosalyn Koo's description of her mother's and aunt's plight is reminiscent of the words of Lu Xun who, in a talk he gave to Beijing Women's Normal College students in 1923, pointed out that it was cruel to "awaken" women by giving them an education when society did not yet offer them sufficient avenues to fulfill their talents and ambitions: "The most painful thing in life is to wake up from a dream and find no way out. Dreamers are fortunate people. If no way out can be seen, the important thing is not to awaken the sleepers."[115]

This was the dilemma experienced by missionary school graduates of the 1910s to the 1930s. By comparing their "Class Prophesies" to the "Alumnae News" section at the back of the schools' magazines in later years, we can see to what extent girls' dreams had become realities. Although McTyeire did produce pioneering professional women, including female lawyer Cheng Xiuling 程修齡 (McTyeire class of 1920) and bank manager Yan Shunzhen 嚴順貞 (McTyeire class of 1910), for the majority of girls the reality upon graduation was marriage and motherhood unless they went into higher education or teaching.[116] It was not until the mid- to late 1930s, when the second Sino-Japanese War brought opportunities for women to pursue a career alongside marriage, that this became a real possibility for many women of their class. A shift took place for women who graduated later in the 1930s on the eve of the second Sino-Japanese War, when women demonstrated their ability to work in society alongside men. Kuan Yu Chen (Chen Guanyu) explained this shift in opportunities:

> In those days all the girls were preparing themselves to get married and not a career. Well, I already belonged to a later generation. I am thinking of those students of the twenties and early thirties. Of my generation, I would say half of us prepared to go to college. To be so mature already and so sophisticated as ladies. They were married, and no one worked. It was not because of McTyeire, but because of the whole society at that time. There was no opportunity for women to work. But hard times came, the Japanese came.[117]

In 1937 Dou Xueqian 竇學謙, a sociology major at Yanjing University, documented the increase in the numbers of working women and professions opening up to women. According to Dou, by 1937 women could work as teachers, librarians, doctors, nurses, editors, journalists, translators, interpreters, lawyers, lab assistants, pharmacists, accountants, secretaries, typists, stenographers, and telephone operators. Social attitudes toward married women working were changing, and it no longer carried the stigma of economic desperation that it had before the war.[118] Although in the post-war period, as in Europe, there were patriarchal calls for women to "return to the home," and women were the first to lose their jobs when post-war unemployment replaced the wartime demand for their skills and labor, women's wartime experience of the workplace was a dramatic turning point.[119]

The School as a Lab: Conducting Gendered Experiments

The missionary school for girls was an experimental space that produced unexpected results. It was set up under tightly controlled conditions, designed to produce the perfect Christian wife and mother according to very conservative gendered ideas about women's roles. The parameters for the experiment also accorded with Chinese government visions for women's education, which during the 1930s stressed women's domestic roles as the foundation for a rejuvenated nation. In reality, the outcomes were rather different from those anticipated.

As the first generation of Chinese women to study abroad, missionary schoolgirls positioned themselves as representatives of "New Chinese Womanhood" to the world. The "New" woman that missionary schoolgirls envisioned was a hybrid and rather paradoxical figure: a fusion of their Christian, gendered, class, and patriotic identities. The modern Chinese woman should be a patriotic consumer of her country's goods, conservative in her Chinese mode of dressing, but fluent in English and fully equipped with Western manners and social graces. She should always be thinking about how to serve society and be aware of national politics, but should devote the majority of her time to caring for her family.

While girls participated in the construction of conservative Christian and Chinese government-sponsored visions of Chinese womanhood, they also used their schools to transgress or go beyond them. Within the safe all-female refuge of the girls' school environment, students sought to equip themselves with the skills necessary to become economically independent, go to college, and escape marriage. In addition, it provided a space where they could perform experiments with their gendered identities. Schools afforded some pupils the freedom to take on traditionally defined "male" roles, expressing these more fluid-gender identities in their dress, extra-curricular dramatic activities, leadership roles, and same-sex relationships. These same-sex relationships, which could last a lifetime, often seemed a desirable alternative to marriage, in a period when gendered roles for women were still deeply entrenched, and the ideals of companionate free-choice marriage had yet to become a reality.

This brings us to what was, for most of the Republican era, the fundamental tension at the heart of missionary education for girls. At school they learned that they must be useful to society and found scope to develop qualities of leadership and assertiveness. However, upon leaving school they found a society which was not yet ready for them. Until the eve of the Second World War, the career options open to elite women before marriage were limited, and after marriage most were expected to give up work. Although some graduates in the 1920s and 1930s did manage to stay single and pursue a career, the reality for many was an arranged marriage—a far cry from the professional career woman who also found happiness in a companionate marriage that these girls had envisioned. The Second Sino-Japanese war was a rather rude "awakening" for missionary schoolgirls. It not only offered women new opportunities to work outside the home through wartime relief work; it was also a moment of political conversion. Witnessing the suffering that the war wrought, girls started to question the stark inequalities between their own privileged lives within the safety of their boarding schools and the conditions of poor women and children beyond the school gates.

4
Awakening
The War, 1937–1945

In the 1938 edition of the St. Mary's *Phoenix*, pupil Tsang Sieu-ai (Zhang Xiuai 張秀愛, class of 1938) describes her experience of commuting to a new school building on Nanjing Road during the Japanese occupation of Shanghai in a piece entitled "The Centre of a Tornado":

> Sitting in the comfortable classroom and listening in a leisurely way to what the teacher is saying is like hiding at the center of a terrific tornado, which seems to be whirling the whole world around. Though we feel that we are safe, yet the terror outside our center keeps roaring around us, calling our attention to it. To reach this place of safety is also not without labor. You have to pass through the tornado in order to reach the center. . . . Even at the center of the tornado, which you have reached through so many hardships, you cannot be quite at rest. First of all, the smell of noonday lunch, keeps you feeling "the wrong place." (There is a whole family living in the room right next to us you see.) Then, during classes, the teacher is forced to stop for a few minutes though most apologising, with a sorrowful eye towards the window, outside of which, either a bombardment is taking place too noisily, or the newspaper boys are having their daily "revolution."[1]

The feelings Tsang captures here provide an insight into how missionary schoolgirls experienced the Second Sino-Japanese War in Shanghai. She is aware of being apart from but not cut off from the war. There is an awareness of her own privilege, gratitude for the "refuge" which their school provided, and a sense of novelty. However, they are not cut off from the "tornado"; the war is very close at hand, the sound of bombing drowns out their teachers, and girls have to pass through its tempest, confronting challenges and dangers on their way to school. Tsang is also aware of the national politics and debates taking place around her, and the "terror" of fighting is not far off.

Dreaming the New Woman. Jennifer Bond, Oxford University Press. © Oxford University Press 2024.
DOI: 10.1093/oso/9780197654798.003.0005

The recollections of missionary schoolgirls during China's war with Japan are both fragmentary and contradictory in nature. Students recall the "fun" of doing homework by candlelight, "excitement" of air raids and the wealth of new sights, sounds, and experiences they encountered on their daily commute to school. However, at the same time, the danger was very real and close to the surface of girls' recollections: a Japanese teacher banged his baton on the table to threaten girls into silence, students were forced to bow as they passed the Japanese checkpoints in the park on their way to school and fled from soldiers who tried to corner them alone. Nonetheless, the fragmentary moments of fun and excitement which emerge from missionary girls' recollections do not fit into established narratives, which tend to depict the war as a period of uniform suffering, particularly for Chinese women.[2]

Although studies of the Second Sino-Japanese war have proliferated in recent years, few studies examine the lived experiences of women in the wartime. Reflecting available archival evidence, they tend to tell us more about representations of women during the war than about what they actually did.[3] In general, two tropes of women in wartime China have emerged from the existing literature: the woman "warrior," who abandons her femininity to fight the Japanese, and the passive female "victim," who is raped or exploited by Japanese soldiers.[4] In the literature on wartime education in China, we know much more about the students who made the arduous trek to "free China," joining the GMD resistance in the West or the CCP in the Northwest and central China, than we do about the schools which remained and tried to continue under Japanese occupation in East China. Comparatively little research has focused on middle schools, particularly those that remained in occupied areas.[5]

In addition to a lack of source materials, much of this focus has to do with the overriding narrative of Chinese patriotic "resistance" which privileges the clear-cut memories of those who went West versus the more complicated, and at times uncomfortable, memories of those who remained in Japanese-occupied areas. Missionary schoolgirls' writings and memories provide us with an important lens into the everyday life experiences of female students in wartime Shanghai. Their memories complicate the neat binaries of heroines versus victims and resistance versus collaboration. Although both female and children (normally powerless subject positions), they had agency to test, rebel against, and in some cases invert the power dynamics between Japanese invaders and Chinese civilians.

Missionary schoolgirls' writings and memories also offer us a lens into the impact of the war on girls' political worldviews. Although in the early years girls were sheltered from the horrors of warfare, safe within their schools' foreign-owned campuses, after they were forced to move out of their campuses to other locations in the city, the realities of warfare hit home. They were no longer in an "ivory tower" but exposed to a wealth of new experiences brought by the war. On their commute to school, they witnessed the plight of refugees who flooded into Shanghai's international concessions for safety. While some students remained in a comfortable elite bubble, removed from the suffering around them, for many the war was a decisive turning point or a moment of awakening. The psychological shock of the war caused some students to turn toward communism, rather than Christianity, to make sense of the inequalities they witnessed in society. Although participation in Christian- and Communist-organized activities could provide some sort of escape, a feeling of being useful to society, and perhaps help to assuage their feelings of guilt for living privileged lives in the midst of so much wartime suffering, it did not necessarily turn them into "heroines" or "tough resistors" to the Japanese, as typically portrayed in communist historiography of student CCP members in this period.

On the Move: Relocation of Missionary Schools

The most dramatic change missionary schools underwent during the Second World War was their physical relocation or, in more cases, closure. After the Marco Polo Bridge incident of July 7, 1937, as Japanese troops advanced into central and eastern China, many schools were relocated, merged, or disbanded. In Japanese-occupied areas, 110 middle schools with more than 41,700 students were forced to relocate or shut down, and the wartime minister of education, Chen Lifu 陳立夫, wrote that half of the nation's 571,800 middle schools were directly affected.[6] Many missionary middle schools in East China followed other government schools and universities to "Free China," relocating in the GMD wartime capital of Chongqing, Sichuan province, or to Kunming in Yunnan, among other locations.

Christian schools and colleges were more likely to remain in East China than their government counterparts were. Missionary schools sought to use their foreign connections and close location to the treaty ports to protect themselves, either by moving into the nearby foreign concessions or by hoisting foreign flags to try to become "islands of extraterritoriality."[7] Before the Japanese occupation of Hangzhou on December 24, 1937, Hangzhou Union Girls' School moved to Jiande 建德, a mountainous region east of Hangzhou, and shortly afterward to Shanghai, where it joined the East China Christian School Association (Donghua qu jidujiao xuexiao lianhui 東華區基督教學校聯會) of fifteen middle schools that had been forced to relocate to the international concession during the war.[8] After the Japanese attack on Pearl Harbor in December 1941, the East China Association of Christian Schools was also disbanded, and some students traveled to attend schools in inner China.[9]

Other schools, such as Riverside Academy, decided to move to the Zhejiang countryside rather than to risk the move to Shanghai. In November 1937, Riverside narrowly escaped a direct hit during the Japanese bombing of Ningbo. It was decided that for safety, the school should relocate to Tinghsing, the hometown of principal Shen Yixiang, 100 li (about 31 miles) from Ningbo. Shen Yixiang was able to use the Shen family ancestral hall and the village temple as a temporary school.[10] One hundred seventy boarding-school pupils made the arduous twelve-hour journey by bamboo raft, racing each other to keep themselves awake, to the remote village where classes were conducted from 1937 to 1945.[11] In Zhejiang province, the network of waterways aided the movement of schools in exile, whereas those who followed the GMD government to inland provinces often had to make the dangerous journey on foot.[12]

Middle schools in exile in Zhejiang province during the war had a difficult time. Having to relocate several times to avoid Japanese troops, students faced difficulties in getting enough to eat, lack of adequate accommodation, and lack of medical supplies. Pressures put on limited food and other resources caused by an influx of students often resulted in tensions between students and locals. Much depended on the character of the Chinese principal running the school.[13] Riverside seems to have come through the war relatively well, compared to the dire situation that many students in Zhejiang faced. This was mainly thanks to Principal Shen Yixiang, whose family connections smoothed relations with locals and crucially ensured that students had enough to eat. Presbyterian missionary teacher Esther Gauss reported:

> The fact that the village is Miss Sing's home place ensured friendliness and paved the way for more or less difficult things such as securing enough extra bags of rice to feed such a sudden influx of population, or securing

the temporary use of a temple that when we arrived was being attractively partitioned and arranged for a provincial free clinic, but that would not be used for that purpose until several weeks later.[14]

Keith Schoppa questions the quality of learning that could have taken place under such conditions, but argues that the life skills, practical survival lessons, and an awakening to the conditions of their impoverished countrymen might have been the real lessons imparted in this period.[15] According to missionary teachers, Riverside students also gained from this real-life educational experience. Esther Gauss wrote upbeat letters to the Presbyterian Missionary Society about the continuing good spirits of her pupils throughout the war. Indeed, there is an element of "summer camp" feeling in Gauss's letters home, which describe the beauty of the rolling hills and rivers which surround the temple-cum-school. She seems to relish this

Presbyterian missionary teacher Esther Gauss poses with a group of Riverside Academy students who have been evacuated to the Zhejiang countryside during the war. Riverside staff and pupils lived in difficult conditions, using a temple as a temporary school, and they struggled to secure books and equipment to keep the school running. *Courtesy Presbyterian Historical Society Archives, Philadelphia.*

experience as a chance to get back to nature and live in closer proximity with the Chinese students and staff:

> We with 24 students and three other members of the faculty secured rooms in a new house situated high up on a hill overlooking most of the village.... Our cooking was simple as we took our noon meal in the school, eating Chinese food with the students and teachers. A long veranda running the length of the building and facing south gave us our morning and evening dining room, where the beauty of the mountain scenery proved a fine appetizer. I found the country life even more fascinating than it had seemed to me when I had been in "_" towards the close of the previous school year.[16]

For foreign missionaries, who tended to live in separate Western-style accommodations on middle-school campuses, it is easy to imagine how they might have seen this as a particularly bonding experience: living, eating, and sleeping in the same spaces as their Chinese colleagues and students for the first time.

But not everything was smooth sailing for Riverside-in-exile. Doris Coombs, the other missionary teacher who accompanied the school into the countryside, complained of a chronic lack of funding and equipment, including library books and blackboards. In May 1939 she appealed to the Presbyterian mission board for $5,000 of emergency funding.[17] Esther Gauss also lamented the "noisy and not infrequent interruptions to classroom work" caused by the frequent groups of mourners who came to commemorate the dead: "The wailing, loud beating of gongs, and firing of large firecrackers of course stopped all recitations for the time, but the intrusion seldom lasted for more than ten minutes. In the temple we as a school made no use of the stage and carefully refrained from any use of the central section running straight to the idol and altar."[18] While missionaries' disapprobation of such "idolatrous practices" is unsurprising, we are given no clue as to how their Chinese colleagues and pupils felt about the conditions under which the school was operating in their letters.

Girls who attended missionary schools in Shanghai had a distinctive experience of the war, due to the city's international concessions, which afforded it a special position. Along with Macau, Hong Kong, and other foreign-controlled concessions, it became a so-called "lonely island" (*gudao* 孤島) of neutrality within Japanese-occupied China during the period 1937 to 1942. In fact, these international concessions were by no means cut off from the turmoil of the war or the wider political situation; they not only had to deal with the effects caused by an influx of refugees from surrounding areas, overcrowding, food shortages, and spiraling prices, but also in some cases benefited from a new cosmopolitanism that refugees brought.[19]

On August 13, 1937, when girls were on summer vacation, the Japanese army started their invasion of Shanghai. After three months of fierce battle, Shanghai fell to the Japanese forces. The Methodist Episcopal Church decided that, for safety, St. Mary's, which was located on Brenan Road, close to the fighting near the West train station, should move with St. John's University and Middle School to the Emporium Building, a commercial building within the international concession on Nanjing Road.[20] St. John's rented twenty rooms on the fourth floor of the building and allocated several rooms for St. Mary's to conduct junior and senior classes.[21] Because space was limited, classes had to be conducted on a half-day basis, with girls coming to school to start lessons at 1:30 p.m. and finishing at 4:30 p.m. There were no facilities for sport, music, or dance classes, which had formed an essential part of missionary school life. Religious services took the form of a twenty-minute worship session held before classes each day. In the autumn of 1939 St. Mary's was able to move into a building called "Graves Hall," named after Bishop Graves (Feiwei tang 斐蔚堂), on the St. John's university compound. With more space, St. Mary's could resume whole-day lessons and make use of the physical education and music equipment and the chapel facilities that St. John's offered, although there was still no accommodation for girls to live on campus.

If the latter years of the war were a relatively easier time for St. Mary's, the reverse was true for McTyeire. Due to its location on Edinburgh Road, close to the international settlement, McTyeire suffered comparatively less disruption during the early years of the war (1937–1941). After the bombing of Pearl Harbor in December 1941, Japanese troops expanded their occupation into the international settlement, ending the *gudao* ("lonely island") period. This wrought dramatic changes for McTyeire, an American missionary school. During 1942 Japanese patrols periodically searched McTyeire and positioned military police outside its gates. In the spring of 1943 the American teachers, along with all allied civilians in Shanghai, had to enter Japanese internment camps, and in the summer of 1943 the school was requisitioned by the Japanese army to become the Number Two Military Hospital. McTyeire was relocated to a former British girls' school known as the Cathedral Girls' School at 425 Avenue Haig.[22]

Students' memories of the war were defined by the forced removal from their beautiful campuses, which were also their homes for five days a week. Before they moved campuses the war felt rather remote, but after having to

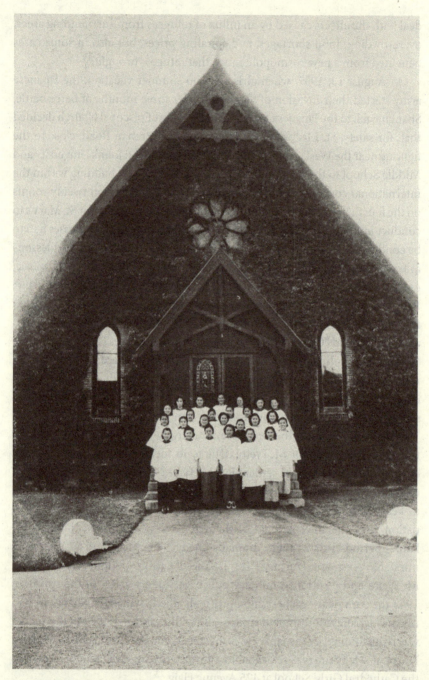

St. Mary's girls in choir robes on the steps of St. John's University Chapel. During the war, St. Mary's, which was run by the same missionary society as St. John's, part of the American Episcopal church, moved onto the latter's campus. *Photo from The Phoenix (1940), Shanghai Number Three Girls' School.*

move out (St. Mary's in 1937 and McTyeire in 1943), the realities of war sank in. The students experienced mixed emotions about the campus move. In the 1938 *Phoenix*, student Yau Ding-Vi Yao (Yao Meidi 姚梅棣, St. Mary's class of 1942) recalls with sadness having to leave "the quiet classrooms, the majestic corridor, the beautiful lawns, and the large gymnasium of St. Mary's Hall behind."[23] Other students found the move a novel and exciting experience. One of the strongest memories of the war for McTyeire student Xu Meizhen (徐美貞, class of 1946), was having to help move the library books from McTyeire to the new school on Avenue Haig:

> Our school library had very many books. So the school asked us to volunteer to help find a way to transport all of our library books from the old building to the new school. So we just put them on bicycles, on pedicabs, to take them to the new place! (Laughing). At that time our principal, she was very capable. She negotiated with the Japanese. She said to them our school has music classes, we have many pianos, we want to find a way to move them, can we use your army trucks? Later they agreed, and they used the army trucks to take the pianos to the new place. This was Principal Xue Zheng.[24]

Girls' memories of the excitement they felt in moving campuses challenge straightforward narratives of patriotic resistance to violent Japanese forces presented in the official histories. The fact that Principal Xue Zheng was able to negotiate with the Japanese in order to secure the safe transfer of the musical instruments and books highlights the complex and blurred boundaries between "resistance" and "collaboration" in the daily survival strategies of Shanghai residents during the wartime.[25] Teachers and students made the best of the difficult situation they were faced with, and they worked with the resources they had at their disposal in order to ensure the survival of their school. This trend of "making the best of it" is revealed in girls' experiences of their Japanese-language education.

Academics: English and Japanese

After the internment of their English and American missionary teachers in 1943, St. Mary's and McTyeire had to hire Chinese teachers of English for the first time. Kuan Yu Chen (Chen Guanyu 陳觀裕, McTyeire class of 1936), a St. John's English Literature graduate, was invited to become the first

Chinese teacher of English at McTyeire. Chen was put in charge of the curriculum and given responsibility for finding other suitably qualified teachers. She recalled: "Then Pearl Harbor. They were in a concentration camp, then evacuated. Then there was a vacuum in the English department, and we had to fill it. So I had to take over teaching senior high school English."[26] For Chinese teachers at McTyeire, the absence of the foreign staff also fostered a feeling of greater autonomy, as they no longer had to consider missionary demands or interests. Students and staff came to describe their pre-1943 experiences as "Alice in Wonderland. After that we had to grow up fast."[27] These words reveal that the war was a profound turning point in the experience of teachers and students at missionary schools. Indeed, they also echo the prewar (or pre-campus removal) sense of utopian "daydreaming" in the safe space that schools afforded. It was during the war that harsh realities broke into their daydreams and forced teachers as well as students to wake up to the real world.

Schools in Japanese-controlled areas of China were obliged to teach Japanese language as part of the attempt to create a "Greater East-Asia Co-Prosperity Sphere."[28] In the official history of McTyeire, Japanese-language instruction is depicted as a complete failure due to the patriotic resistance of McTyeire students to their Japanese teacher.[29] Alumnae's memories, however, complicate this straightforward narrative of patriotic resistance. Although many students started off by narrating their experience of Japanese education in a familiar and approved language of hatred and resistance, as I probed deeper into girls' memories of their Japanese education, a range of feelings came to light, from resistance and hatred, to pity and ridicule, and even some moments of fun.

At McTyeire a Japanese language teacher named Ishikawa was recruited alongside thousands of other educators who came to teach in China during the war.[30] Alumnae memories revealed that the gender dynamics at an all-girls school rendered their male Japanese teacher a rather powerless and pitiful figure. Ishikawa found himself at the mercy of his female Chinese students, as he was forbidden to physically punish the girls and could only verbally reprimand them. Lucy Hong remembered: "At that time the Chinese teachers were in charge of the school and the foreign teachers were forced to go to the concentration camps. We were all girls, and the teacher was a man and he had to be polite to us. He was not too serious.... We just went to his class to waste time, not to really study." Lucy then added, almost as an afterthought, "Of course with hatred in our hearts but we could not show it."[31] At their fiftieth anniversary reunion, the class of 1947 recalled rather humorously that the Japanese teacher used to bang his baton down on the table in an attempt to restore order and make girls listen to him in class, without much effect.[32] Xu Meizhen gleefully remembered their Japanese teacher's powerlessness to control the class:

> The Japanese army enforced Japanese lessons and sent a Japanese teacher from Japan to teach us. They sent a male teacher. Now Xue Zheng, she was very firm. She said to them: We are a girls' school. You are not allowed to hit the students. Because the Japanese would try to hit the students. So they agreed. But who wanted to study Japanese? So this young male Japanese teacher, he had a baton. When we were in his class we all did not listen, we just chatted to each other, he was so angry... but he could not hit us.... So he whacked his baton on the desk so hard that it broke in half! [Laughing]. We didn't want to learn Japanese so we just played up in his classes.[33]

While narrating their memories in the patriotic language of "resistance," girls at McTyeire actually came to sympathize with and pity their Japanese teacher when they found out that he was forced to live away from his wife and son, who subsequently died on a boat from Japan to China. Xu Meizhen recalled: "Later we learned that he also did not want to come to China. He was sent by the Japanese government. In his own country he was also a teacher. He had a wife and children, and he really missed them. He had photos and let us look 'this is my wife, this is my child.'"[34] Students also remember humorous incidents that resulted from miscommunication with their teacher. Xu Meizhen explained with great mirth:

> Because we couldn't speak Japanese, we learned the English alphabet. So it was very difficult for us to communicate with him. But he understood Chinese characters, because Chinese and Japanese have this traditional connection. There was a classmate who injured herself falling off a horse. She did not come to class. This Japanese teacher asked us, why is she not coming to class? We all didn't know how to tell him what had happened to her. We just knew that in Japanese "wuma" meant horse. We told him "wuma boolongdong" (onomatopoeia in Shanghai dialect to describe the sound of an object falling from a high place) [Laughing]. The teacher understood somehow.[35]

The Japanese teacher eventually gave up trying to teach these unruly girls and, directed by the students, taught the girls how to sing songs in

Japanese: an experience that many girls seem to have enjoyed. Rosalyn Koo (Chen Jinming 陳晉明, McTyeire class of 1947) explained how the students suggested that they learn to sing Japanese songs as a compromise:

> And we would be talking, totally ignoring him. He would use his sword and bang it on the teacher's desk, stomp out, bringing Xue Zheng. She would be very severe. Then this lieutenant, still mad, would try to teach. Of course, he had no idea how to teach girls. We made sure he didn't know how to teach anybody. Then we decided this wouldn't work, because this guy was not going to disappear. Then we asked him, "What do you like to do? What do you like? Would you like to sing?" We were trying to find out anything to distract us from teaching us Japanese. And then, you know, kids are good singers. So, they say, "Sing!" And he finally got the drift. He said "Yes, let's sing." So we asked him to teach us singing in Japanese. We thought that would be a good compromise. And this is how we went through the year in Japanese. Didn't learn a single word! Later on we found out that his family, his wife and children, were planning to join him in Shanghai and their boat sank. And so he lost his entire family. And we never saw him again.[36]

Girls at McTyeire took the lead in their Japanese education, dictating to their teacher what and how they should learn. Girls' experiences of their Japanese education—from defiant resistance to pity, ridicule, and even some moments of fun—provide further nuances to our understanding of the ways in which girls negotiated their lives during the Japanese occupation period. Indeed, in the case of McTyeire and St. Mary's, the gendered relationship between an all-female student body and a male teacher (who was powerless to discipline the girls) worked to effectively reverse the power dynamics between Japanese aggressor and Chinese civilians. Girls' memories, which reveal the sympathy they felt after the tragic loss of his family, also show that they regarded him as a human being—a real-life Japanese person whom they pitied, as opposed to the "evil predators" that dominate other narratives.

Life in Wartime Shanghai

The war also wrought changes in the student body at St. Mary's and McTyeire. The new school campuses did not have room for students to board, and those who lived too far away to commute to school on a daily basis could no longer attend. Students whose fathers worked for the Nationalist government had to relocate to Wuhan and then Chongqing following the retreating GMD during the war. Others temporarily moved to inner China for safety. For example, Rosalyn Koo's father, who worked for a bank in Shanghai, out of concern for his family's safety, decided to relocate them to Chongqing for one year in 1937–1938.[37] At the start of the war, students whose families lived in Chinese-owned areas of the city joined the flood of refugees into the concession area for safety. The trauma of leaving home permeates the memories of these students, some of whom were too young to really understand what was happening. Yang Zhiling 楊之嶺 (St. Mary's class of 1951), who was only four years old at the time, was layered up in her best clothes by her mother. Her father fought to find a taxi in the scramble to get into the safety of the concessions. Upon arrival, the family of eight had to divide themselves across the homes of their friends and relatives: "No family could house so many people. So some of us stayed at my grandmother's place, some of us stayed with my grandfather's friend, and I was in one of my distant uncles' homes. So like that, all divided into different places. It was hard not to be able to see our parents."[38]

The experience of being a refugee for elite missionary schoolgirls, the majority of whom had wealthy friends and family residing in the concessions with whom they could stay, was a world away from the plight of poor refugees who flocked into the city's public spaces looking for places to stay and with rapidly increasing food prices, trying desperately to feed themselves.[39] During the wartime, inflation rose to the extent that in Shanghai by December 1943 rice cost 2,500 dollars for one picul or *dan* (approximately 60 kilograms) and wages could not keep pace with prices.[40] Indeed, hyperinflation during the war meant that currency was soon almost worthless, and many people were paid in rice rather than cash during this period.[41] Daily necessities such as grain, coal, and cooking oil became difficult to procure. As a result, a flourishing black-market trade in such commodities became rife. Although they were from wealthy families who could generally afford to buy food at inflated prices on the black market, some St. Mary's and McTyeire students also experienced the struggle to buy rice. Tsu Foh-Pau (Xing Fengbao 邢鳳寶, St. Mary's class of 1941) wrote in 1941:

> The second new experience for me is the shortage of rice. As our native rice is not available, we have to buy imported rice, which is much inferior in flavour to our own rice. Moreover, there is great difficulty in getting the rice.

The purchase is limited to one dollar each buyer, and one has to wait hours and hours before he can get a dollar's worth of it. There is often a big crowd of people lined up in front of the rice shop under the supervision of a policeman. We have never known such troubles of living.[42]

Alumnae from McTyeire also remembered the rationing system and queuing up to get rice. Their experience of rationing was also highly inflected by their status as children. Xiao Jiaxun 肖嘉珣 (McTyeire class of 1952) explained that she and her sister were sent to buy rice but were too young to understand how the system worked. They were consequently overlooked in the queue for rice and had to start all over again.[43]

Frustration and excitement are also exhibited in alumnae's childhood recollections of the bombs which the Japanese (1932, 1937) and then the Americans (1945) rained down on Shanghai. The terror of bombing cut across the class divide in Chinese people's experience of the war. As Danke Li reveals, the experience of running to air-raid shelters and taking refuge together regardless of class, age, or gender was present in many women's memories of wartime Chongqing.[44] In Shanghai the most notorious bombing incident was actually a tragic case of friendly fire, known as "Black Saturday." On August 14, 1937, Chinese bombers, attempting to hit the Izumo, a Japanese naval ship moored in the Huangpu River, hit civilian targets by accident, including the Sassoon House (today the Peace Hotel) and a busy intersection in front of the Great World amusement center on the Nanjing Road. Over 1,200 were left dead and many more wounded.[45] Girls' memories of bombing and aerial battles in Shanghai are distinguished by their status as children. In her article entitled "A Dangerous Outing" in the 1938 *Phoenix*, the war becomes a game or adventure to student Tsang Vung-Chung (Chen Jianqing 陳簡青, St. Mary's class of 1939), who describes her excitement at watching an airplane battle over the Bund:

> We reached the Bund and waited for a long time in a park over there, but the aeroplanes seemed as if they would never show up. As we were impatient of waiting, we started for home, but just then we heard the sound of many planes. We returned and intended to feast our eyes on the site. Hardly had we sat down when the machine guns in the aeroplanes had begun to work! How awful that "Pa-pa" noise did sound to us! Fearing to get some stray bullets, we jumped to our feet and tried to get out from that terrible place, but it was not a very easy thing to do as crowds of people were also

coming out from the Bund. In a twinkling we heard some horrible sounds again. This time the noise was "bon-bon" sound of some tremendous bombs thrown down from some bombers. In an instant an eight-storied building a few metres from us was hit, about ten people near us were killed by the shells, and several automobiles some distance away from us burst into crimson flames. . . . When we had recovered our senses, we immediately turned on our heels and ran straight before our noses for our very lives. Our dresses were quite wet through by sweat when we got home. Our dangerous adventure was related not without shudders.[46]

Whether or not this story was a record of Tsang's actual experience or a fictional piece, or some mixture of both, is difficult to ascertain.[47] Students clearly felt some excitement and curiosity surrounding the danger of warfare; it was a "spectacle" and a "dangerous adventure" to be witnessed and related. Similarly, Theresa Chen (Chen Zongci 陳宗慈, McTyeire class of 1951), recalled much later toward the end of war when the Americans started strategically bombing Shanghai, the "colorful" experience of doing her homework by candlelight, ensuring that the blackout blind covered the windows, so not one speck of light could escape to attract the attention of bombers:

This was when we were in Shanghai and thinking back it was really colorful. We were all crowded in one bedroom. And my brothers were living with my uncles. And so she (my mother) has five children and he has seven, so it was a whole dozen! At that time the Americans were bombing Shanghai, and I remember that at that time we had to have black drapes and then you would hear the warning siren that the American planes were coming, so then we all closed the drape, and no electricity was allowed. So on a small table in our bedroom all the little kiddies were sitting there, and there's no light, there is an oil lamp, with just one oil wick, so this oil lamp, the brightness is less than a candle light. Just study. And that is an amazing picture. And not a whole lot of conversation.[48]

Alumnae's memories of the excitement and novelty that the war brought, as well as a sense of very real danger and terror, complicate this period as a universally dark time for Chinese women. Indeed, this mixture of emotions is also apparent when we examine alumnae memories of their experiences of commuting to school, which was both an eye-opening and dangerous experience for them.

Commuting to School: Novelty and Danger

Students who remained in Shanghai had to face a long and difficult commute to school via foot, bicycle, bus, or rickshaw on journeys which traversed the different administrative sections of the city. On the way, they were forced to pass Japanese checkpoints, where they had to bow to the Japanese guards. Rosalyn Koo recalled her feelings of nervousness, frustration, and anger when she passed the checkpoint on the Waibaidu Bridge (*Waibaidu qiao* 外白渡橋) on her way to school:

> I remember I was generally nervous, restless every day, especially when we had to move to the temporary site, and I was worried about the Japanese military and they were on the street everywhere. We had to get off the bicycle and then bow and then go. And one time I decided not to bow and I just rode my bicycle. Just to get away really fast. That's no good if they should catch you. It's humiliation, in your own country you had to do this.[49]

Lucy Hong (Hong Lüming 洪侶明, McTyeire class of 1948) explained that her father, Hong Deying 洪德應, an Anglican pastor and faculty member at St. John's University, used to take a much longer, circuitous route on his daily commute to the university in order to avoid having to bow to the Japanese on the bridge.[50] For one McTyeire student this was a particularly sensitive point, as her mother was Japanese, and she therefore had a special pass which allowed her to cross without bowing. Zhu Lizhong 朱麗中 (McTyeire class of 1950), who was attending the junior school linked to McTyeire at the time, recalled the painful isolation and ostracism she experienced due to her Japanese heritage:

> We had to cross two bridges going to school, and everyone has to get down from their pedicab or rickshaw and then you had to bow to the soldiers standing guard. My mother refused to bow, so she was taken to the military border police, and she said, I am Ashikaga, how should I bow to a no-name soldier? She refused to bow. Then she got special permission, she doesn't have to bow.... I was ostracized by my classmates, so I did not have close friends.[51]

Although identifying herself as "more Chinese than Japanese," Zhu Lizhong remembered that her mother used to dress her in Japanese clothes during this period, perhaps for her own protection, which sealed her status as an outcast at school: "Our mother was the descendant of the two Japanese shogun families, Ashikaga of Muromachi period, and Tokugawa of Edo period. When we were in the elementary school, it was during the eight years [of] Sino-Japanese war. I was more Chinese than Japanese, although my mother used to dress us in Japanese students' attire. I did not have friends as I was outcasted."[52]

Passing the Japanese checkpoints across the city was not just humiliating, it also posed a very real sexual threat to young women. Yang Zhiling remembered her mother's advice on how to safely pass Japanese soldiers while escorting her younger sisters to school:

> We had to walk to school, and my mother was so afraid of the Japanese soldiers, and we were all girls.... Because every day my mother was afraid for us, and we did not laugh and giggle, make noise, we did not want to attract attention when we had to pass Japanese soldiers. One day, I was escorting my two younger sisters and some Japanese soldiers were walking close to us, and you cannot run, otherwise you would attract attention, my mother told me, just walk slowly and do not look at their eyes. Just lower down your head and walk. It was scary.[53]

After 1939, St. Mary's was able to move to Graves Hall within the grounds of St. John's University. To reach the relative safety of the campus, many girls had to traverse Jessfield Park (today Zhongshan Park 中山公園), where there was a Japanese patrol stationed. Girls often crossed the park in groups or waited for older, male students from St. John's University to escort them. Girls who rode bicycles to school had to dismount and push their bikes across the park. Ying Manrong 應曼蓉 (St. Mary's class of 1945) narrated her narrow escape from sexual assault by a Japanese soldier one rainy day as she tried to cross the park from campus to her home:

> During the war I had an experience that had a great influence on me. When I was in Senior Two, one day I was studying in the library, I was reading for a very long time, suddenly the sky went very dark and heavy rain started falling. I decided to leave quickly. There was nobody in the library. I was pushing my bicycle across Zhongshan Park, you could only push your bike they wouldn't allow you to ride it. However whilst I was pushing it on the way there was absolutely no one there, there was no one there ... [voice

shaking]. Suddenly I saw in front of me, about, about, five or six yards away a man, wearing a dark raincoat, very big coat, I was very afraid because he was Japanese. He had a demonic grin on his face. As soon as I saw him I was very afraid, he certainly had bad intentions. Although I saw that he did not have a gun, he took out his sex organ from underneath his raincoat, I had never seen this before. I have never told this to anyone before. You know when Japanese soldiers saw nobody was around they would rape women. I saw there was a music bandstand close by where there was a young couple. When I saw them I made a run for the bandstand. I did not care if I was disturbing them, I just wanted to save myself. Later I found out he was one of the Japanese Military Police, who had been stationed in the Zhongshan Park. Although they patrolled there they also preyed on women. Oh! I was scared to death. [with anger in her voice] All Chinese women at this time never had a day when they felt safe, even us students who studied at a prestigious school, even we encountered this kind of danger! If there was not this young couple in the bandstand I am afraid I would have been raped. To encounter this kind of thing! At that time I was not very strong.... I had almost forgotten this thing. That's why I know how terrible those Japanese troops were. Can you imagine, how many Chinese women did the Japanese rape?[54]

Ying Manrong recounted this story with great emotion in her voice and facial expression: the fear and anger in her narrative came through strongly, even after sixty-two years. The sexual threat from Japanese soldiers faced by Chinese women has been highlighted in many studies of the Second Sino-Japanese War. While there has been much scholarly attention paid to the rape of women in notorious instances, such the Nanjing massacre, and women who were forced into sexual slavery as "comfort women" for Japanese soldiers on the front lines, there has been limited attention paid to the sexual threat that women of all social classes had to face on a daily basis in occupied wartime Shanghai.[55] Ying Manrong was narrating a personal experience and it is impossible to determine the number of women who were raped during the occupation period in Shanghai. Her outrage toward the end of her narrative where she states, "Can you imagine, how many Chinese women did the Japanese rape?" may have also been influenced by later depictions of Japanese soldiers at Nanjing. In Ying Manrong's retelling, her anger is also closely connected to her class status—even elite students such as herself became vulnerable to the sexual threat of Japanese patrolling soldiers during this period.

After the bombing of Pearl Harbor and the entry of Japanese forces into the foreign concessions, life became even more difficult and dangerous for girls commuting to school. Julia Tsai Li (McTyeire class of 1945) remembered that Japanese soldiers could regularly be seen outside of McTyeire, and on one occasion the principal ordered the girls to hide from the soldiers who wanted to enter the school:

> Oh let me tell you about that one incident I can never forget. It will stay with me until the day I die. I was in my junior year and school usually got over at 3:00 or 3:30 right? Just before the end of the school day all of a sudden, Miss Xue gave us a hush-hush and then shooed us all away to the top of the school, I think the fourth floor, the top of the building. And as children at that time, well, you don't ask questions. Whatever the teacher asked you to do, just do it. So, we all went upstairs and then were very quiet. We didn't know the reason why until later on. We were let out, and we were asked to go home. Then we were told that one troop of Japanese soldiers, they were all six footers, were outside the school and they knew that this was a girls' school. So they wanted to crash in. I don't know how she had got wind of it. She had all girls. I could never forget that incident.[56]

Despite the very real dangers and humiliation that encountering Japanese guards brought, they do not represent the totality of girls' experiences of commuting to school. Indeed, in the school magazines of the period, we also find evidence that this period was eye-opening and fun for some girls, who experienced more independence in commuting to school every day than they had been able to do when they lived in their elite boarding schools. Their recollections complicate the dominant narrative of women's wartime experience in Shanghai, which, by focusing on the hunger, deprivation, and danger wrought by the Japanese, serve to repress positive memories of the war for women.[57]

Girls found enjoyment in their exposure to all sorts of people who they would not normally encounter in the elite social circles their families moved in. For example, Sung Sing-Ling (Shen Shuqin 沈淑琴, St. Mary's class of 1941) wrote in 1938:

> Now that I'm not a boarding student, I have to take much pains in getting to school, which is quite a distance from my home. . . . We also see many different kinds of people on the bus. There are noisy American schoolgirls, eating, joking and sending laughter through the whole bus, making everybody turn his head and stare at them. There are many workmen, curious sightseers, and serious businessmen who knit their brows if the bus becomes too crowded. Beside these, there are sights to be seen on the

138   DREAMING THE NEW WOMAN

St. Mary's students walk to their relocated school campuses during the war. Students' experiences of their journey to school during this period were mixed. They faced a difficult and dangerous commute via foot, bicycle, and rickshaw, having to bow to Japanese guards at checkpoints as they traversed Shanghai. Some also enjoyed the newfound freedom and experiences that their commute brought. *Photo from The Phoenix (1938), Shanghai Number Three Girls' School.*

> streets and sidewalks. We often see anxious people trying eagerly to get a chance of purchasing a dollar's worth of rice. There are, too, occasionally street fights and people getting into each other's way in their hurry. There are so many exciting things that you don't get to see when you're riding in a car.... Though there is much that is uncomfortable about riding a bus or tram, yet we enjoy it thoroughly.[58]

We might question whether Sung is being genuine in her excitement or using a sarcastic tone in this article. However, it is clear that the war provided new life experiences for the previously sheltered St. Mary's girls, albeit witnessed from the safety provided by the bus window. In her article entitled "Why I Like Day School," Zia Ung-sing (Ji Qixian 吉琦仙, St. Mary's class of 1940) goes as far as to write that she prefers life in the "New St. Mary's" to their old boarding school:

This year we are studying in the Continental Building instead of in St. Mary's Hall, because the places around our school are occupied by soldiers. We cannot stay in the Continental Building during the night, so all the students must go from their homes to the building every day. Though it seems very inconvenient, yet I like the day school better, because there is plenty of time for me to study my lessons in the morning. Another reason why I like day school better is that if the weather were very cold in the morning, the time which I could spend in sleep is longer than in St. Mary's Hall. The third reason is I can see a great many interesting things which we could not see in school. These are the three reasons why I like day school better than boarding in St. Mary's Hall.[59]

Although many of her classmates do not go so far as to agree with Zia that they enjoy their new school life more than their old one (in fact many bemoan their new situation and look forward to the time when they can return to their old campus), pupils had a range of experiences and reactions to the war—both positive and negative, but many eye-opening and new. Going to school on foot, bus, bike, or pedicab enabled girls to interact with and experience the city in a new and much more independent way than they could do before the war. Girls' excitement about their new experiences and more independent lifestyle provides a more complex picture of the daily lives of female students in wartime Shanghai. These experiences of being exposed to a much broader swathe of society on their way to school also had a profound impact on their worldview. It was during the wartime that girls started to question the stark differences between the privileged and luxurious lifestyles that they saw still being lived in their homes and their school and the desperate plight of the refugees who they encountered on their way to school.

Making Sense of the War: Christianity and Wartime Relief Activities

On their journey to school, girls came into contact with and witnessed firsthand the suffering of refugees who flooded into Shanghai's international concessions. During the war over sixty million people, one-seventh of China's population, became displaced.[60] This situation was compounded by the GMD's own ruthless scorched-earth tactics and inadequate provision of relief for the refugees who were fleeing from a famine in Henan province during which approximately two million people starved to death.[61] Massive loss of human life and displacement of people also resulted from the deliberate breaching of the Yellow River dykes in 1938 by the GMD in a futile attempt to halt the Japanese advance on Kaifeng.[62] While some fled their devastated homes to "Free China" in the West or joined the Communists in the North, others moved into international concessions in Shanghai and other foreign-administrated areas such as Hong Kong and Macau.[63] Girls' reactions to this large-scale human suffering that they witnessed for the first time varied: some turned to Christian social service as way to assuage feelings of guilt for living privileged lives, others were content to remain in a privileged bubble of wealth. A few started to question the status quo and turned to communism rather than Christianity as the most effective solution to the suffering that they witnessed in society.

The psychological shock that the war brought to girls can be seen in their writings about the refugees who they encountered on their way to school. For some, a sense of pity pervades their descriptions of the refugees, and the encounter seemed to reinforce their gratefulness for their relatively privileged positions. They often felt powerless to help.[64] Coming face to face with other girls of their own age, but who were in a much less fortunate position than themselves, left a particularly deep impression on students. Tseu we-kyoen (Zhou Huijuan 周惠娟, St. Mary's class of 1940) recounted her experience of encountering a refugee family on the way to school:

> A very pitiful scene appeared before my eyes. It was a group of poor refugees. When I looked at them, I saw a very old man, a young girl and a group of small children. The girl was carrying an infant about six or seven months old. One boy about eight years old went hand-in-hand with the old man. Some of the children were crying. I forgot about the rain and went towards them and question them. This is the answer which the young girl gave me. "Oh, Miss! I do not know what to do with these children and my old grandfather. They have not eaten for three days. Look at them—so thin! We came out from Pootung. Before the war we could have enough food to eat, and enough clothes to wear. But now they are all gone! My father is forced to carry things for the soldiers, and my mother died on the road. These are all my poor brothers and sisters. Ah! I hope we can find a place to live in!" . . . She cried because all the sad things which had happen to her. I looked at the old man who was also very hungry and tired, sitting on the wet ground with tears in his eyes. The children trembled and cried, because

they had not enough clothes to wear. Ah! Two tears rolled down my cheeks. Did not know what to do, so I gave the people money and left them in the street.[65]

Perhaps to assuage feelings of guilt for their relatively privileged positions, some students threw themselves into charitable wartime relief work. As in many countries during the wartime, the work of keeping up morale, and promoting resistance and national consciousness, became highly gendered work. The figure of the female nurse or social worker (along with women such as Xie Bingying 謝冰瑩, who joined the army to fight the Japanese), have come to epitomize patriotic "heroines" in traditional tropes of women's wartime work.[66] We know much more about women's wartime work in "Free China" than in the occupied East. The Women's Advisory Council (WAC), headed by Song Meiling, coordinated women's' wartime relief work, which included promoting wartime national consciousness, education, children's relief work, rural work, life guidance, literary training, and hygiene training.[67] Female middle-school students in Chongqing remembered taking part in a variety of activities to raise money and national consciousness among Sichuan people in the period 1938–1945, including speeches, plays, and street performances.[68] Girls at Ginling College, who moved to Chengdu in 1937, conducted a variety of relief activities and social work in "rural service stations" which they helped establish in remote villages in Sichuan province. Sixteen Ginling students spent the summer of 1940 at Zhonghechang Station, carrying out various activities including nursery play groups, parents' meetings, women's classes, medical work, home visits, and research work.[69]

This wartime work also expanded the roles it was possible for women to do outside the home.[70] The WAC and other wartime relief associations such as the Women's Association for National Salvation (Funü jie jiuguo hui 婦女界救國會), founded in Shanghai in 1935, allowed women to demonstrate that they were ready and able to serve China as her future national leaders and organizers.[71] In order to legitimize and underline the urgency of their wartime contributions, Ginling students used a martialized language to describe these traditionally sanctioned female roles: "These 'Women Soldiers' as they were called by the local people, were very energetic, enthusiastic and delightful vanguards in the battle against ignorance, disease and selfishness."[72] Women's wartime relief work was thus highly gendered and, in many ways, can be seen as an extension of their prewar patriotic and Christian social service activities. The war underlined the urgency of their patriotic contributions.

Girls at missionary schools in occupied East China also enthusiastically participated in gendered wartime relief activities. These included collecting clothes and raising money for refugees, teaching children in the refugee camps, and volunteering as nurses. In the 1939 edition of *The Phoenix*, Loh Oen-vung (Lu Anwen 陸安文, St. Mary's class of 1939) outlined the wartime relief work that St. Mary's girls were involved with:

> As we are now living in this isolated island, the Paris of the Orient; what we now realize is that it is the paradise of a few and the grave of the many.... Since we are citizens, we cannot stand by and watch our country fellows being starved and frozen to death. Sympathy and pity are of no use to them unless we put our sympathy and pity into practice with our whole heart. That is the real way to help them and save them. Rich people can contribute money, while the others can offer their wits and energies. Everybody can help others in different ways. In the past year we, young people, did a lot of such kind of work. In our school we contributed money, certainly as the most important work; collected old clothes; taught poor children in the refugee camps; and helped to sell tickets for the Charity Bazaar during the Christmas season. All of those had quite good results.[73]

Wartime relief work also provided opportunities for girls to gain new skills and training. In 1938 a group of ten St. Mary's girls undertook a four-week training program in nursing and then volunteered as student nurses in the Red Cross Medical Corps. Loo Kyan-Faung (Lu Jianfang 盧鑑芳, class of 1938) described girls' experiences at the hospital:

> On our mark—we began our work, getting everything ready for the doctors, helping them change the uncleaned bandages of the wounds, and lifting patients up carefully while the doctors were washing their wounds.... Thrice this day we took the patients' temperature, respiration and pulse. At recess, we wrote letters for the soldiers to their families or friends; conversed with them and sang for them when they asked us.[74]

For some girls, this relief work was not just a patriotic imperative but also a fundamentally Christian enterprise. Like their missionary teachers, they sometimes used wartime relief work to preach the gospel among the unfortunate people they encountered. For example, in a letter to her classmates in the 1940 *Phoenix*, St. Mary's alumna Loh Oen-vung (Lu Anwen 陸安文, class of 1939), describes her work at the Christian-run Child Welfare Centre where she volunteered her time:

> I reserve one day a week for calling on the families of our children in order to keep in touch with their home conditions and needs. Here again the wonderful opportunity for Christian social service presents itself. . . . Is it not a true fact that our Christian religion is the only valuable means of comfort? . . . We try to comfort the old grandmother by telling of the endless love and strength of Him who dwelt among man and died that we might live. The daughter-in-law has since become interested in Christianity and attends services and meetings when possible.[75]

Christianity also helped girls make sense of the war and provided some psychological relief to students themselves. The war had a particularly disturbing impact on Christian students' psychology, as a utopian vision of a bright Christian future for Chinese women receded and was replaced with feelings of powerlessness, hopelessness, and despair.[76] Christian organizations for women, such as the YWCA, recognized the increasing need for student counseling during the war. In March 1945 YWCA student secretary Winifred Galbraith reported that:

> Their need gets more and more desperate as the war drags on. Our latest Y.W.C.A. secretary from the United States says of the students she has met "I have lost count of the number of students who have told me that they feel 'lost all the time.' The reasons are obvious—their families live in occupied territory, their personal futures are insecure, their country's future uncertain, their daily fight for bare existence is a hard struggle."[77]

Recognizing the increasing psychological pressures on students during the wartime, Ginling College installed a system of Christian-trained counselors in its dormitories to help students cope with life problems ranging from vocations, marriage, and relationships to religious and health issues.[78]

According to missionary teachers and YWCA workers, there was not only a great need for Christianity among students in the wartime, but also a renewed interest in the faith. Although we must be careful not to take missionaries' ever-hopeful words at face value, it appears that for some students a renewed sense of Christian faith helped them to weather the psychological impact of the war and try to make sense of the suffering and destruction going on around them. In her memoir, McTyeire Methodist missionary teacher Ruth Harris recalls the letter of a student who uses Christianity and the theme of rebirth to describe her wartime experiences:

> This is my Father's world. I thought that Spring would never come. And then this morning when I woke and went out front to get the newspaper, I noticed a bud on the tree. I ran into the house and got my bike and started to ride out to the little village where my brother and I had such fun in the summer when we were children. As I rode along, I forgot about the horrible war we [had] just been through, and I began singing my favorite song, "This is my Father's world." Before I knew it I had reached the village—only the village wasn't there. In place of the village there were demolished houses. Dead, unburied bodies were scattered about. A great big sob came up in my throat. I turned round and crossed the little bridge that led back to town. As I crossed the bridge, I heard a trickle of water. The water was running under the ice. I stopped and looked down, and there by the side of that icy little stream, there was a tiny wildflower that had pushed its way through the earth. I picked it up and stuck it through the buttonhole of my sweater. I got back on my bike and pedalled back to town singing to myself "This Is my Father's World."[79]

During this difficult period, some girls used their Christian faith, concretized in hymns and songs, as a coping strategy to make sense of the death and destruction which they witnessed around them.

Not all girls were engaged in these patriotic and Christian relief activities. Others seemed content to remain in a privileged bubble. Indeed, the extent of their awareness about the war and the suffering it was causing, aligned with the extent to which it directly affected their own lives. Toby Lincoln has highlighted the need to carefully analyze the special geographies of wartime violence when attempting to understand the lived experience of warfare for residents in the lower Yangtze region.[80] The school yearbooks make it clear that it was not until they were forced to move campuses that the war significantly influenced their daily lives. For St. Mary's girls, the early years of the war (1937–1939) were particularly difficult as they were forced to commute to their temporary school building on the Nanjing Road. For these years, a large proportion of their writings touch on the war, compared to their writing in the later years (1940–1941) when they were more comfortably ensconced within St. John's campus and the war seemed more remote. In contrast, for McTyeire students who remained in their original campus until 1943, these early years were ones of comparative safety, and the war features remarkably little in their writings. The McTyeire magazines of 1937–1941 continue on lighthearted topics about girls' dress, appearance, and social life.[81] The magazines for these years are still full of news of sporting competitions, plays, and pageants that girls were performing, suggesting that the war had not deeply affected girls' daily lives and thinking up to this point.

Girls' retrospective writings about the war also suggest that their schools provided a safe haven or "refuge" where they could escape the realities of the outside world. Children's writings about the war invariably reflected adult resistance propaganda.[82] This is evident in girls' narratives of "carrying on" against the odds during the wartime. For example, in the "Class History" of 1945, McTyeire student Hsueh Nying (Xue Yin 薛吟) writes:

During the period of time that we studied in McTyeire a tremendous change has taken place in the world outside, but inside the four walls of McTyeire life was calm and peaceful. Some said that we were most unfortunate to have the golden years of our youth pass in such a hard time, but they did not know that the happiness that McTyeire gave us was enough to make up for everything.[83]

This spirit of "carrying on" is also reflected in the McTyeirean class history of 1943, where Chang Ching Yu (Zhang Jingyu, 張景瑜, class of 1943) writes: "The war did not dull our youthful zest or mar our childish happiness."[84] These writings were published retrospectively in 1946 after war had ended, and thus girls could afford to look back on the war years with a triumphant mindset.[85]

In interviews conducted with graduates living in the United States many years later, McTyeire graduates not only spoke about their school as a welcome "refuge" but also as isolating and cutting them off from the wider political events going on in the country. McTyeire teacher and alumna Kuan Yu Chen (Chen Guanyu) remembered that before the school was forced to move campus, it was to some extent sheltered in a privileged bubble of extraterritoriality, and the war seemed very remote:

> Well, we were the privileged ones. We lived in the international concession, so we were protected by colonialism. So the bombing didn't bother us. We heard of refugees, of course, people who lived close to the Chinese territories, who fled to the international concession to take cover. But we never really directly experienced bombing. Or like the massacre in Nanjing, those things are very remote. I learned about Chinese history and all of those terrible things that happened to us, the famine, and the floods, after I had grown up and gotten out of China. I read a lot about Chinese history written by Western scholars like Fairbank and I got a more accurate understanding of China. For heaven sake! We didn't know anything about our own country.[86]

After the Japanese moved into the international concessions, their foreign teachers were interned, and they had to move out of their school and face a daily commute, the realities of the war hit home, even for these privileged girls from elite families. Kuan Yu Chen (Chen Guanyu) recalled working as a teacher at McTyeire after 1942:

> Especially when we moved campus, that was a great change. From then on, it was not an ivory tower. We had no fuel, everybody was on bicycle. There was no boarding, and from that time on it was such a deterioration. The inflation was astronomical, and deterioration, deterioration. That generation of students is much more practical. Oh, I'm talking about clothing, they are more socially conscious. I don't know how much we were politically aware, only socially more conscious. And everybody had a hard time, and so many people lost so much during the Japanese occupation.[87]

Students' varying levels of political and social engagement during the war is also revealed in the writings of pupils who criticized their classmates for not doing enough to help their less-fortunate counterparts. For example, in her article in the *Phoenix* of 1939, student Ling Kuo-fen (Ling Guofang 凌國芳, St. Mary's class of 1941) berated her classmates:

> And when we compare wealthy playboys and girls, who continue to squander their money on amusements, with the pitiful refugees, who are lying cold and hungry so nearby, one cannot feel that people in Shanghai can really lend more of a helping hand to the unfortunate ones than they have been doing. In this school alone, I see many students who spend a

great deal on amusements without a thought of the poor refugees. It is not that they want the refugees to die or are unwilling to give when asked, but that they are just sometimes thoughtless. Are we extending a helping hand? Are we doing our part in helping our countrymen? The answer is "No"—at least for many. Now with Christmas near hand, a time of goodwill and helping others, I sincerely hope that many will recall and bear in mind the verse in the Scriptures: "inasmuch as ye have done it unto the least of these my brethren, ye have done it unto me."[88]

Ashamed by their classmates' complacency, some students threw themselves into the Christian social work described above as a way to make sense of and relieve the suffering they witnessed in society. It was also during the wartime that a handful of these very patriotic and Christian students, through these social service activities, started to turn toward communism, rather than Christianity, as the most effective solution to the suffering that they witnessed in society.

Political Awakening: The Case of Ellen Cao

The war was a political awakening for some students. Shocked by the scale of human suffering they witnessed, girls started to question why they could live in relative safety and ease, while beyond the walls of their elite missionary schools, other children their own age starved to death, or were sold into indentured labor. Girls who became interested in joining the CCP in this period were often the most Christian and socially minded students. During the 1930s the CCP started to infiltrate Christian women's organizations including missionary schools and the YWCA. In particular, they found in the YWCA a pool of well-trained Chinese women, adept at organization and leadership, who were deeply committed to the social gospel of "serving" their less fortunate counterparts. The CCP utilized the networks of the YWCA and other Christian groups to recruit members in this period. For example, YWCA industrial secretary Deng Yuzhi 鄧裕志 helped the party contact women working in Shanghai's cotton factories through her night-time literacy classes.[89] The YWCA also conducted summer camps for students in the wartime which sought to raise their political awareness. Apart from talks on Christianity, skits, and sports activities, Lucy Hong and Cao Shengjie 曹聖潔 (a graduate of the Baptist Jinde Girls Middle School in the class of

1949) remembered that the summer camps also included political elements. YWCA student secretaries would discuss progressive ideas with girls, who also performed plays which critiqued political enemies, such as the collaborationist Reorganized Nationalist Government leader Wang Jingwei 汪精衛 (1883–1944).[90]

The CCP made good use of students' patriotism during the war. While many followed the GMD into exile in Chongqing, others decided that the Communists offered the more compelling solution to China's problems. Progressive students and intellectuals flocked to join the CCP in Yan'an during the war.[91] The experience of Ellen Cao (Cao Baozhen 曹寶貞, McTyeire class of 1939) provides a case study of the political conversion that some missionary schoolgirls underwent during the war. Cao recalled that during the war it was through the Shanghai YWCA that she "learned to feel patriotic":

> Shanghai YWCA had many activities. Such as activities to promote the anti-Japanese war. When I attended Shanghai YWCA activities . . . they told me, you must be patriotic. They taught me how to be patriotic. . . . I wanted to go to Yan'an but I was only fifteen years old. I had an older friend within the YWCA who asked me to write a letter to explain what I knew about communism. When she saw the letter, she realized I knew what I was talking about. It was about a 1,000-word report, about what nationalism meant.[92]

Ellen Cao was born in 1924 into a devout Christian family. Her father and mother were both Christians from Ningbo. They had ten children, all of whom were sent to missionary schools. Her father was educated at Nanjing University medical school and played an important role in the founding of the Three-Self Patriotic Movement (Sanzi aiguo yundong 三自愛國運動), which moved the Christian Church in China away from foreign missionary control. Cao had a very religious upbringing. Her parents taught her the Christian parable of charity in Luke 3:11, that "if you have two pieces of clothing you should give one to those in need." However, the futility of the Christian social gospel in the face of the extraordinary suffering of the Chinese masses, particularly women's suffering, was hammered home to her one day when the Shanghai branch of Chinese YWCA organized its student members to visit a factory to inspect the conditions of Chinese girls sold into indentured labor:

Now I will tell you about the time I joined the YWCA. They organized us to visit indentured workers (*bao shen gong* 包身工). This place was full of girls whose families had sold them into labor. They thought they would have a good life, but as a result, these girls (they lived in Shanghai near the Suzhou creek), they did not even have beds and lived in huts made of grass. They did hard work at factories. Because their lives were so bitter and everything they earned were taken by the person who bought them, they were afraid they would run away. So these girls, when they went back to their dormitories they were completely naked. They were not allowed to have clothes in case they would run away. If you don't have clothes you can't run. So when I saw these girls, lying on the ground with very thin grass beneath them, so miserable! This experience had a really deep influence on me. I thought giving one piece of clothing to them, can't solve the problem at all! The real problem is the corrupted government and the structure of the society. Therefore, after I had read books, I thought that this society was really not equal, and it must change. Change how? So this was an important factor as to why I joined the Communist Party. My family taught me that human love had no social class barriers, so that is why I joined the Communist Party.[93]

In our interview, Ellen Cao stressed her feeling of shock that these girls lived just around the corner from her own home where she led a life of wealth and privilege. Her sense of anger at the injustice that she could have such a privileged life while these girls lived in such pitiful conditions came through strongly in our conversation. After attending YWCA meetings and activities Cao was invited to dinner by YWCA secretaries dedicated to working amongst student members in Shanghai, where they discussed China's political situation and Communist ideas.[94]

Cao was a precocious student. Having entered McTyeire at age nine, she was much younger than many of her classmates, who were interested in what she considered frivolous topics: clothes, makeup, and getting married.[95] Her serious and detached nature perhaps made her an unpopular student. She was the only student not to provide a photo in the yearbook page dedicated to each girl in the graduating class, and there is no description of her by a friend, which normally accompanied the photo. Instead, she cryptically wrote: "She is a person" beside her name. Where her image appears in another picture in the magazine, someone has graffitied on her face.[96] Though this may have occurred at a much later point (perhaps during the political turbulence of the Cultural Revolution), it is clear from the school yearbook that Cao considered herself a bit of an outsider and she formed friendships with other like-minded students who joined the YWCA.

Witnessing the complacency of her classmates toward the suffering of other girls and women during the war was the final straw for Cao. She consciously rejected her elite boarding school and planned to run away to Yan'an to join the Communist Party. Although she did not make it to Yan'an, she did become a member of the underground Communist Party in 1939. Taking part in activities organized by the YWCA also helped Cao to hone her organizational skills, which became important training for her work as an underground Communist Party member. She worked to contact other students at her school clandestinely to interest them in the Communist cause. After her graduation from McTyeire in 1939 she went on to study and eventually work as a teacher at St. John's University, where she continued her work as an underground party member.[97]

At the Crossroads

We cannot underestimate the importance of the war as a turning point in girls' political consciousness, as it was for many people in Chinese history.[98] While their schools may have provided a "refuge" for girls during the periods that they were allowed to remain, after they were forced to move campuses the realities of war hit home. Rosalyn Koo recalls how this moment of "waking up" for McTyeire girls actually happened in 1943 rather than 1937: "During the war, [by] going to the campus you were able to shut everything out, you just study, it's like a refuge. You can peruse Charles Dickens, Thomas Hardy, and not worry about anything else happening outside the school. However, in ninth grade, tenth grade, no matter what, the soldiers came in, and we had to get out."[99] Girls' memories of the war complicate our traditional tropes of women's wartime experience. Indeed, Rosalyn's words remind us that we need to pay attention to the rich multiplicity of individual lived experiences if we are to better understand the impact of the Second World War on Chinese society.

The war, when it affected girls' lives in a material way at different points, served as a rather rude awakening from a period of relative safety and ease. Students experienced and interpreted this awakening in many different ways, and while it brought both positive and negative experiences, there could be no return to the utopian "daydreams" of their pre-war existence. Exposed to the suffering of their compatriots in a more direct way than ever before on their journeys to school, some girls used Christianity to fulfill their wartime patriotic and Christian social service responsibilities and make sense of the suffering they witnessed. Some remained more complacent and continued to enjoy their privileged lifestyles at home and within their schools. For others, such as Ellen Cao, communism rather than Christianity became the most effective solution to the plight of poor Chinese women and children. In the post-war period, these divisions within the student body deepened. The stark contrast between the privileged lives being enjoyed by students in their school and the mass suffering of Chinese people outside the school walls, drove increasing numbers of missionary schoolgirls into the arms of the CCP.

5
Negotiating Christian and Communist Identities

One evening at the end of December 1946, eighteen-year-old Ying Manrong 應曼蓉 (St. Mary's class of 1945), a recent graduate of St. Mary's and an English Literature major at St. John's, decided to stay up all night to translate a newspaper article about the rape of a Peking University student, Shen Chong 沈崇, by American soldiers. Seventy years later, in 2016, Ying Manrong recalled the deep impact this translation activity, organized by the Communist Party, had on her political thinking at the time:

> At that time, I experienced a great internal change. There had been so many times, when my friends had come to ask me to join in with political rallies and I just went along, because they wanted me to. But during this student protest, I wanted to take an active part. The Japanese had hurt us. The Americans, although they pretended to be our friends, actually also harmed lots of Chinese girls.... So I understood that Japanese and Americans were really the same, they all treated China as their colony.... Therefore, when my friends asked me to translate this newspaper article about the rape of Shen Chong into English for the *China Press*, I agreed to do it.... I really didn't know how to translate their big expressions into English. I had never seen this kind of newspaper as well. I decided to use a language that I thought English and American people would understand.... I wrote it according to how our missionary teachers taught us—we had come across speeches such as the Gettysburg Address by President Lincoln.... It was almost 6 am when I submitted the translation. I thought maybe the newspaper had decided not to publish it, so I thought, "Oh well, maybe they found someone else to translate it." On the fifth day, I found out that it was published! This was an activity led by the Communist Party and there were leaders in the Party who understood English. So after this I thought I should join the Communist Party; not only did I feel they could liberate women, but I felt I could also make a contribution with my English education.[1]

The rape of Shen Chong on Christmas Eve 1946 ignited student resentment at the failure of the Nationalist Party to restore China to full sovereignty after years of invasion by allowing a continued American military presence after the war. The incident sparked waves of protests across the country. Students in Beijing formed the Association for Protesting against American Atrocities. They held strikes on December 30 and 31, 1946, and placards and posters appeared denouncing American imperialism, demanding an official apology, compensation for Shen Chong, and immediate withdrawal of all US troops in China.[2] Ying Manrong's memory of her participation in the nationwide student demonstrations that occurred after this notorious case provides insight into how and why missionary school students gradually turned toward the Communist Party in the post-war period. Ying Manrong's personal reaction to the Shen Chong case was compounded by the fact that she herself had narrowly escaped from rape by a Japanese soldier patrolling in Zhongshan Park during the war. In her memory, Japanese aggressors, and their humiliation of Chinese women during the wartime, had become inextricably linked with later American presence in China. Indeed, when asked about her experience of going to school in the wartime, Ying Manrong told me of her own close escape from rape, which immediately triggered her memory of the rape of Shen Chong. The two events had left an indelible connection in her mind. For female students, their anger was closely connected to Shen Chong's class status; she was not a "common" prostitute or even a "tacky" GI girl who threw herself at American soldiers in bars but, much like themselves, was from a respectable family and was studying at one of China's most prestigious universities.

Within the fierce debates that ensued over this case in the newspapers, female students expressed their outrage in terms which drew on long-standing ideas about the importance of female chastity. Although we cannot be certain that this was the article Ying Manrong translated, a piece entitled "Some Co.eds' Views" and signed by "Some Twenty Sympathetic Girl Students of St. John's" appeared in the *China Press* on January 5, 1947, five days after the student protests in Beijing began.[3] In the article, Shen Chong's class status as the granddaughter of the former governor of Jiangsu, Anhui, and Jiangxi was stressed, as well as her near suicidal mental status. Compounding this very traditional gendered debate, a 'concerned mother' wrote a strongly worded response to the female students' article that berated these irresponsible girls for giving information which revealed the identity of Shen Chong, and thus bringing her further pain and shame. If Shen Chong was indeed to commit suicide, her blood would be on their hands, she exclaimed.[4] If this was the article that Ying Manrong translated, it is fascinating to see how Communist-led student protests were still couched in the language of female chastity, the cult of which had been decried by many leading Communist Party members since the May Fourth period.[5]

This outrageous insult to one of their own in 1946 came too close to home for students at St. Mary's and McTyeire, many of whom were due to continue their studies at Peita (as Peking University was known), and marked a profound turning point in their political thinking. For Ying Manrong and several of her classmates it was this incident of gendered violence against an upper-class woman that sparked her interest in the Communist Party. Unlike the GMD, the CCP promised to restore China's sovereignty and stand up for Chinese women against colonial oppressors. Ying Manrong's memory also reveals another, unexpected reason for her conversion to the Communist cause: she felt her high level of English could be useful to CCP. After so many years of feeling powerless and frustrated during the war, Christian-educated Chinese women now saw a direct and very practical way of helping their country.

During the immediate post-war period, students in missionary schools in East China gradually turned to the Communist Party as the most effective solution to restore their country's sovereignty and national pride. It was often Christian, socially minded pupils who first made the transition to the Communist cause and started to work to influence other pupils in missionary schools. Paradoxically, St. Mary's and McTyeire's status as elite all-female Christian schools, for which they would later be criticized, actually aided the CCP cause in the Civil War period. Library books remained uncensored, and male GMD secret police were prevented from entering the campus because of their sex.

There were also surprising continuities at missionary schools for girls during this period of profound political change. After 1949, religious activities continued, and there was even a surge of new interest in Christianity as students and teachers harnessed communism to the social gospel in their social-service activities. From the missionary perspective, the Communist Party even drew upon the organizational structures and meeting formats of long-established Christian organizations in China. This borrowing of form and adaptation of content by the CCP in some ways mirrors the process that missionary schoolgirls themselves had employed since the early twentieth century as they harnessed nationalism to Christianity.

The real turning point for missionary schools came shortly after the outbreak of the Korean War in 1950, rather than in 1949, after which American missionary teachers were forced to leave and the English curriculum was radically altered. By 1952 all remaining missionary schools were disbanded, merged, or renamed in the reorganization of the educational system by the PRC government. By highlighting the continuities, as well as the changes that occurred to missionary schools in the period 1945–1952, missionary schoolgirls' memories help to redefine conventional chronologies of this period, which center around 1949 as the watershed moment in modern Chinese history.

"Never Forget National Humiliation": Recovery and Anger in the Post-War Period

Students' most vivid memories of the immediate postwar period were of the destruction that the war had wrought on their formerly beautiful school campuses and the slow and painstaking process of restoring them to their former glory. At McTyeire, which had been used by the Japanese as a military hospital, there were five large water-filled holes in the beautiful grass lawns, with an air raid shelter under the wide palm tree and debris strewn everywhere. The school's desks, chairs, and sports equipment had all been destroyed.[6] Principal Xue Zheng reported that all the doors, windows, and washroom equipment in the school had been broken and all the science equipment was gone, with a total estimated damage of 200,000 yuan.[7]

In order to start the laborious restoration work, Xue Zheng organized the students and teachers to work in small teams to help clear the debris. After three months the school was able to resume classes full-time, albeit in somewhat dilapidated surroundings. Donations from parents and alumnae helped to pay for the cost of restoring the school, and students themselves played a part in helping raise the funds needed through ticket sales for their Christmas pageant. Girls took direct responsibility for restoring their campuses to their former glory, and their feelings of sorrow and anger at the destruction wrought by the war come through strongly in students' writings.[8]

Students' anger was not aimed just at the Japanese aggressors who had wrecked their beautiful campuses, but increasingly toward a government that had not done enough to defend China during the wartime.[9] Many alumnae recalled that it was during the post-war period that they became disillusioned with the Nationalist government and started to turn toward the Communist Party for inspiration. On her birthday in 1946, Zhu Lizhong 朱麗中 (McTyeire class of 1950) wrote in her brother's autograph book: "Never forget the National Humiliation" in decorative Chinese characters. In our interview in California in 2016, Zhu Lizhong did not remember feeling particularly patriotic during her schooldays, but said she "must have been" at that time, citing the evidence from her brother's yearbook. Although this could be regarded as a formulaic expression of patriotism, which was characteristic of all students in the post-war period, it is also worth considering the fact that, having been ostracized by her classmates due to her Japanese ancestry during the war, Zhu Lizhong perhaps felt she could make up for this by a show of intense patriotism after the war.[10]

Anger toward the GMD government was compounded by the continuing American military presence in China, which, at missionary schools, flared most dramatically after the rape of Shen Chong by American soldiers in

A doodle by Zhu Lizhong (McTyeire class of 1950) reads "Never forget the National Humiliation," which she drew in her brother's autograph book in January 1946, shortly after the end of the war of resistance against Japan. The war was a moment of social and political awakening for many students, who started to question the inequalities they witnessed in society. *Courtesy of Zhu Lizhong.*

Beijing. The continued American military presence was felt, from McTyeire and St. Mary's students' perspective, as a highly personal and gendered affront, and the incident could not but remind them of the exploitation that Chinese women had faced under Japanese occupation during the wartime. In the eyes of Chinese female students, American soldiers, just as the Japanese had done, were exploiting Chinese women and making China into their colony. Indeed, some students at St. Mary's were particularly angry at the ways in which some of their female compatriots were consorting with the Americans in the post-war period. Ying Manrong expressed her disgust at the "GI girls" who went out to bars with American soldiers:

> These kind of GI girls . . . did lots of things to make Chinese women lose face. I thought these people, they all come to make China into their colony, and they had all come out of the system of extra-territorial privileges. These GI girls would be taken out by American soldiers to bars and get drunk. This was a result of the continued colonial invasion of China. These kind of girls were really the lowest![11]

Focusing on the sexual promiscuity of some Chinese women who went to bars with American soldiers, they condemned their compatriots in highly gendered terms. This traditional concern for female chastity chimed with post-war anxieties about the nature of Chinese women's "collaboration" with the Chinese puppet government of Wang Jingwei during the wartime.[12] Even those women who were forced into sexual slavery for the Japanese, known as "comfort women," were criticized and stigmatized by their local communities for having provided sex to the Japanese, albeit against their will.[13]

Students' disillusionment with a government that had failed to restore full national sovereignty was also fueled by the continuing inequalities, corruption, and economic deterioration after the war. With tens of thousands of kilometers of impassable roads and destroyed villages, agricultural production down by 50 percent in some provinces, the dikes of the Yellow River unrepaired, millions of displaced people struggling to survive each day, and civil war brewing as support grew for the Communist Party in the North, the GMD faced an almost herculean task to stabilize China's economy and unite the country politically. Indeed, American military and humanitarian aid was deemed essential for the GMD to survive, with UNRRA (the United Nations Relief and Rehabilitation Administration) giving $518 million to help relieve starvation and providing seed, fertilizer, animals, clothing, and shelter for refugees.[14] The situation was not helped by the lavish lifestyles, violence, and corruption that continued to be rife among the upper echelons of Chinese society. Despite issuing a new currency in 1948, the GMD struggled to get inflation under control, and the new money became worthless almost overnight. Many middle-class Chinese suffered disastrous losses after they had been compelled to exchange their old currency for the new Gold Yuan.[15] Wang Shaolan 汪紹蘭 (McTyeire class of 1949) described her feelings of increasing disenchantment with the government:

> During the time when I was in the senior classes, after the war of resistance had been won and the Japanese had surrendered, the GMD started to fight a civil war to break the Communist strength. Under its reactionary government, prices rose, people had no means of livelihood, I was disconcerted and full of resentment. At that time all Shanghainese were struggling for democracy and peace, against hunger, against war, against the destruction wrought by war, which came in wave after wave.[16]

Students' disgust at the extravagant lifestyles some were leading during and after the war was not confined to political leaders but also extended to their own families, classmates, and teachers. Zhu Lizhong reminisced about how she and her classmates rebelled against their Home Economics teacher who was encouraging girls to behave in a wasteful and unpatriotic way during the civil war:

> This teacher suggested that we should use milk to wash our faces to have beautiful facial skin, as the wife of Shanghai mayor [Wu Guozhen] 吳國楨, and use egg white to wash our hair to make it shiny. The daughter of the mayor [Wu Xiurong] 吳修蓉 wrote a piece on our weekly board publication named [Kuangbiao] 狂飆, sharply criticized that this person was unqualified to be a teacher, when the country was torn with civil wars and millions dying from hunger, to suggest using edibles to selfishly beautify ourselves. The teacher was furious and wanted the school authority to punish the writer, but the whole class united together and did not reveal who the author was. The school listened to the students, and fired the teacher. That was one of our class victories.[17]

Though this story may also be read as a student's defense of her mother (no doubt Wu Xiurong was afraid that her mother would be criticized if the students believed that she behaved in this way), other students also recall feeling angry at their teachers and parents for what they considered to be wasteful, frivolous, and unpatriotic behavior. Rosalyn Koo (Chen Jinming 陳晉明, McTyeire class of 1947) remembered that she accused her father of being "decadent" for hoarding food when so many people were starving during and after the war: "I went home and I called my dad. I said, 'You are decadent. I will have nothing to do with you. You are corrupt, you are a hypocrite. You store things on the black market, people are starving. You store everything and you have servants.' It was a guilt trip."[18]

Girls came into contact with Communist ideas via a range of sources, including their library books, teachers, classmates, and family members who had become members of the underground Communist Party. Students' political awakening at missionary schools was also aided by the Communist Party's infiltration of Christian schools and institutions, including the YWCA. Qu Mingming 瞿明明 (McTyeire class of 1950) first came into contact with the CCP through her strong Christian background and involvement in the YWCA. Qu was a Christian student from a wealthy middle-class family. Her mother died when she was in Senior 3, and she saw the school as a surrogate family. In 1947 Qu attended a meeting of the YWCA student section at the Community Church (Guoji libai tang 國際禮拜堂) on Hengshan Road. She remembered: "There I attended the welcoming spring festival, listened to speeches, participated in visits, travels, campfires, such activities, where I received progressive ideas, which opened my eyes. We formed a Christian students' fellowship and I became the vice-chairman, we organised meetings, published small reports, organised excursions. It called students to strive for freedom and promoted their zeal for progressive ideas."[19] At missionary schools it was thus progressive Christian students, such as Ellen Cao and Qu Mingming, who first turned toward the Communist cause as the most practical means of helping their countrymen.

By the end of the war the CCP had infiltrated many schools across China. Even in exclusive missionary schools, such as St. Mary's and McTyeire, there were underground party members who worked to influence other students and teachers. McTyeire teachers Zhang Xiaoru 張小如 and Yuan Weitong 袁煒彤 were part of a Communist group of middle-school teachers operating under the name of the Middle School Education Research Group (Zhongdeng jiaoyu yanjiu hui 中等教育研究會).[20] After the war had ended, Zhang Xiaoru restarted Yiwu Primary School (Yiwu xiaoxue 義務小學), a charitable school for poor neighborhood children that McTyeire students had run before the war in order to gain teaching practice. Zhang used the school to recruit socially minded students to the Communist cause, and the school became a secret base for underground Party members to organize their activities as liberation drew near. Qu Minming recalled: "After victory in the War of Resistance against Japan, Zhang Xiaoru started the Yiwu Primary School within McTyeire. I became a student teacher. It was through visiting the families of the poor students that I became to recognise the corruption of the GMD government."[21] For Qu Mingming, like YWCA industrial secretary Deng Yuzhi 鄧裕志 (Cora Deng), there seemed to be no conflict between Christianity and communism in her thinking.[22] Rather, one led to the other as she naturally applied Communist ideas to the social service activities that had been central to missionary school life before the war. It is easy to see how missionary schools and other Christian women's organizations, such as the YWCA, with their long history of stressing social service and the complementary tenets of Christianity and nationalism became fertile ground for the Communist Party.[23]

Aside from social service, which naturally lent itself to communist ideas, interviews with alumnae reveal that they gained an understanding of communism from the left-wing books in their school libraries. Underground Communist Party teachers encouraged girls to think critically about the inequalities in society in their academic work and wider reading. They used subtle methods to encourage socially minded students to join the CCP, praising students' written work that contained progressive ideas. For example, Chen Tianmi 陳添彌 (McTyeire class of 1952) remembered that her Chinese teacher, Yuan Weitong, gave her progressive books to read and that Zhang Xiaoru praised her for an article she wrote in December 1948 entitled "Why I Don't Want to Write about Christmas":

> There was a teacher in the library called Zhang Xiaoru. At Christmas there [were] some activities, this teacher said, you guys can write whatever you feel like writing about, choose the topic yourselves.... I read a lot of books, including Lu Xun's books. From Junior Three I had a read a few books that had been passed down to me in the school, including books about American imperialism in China and Mao Zedong's writings.... I got many chances to get access to these books. Including a book written by that author living in the revolutionary base areas [Ding Ling], *The Sun Shines Over Sanggan River*. This is a novel about farmers' struggle against their landlord to regain their rights. I really liked reading these books, especially Lu Xun novels, I read all his works.

So after I had read all these books, I thought my country really has suffered so many humiliations and hardships. So at Christmas I rebelled. Everyone was writing about welcoming Christmas. I wrote an article entitled "Why I don't want to write about Christmas." Because I had this idea that China had suffered from so many hardships. In the end I wrote, "Only when everyone in China is in a position to enjoy and welcome Christmas, would I like to write an article about Christmas." My teacher was very happy when she saw this article. She gave me a very high mark. Although naturally it could not be published in the school magazine, she gave me a high mark and she encouraged me.[24]

According to Qu Mingming, there was a "treasure trove" of left-wing literature at McTyeire even before the war, accumulated by underground Communist Chinese teacher Dong Ruijin 董瑞瑾 and librarian Zheng Peide 鄭培德, who worked at the school from the 1930s:

Dong Ruijin introduced students to progressive books. She encouraged students to start a wall newspaper and a small library.... Every month Miss Deng and Miss Dong would buy books and magazines for the library. They brought left-wing books of the New Culture movement of the 1930s. They also brought translations of progressive foreign language books, and foreign classics. These included Xiao Jun's 蕭軍 *Village in August* (*Bayue de xiangcun* 八月的鄉村), selected works by Qu Qiubai 瞿秋白, and other authors including Ba Jin 巴金, Mao Dun 矛盾, and Lu Xun 魯迅.[25]

This store of progressive literature was also added to, perhaps unwittingly, by foreign teachers who brought with them influential books in English when they came back from their furloughs in England or America. For example, one summer Miss Robinson brought back with her a number of left-wing writers' works such as Karl Marx's *Capital*, John Reed's *Ten Days that Shook the World*, and Vincent Sheean's *Personal History*.[26] By the 1930s McTyeire had built up a rather unique store of books containing progressive ideas.

Alumnae revealed that their library books were not subject to the same censorship as in government schools, and students thus had access to a wide range of political ideas in their reading materials. One McTyeire student remembered: "What I liked about McTyeire was its liberal atmosphere... we were not controlled by the KMT like a lot of public schools. We could read whatever we wanted. From Karl Marx to Byron, everything was on the shelf waiting. It was a joy. We were so young at the time. We were interested in everything from Hamlet to Hitler."[27] McTyeire's status as an elite all-girls institution also protected the school's underground CCP members during the civil war years when the GMD ruthlessly arrested students who they suspected of being Communists. Chen Tianmi remembered that on one occasion GMD police were prevented from entering the school grounds on the grounds of their sex:

> The school was quite tolerant of such independent thoughts. However, because it was a missionary school, they did not encourage us to get involved in any political activities. Later, the secret police of National Party had suspicion about communist ideas spreading in the school. Once they tried to burst in and arrest students. However, because these secret police were all men, the guards at the gateway did not let them in. That was a rule of missionary schools, men were not allowed in the school gate. After liberation we found out that Zhang Xiaoru was an underground Communist Party member, as was Yuan Weitong. So the school definitely had these kinds of underground activities.[28]

By the spring of 1949, three progressive students in McTyeire, Qu Mingming (who was an official Party member), Wang Shaolan, and Luo Mingfeng 羅明鳳, encouraged by their teachers, set up a small underground Communist Party group within the school called the McTyeire New Democracy Youth Group (Zhongxi nüzhong xinminzhu zhuyi qingnian hui 中西女中新民主主義青年會). Girls in this group (who numbered twenty-one by May 1949), together with their teachers, worked to encourage others to join the Party and get involved in progressive activities both within and outside of the school. They used Yiwu Practice School as a recruiting base and met secretly at the home of Zhang Qiying 張啟瑩, whose family had already fled to Taiwan.[29] Chen Tianmi also remembers being influenced by Qu Mingming to join a student rally at Jiaotong University in April 1949 to protest the killing of three university students by the GMD. Chen recalled that, although she just "went along" with other students, attending this rally was an important turning point in her political thinking:

> The whole of Shanghai was liberated on May 27, 1949. Shortly before liberation in Shanghai, in April, I attended a student meeting at Jiaotong University which I believe Qu Mingming organized us to attend. Three students from Jiaotong University had been killed by the GMD. I don't

know why I went, but several of our students from McTyeire (about forty to fifty students) went along to attend the meeting. We went to Jiaotong University to commemorate the sacrifice of these three students. Their bodies were buried at the Jiaotong University campus. They built graves for them as well. We sang a song called "*Wu yue de xianhua*" [Flowers in May]. This song was from the war of resistance against Japan. These student pioneers had sacrificed themselves for the country's future. When I listened to these songs, I felt quite shocked. The atmosphere at that time was very solemn and quiet.

So this made me feel that strongly, that the future of our country was in the students' hands. At that time I realized we were responsible for this country's fate. This was a Communist Party–organized meeting. I am not sure why I went. . . . Some of my classmates asked me, "Are you going to come?" So I just followed along with them in a muddled way. . . . But when I went I realized students' responsibility for our country.[30]

Chen Tianmi, like many of her classmates, narrates her memories of becoming more interested in communism, as starting with just "going along" with friends or classmates. It was particular historical moments, such as the rape of Shen Chong and the killing of three Jiaotong students, that sparked a moment of conversion when they realized that elite students like themselves could become victims of American or GMD violence, galvanizing them into actively taking part in revolutionary activities.

Vice-Principal Kuan Yu Chen (Chen Guanyu 陳觀裕, McTyeire class of 1936) observed that students who became interested in the Communist Party before 1949 were from what she called "broken families," girls with unhappy family backgrounds: "Very interestingly they were students from troubled families. Broken families, problem families, and those students found somehow an outlet in revolution. They were dissatisfied with their personal family life, and they had a cause to embrace, to give themselves to."[31] Although this was not the case for many patriotic Chinese students who came from a variety of backgrounds and joined the Party, this assessment does seem to apply to several girls from elite missionary schools such as McTyeire. With parents who were often GMD politicians or big businessmen with interests in the regime, these girls might have been prompted by unhappy family relationships to rebel in a way which would appall their parents.

Rosalyn Koo explained how she had suffered from gender discrimination at home all her life—and was therefore naturally drawn to the Communist cause. She was particularly angry at her father, who treated her differently from her brothers and made her mother unhappy by having several extramarital affairs. However, Koo never became a CCP member. Upon her graduation from McTyeire in 1947, her parents shipped her off to an elite liberal arts college, Mills College, in the United States. They feared that their headstrong, feminist daughter would inevitably become a Communist if they allowed her to study at Yanjing University as she wished.[32] She recalled:

> I always wanted to go to Yenching. Always planned my life that after McTyeire I would go there. Because my grades were quite good, I only had to take two subjects to pass the exam, which I passed easily. You see my mother went to Yenching [University]. My father went to Chinghua [University]. So all my young life the idea was that I shall go to Yenching. But that was 1947 and the communists were coming down from the North. And my parents put their foot down and informed me that I cannot, because they feared I would become a communist member for sure....
>
> I would discuss with my mother the kinds of injustices going on. For instance, very close to home, we would have servants. We would have a wet nurse. And the woman would abandon her child to come here because her family was in the countryside.... I really felt it was so unjust.... Now where did I get this? I got it from my mother. My mother said to me, "Everyone has some place in Christ" but somehow she did not practice it. Then I enjoyed it. We had a chauffeur. I mean we enjoyed it. But I always had this big guilt trip about the unfairness. So I always said to my mother—that's why she got so scared—the reason I wanted to go to Yenching is I want to advance myself intellectually—wanted to help the poor. I wanted to go to the countryside and help the farmers. My mother said, "Where did you hear about all this?" And that's why she put her foot down saying, "You will become a communist member for certain." I probably would have because I have a basic sense of the society being unjust and also, I have an anger about being treated like a second-class citizen.[33]

In her narrative, Rosalyn Koo seamlessly blends the different ideological influences that had molded her upbringing and education. Her family background unintentionally reinforced the feminist (through her sense of unfair treatment as a girl) and Christian ideals she imbibed at home and school, making her more socially conscious and interested in the Communist cause. While girls at missionary schools were to some extent sheltered by the elite family background and prestigious education environment in the years 1946 to 1949, their recent experiences of warfare meant that they were by no means isolated from China's wider political situation.

1949: Liberation

As the People's Liberation Army (PLA) advanced toward Shanghai, progressive students at McTyeire prepared for the political change. On the eve of liberation (the term used in China to refer to 1949) in Shanghai, May 24, 1949, Qu Mingming, leader of the McTyeire Student Union New Democracy Association, led her progressive classmates in activities to welcome the People's Liberation Army:

> When Shanghai was liberated my classmates and I formed a team to help spread the news amongst the people. Wearing armbands, we proclaimed to the residents and workers of Shanghai: "Shanghai has been liberated", "the Guomindang has collapsed", "Power has been returned to the people", "Welcome the Peoples Liberation Army to Shanghai". Within a few days, McTyeire was seething with excitement, and these young ladies who had been shut up in an ivory tower rushed out of their cage and like small birds, spread their wings and began to soar.[34]

A few days later, on May 27, 1949, McTyeire and St. Mary's students represented their schools, among other middle schools in Shanghai, in a parade to celebrate the Communist victory. Dong Yue 董悦 (St. Mary's class of 1951) recalled her excitement at participating in the parade, where she wore Shaanxi-style clothes and learned to play the drums from that region.[35] Not all students took part in these activities or felt like "birds" suddenly released from a "cage." According to missionary teacher Ruth Harris, some students and faculty members at McTyeire had hidden in their closets and behind mattresses, frightened by the sound of gunfire as the PLA advanced on Shanghai.[36]

After the Communist victory, a tangible shift took place in the power dynamic among the student body at missionary schools as underground students and teachers revealed their identities as CCP members and began to lead their school. On December 9, 1949, McTyeire became the first Christian school in Shanghai to set up a general branch of the Communist Youth

League, with ninety-seven members. Qu Mingming became the General Secretary of the League, and Chinese teacher Zhang Xiaoru became the Party Secretary at the school. Members of the McTyeire Communist Youth League organized their classmates to take part in political activities and rallies alongside other middle-school students in Shanghai to show their support for the new government. To celebrate the first anniversary of the PRC, in 1950 the whole McTyeire faculty and student body represented their school in a parade alongside other schools in Shanghai. Some students carried the national flags, with others following with drums and other musical instruments.[37]

Alumnae's memories complicate this rather seamless transfer of power and ideological conversion that the official histories of the school present us with. One of the most dramatic changes that missionary schools experienced after 1949 was a physical change in the makeup of their student bodies. In the period leading up to liberation, many students whose families worked for the GMD government or who were wealthy businessmen left China for Hong Kong, Taiwan, and the United States. After 1949 there was an influx of new students who were from less elite family backgrounds. The new students were not required to pay the tuition fees or meet the previous entry requirements in English. This changing class and academic makeup of the student body was resented by some of the more senior girls, who still prided themselves on their school's elite status and illustrious academic reputation. Tao Xiafang 陶霞芳, who entered McTyeire in 1950, felt that the senior girls looked down upon newcomers, such as herself, for being from less socially elite families.[38] According to some alumnae, the academic standard of the student body as a whole dropped as the new students were not as advanced in English. Jean Craig recalled: "The greatest obvious change was the increase in enrolment. Students were still admitted by examination, but they no longer had to meet our former requirements in English. This meant that Junior I students began using the new government English texts!"[39]

Immediate changes to the curriculum included the complete replacement of previous textbooks with new government-approved ones; teachers were required to train in the new curriculum. Jean Craig recounted how, at McTyeire, "by September 1950 the government had rewritten and printed all textbooks from kindergarten through high school and these texts were used in all the schools. Instruction in the use of the new curriculum was required, and classes according to subject matter were organised."[40] Doris Coombs reported the changes in the curriculum at Riverside Academy: "The curriculum and the textbooks were changed dramatically. Apart from time spent in various political exercises, long periods were given to working on the land, etc. The history books were scrapped and new ones were so meagre that the teacher told us privately he had finished well before the end of term and he used time in telling them stories. The classics were banned."[41] Ruth Harris detailed the content of the new textbooks at McTyeire: "Our study books told of foreign imperialism and colonialism, they dealt with the hundreds of years of unequal treaties. . . . They described the Opium War of 1839–1842, when the British forced China to continue receiving shipments of opium and China was forced to cede Hong Kong to Great Britain. They detailed the unequal treaties with other European countries and finally with the United States too."[42]

Some alumnae also remembered this period of transition just after liberation as one of academic disruption and confusion. One McTyeire alumna from the class of 1951 remembered:

> Just after liberation when I was in Senior Two and Senior Three, the curriculum was in chaos, because some teachers had to leave. . . . For those who stayed they were not allowed to rely on the old textbooks, so there was lots of confusion about what they should teach us. You can understand at that moment of great change, there was lack of clarity. Also, there were lots of political activities, and everyone had to attend, so there was less emphasis on the academics which got weaker. Nobody was really paying attention to the academic side of things. It was a bit chaotic . . . but of course every country goes through those periods of change.[43]

Academic work was also disrupted by the new political activities in which both staff and students were expected to participate. Doris Coombs reported how exhausting trying to balance academics with political activities was for girls at Riverside Academy:

> This term we are having great difficulty trying to keep our educational work anywhere near normal standards. There are many competing demands on the girls' time and strength. To begin with, there is the study-work scheme, where they are trying to earn the fees their parents are unable to pay. The biggest project is vegetable gardening, not only on our own land, in the former lanes and playing field, but also a large piece of ground outside the west gate. Apart from that there was one day last week when all the schools went out to the country to catch worms which spoil the crops. I heard

that the farmers were not as appreciative as they might have been because some of the young rice was trampled down! Girls left school soon after 5 am, walked about 6 miles to the appointed place and worked till evening. Then most of them returned, but several stayed to put on a propaganda programme for the villagers and didn't get back till midnight. Last, but not least, there have been innumerable celebrations—Youth Day, Labour Day, the recent liberation of Chusan and yesterday the anniversary of the liberation of Ningbo.[44]

Missionary teachers, along with their Chinese colleagues, had to go to political education meetings and self-criticism sessions. At Riverside Academy all teachers had to be in the staff room from seven to eight o'clock in the morning to study books on Marxism-Leninism, and periodic meetings were held to test them. Although Coombs and Gauss started to attend, they were later excused on the grounds of not being proficient in reading Chinese. Coombs also described the weekly staff criticism meetings where teachers were expected to confess their errors and criticize each other:

> I remember that on one occasion one of our Christian teachers was accused of neglect of duty because she had taken some girls to a revival meeting instead of encouraging them to study. At the end of term each of us received triplicate forms which we had to state all kinds of details—how much time is spent on reading, what books you read, how long we were in bed, did we live frugally.... A meeting was held where we read our declarations and had a chance to alter them if our critics persuaded us to do so. The forms were then next studied by the school council which included servants and students, and they amended or added as they felt necessary and finally sent them to the education authority of the city. In this way records were kept of everyone. In addition to all this, two teachers at a time had to go to two-month indoctrination courses, and if they didn't satisfy the authorities they were kept longer. I believe they were asked to admit that it was wrong to believe in God, amongst other things. What could they do? I'm afraid most of them used the Chinese lie, saying what they were supposed to say while realizing that both parties knew it was not a fact. This was how one "saves face" and it obviated their having to prolong their stay.[45]

Although tensions between missionary students' identities as Christian and Communist grew over time, they were not irreconcilable in the years immediately after liberation. Missionaries also still hoped they could find ways to continue their work in China.

Changes in students' dress, hairstyle, and deportment were an external sign of student commitment to the new way of thinking. Ruth Harris documented the physical changes in the student body which resulted from this outward adoption of a new ideology: "It was astonishing how soon changes came to our elite student body. Very soon, everyone was wearing plain blue cotton clothing, no jewellery or makeup and simple hairdos. Anything that symbolised identification with 'the people' was in; everything that suggested separation from the people was out."[46] Adopting dress and hairstyle of "the people" was particularly important for those whose political loyalties might be in question. When Shanghai was liberated in May 1949, McTyeire principal Xue Zheng was studying for her doctorate in Education at Columbia University in the United States. According to the official school history, she rushed back to China, selflessly sacrificing her chance of finishing her doctorate. After she underwent a hasty political "re-education" in Beijing, the Shanghai education authorities confirmed that she could continue in her post as headmistress, and she reappeared on the McTyeire campus in April 1950 wearing a Lenin suit (a military-style jacket and trousers). According to the McTyeire history volume, her clothing represented the fact that she wanted to "conform to the new tide" and was firmly resolved to dedicating herself to the work of education in New China.[47]

In reality, more self-interested and pragmatic decisions may have driven many patriotic Chinese who were studying and working overseas back to China immediately after 1949.[48] These educated and idealistic patriots believed they could help the new government, but also wanted to distance themselves from a country which might taint their reputation if they remained too long.[49] Xue Zheng wanted to secure her position as headmistress of McTyeire and ensure the smooth transition of power, which might have been jeopardized if she had remained in the United States for an extended period after liberation. Not all missionary school principals were as ready to bend to the new tide in their dress, behavior, and political thinking as Xue Zheng. For example, at Riverside Academy, principal Shen Yixiang refused to denounce American education as "imperialist brainwashing," and in 1952 she was imprisoned as a counter-revolutionary.[50]

Xue Zheng's conscious adoption of socialist dress to prove her political conversion contrasts sharply with how another teacher, Yu Huigeng 俞慧耕, decided to present herself to the student body at St. Mary's. Yu Huigeng was a graduate of American Presbyterian Mary Farnham Girls' School (Qingxin nüxiao, 清心女校), another elite all-girls institution in Shanghai, and a recent graduate of St. John's University's English department. She had also become an underground CCP member while at St. John's. With her political loyalties not in question, Yu Huigeng could afford to present herself very differently from Xue Zheng, dressing in a way that would enable students to trust and identify with her. Yu Huigeng remembered:

> In September 1949 when I strode into the high walled, yellow and red tiled campus, a group of innocent and lively girls were craning their necks from the second story classroom window in a state of great curiosity and anticipation to have a look at me. They expected, that because I was sent to them by the military education bureau, that I would certainly be wearing a military uniform, have a military cap on my head and on my feet a pair of straw sandals, such as those worn by the female soldiers of the Eighth Route Army. Contrary to their expectations, there came this young teacher fresh out of St. John's University, wearing a finely tailored green *qipao*, with white leather shoes, no military cap on her head, who even had waved hair. There were some students who really didn't expect this and they called out in surprise: "Oh! How did that happen?" In this exclamation of "Oh!" I entered their lives and hearts.[51]

According to the alumnae, Yu Huigeng was very successful in winning over the girls' hearts and minds. She was appointed to teach politics at St. Mary's, and her ex-students all reported fondly that they enjoyed her classes. This memory is somewhat complicated by the ongoing personal friendships between teacher and former pupils. In 2016 Yu Huigeng was one of the oldest organizing members of the St. Mary's Alumnae Association in Beijing and still acted as a teacher to her former students in reunions. She showed the seventy- to eighty-year-old alumnae how to keep as subtle and healthy as she at ninety-three years old.[52] Yu Huigeng explained:

> The country sent me to St. Mary's after St. John's. Why did they send me to St. Mary's? Because I had graduated from St. John's and St. Mary's was the girls' middle school linked to St. John's. I taught girls politics at school, explaining to them why it was necessary for liberation, to have an equal society. Because my class background was the same as theirs. So I could really understand them. I was not there to criticize them. They were all from

wealthy family backgrounds, just like mine. So I could really understand these kind of girls' way of thinking. So gradually their thinking changed, until eventually some even signed up for military service. They realized that I had the same class and educational background as them. They all listened to me. I wasn't from a peasant or revolutionary family background. So we had a very good relationship, even until today the girls all listen to me.[53]

Yu Huigeng's memory typifies the softer, more gradual approach to political change that the newly empowered Communist government employed in the period just after 1949. Historians have explored how the "New Democracy" period (1949–1953) was marked by fluidity, accommodation, and continuation of older forms of political and social organization.[54] The Party was keen to co-opt China's capitalists and industrialists, on whom it was reliant for China's economic reconstruction after eleven years of almost continuous warfare. In order to make sure that these entrepreneurs did not all flee to Hong Kong, Taiwan, or the United States, the Party stressed that their interests would be accommodated and that they would even have an honored place in the new regime if they stayed to help build a New China.[55] St. John's Middle-School alumnus Tao Shuyu 陶樹玉 explained that his father, Tao Xinde 陶信德, who owned several textile factories in Jiangsu and Zhejiang, was rewarded for donating his enterprises to the country by being made a People's Representative for Jiangsu province.[56] This period of accommodation, continuity, and gradual transition which characterized the New Democracy period was also felt in missionary schools, where teachers and students experienced a surprising period of spiritual revival in the immediate period after 1949.

Spiritual Revival at Missionary Schools for Girls

The religious atmosphere at some missionary schools for girls just after liberation was remarkably characterized by a short-lived revival of interest in Christianity. For some in the Christian Church in China, the period after 1949 was experienced, like the period after 1927, as a moment of elation and new-found independence.[57] Pastor Cao Shengjie 曹聖潔 (a graduate of the Baptist girls' school, Jinde nüzhong 進德女中) felt that after 1949 the Three-Self Patriotic Movement Christianity in China away from individual denominations, in which foreign missionaries still had influence, to a truly Chinese non-denominational Church.[58] Some Christian Chinese leaders therefore welcomed the CCP, aligning Communism with Christianity in their thinking, while using the new political situation as an opportunity to move away from the interfering control of foreigners. Christian churches sought to elect new leaders for their institutions who would not only be politically acceptable to the new regime but also could be trusted to carry on the work of the Church in China. For example, YWCA Industrial Secretary Cora Deng (Deng Yuzhi), who was left-wing and a Christian, became the National General Secretary of the YWCA in 1949.[59]

Foreign missionaries were surprised at the level of Christian activities that were able to continue in the mission schools after 1949. Although formal religious classes were banned, Christmas and Easter celebrations, always an important part of the missionary school calendar, continued. Religious services carried on as normal, but off-campus. Doris Coombs reported that religious activities were able to continue and actually flourish at Riverside Academy, and that many students became interested in Christianity for the first time immediately after 1949:

> RE was banned, of course, but our principal had rented a large house next door to the school, where she installed her mother. A door was made in the wall and Christian activities continued there, not on school premises. After eighteen months of liberation there were two or three times as many girls attending meetings as before. This was chiefly due to courageous witness of the Christian students. When wall posters were put up ridiculing Christ and the Christian religion, the Christians would put up posters refuting the anti-Christian arguments, and their refusal to deny their faith caused many who had wavered to side for Christ.[60]

This surprising new interest in Christianity was actually fueled by the challenging new political climate. Ruth Harris, who was posted to teach at McTyeire after the Second World War, experienced 1949–1950 as a time of spiritual and political awakening for herself and a revival of the Church in China:

> Every student at McTyeire was now required to take the course on political thought. Previously a weekly chapel service had been required. But this could no longer be held. In these circumstances, however, a new church

was born, made up of those students and teachers and neighborhood people who were Christians. Of the 1,800 students, fewer than 100 attended church. A wholly new situation developed as these students asked one another for prayer, and each phase of the hymns we sang had real meaning for our lives. The Church began to come remarkably alive when it was standing up to be the Church.[61]

Under the new political conditions, Christian students at McTyeire continued their social service activities. Harris organized charity activities including a summer camp to the countryside near Suzhou which, remarkably, was granted permission by the new government authorities:

The Youth Fellowship of the new Church, influenced by a new awareness of the people and their suffering, began to see the gospel in a new light. Young people became interested in their neighbours and questioned for the first time, why there were glass shards on the tops of the walls surrounding the school. We made plans to organise a summer work camp with women and children in the countryside near Suzhou. . . . I explained that our goals for the work camp were the same as the goals of New China: to serve the people, to learn about the living condition of poor rural folk, and to work for their liberation from poverty.

To everyone's amazement, including mine, we were granted travel permits. We had not heard of anyone else being allowed to leave Shanghai at that time. That summer experience proved to be the highlight of my three years in Shanghai. We deepened our knowledge of the Christian faith and our understanding of the lives of people living under the oppression of poverty. . . . Later an American friend in Nanking asked me with much concern: "How are you?" I answered with complete conviction: "I'm great! I never realised the Church could be like this." That expressed my amazement and excitement at my first experience of the Church alive in that small faithful community in Shanghai.[62]

That Christian faith could be complementary to the new political conditions is revealed in the surprising overlaps between missionary and Communist structures of meetings and organizational activities. Doris Coombs remarked on the similarity of tactics used by the CCP in their meetings to the ones traditionally employed in churches:

The Christian teachers and girls had a meeting, and we decided to have a fellowship for the Christians, meeting on Sunday at 4.30. After the afternoon series, they will also have daily morning watch and evening prayers and twice a week there will be a meeting when we hope enquirers will also come. It will be led by a fine Presbyterian woman evangelistic worker. The first meeting she will introduce a subject and will prepare questions, which will be discussed at the second meeting. At the third meeting the groups will give their reports, and the fourth meeting will be a summing up by the leader. That is the latest Communist method, but it [is] also that which has been used in our summer conferences for many years! We are going to try it.[63]

According to Gauss, the Communist Party borrowed from the form and structures used by the Christian Church in China but adapted the content. This is not too surprising when we consider the history of the infiltration of Christian women's organizations by the CCP before 1949, such as the YWCA. Left-wing YWCA secretaries and student members, such as Deng Yuzhi (Cora Deng), Ellen Cao, and Qu Mingming may well have learned from the organizational forms of Christian women's organizations and applied those to their own organizing activities and structure for meetings.[64]

The Korean War

Despite missionaries' rather upbeat perspectives on the future of the Chinese church in the immediate period after 1949, their reports also hint at the tensions between Christian and non-Christian students and staff that was building at the schools. These tensions came to a head in 1950 as the Korean War broke out and China went to war with its former ally, the United States. Left-leaning missionary teacher Ruth Harris was happy to adopt proletarian dress and teach McTyeire girls new political songs that celebrated the founding of New China and extolled the valor of the working classes. She was not willing, however, to openly criticize her own country by teaching girls anti-American songs during the Korean War. Harris also got into trouble with principal Xue Zheng for attempting to continue religious meetings for McTyeire students off-campus.[65]

In sharp contrast to Riverside principal Shen Yixiang, who installed her own mother in a building adjoining the school to enable religious activities to continue off-campus, Xue Zheng was much more keen to toe the party line and ensure her own survival, particularly as political tensions ramped up after the outbreak of the Korean War. Shen Yixiang identified as a devout Christian, but Xue Zheng's commitment to Christianity is more open to question. Indeed, many McTyeire alumnae could not say whether or not Xue Zheng was a Christian.[66] At Riverside, Doris Coombs refused to teach singing and made sure that her students knew she did not endorse the political message of the new English language curriculum which she was required to deliver: "Needless to say I ceased to teach singing at all as all the songs were propaganda. The English periods were curtailed and I had to use an English translation of one of Mao's writings, though I made it clear to the girls that I was merely teaching the English language as I didn't agree with all the ideas!"[67]

Older, more experienced missionary teachers who had taught in China before the Second World War were much less sanguine than post-war newcomers, such as Harris. The words of American Episcopalian missionary Deaconess Ashcroft, as remembered by one St. Mary's alumna, give a flavor of the increasingly difficult position that foreign missionaries found themselves in after 1950:

> Deaconess Ashcroft said something to me one day which had a very deep impact on me. At that time, it was just after liberation, so we all thought how great it was that the CCP had come. We were just kids and we didn't really understand. Deaconess Ashcroft called me aside and she said to me: "Did you know that you should not call everything 'Imperialism'"? I thought about it and realized she was correct. Was America an imperialist country? Today we don't think of it like that. So I thought her words were correct. At that time Deaconess Ashcroft was correct. She said to me: "You don't understand what imperialism is." When I heard her words, I was very young, I didn't really understand. But now when I think about it she was correct. Deaconess Ashcroft! She said, "You should not call everything imperialism or everyone your enemy."[68]

Although this alumna is applying her twenty-first century understanding (in light of the reestablishment of China–US relations since 1971) of what might be considered Deaconess Ashcroft's quite patronizing words to her as a teenager more than seventy years before, her memory of this incident reveals the growing tensions between Christian and non-Christian elements of the school body and the increasingly uncomfortable environment missionary teachers operated in after 1949.

After the outbreak of the Korean War, it became apparent to missionary teachers that their presence in China was no longer welcome. Indeed, they were becoming a hindrance and an embarrassment to their Chinese colleagues. At McTyeire, tensions grew in the student body between students who belonged to the Christian Fellowship and students who were members of the Communist Youth League. The two groups competed for control of the Student Union. Chen Tianmi recalled:

> Just after liberation, when I was in Senior One, there was a split in the student body at McTyeire. . . . Students were in these two different factions, the CCP faction against the non-CCP faction. There was a group called the Christian Fellowship, and most of the students were Christian. Each faction had a student who was competing to be the leader of the student union. . . . This rivalry was very clear in the school. Before liberation you could not see this kind of rivalry, but afterwards it was very apparent. Each faction sang songs and made speeches to try to win over the students and get their candidate selected as student body president.[69]

These tensions also affected the faculty as well. Xue Zheng wrote in a letter dated 1950:

> There are conflicts among the faculty in McTyeire. . . . The progressive group is against the conservative one, the non-Christian group is against the Christian group, and a certain group is against the American group, although the latter does not realise the opposition and is also too busy at work but that certain group just wanted to create this feeling. All these feelings should be wiped out as soon as possible in order to prevent troubles in the future.[70]

At Riverside Academy, animosity grew between Christian students who supported their missionary teachers and more radical, non-Christian students who objected to their continued presence in China. Doris Coombs reported: "It was our custom to hold a sunrise service in the compound on Easter morning. Nearly a year after liberation the principal decided to go ahead and hold the service in the compound as usual. Most of the girls attended, but we were saddened by group of girls in a room on the opposite side of the campus singing propaganda songs and shouting slogans."[71] Coombs added with irony and amusement in the same letter that "a smaller service was held in our Methodist compound and an interested group of soldiers climbed over the wall and listened in, one of them joining in the egg hunt which followed."[72]

In many teachers' and students' memories, the battle for ideological control of the school between Christian and Communist students was fought using songs as a musical form of "ammunition." Girls tried to drown each other out or out-perform each other's displays of zealous devotion to their cause in a display of musicality which had always been a core and celebrated part of the missionary school curriculum. In both Christian and Communist ideology, songs and music were a tool for conveying key tenets and a very persuasive and emotive way to influence or indoctrinate the listener. In the alumnae's memories of their schooldays, songs—both Christian and Communist propaganda songs—stand out in their recollections. Often my interviewees broke into song to narrate a certain period of their life or to illustrate why they were so moved by a particular idea or campaign.[73]

The Korean War also marked a significant decline in the power of the principal and faculty members to control the students, who increasingly took charge of mobilizing their classmates to take part in the patriotic efforts. At Riverside Academy in Ningbo, Doris Coombs explained that the power of the principal was greatly diminished and the school was being run by a committee of seven teachers, including the principal, and two students who were elected by their fellow students.[74] Kuan Yu Chen (Chen Guanyu), who was acting principal of McTyeire from 1948 to 1950 while Xue Zheng was in the United States studying for her PhD, remembered the shift in power from faculty to students and her struggle to balance competing tensions and retain her own authority in the new political landscape:

> You didn't talk about politics if you are liberal, because you'd be labelled. In those days the Christian schools taught us we should be above politics. Politics is a dirty thing. And yet, it's just the reverse when the Communists came. They wanted you all to be involved in politics, to know the ideology, to know the government directives, to form into small discussion groups. They were trying to embrace everybody. . . . We were walking on eggs. Students revolted, faculty revolted, servants revolted. Then there was a group of radical students already underground and teachers who ate with me for several years emerged from underground and began to join the

Communist Party.... We never stopped the school. They wanted us to keep the school open.

Those radical students, the radical students just didn't care. They went off to rallies in the evenings, and the Dean tried to follow the old rules and called up the parents. She could be attacked as reactionary or anti-revolutionary. I worried about these older rigid faculty members, and I was supposed to be acting principal! I was young and inexperienced and they were so stubborn. After every city fell they wanted each unit, factory, school, to send a contingent of people marching, to parade. They would tell the students to parade, and, oh, you really have a hard time if you didn't have a contingent. It was all on my shoulders. If you don't have one it's my fault. I was prepared to be attacked at any time. And they can ring bells. They would assemble in the auditorium. They could have asked me to go on the platform. They could have had those accusation meetings. They could have made me a target. Why? I was a Christian. I went to America, just got back. I taught English, and I was very friendly with the missionaries. They were my teachers, we were on good terms. I was still in charge, but really the student government was in charge.... I took the lead, I had to, for the sake of the school. Otherwise the school would be in trouble. In one of the old pictures, I carry a red banner. And the terrible thing, down with the Americans, the Korean War. All along the road the students sang "Down with the American Devils, up with the Koreans!" And I carried the banner.[75]

Although Chen is narrating her experience several decades later, after she had emigrated, first to Hong Kong and then to the United States, we get a real sense of how this was a period of great anxiety for her as she struggled to manage both the staff and student body to ensure her own and the school's survival.

The political Campaign to 'Resist US Aggression and Aid Korea' (Kang mei yuan chao 抗美援朝), became an immensely successful tool for promoting patriotic support for the new regime in all sections of society. At McTyeire and St. Mary's, many students also enthusiastically participated in activities to support the Korean War effort. At McTyeire, students put their theatrical and musical talents on display to the public once more, this time acting out plays to represent their classmates' political conversion. For example, in 1951 Wu Yiyun 巫漪雲 directed a play entitled *Deng Yiliu's Transformation*, which "depicted the life of a girl from a capitalist family, who from a life of privilege which was deeply influenced by American television, realised that the importance of humanity lay in devoting her strength to building and preserving the New China."[76] The narratives of a struggle toward a "moment of conversion" and a theme of "redemption" perhaps struck a familiar chord with their Christian education. The new revolutionary zeal with which students carried out their political and social service activities can be seen as a continuation of the energies which they had applied to their earlier Christian social service activities, backed up by a new political message.

How deeply these girls were committed to the ideological underpinnings behind their actions, like their previous commitment to the doctrine of Christianity, is similarly difficult to determine, however. The alumnae's memories complicate the official picture of a smooth ideological conversion among students. Some students admitted that they only joined in these political activities because all their classmates did so. Acting principal Kuan Yu Chen (Chen Guanyu) put it like this: "Some tried to be, well, whatever the wind blows. It was an east wind blowing so they joined in."[77] In their joint recollections recorded at the fiftieth anniversary of their class entering McTyeire, alumnae from the class of 1947 felt that their Christian education, which exhorted them to "love" and "understand" each other rather than "criticize" and "hate", was a stumbling block to their political conversion: "We had to remold ourselves, to rebuild our connections. How should we look upon them in a new way, according to Marxism? So that's a struggle to change one's values. This was difficult. And then the movements came up. According to our education we were supposed to love, and here now we have to struggle, to hate your enemy. But we were brought up to love your enemy. This was really a struggle."[78]

Other students became determined to serve their country by joining the army during the Korean War. Between July 1949 and July 1951, forty-two McTyeire students signed up for military service, trained as nurses, or volunteered to work for their country wherever they were most needed.[79] Although six McTyeire students were approved to join the army and intended to go to Korea, ultimately many were prevented by the rapid end of the war. One McTyeire alumna described her conflicted feelings about signing up to the army during the Korean War:

> In Senior Two I decided to sign up for the Army, so I did not graduate from McTyeire. Why did I decide to join the army? Because in 1950, the War to Resist America and Aid Korea had started. At that time, many patriotic

youth decided to sign up for the army. I was one of these patriotic youth, I wanted to protect my country. But I also had a struggle in my mind about this choice.... I was from an intellectual family, I wanted to study mathematics at university like my father had done and become an engineer. I didn't really think much about politics. However, this campaign to Resist America and Aid Korea (Kang mei yuan chao 抗美援朝) was very fierce. We patriotic youth must defend our country. I wanted to go to help people in Korea. But I had this dream of becoming an engineer. But I was afraid I might die at the frontier. It was a dilemma in my thinking. Many students signed up. All my good friends decided to sign up. They encouraged me, "Your country needs you," so I signed up to be an artilleryman. Because I thought I should use my skills in mathematics. Many students who liked Math signed up for the artillery.... I like mathematics and I am very good at it. In the end, only I and other five students were approved to join the army....

However, although I signed up for the army, I never went to Korea. They sent us to the medical unit of the army to train as medics. Because we were from a girls' school, many of my classmates wanted to study medicine. I was not interested in medicine. I was more interested in mathematics. But they sent me to train as an army medic. They asked us to train in basic medical knowledge. I did the training, but I never went to Korea. Although I did help to lift the wounded soldiers and donate blood. They thought the war might end very soon and so we did not go to the frontier. So after training for several months I was sent to study medicine at Medical School (Yike daxue 醫科大學) for six years. So in reality, I never went to war....

After I graduated, I completed some medical research, so I never acted as practicing doctor, I just did foundational medical training of six years. Therefore, I did not actually graduate from McTyeire. I left in Senior Two, but I never picked up a gun.[80]

This alumna's frustration that she was not allowed to pursue her natural interests in Artillery and Mathematics, because it did not accord with continuing gendered expectations about women's caring roles in society, is apparent in her narrative. Despite the CCP rhetoric of female equality and liberation, in practice in the early 1950s, girls who signed up to serve their country in military service were still confined by a doctrine of femininity.[81] These continued gendered expectations for women have striking parallels with an earlier generation of missionary educators, who had frowned upon the military participation of their female students.

Six McTyeire students signed up and were approved to join the army during the Korean War. *Photo courtesy of Chen Tianmi.*

After the outbreak of the Korean War, conducting religious activities at school became fraught with difficulties, and life for foreign missionaries became increasingly tenuous. In 1951 the American Methodist Bishop of China, Ralph Ansel Ward, suggested that all missionaries should leave following the 1950 move by the People's Government to take over all

American educational institutions. The government declared missionary schools a "tool of cultural imperialism" in a new wave of Chinese nationalism that echoed the anti-Christian and anti-imperialist movements of the 1920s.[82] Ruth Harris was saddened that the Korean War made it necessary for missionaries to leave in order to avoid causing "more harm than good" by bringing trouble and embarrassment for their Chinese colleagues:

> There was no way to anticipate the effects of the Korean War on the Christian community in China. Often over the previous two years, I had marveled at the fact that I was still there, an American teaching Chinese young people. I thought of the ways Germans and Japanese had been treated in my country during World War II. How could the Chinese be so accepting and trusting? But now the time had come when no American could make a positive contribution. Now I was a liability to my Chinese friends and colleagues. . . . It was time to leave China. If I stayed, I could do more harm than good, mostly in bringing suspicion on my friends and students. Signs of friendship to me might be difficult for them, perhaps even dangerous.[83]

Similarly, Doris Coombs at Riverside Academy reported that as time went on the remaining missionaries felt that they were becoming "an embarrassment to our Chinese friends" and decided to apply for permits to leave the country.[84]

The Korean War and departure of the missionary teachers brought dramatic changes to the English curriculum. No longer allowed to use the texts that had comprised the missionary school curriculum, the Chinese teachers in charge of teaching this subject struggled to come up with suitable, politically correct teaching materials, particularly for girls with advanced English levels in the higher grades. At McTyeire, students felt that their English suffered when all the foreign teachers had left the school. During the Korean War little attention was paid to the English curriculum and the school struggled to find appropriate teaching materials. One alumna regretted that she was no longer allowed to study the foreign novels which she felt would have improved her English at a quicker rate:

> When the English teachers returned home, who was going to teach us? What would they use to teach us? At that time nobody was really paying

attention to this. The principal, she was sometimes absent and she couldn't pay attention to these really particular matters.... The result was that they invited an alumna, Miss Zhu, to come and teach English; however, after talking with her we realized she really did not know how to do this. She was not allowed to use the old material, so what could she use? She was also not familiar with teaching, and this was a really big change [after liberation]; as a result she came to find me, as the class leader, she said, "You come with me and help me to find some teaching materials."

So she put this responsibility on me, and I thought, how am I meant to find teaching materials? At this time we still had English class, but what should we use as materials? How should I know? Later I found a few foreign English Language newspapers, which were quite modern to teach the class. When we were in Senior One we read *Ivanhoe*. Now this book was very interesting, but also wasn't very easy. It's all about English history. Originally, my English wasn't that strong, but in Senior One something that left a very strong impression on me was that we read *Les Miserables* [in English translation], and I was very moved by this book, and then I really started to like English class, and I became very diligent. And *Les Miserables* was a very thick book, not only did you have to get the content, but also understand all of the vocabulary, and the feeling behind the story. So, I started to like English after reading this book. In Senior Two we read *A Tale of Two Cities*, now this is not a very easy book to read, but I also liked reading it.... Then after Senior Two all of the foreign teachers went home. What were we supposed to read? Just randomly reading books from the library was not suitable because I still needed help to grasp the meaning. So after liberation what should we do? Finally I thought of a way to find some kinds of newspaper materials. However, compared to the original material, the gap in level was so big, so I said to the teacher, "Okay, I will go out of the school to find some newspapers," and she said, "Okay." In reality, I really didn't learn anything. This was the situation in English class.[85]

Although missionaries detail at length their sadness upon their forced departure from China, ascertaining how students felt about the departure of their foreign teachers is somewhat more elusive. While some students remembered tearful farewells, others, whether out of political correctness or simply disinterest, did not seem to attach much emotional significance to their teachers' departure. Indeed, other students and teachers were relieved and happy to see them go. By this point missionaries had become somewhat embarrassing appendages rather than central characters in the life and running of the school. What seems to have left a deep impression upon girls' psychology in 1952 was the ending of their schools' independent identities as they were renamed, merged, or disbanded in the nationwide reorganization of the educational system. In Shanghai, McTyeire and St. Mary's were merged to form Shanghai Number Three Girls' School based at the McTyeire campus on Jiangsu Road. Tan Ying 覃英 was appointed principal and Xue Zheng vice principal.[86] Riverside Academy became Ningbo Girls' Middle School (Ningbo nüzi zhongxue 寧波女子中學), and Hangzhou Union Girls' School became Hangzhou Female Middle School (Shengli Hangzhou nüzi zhongxue 省立杭州女子中學). The Laura Haygood Normal School was disbanded and the original campus became part of Jiangsu Normal College (Jiangsu shifan xueyuan 江蘇師範學院), today Suzhou University (Suzhou daxue 蘇州大學).

A Turning Point

The seven years following World War II were a transitional period for missionary schools for girls in East China. Seeds of the divisions between politically engaged students and those who were content with the status quo, sown during the war, germinated into real tensions in the post-war period. In many schools it was Christian students who started to realize the applicability of their charitable social service activities to the Communist cause. Ironically, as elite all-female spaces, missionary schools also provided the perfect cover for underground Communist students' activities and gave them access to relatively uncensored progressive reading materials.

Although 1949 did represent the start of a new political era at missionary schools, it was also a period of continuity and accommodation. Christian students and staff continued their religious activities off-campus and found in the new political environment opportunities for recruiting new followers, bringing about a surprising, if short-lived, revival of the Church. There were, however, dramatic changes to the curriculum, with new political campaigns and study groups to attend, as well as changes in the make-up of the student body, and a power shift from staff to students.

Girls experienced these changes in different ways. While students who were already operating as underground Party members were able to come out and take charge of their classmates' and teachers' political re-education, other alumnae's memories of this period were more ambivalent. Some attended political meetings as a matter of course, rather than out of any real conviction or enthusiasm; others were disenchanted that their education had to suffer as a result of these disturbances.

In alumnae's memories, the more dramatic turning point came in 1950 with the outbreak of the Korean War. The war brought to a head growing tensions between Christian students who supported their few remaining missionary teachers and students who wanted their foreign teachers to leave. Their departure evoked sadness in some girls and nonchalance in many others. Although their English suffered as a result, girls had little time to brood over this; very soon the history of their schools would end abruptly with their merger into the government education system in 1952.

6
Reimagining Missionary Schools for Girls

On July 5, 1952, McTyeire and St. Mary's students filed into McTyeire's spacious auditorium, Richardson Hall. This was a painful and rather anticlimactic moment for many girls. They had grown up in a school environment that fostered unique identities as a St. Mary's girl or a McTyeirean. On that day, however, the classes of 1952 from both schools received diplomas which named them as the first graduates of the newly inaugurated Shanghai Number Three Girls' School. On the stage, Xue Zheng, representing McTyeire, and Yu Huigeng, representing St. Mary's, gave speeches to inaugurate the new school. After the speeches the girls paraded to the school gate where they hung a sign bearing the new school name.[1]

This moment was symbolic of the ending of just over one hundred years of history of missionary schools for girls in China (1844–1952). Despite the celebratory rhetoric that is used to describe this historic change in the official school histories, the alumnae's memories testify to their sadness at this sudden end to their schools' identities. This was particularly true for St. Mary's girls, who had lost their beautiful campus and were now "guests" in their rival's domain. Zhang Luoluo 張羅羅 (McTyeire class of 1947), who attended the opening of the Number Three Girls' School in her capacity as reporter for the Wenhui Bao newspaper 文匯報, recalled the sadness of the St. Mary's pupils at the opening ceremony: "That day I sat on the first row and saw the faces of the St. Mary's girls, they were all extremely sad. . . . Our McTyeire campus was still here, we still had our auditorium, but I felt that St. Mary's girls were just guests in our school."[2]

Despite becoming the first class of girls graduating from the Number Three Girls' School, McTyeire and St. Mary's students who graduated in 1952 continued to identify with their almae maters as the last class of St. Mary's girls and McTyeireans. Alumnae from the class of 1952 belong to separate McTyeire and St. Mary's alumnae associations, and their names are listed in the back of their schools' respective history volumes.[3]

However, this is not quite the end of the story. In 1981 McTyeire alumnae succeeded in restoring their old school campus, which had become

Dreaming the New Woman. Jennifer Bond, Oxford University Press. © Oxford University Press 2024.
DOI: 10.1093/oso/9780197654798.003.0007

co-educational in 1966, as an all-girls' school.[4] This remarkable restoration of the school's link to its prestigious Republican predecessors came about in the period since the reform and opening policies of Deng Xiaoping, which has witnessed the re-emergence of demand for Western (particularly American and British) education. In a new social and political context in which Western-style social graces, fluency in English, and overseas study experience re-emerged as markers of elite status, alumnae took the opportunity to recapture their school's history and celebrate its and their own prestigious status in China once more. That the alumnae decided to invest significant sums of money to re-instate their school history as soon as they were permitted to do so also points to the long-lasting impact that going to missionary school had made on them. For alumnae who left China at the cusp of the 1949 revolution, their schooldays constituted some of their most salient memories of their childhoods in China.

Many alumnae suffered during the Cultural Revolution because of their family background and for having attended a missionary school. Xue Zheng was removed as headmistress.[5] Riverside Principal Shen Yixiang spent years in prison for refusing to denounce American education as imperialist brainwashing.[6] Despite the hardships that many faculty and alumnae endured during the turbulent political changes that took place after 1949, their sense of loyalty and identity to their school has withstood the test of time, notably in the re-emergence of the alumnae associations since the 1980s. The alumnae chapters established in Shanghai, Beijing, and the United States host annual reunions where students' sense of love and loyalty to their almae matres is palpable. Whether born out of old age, nostalgia, a desire for longevity, or the shared suffering they have endured, these students' loyalty to their school has certainly had an impact on their schools' successor institutions.

Alumnae strive to keep the memory of their schools alive in their reunions, newsletters, book publications, and financial investment in the Number Three Girls' School today. Generations of alumnae and teachers have successfully transmitted their school spirit, which stressed the importance of girls' education, into the culture of the Number Three Girls' School. Jean Craig remarked upon her return to the school shortly before the centennial anniversary in 1982: "McTyeire has lost her name but not her spirit! She lives on in the lives of her daughters: women of strength and faith, women who have dared to make their school motto central in their living. Scattered now in faraway places and in many lands, McTyeire alumnae continue to be women of distinction and persons who care. Some, though very old, carry heavy leadership responsibilities."[7]

What did alumnae feel to be the most important and lasting impact that going to a missionary school for girls had upon their lives? The lives of famous and accomplished alumnae, including translator Chen Hongbi 陳鴻璧 (McTyeire class of 1902), Madame Chiang Kai-Shek, Song Meiling 宋美玲 (McTyeire class of 1907), pioneer female aviator Hilda Yan (Yan Yaqing 顏雅清, McTyeire class of 1923), diplomat Gong Peng 龔澎 (St. Mary's class of 1933), novelist Zhang Ailing 張愛玲 (St. Mary's class of 1937), and Nobel prize–winning scientist Tu Youyou 屠呦呦 (Riverside class of 1951), are well known. However, the more typical career paths and life trajectories of other graduates, who became businesswomen, educators, writers, wives and mothers, lawyers, bankers, architects, engineers, translators, army officers, politicians and diplomats, among many other occupations, are less well documented. The afterlife of missionary schools for girls and the experiences of the alumnae post-graduation reveals much about the cyclical history of the making and unmaking of elite identities for women in modern China.

Looking Back

During a focus-group interview in Beijing with four alumnae who graduated from St. Mary's between 1947 and 1953, following the suggestion of their former teacher, Yu Huigeng 俞慧耕, I started by asking the group an open question: What was the most important influence you feel that going to St. Mary's had on your life? Naturally, the answers they gave varied with their personal experiences and storytelling style. However, three clear themes emerged: alumnae felt it had given them a strong foundation in English, which was important for their later careers. They had formed life-long friendships at school that had survived and supported them during the tumultuous decades of political changes through which they had lived. Finally, and perhaps most difficult to define, it had "cultivated their characters": taught them how to "love," how to "forgive," and how to be "a good person."[8]

Unpicking how far their experiences at missionary school were influential in directing the course of their later lives is a difficult and potentially misleading exercise. Although their experiences at school were formative, we must place them in context to other influences, including their family background and career choices, not to mention the momentous social and political changes that China went through, rendering many ordinary Chinese people with little direct control over important decisions in their lives. This is especially true for alumnae who graduated from middle schools and universities after 1950. No longer could they choose their career paths or where they worked, but were sent where the country deemed them to be most useful. One alumna who I interviewed went to great lengths to maintain her freedom of choice upon graduation. Determined to devote her life to serving the church as a priest, Cao Shengjie 曹聖潔 gave up a scholarship at St. John's University and transferred to finish her degree in theology at Nanjing Theological Seminary. She explained that if she had graduated from St. John's, she would not necessarily have been able to enter the ministry, as the government may have assigned her to another profession.[9]

In some cases, there is an obvious correlation between alumnae's missionary school training and their later careers. Many of the alumnae I interviewed went on to work as teachers and translators because of their advanced English. Ying Manrong 應曼蓉 (St. Mary's class of 1945) realized she could serve the Chinese Communist Party with her English skills by translating a newspaper article about the rape of Shen Chong.[10] After the Cultural Revolution had ended, Ying Manrong was invited to help compile the Chinese–English dictionary published by the PRC in 1978.[11] Although English was replaced in the curriculum by Russian after 1951, since the late 1970s their proficiency in English has subsequently proved an asset in many alumnae's careers, even if they did not advertise too widely where their fluency had come from in the years immediately following the Cultural Revolution.

Yang Zhiling 楊之嶺 (St. Mary's class of 1951) felt that the high level of English that she acquired at St. Mary's had a profound influence upon her later career. Yang Zhiling remembered that although she had originally aspired to become a doctor, upon her graduation from St. Mary's in 1951 the country was short of teachers. She therefore went to Beijing Normal University (BNU), graduating in 1955. Upon graduation she worked as an administrator for BNU, assigning students jobs upon graduation. During the Cultural Revolution she was denounced as a "capitalist roader" and felt she could no longer do her job. In 1973, toward the end of the Cultural Revolution, she applied for a job at BNU's Institute for Research on Foreign Issues (Waiguo wenti yanjiusuo 外國問題研究所).[12] During the interview she convinced her boss to hire her by being able to recite to him a passage from Charles Dickens' *A Tale of Two Cities*, which she had studied at

St. Mary's. When delegates were chosen to go to the United States to study comparative educational systems in 1980, Yang Zhiling was selected. She was invited to tour fifty-three cities across eighteen states to give talks about modern Chinese educational developments.[13] Yang Zhiling decided to pursue her studies in education to the PhD level at Kent State University in Ohio, and when she graduated in 1982 she became one of the first Chinese nationals to receive a PhD degree in the United States since re-establishment of diplomatic relations. She later worked as a professor of education at several universities including Beijing Normal University, the University of Minnesota, University of Utah, and California State University. According to Yang Zhiling, throughout her time in the United States, people were interested in her educational background and felt that she was "different" from most Chinese people they had met before. She felt that her Western manners, knowing how to say "Yes, please" and "No, thank you" acquired at St. Mary's, were probably the reason she seemed different and was invited on the lecturing tours. Yang Zhiling has had a successful career in the education world and she has been invited to more than twenty countries to give talks and lectures. She attributes a large portion of her successful career to the training she received at St. Mary's.[14]

Other graduates had careers as translators and interpreters for important politicians and diplomats. After graduating from St. Mary's in 1947, Zhao Fengfeng 趙風風 studied for one year at St. John's University and then in 1949 transferred to Tsinghua as her sister was studying in Beijing. She originally majored in Education, but later switched to foreign languages. She graduated from Tsinghua in 1952. After graduation she entered the Chinese foreign service, acting as translator for several important political figures and foreign visitors to China. Her longest assignment was as the personal secretary of American left-wing writer and political journalist Anna Louise Strong. Strong visited China six times in total, starting in 1927. On her final stay, which lasted for twelve years (1958–1970), Zhao Fengfeng accompanied the seventy-two-year-old Strong on her visits all over China and overseas, acting as translator at her meetings with a variety of important political figures including Vietnam's President Hô Chí Minh.[15]

Similarly, Liu Zechi 劉澤墀, upon graduating from McTyeire in 1947, studied at St. John's University for one year before transferring to the education department at Yanjing University. Upon graduation she worked as a translator at the Beijing Foreign Affairs Office and met several political leaders during her work there, including Mao Zedong.[16] Other graduates used their English as translators for news agencies and other cultural bureaus. For example, Wu Qihui 吳其慧, who was particularly strong in English, was one of the top three students graduating from the St. Mary's class of 1947 and was therefore able to enter St. John's University without taking the entrance examination. She majored in English, and after her graduation in 1952 went to work for the Xinhua news agency until her retirement at the age of sixty-five. After retirement she worked as an editor for the *New China* magazine.[17]

How the "moral training" that St. Mary's girls emphasized as an important legacy of their missionary school experience affected girls' lives is more difficult to define. By the 1930s only a minority of girls who went to missionary schools for girls identified themselves as Christian. However, some Christian teachings, such as forgiveness, seem to have stayed with girls and sustained them through difficult periods in their lives. Two alumnae took pains to try to define this intangible moral education. According to these alumnae, girls were influenced by the Christian environment of the school in an intangible or imperceptible way. Christian values were inculcated through the literature they studied and the music they sang. Yang Zhiling defined it in this way:

> Forgiveness. According to the school, if you did something wrong the dean would call you into her office, and talk with you and tell you what is right and what is wrong, they did not seek to punish people. If you changed you would be allowed to remain, if not, according to the schools rules you would be allowed to leave. In a lot of literature [that we studied], such as *A Tale of Two Cities*, Dr. Manette because of the son-in-law, he was in prison because of that family. But after he knew about the son-in-law's background he tried to forgive. This kind of thing is so powerful, not like instruction, telling you what to do, but the literature is penetrating into your blood, into your mind and your thinking and your feelings and everything.... During the Cultural Revolution I can remember, not only myself, but a lot of classmates, and younger classmates were persecuted because of our background. But after that we tried to forgive these [people], because they are all young students and we need to teach them. And at this time if you did not have this kind of attitude you would hang yourself. So this is something very important.[18]

Yang Zhiling's interpretation of the impact that a Christian education had on her life is also echoed in some of the "scar literature" produced by survivors of the Cultural Revolution in America in the 1980s.[19] Theresa Chen (Chen

Zongci 陳宗慈, McTyeire class of 1951), also felt the same "imperceptible" Christian or moral influence was inculcated at her school through the influence of music and songs:

> De, zhi, ti, 德智體, Morality, Academics and Physical education. These are important aspects. But McTyeire had another one that [made] the students very vivacious [*huoyue* 活躍]. . . . This was not very obvious, but there was this kind of underlying [education], there is a cultivation of people's characters. At McTyeire, in addition to this de, zhi, and ti, there was music. Music is that emotional appreciation, that art appreciation, that uplifting appreciation. And to me, because by this time we did not have religious classes, this was our religious education. There was this fellowship thing. For me, music is where I got my religious education. Because in that music there was a lot of praise. Hymns are where I got my religious education. It was also from art. If you look at the hymns they are very poetic. And so it cultivates your appreciation for art. I was part of Miss Harris's Choral Group. Out of the choral group she selected twelve students and I was one of the twelve, when I was in my last semester. We even went out and we sang a cappella. We went by train out of town to a little place, we sang to the people there. It was a field trip. I was second soprano.[20]

For other missionary school graduates who consciously identified as Christian, or at least came from a Christian family background, their missionary school education was to help them in a more tangible way by providing them with a stepping stone into careers for the Church. These Christian students were co-opted by the new regime to staff their religious affairs bureaus and other cultural and religious organizations under the new Communist government control, such as the China Christian Council (CCC), Three-Self Patriotic Movement (TSPM), and YWCA. For example, Lucy Hong (Hong Lüming 洪侶明), who attended McTyeire from 1943 to 1946, graduated from St. John's as an Education major in 1952. Upon graduation she was assigned to work in the Shanghai Cultural Bureau (Shanghai shi wenhuaju 上海市文化局) editing films, TV dramas, and comics. In 1953 she was transferred to work in the Shanghai Culture Publishing Company (Shanghai wenhua chubanshe 上海文化出版社) and was responsible for helping to edit novels. In 1954 Hong transferred to work for the CCC as an assistant editor of its Christian magazine, *Tianfeng*

天風. She recalls that at this time the government needed people with a Christian background to staff the CCC. In 1953 she married Shen Yifan 沈以藩, who became the last ordained Episcopal bishop of China before the Cultural Revolution.[21] After the Cultural Revolution, Hong started working for the YWCA and she became the Vice-General Secretary of the Shanghai YWCA. In 1988 she was selected for one year of study at Manchester University Seminary in the United Kingdom, funded by the China National YWCA. In her retirement she taught the organ at the East China Theological Seminary.[22]

Similarly, Cao Shengjie, whose adopted mother and grandmother were devout Christians, was a graduate of a Southern Baptist school for girls in Shanghai, Jinde nüzhong 進德女中, in the class of 1949.[23] Upon graduating from Nanjing Theological Seminary in 1953, Cao worked as a church worker at St. Peter's Church in Shanghai (Shanghai shengbide tang 上海聖彼得堂), and she was also a board member of the Shanghai YWCA. After the Cultural Revolution, along with other figures who had been leaders of the Protestant church in China before the Cultural Revolution, such as Shen Yifan and Yao Minquan 姚民權, Cao Shengjie was invited by the Centre for Research on Religion (Zongjiao yanjiusuo 宗教研究所) to do research and conduct interviews about the status of Christianity in China. This study marked the revival of the Protestant church in China. In 1991 Cao Shengjie became the National YWCA Vice-President until her retirement in 2012.[24]

In other cases, the values of girls' education imparted at school created strong-minded women who self-consciously championed women's causes throughout their lives. Rosalyn Koo (Chen Jinming 陳晉明, McTyeire class of 1947), always felt discriminated against at home for being a girl. She was angry and disappointed with her father who had several girlfriends and did not live up to the ideals that she felt his Western educational background should have imparted in his personal life:

> I always think he treated me as a second-class citizen. There should be no excuse for that because he was educated in the United States. What is your excuse? He had girlfriends, he hurt my mother. But my husband's side [of the family] was straight and above board. The concubines would come in, at least the ones who bore children. But my father was supposed to have one wife and three kids, but he fooled around outside. And I said, "You are a hypocrite!"[25]

Koo described McTyeire as a "sanctuary" or "refuge," and it was only at school that she felt she had a free space to truly be herself, dressing as a boy at school and escaping traditional "feminine" stereotypes expected of her at home. After graduating from McTyeire in 1947 Koo left China for higher education in the United States. After pursuing a successful career as a partner in an architecture firm in San Francisco, in 1989 Koo co-founded the 1990s Institute, which supports Asian Americans and promotes constructive US-China relations. Through the 1990s Institute Koo became involved in the All China Women's Federation's 'Spring Bud Project' (Xiwang gongcheng 希望工程), and helped raise funding to sponsor girls from poor families in rural Shanxi, to attend primary school, high school, and university.[26] In narrating her life story, Koo directly relates the education she received at McTyeire, which expounded the importance of girls' education, to her philanthropic work in later life.[27] Indeed, she is in some ways a paradoxical example of a student who fulfilled missionaries' hopes for their efforts in girls' education in China. Although defining herself as a tomboy and a socially minded activist, rather than a lady-like Christian, she dedicated her later life to the cause of serving less-fortunate Chinese women.

Networking: Friendships, Alumnae Organizations, and the YWCA

Perhaps the most long-lasting and tangible impact that going to a missionary school had for the alumnae who I interviewed was the lifelong friendships, concretized through alumnae networks. These alumnae networks were united by a shared school identity and, in some cases, shared experiences of suffering for their elite "foreign-style" education during the Cultural Revolution. Many alumnae felt that the girls who came out of McTyeire and St. Mary's were somehow "different." They are indeed extraordinarily accomplished and determined women who have achieved remarkable things in their lives and careers, both inside and outside of China. As one alumna put it jokingly, "What you can say about McTyeire husbands is that they all married very powerful women!"[28]

The friendships and networks of educated women that missionary schools and their alumnae networks supported were vital to several generations of graduates. For the early generation of missionary school graduates, who were the first Chinese women to receive an education, missionary school and other Christian women's organizations such as the YWCA, provided important networks of support and career opportunities for women trying to take their first steps in the public sphere. Many of the early graduates from missionary schools became teachers, and schools run by the same mission tended to employ each other's graduates. The principals of Riverside Academy (Shen Yixiang 沈貽瓕), McTyeire (Xue Zheng 薛正), and Hangzhou Union (Zhou Juemei 周覺昧) all attended missionary schools for girls. They earned BA degrees from missionary universities in China and then worked for missionary schools as teachers before being selected as school principals.[29] Shen Yixiang and Xue Zheng were also sponsored by missionary boards to study abroad in America for higher MA and PhD degrees in Religion and Education during their tenure as principals.[30]

Organizations such as the YWCA also provided a crucial network of Christian-educated women and a platform for girls to step from school into society upon graduation. The Chinese YWCA was founded in and cultivated its first generation of secretaries from the missionary schools.[31] Indeed, statistics on McTyeire alumnae careers reveal that by 1924, 10 percent of McTyeire alumnae were working for the YWCA as board members, committee chairs, or national secretaries. Other graduates were mainly married and not working outside the home (15 percent), pursuing further study (18 percent), or teaching (34 percent).[32] Critically, the YWCA also afforded married women opportunities to work outside the home in voluntary and part-time roles by serving on committees and sitting on boards.[33] This was particularly important in a society that in the 1920s and 1930s still offered very few opportunities for elite women to work after marriage. During this period, charity and social service work was one of the acceptable occupations for women alongside teaching and nursing. Rosalyn Koo remembered how her mother and aunts were very strong women, who found comfort and support in each other's company within a deeply gendered society:

> I was very much influenced by my mother and aunts; they all attended university. My mother was educated at Yanjing for a couple of years; she didn't finish. And my mother's younger sisters both finished Yanjing. When you get these sisters together, I mean heaven help him! My father would just run. Very strong. But they were also the victims of the circumstances, of society. Even though they may be capable, they cannot work.[34]

Rosalyn Koo and her generation of missionary school graduates (my interviewees who graduated from the late 1930s to early 1950s), faced different challenges and opportunities than their mothers did. Although gendered expectations of women's roles in society were still deeply entrenched, the job opportunities for professional women had widened, particularly after the outbreak of the Second Sino-Japanese War. The early generation of Christian-educated women, such as Xue Zheng and Shen Yixiang, were now their role models, teachers, and task masters. These educated women also formed an important network of support for Rosalyn Koo's generation, by pushing at the boundaries of what it was possible for educated women to do in society. Graduates contributed articles about their experiences studying abroad, going to university, or entering the workplace in the school magazines.[35] The successful careers of alumnae provided girls with aspirational role models, as Methodist McTyeire missionary teacher Jean Craig recalled: "There were role models aplenty—alumnae distinguishing themselves in colleges and universities in China and overseas; alumnae on our faculty and in other schools; alumnae in Shanghai: in the home, in the church, in medicine, in business and even in Law."[36]

The alumnae association thus formed a network of support and influential contacts which girls could access upon graduation to gain higher education and career opportunities. Keeping in touch with its graduates was also ultimately important for the schools. By the 1920s, alumnae who married wealthy or politically influential men could become vital supporters of the school both financially and politically. St. Mary's alumnae established a scholarship for Christian students in financial need, and donations from alumnae helped pay for repairs to McTyeire and Laura Haygood after the Second World War.[37]

During the Republican era, wealthy and well-connected alumnae not only provided valuable role models and financial support for the schools, they also helped to bolster the school's reputation. Going to a missionary school for girls in the Republican period became an important marker of elite status for modern women in treaty-port East China. The girls who passed through their doors performed a careful blending of Christian and patriotic ideas about what an elite, well-educated Chinese woman should be. This vision, which stressed women's contributions to the nation via homemaking skills, also became deeply tied to a state-sponsored vision of modern Chinese womanhood, particularly during the New Life Movement. While they often shored up rather conservative gender views about how an upper-class patriotic modern women should dress and behave, they also used their school as a laboratory to playfully cross gender boundaries and imagine new roles for themselves.

Evidence suggests that this "elite" status was carefully guarded and supported by pupils, teachers, and alumnae during the Republican period. However, it has also become one of the most enduring negative labels attached to missionary schools for girls. One McTyeire alumna recalled how she was bullied by a teacher at a different school in Shanghai, who labeled her as a "spoilt young lady" simply because she had attended McTyeire.[38] In 1989 the Shanghai Film Studio produced a film entitled *The Last Aristocrats* (*Zuihou de guizu* 最後的貴族), based on the novel *Zhexian ji* 謫仙記 (Gone to Earth) by Bai Xianyong 白先勇, which tells the story of four wealthy missionary schoolgirls (apparently based on McTyeire pupils) who leave Shanghai for higher education in the United States shortly before 1949.[39] This "aristocratic" label profoundly affected the alumnae's lives and careers during the Cultural Revolution.

Missionary Schoolgirls in Mao's China

Missionary schoolgirls helped to create a new version of upper-class female gentility in Republican China. After 1949 the state mobilized women to take part in work outside the home, and new proletarian gender identities for women were valorized. This was represented externally by the adoption of androgenous forms of dress and a rejection of traditionally "feminine" attire such as the *qipao*. Socialist feminism sanctioned by the state predominated, and PRC historiography has since dismissed the Republican period as a brief interlude of "bourgeois feminism" directed by foreigners.[40] However, older persistent ideas about femininity and female virtue for all classes of Chinese women continued well into the Mao era and beyond.[41] One of the eight officially sanctioned Revolutionary-model theatrical works during the Cultural Revolution, the ballet *The Red Detachment of Women* (*Hongse niangzi jun* 紅色娘子軍), is a classic example of how even the supposedly androgynous Chinese female soldier could be poised and graceful as she performed jetés and pirouettes in costumes that showed off her legs and small waist on stage.[42] At times when the state deemed it beneficial for China's economy for women to go back home (1955–1956 and 1990s), women's traditional caregiving and household management roles were again valorized, rebranded as the "new socialist housewife."[43]

Because of their class and educational backgrounds, most alumnae remember the Mao era, particularly the Cultural Revolution, negatively. They were forced to give up promising careers, they were persecuted, and they were sometimes physically tortured. However, some alumnae also recalled surprisingly positive memories of this period, alongside narrating the hardship and suffering they endured. For example, Lucy Hong and Cao Shengjie remembered that their educational level won them the respect of the farmers and factory workers who were supposed to be "re-educating" them. During the Cultural Revolution churches were closed and Lucy's husband, Bishop Shen Yifan, was put under house arrest in their home next to the former Episcopal church. Alongside this painful memory, Hong recalled the "fun" she had working with Pastor Cao Shengjie, at the New China Leather and Chemical Factory (Xinhua pige huagong chang 新華皮革化工廠) in Shanghai, toward the end of the Cultural Revolution. In a joint interview, Lucy Hong and Cao Shenjie recalled:

Cao Shengjie: During the Cultural Revolution the religious leaders suffered a lot. We two, we were not leaders back then so our lives were not too bitter. We worked together in a factory for eight years so we are old friends.

Lucy Hong: We worked as assistants at a factory which made plastic bicycle seats and we did night shifts. Although the temperature was over 40 degrees [Celsius—over 100 degrees Fahrenheit] in the factory and the air had poisonous fumes, it wasn't too hard work, we were young. Actually, it was also quite fun [laughing]. The workers were good to us, and took care of us. Because we were cultured (educated) [*you wenhua* 有文化], we also acted as their teachers. We taught the technicians English, because we had graduated from St. John's University. At that time the language had changed back from Russian to English. We intellectuals were still useful and could make a contribution. So we had this experience but we didn't suffer too much.

Cao Shengjie: Actually, it was great. They didn't look down on us for being intellectuals. We worked alongside them.... However, we couldn't talk about religion, we did not dare to during this period. We had a bad-class status. We were classed as "cow demons and snake spirits" [*niu gui she shen* 牛鬼蛇神]. However, we were not big "cow demons and snake spirits."

Lucy Hong: We were part of the six bad classes [*hei liu lei* 黑六類]. However, we were the in the sixth category, the least bad kind. So it was okay, we got to know the workers. We taught them how to read Chinese, a bit of English, and taught them to practice singing. I remember I organized them to have inter-factory singing competitions. . . . Not religious songs, of course. Religion was banned; all the Churches in Shanghai were closed. But nobody could know if you prayed at home in private. Because of our status we were under the authorities' watch so we couldn't invite any Christians to our homes.

Cao Shengjie: Later, after the churches were reopened, I saw that one of the workers from the factory that we worked at showed up [at Church].[44]

There are some surprising continuities in Lucy Hong and Cao Shengjie's memories of their factory work in the Cultural Revolution and the ways in which schoolgirls described their social service work among poor factory workers before 1949. Although they did not undertake this work on a voluntary basis, they were conscious of their different class status (albeit a bad one at the time) and, recalling this episode in the post-Mao era, rather paternalistically positioned themselves as the educated elite. They also used similar teaching materials and methods: English language and songs. Lucy also found that the musical training she received at McTyeire and in the church before 1949 was helpful in training the workers for singing competitions.[45] Hong and Cao's memories of this period are undoubtably influenced by their respected positions within the church in China and the relatively comfortable standards of living that they have regained today. We also do not know what the workers who attended their classes actually thought about these two educated women who were sent to their factory. However, their memories of the respect and social cachet they received for their educational background adds nuances to the conventional picture of the suffering experienced by women of their class, educational, and religious background during this period of Chinese history.

The majority of alumnae who I interviewed in China, like many who lived through the chaos of the Cultural Revolution, did not want to dwell on the hardships they experienced during this period. They quickly moved from their schooldays to their relatively successful careers after the end of the Cultural Revolution. Not wanting to reopen potentially painful memories, I respected their choices about which parts of their personal histories they wanted to relate.

However, the Mao era certainly left its mark on alumnae's retrospective on their school experiences. This can be most vividly seen in the splintering of memories between those who remained in Mao's China and those who emigrated. Alumnae who remained in China and were persecuted for their elite, Christian, and foreign educational backgrounds were far more sensitive about the "elite" label that was attached to their schools and generally downplayed the Christian aspects of the school history. Overseas alumnae, some of whom had become devout Christians since moving to the United States, were keen to talk about the religious education they received at school and were proud of the fact that their schools were considered the most elite schools for girls in China. It is also clear that some diasporic alumnae's concern for their compatriots who remained in China during the Mao years was driven by a sense of guilt for having escaped suffering to relatively easy lives abroad. Rosalyn Koo certainly felt a sense of guilt and obligation to her former principal, Xue Zheng, who she sought out on her first trip back to China after the end of the Cultural Revolution. She was saddened by the dilapidated state of her school and its "down-in-the-mouth" former headmistress, and was determined to restore Xue Zheng's and her school's "old glory."[46]

Reinventing Elite Gender Identities

In today's China we can see a re-emergence of older notions of female gentility in what has become, since the 1980s, a highly unequal society. Many wealthy Chinese parents now send their sons and daughters to elite private foreign schools and universities in China or abroad where they can be "finished off," in remarkably similar ways to how the Republican elite understood the advantages of missionary schools for girls. Advanced training in English and fluency in Western cultural norms and habits are again regarded as desirable, giving them a competitive edge over their mainland-educated counterparts. It has also, until quite recently, been a marker of elite social status and a tool for upward social mobility for families. The new middle-class elite compete to distinguish themselves as a cut above in their clothing and lifestyles. Correct performance of being an upper-class Chinese woman is an important part of this.[47]

This is by no means a straightforward performance and has become increasingly fraught in recent years by a new hardening of Sino-Western international relations, an upswing in patriotic education in China, and, most recently, efforts to close the inequality gap by banning private tutoring (including English) outside of school.[48] Being a modern, Western-educated Chinese woman is perhaps now even more complicated than ever before. The experience of foreign-educated Chinese women today resonates with the patriotic and gendered predicaments faced by their early-twentieth-century counterparts. For example, in 2022, Janny Ye, a graduate from London's Royal Academy of Arts, co-curated an exhibition based on her clothing brand "Seventy Five," which was inspired by the Republican-era women's magazine *Linglong*. Referring to a dress in the exhibition, Ye explained how she was inspired by the student aesthetic of the 1930s: "This is inspired by how in the 1930s the girls liked to add something to their clothes or tops, so this is a simple top and I added a big voluminous skirt, to make it into a dress. And the top is referencing a student uniform and the cut of that little mandarin collar."[49] Reading *Linglong*, Ye was surprised by how many of the problems encountered by Chinese women in the early twentieth century still affected Chinese women of her generation, including how to balance marriage and career, the desirability of lifelong singleness, and the possibilities of same-sex female companionship.[50] Much as missionary schoolgirls carefully positioned themselves as interpreters of Western fashions and lifestyles for Chinese audiences, overseas-educated Chinese women are today acting as cultural intermediaries and trendsetters both inside China and abroad. In doing so they also have to perform a similarly fraught balancing act, a situation that can be paradoxical and confusing for them.[51] Returned students today face issues of being labeled patriotically suspect or slavish consumers of all things foreign, which parallel the predicament of missionary schoolgirls in the 1920s. Janny Ye herself identifies as part of the Asian diaspora. Her clothing design is transnationally influenced but retains some references to classical Chinese clothing, including the way she cuts her clothes with no seams at the armhole opening. This creates more rounded shoulders, giving the clothing a softer and gentler aesthetic.[52]

This is not to say that nothing has changed. The Mao era inexorably altered gender relations in China. In the reform era many social, political, economic, and demographic factors have played into the re-emerging problems faced by modern Chinese women, including: changing work opportunities, rural-to-urban migration patterns, and family-planning policies, to name just a few. One thing is certain: How to be an elite woman in modern China is being formulated and negotiated by Chinese women themselves, as it was in the

Republican era. Dismissing bourgeois Chinese gendered identities as "foreign"-inspired or -directed therefore makes as little sense for the Republican period as it does today. In an age of global capitalism, Chinese women continue to negotiate their intersecting gender and class identities in a conscious and reciprocal dialogue with ideas from beyond China's borders.

The lives of missionary school graduates therefore allow us a unique perspective into how Chinese women who have received a "Western" education have formulated their elite identities according to changing domestic politics. Missionary school alumnae's exclusive identities have survived the decades of the Cultural Revolution, and since the 1980s alumnae have been able to reassert and celebrate their prestigious educational background once more. Missionary school alumnae have sought to reframe their school histories, reinstating their versions of the story of missionary schools for girls in China, through their own oral history projects and worldwide reunions. Now part of a diasporic Chinese global elite, McTyeire and St. Mary's alumnae, in particular, have been able to reestablish what they felt were the most important aspects of their school experience—English, Music, and an all-girls environment—through their financial investment in the Number Three Girls' School.[53]

This endeavor of looking back to the Republican past to confer a newly sanctioned elite status in the post-socialist present is a two-sided process. Alumnae are now actively courted by institutions that wish to promote their cosmopolitan history. For example, advertising their connection to McTyeire and St. Mary's now provides welcome and potentially lucrative publicity for the Number Three Girls' School. In a promotional video advertising the Number Three Girls' School posted online in 2016, the school's prestigious history as the successor to St. Mary's and McTyeire is highlighted.[54] The initials SMH (St. Mary's Hall) and MC (McTyeire) were at one time incorporated into the school's official logo.[55] Another promotional video made for a TV singing contest in which the choir of the Number Three Girls' School performed also featured an interview with four generations of alumnae from the classes of 1951, 1967, 1998, and 2018.[56] The impression given to prospective parents is of an uninterrupted inheritance of rather traditional feminine virtues, which the school inculcates in its girls, producing highly desirable young ladies who will do well in a society in which these virtues again constitute important markers of a gendered elite status, and perhaps also in an urban marriage market where the continuing effects of China's family-planning policies have resulted in women marrying up the social hierarchy.[57]

At the Number Three Girls' School, these virtues are summed up in the acronym "NICE girl": Natural (*shuaizhen* 率真), Independent (*duli* 獨立), Caring (*guanai* 關愛), Elegant (*youya* 優雅).[58]

These ideals which elite Chinese women are meant to aspire to today in many ways parallel the ambivalent gendered virtues promoted by missionary schools and their students in the Republican era. As in the Republican period, the school today is seen by prospective parents as academically excellent, but also as a "safe" option, cloistering girls who will not be distracted by male classmates during the all-important college entrance examinations. It is also highly regarded for its dance, music, and drama programs, extracurricular activities on which both St. Mary's and McTyeire built their reputations in the 1930s and 1940s. The official version of Shanghai Number Three Girls' School's history is largely sanitized from what could be politically problematic, un-patriotic, or embarrassing elements of its missionary school past. While capitalizing on its long and prestigious history, it downplays its Christian and foreign roots in all promotional materials.

Nationalization, Nostalgia, and Commercialization

In a political epoch when China is attempting to spread its economic and soft power beyond its borders, missionary schools have themselves been reinterpreted as sites of Sino-foreign exchange and have become a thoroughly nationalized part of the story of China's place in the world. Local governments seek to stress the cosmopolitan history of their cities' educational establishments, at least on a surface level. This is particularly the case for missionary school buildings, some of which partially survived the religious iconoclasm of China's Cultural Revolution and massive urban redevelopment since the 1980s. In 2003 the Ningbo municipal authorities decided to preserve the derelict Riverside Academy building, and in 2013 at the cost of 15 million Chinese yuan re-opened it as the Ningbo City Education Museum (Ningbo shi jiaoyu bowuguan 寧波市教育博物館) with an exhibition dedicated to the history of women's education. The renovation was done according to the original 1922 building plans, which are still extant in the Ningbo City Archives.[59] The introductory plaque that introduces the school's history, although celebrating Riverside's forerunner as the first school for girls in China, makes no mention of its missionary roots.[60] While appropriating the aesthetics of Republican-era Western-style architecture for commercial gain, authorities do not want to draw too much attention to who the original founders of these buildings were, where the money came from, and why they were in China in the first place. Although the museum tells in detail the story of China's national humiliation by foreigners, externally, at least, the government wishes to present a strong and confident cosmopolitan China which takes pride in its cultured Republican past and looks forward to its bright future.

Today, missionary school architecture has become part of a cosmeticized cultural nostalgia as the Republican past is appropriated and repackaged for a post-socialist Chinese present. If we examine the ways in which former missionary schools have been integrated into the surrounding urban redevelopments, it is clear that commercial developers have capitalized on an appreciation for Republican-style heritage architecture aesthetics, appropriating a nostalgia for a romanticized Sino-Western cultural past (in a sanitized form) to market a modern, cultured, and cosmopolitan lifestyle to consumers today. Riverside sits adjacent to the 1844 Arts and Culture Shopping Center in Ningbo (Ningbo 1844 heyi yishu shenghuo zhongxin 寧波 1844 和義藝術生活中心), which uses the date of the school's earliest predecessors' foundation, 1844, as a historical marker to advertise the shopping mall as a center for those wishing to consume a refined and artistic lifestyle.

Republican-era blue and red brick buildings, with features such as arches, porticos, and porches, have been preserved, restored, and imitated in commercial redevelopment projects in the past few decades. In Shanghai's former French concession, many Republican-era mansions have been preserved as part of the city's architectural heritage. Newly built luxury housing and shopping developments that imitate this style can also be found in this part of the city, providing a startling juxtaposition to the glass skyscrapers nearby in Jing'an district.[61] Arif Dirlik has explored how the global architecture in Shanghai is itself a form of "occidentalism—a sort of imagined futurism."[62] When this imagined futurism, in the form of revolving restaurants at the top of glass skyscrapers, is placed alongside nostalgic but nationalized visual references to the Republican past, this occidentalizing effect, essentializing the West, is magnified. But it also underlines a larger politicized national story: such a contrast invites the viewer to marvel at the speed of China's development and modernization in the past 100 years, conveniently erasing the traces of the political and economic disasters of the Mao era. It also reminds the well-heeled inhabitants of the new luxury apartments and shops of the long history of their city's interaction with the West, signaling their global modernity.[63] In an era of transnational capitalism, highlighting links to this history of Sino-foreign interaction has been a very desirable (and thus lucrative) image for commercial, retail, and housing developments in China.[64]

A pertinent example of this can be seen in the redevelopment of St. Mary's in Shanghai. In 2016, a Singaporean-sponsored retail project rebuilt St. Mary's School in mock-Spanish style on its original site, turning it into part of a shopping center.[65] The St. Mary's chapel, the only surviving original building, has been renovated, and although its exterior remains intact (minus the Christian crosses that sat atop the Church), the interior has been stripped away, with all religious elements (pews, altars, and iconography) removed. Indeed, the church, originally designed to be at the heart of the former St. Mary's campus, now forms the hub of this shopping center. Its main purpose seems to be for the aesthetic pleasure and amusement of its patrons, akin to the promotional displays and amusements which are normally found on the ground floors of shopping centers. Its Spanish-style architecture also functions as an effective advertisement backdrop for the Western brands and lifestyles for sale in the shopping center. The idea that missionary schools are spaces for the Chinese upper classes has been reinvented in small visual details of the St. Mary's Church renovation. Floating white cloth hung over wooden frames, providing shelter from the sun on the lawn in front of the church, are reminiscent of enclosed sun loungers at luxury hotels. Such visual references provide the perfect marketing material, effectively promoting Raffles City as a high-end shopping center where the new global elite of Shanghai can consume a luxurious lifestyle.

A 2016 promotional video advertising the shopping center made direct reference to the school's missionary past. In the video advertisement, a high-powered, Chinese female executive gazes down at St. Mary's from the height of her adjacent glass-fronted office building. In her mind's eye, she is transported back to the Republican past as she imagines the life of a missionary school student at St. Mary's. Sepia-tinted Republican past and technicolor post-socialist present slide seamlessly into one another from the gendered gaze of the modern Chinese businesswoman. Infused with a sense of nostalgia, the video invites the viewer to marvel at how far women have come in the past one hundred years and perhaps even depicts girls' schools as the starting point for such changes. It places the Chinese woman on an upward trajectory of progress, liberation, and self-determination, enabled by her education, until she has arrived at her present status with the

The former St. Mary's chapel is now part of the new Raffles City shopping center, located at 1191 Changning Road, Changning District, Shanghai. The chapel, the only original building that remains, is dwarfed by the gleaming dark reflective glass walls of the shopping center, which tower above and protectively encircle it. White cloth hung over wooden frames provide patrons of the shopping complex a shaded place to relax on the artificial lawn in front of the chapel.
Photo by Jennifer Bond, June 2017.

independent capital to buy expensive brands in the shopping center below. Again, while appropriating Western architecture on a purely aesthetic level, potent religious symbols and all traces of the turbulent history of missionary schools in China remain largely absent from such images.

The idea of the missionary school as a place where Chinese women were *dreaming* of their future personal and patriotic roles in Chinese society carries over in the ways in which the history of St. Mary's is narrated at the shopping center today. The engraved glass introduction sign for the dormitory building, Pott Hall, states: "Today this building no longer shelters slumbers, but dreams still live under its roof."[66] The pervasive political rhetoric of the "China Dream" (a political slogan of Xi Jinping which promises a bright future in which every citizen can simultaneously strive for individual and national prosperity) serves as a useful metaphor in many marketing campaigns. In the case of St. Mary's, it also serves as a translation device, helping to make these Republican buildings legible and identifiable to the modern Chinese female consumer, who is pursuing her own patriotic and personal China Dream. This imagery of missionary schools as a place to "dream" has also been taken on board by alumnae and their relatives who have visited their school site since its reopening as a shopping center. After his visit to the school site in 2019, George Wu, whose mother Xu Ren 徐仁 attended St. Mary's from 1936 to 1941, commented in an email to St. Mary's alumnae:

> During [the] 1930's and 1940's, my mother, her three younger sisters, and her youngest aunt (my grandmother's baby sister) all spent their middle school years here in this building. All of them must have [had] an abundance of dreams and plans for their future when they lived here. They might also have [had] a lot of beautiful and sweet memories on this building when they were old.[67]

However, as in the case of Riverside Academy, the commercial redevelopers of St. Mary's have placed more emphasis on utilizing the building's aesthetics than on telling the story of missionary schools for girls in China. Indeed, all reference to the school's foreign origins and the role of missionaries in its foundation have been eliminated from the information signs, which are constructed from engraved glass and are difficult for visitors to the shopping complex to notice or decipher. The new St. Mary's at Raffles City is an example of the nationalization of colonial-era architecture since 1949.[68] On the plaque, the name of the first Chinese principal of St. Mary's, Huang Su'e 黃素娥, is highlighted. Viewers are left with the impression that it was a Chinese woman, rather than foreign missionaries, who founded and funded St. Mary's. Developers and government authorities have thus sought to rebrand missionary schools as patriotic, aesthetically Western, but essentially Chinese institutions, which made a great contribution to Chinese women's education.

While this rather sanitized or retouched version of their schools may be a long way from girls' real lived experience or memories of these experiences, the fact that their schools are being partially preserved elicited mostly positive reactions from alumnae who accompanied me to the sites of their old schools.[69] None of the alumnae who walked around their former school grounds with me made any comment on the commercialized or nationalized uses to which their schools were being put today. Having lived through the

Cultural Revolution, when their schools were again denounced as "tools of foreign imperialism," it would be surprising if alumnae did not find some of these commercial developments by overseas developers rather ironic. Having learned to keep a low profile and not air their real opinions in public, however, their lack of comment on this is understandable. The overriding feeling of most alumnae and their relatives is one of relief and delayed gratification that they can once again take pride in their schools, and that their schools' and their own roles in modern China's educational history are finally being acknowledged. For example, George Wu explained in his email to a descendant of Francis Lister Hawks Pott and Huang Su'e (the first Chinese principal of St. Mary's):

> The inscription acknowledges that your great-grandmother, Madam Su'e Huang Pott, was the founder of St. Mary's, and the building is named after her. I was more than happy to see her name in public view here. There may be in some places (like museums and libraries) in China that carry your great-grandfather's name, but this maybe the only place where your great-grandmother's name is in public display. The English name for the building is called Pott Hall. However, I like its Chinese name better, which can be literally translated into "The Hall for Remembering Pott." The word "remembering" in Chinese inspires reverence, respect, dedication, and reminiscence on the viewers. Your great-grandmother is remembered in this ever crowded and jostling business center in Shanghai today.[70]

The story of missionary schools for girls in modern China has therefore, in some senses, come full circle. From humble beginnings, they grew to become some of the most prestigious educational institutions for women in China. They also unintentionally gave the generations of Chinese women who passed through their doors (from wooden posted gates, to grey-brick archways, to the revolving glass of shopping centers) a space to "dream" new roles for themselves in China's future. As the power of foreigners and foreign institutions in Chinese society was eroded by the rise of Chinese nationalism, the schools gradually became more "Chinese" over time, until it was a generation of Christian-educated Chinese teachers and students who directed the culture of the schools. Women at missionary schools combined the most salient aspects of their educational experiences to envision a new modernity for Chinese Christian women from their own understanding of how Christianity could best serve Chinese society. These Christian-inflected gendered identities which girls created became part of an elite identity for Chinese women in Republican-era East China. Today, alumnae celebrate their alma maters' history with pride and seek to transmit their schools' unique identities, traditions, and rites of passage to younger classes as new elite identities for women are reinvented in modern China.

APPENDIX

List of Interviewees

Chinese Name	English Name/Pinyin	Left School[1]	Interview Date	Location	Notes
進德女中	**Jinde Girls' School**				
曹聖潔	Cao Shengjie	1949	October 22, 2016	Shanghai	Group Interview with Lucy Hong
			December 12, 2016	Shanghai	
			July 3, 2017	Shanghai	
景海女校	**Laura Haygood**				
戴麗貞	Dai Lizhen (Mary Jean)	1937	April 12, 2019	Shanghai	
弘道女中	**Hangzhou Union**				
范海蘭	Fan Hailan	1937	April 27, 2016	Shanghai	
方蓮蒂	Fang Liandi	1951	November 30, 2016	Hangzhou	Telephone interview
金國英	Jin Guoying	1948	November 30, 2016	Hangzhou	
陸月清	Lu Yueqing	1949	November 30, 2015	Hangzhou	
許老師	Xu Lucy	1952	December 6, 2015	Hangzhou	Requested to be anonymous, pseudonym used
聖瑪利亞女校	**St. Mary's**				
陳潘瑛	Chen Panying (Diana)	1949	November 10, 2016	San Mateo	
程錦倩	Cheng Jinqian	1944	July 21, 2016	Beijing	
刁蓓華	Diao Beihua	1952	October 15, 2016	Beijing	
董蔚君	Dong Weijun	1948	November 23, 2016	Beijing	
董悅	Dong Yue	1951	November 21, 2016	Beijing	
顧美誠	Gu Meicheng (Catherine)	1948	May 11, 2016	Beijing	St. Mary's group interview
			May 12, 2016	Beijing	
郭誠錫	Guo Chengxi	1939	May 11, 2016	Beijing	
郭琳	Guo Lin	1951	November 28, 2016	Shanghai	
梁郇德	Liang Xunde	1950	March 1, 2016	San Francisco	

Chinese Name	English Name/Pinyin	Left School[1]	Interview Date	Location	Notes
李葵	Li Kui (Gwendolin Lee)	1952	October 17, 2015	Shanghai	
邵莉楣	Shao Limei	1950	November 24, 2016	Beijing	
沈郇望	Shen Xunwang (Harriet Sun)	1948	November 11, 2016	San Mateo	
吳其慧	Wu Qihui	1947	May 11, 2016	Beijing	St. Mary's group interview
			June 15, 2016	Beijing	
徐乃玎	Xu Naiding	1952	December 7, 2016	Shanghai	
徐乃珩	Xu Naiheng	1954	November 22, 2016	Beijing	
徐仁	Xu Ren	1941	November 18, 2016	Shanghai	
徐信	Xu Xin	1950	December 15, 2016	Shanghai	
楊小異	Yang Xiaoyi	1952	March 14, 2016	Shanghai	
楊之會	Yang Zhihui (Beatrice)	1946	February 28, 2016	San Mateo	
楊之嶺	Yang Zhiling	1951	July 20, 2016	Beijing	
姚惠娟	Yao Huijuan	1948	October 15, 2016	Beijing	
葉美娜	Ye Meina (Mina Yeh)	1951	April 10, 2016	Nanjing	
應曼蓉	Ying Manrong	1945	October 15, 2016	Beijing	
			November 25, 2016	Beijing	
俞慧耕	Yu Huigeng	Teacher 1949 - 1953 (Graduate of Mary Farnham School, 清心女校)	May 11, 2016	Beijing	St. Mary's group interview
			June 16, 2016	Beijing	
張瑞雲	Zhang Ruiyun	1952	May 10, 2016	Beijing	
張如蘭	Zhang Rulan (Lannie)	1953	April 18, 2016	Shanghai	Group interview with Lucy Hong
張祥保	Zhang Xiangbao	1938	July 22, 2016	Beijing	
趙風風	Zhao Fengfeng (Florence)	1948	May 11, 2016	Beijing	St. Mary's group interview
			June 14, 2016	Beijing	
朱文佼	Zhu Wenjiao	1952	June 17, 2016	Beijing	
朱文倩	Zhu Wenqian (Lydia)	1953	May 11, 2016	Beijing	St. Mary's group interview
朱雅蘭	Zhu Yalan	1948	November 12, 2016	San Mateo	Group interview with Zhang Luoluo and Zhang Weiliang
朱亞新	Zhu Yaxin	1950	December 6, 2016	Shanghai	
朱燁	Zhu Ye (Emily)	1956	November 23, 2016	Beijing	

APPENDIX 213

Chinese Name	English Name/Pinyin	Left School[1]	Interview Date	Location	Notes
中西女中	**McTyeire**				
曹寶貞	Cao Baozhen (Ellen)	1939	November 25, 2016	Beijing	
			November 26, 2016	Beijing	
曹珍家	Cao Zhenjia (Anna)	1947	November 8, 2017	St. Louis Obispo	Telephone interview
陳晉明	Chen Jinming (Rosalyn Koo)	1947	November 5, 2016	San Mateo	
			November 6, 2016	San Mateo	
			November 7, 2016	San Mateo	
			November 8, 2016	San Mateo	
			November 9, 2016	San Mateo	
			November 10, 2016	San Mateo	
			November 12, 2016	San Mateo	
			November 13, 2016	San Mateo	
			November 5, 2017	San Mateo	
			November 6, 2018	San Mateo	
陳桂珩	Chen Guiheng (Pearl)	1949	November 7, 2017	San Mateo	Group interview with Zhang Luoluo
陳老師	Chen Sally	1945	November 7, 2017	California	Requested to be anonymous, pseudonym used
陳添彌	Chen Tianmi	1952	May 17, 2016	Beijing	
陳宗慈	Chen Zongci (Theresa)	1948	November 10, 2016	San Mateo	
丁毓明	Ding Yuming	1941	November 9, 2016	Palo Alto	
龔正冠	Gong Zhengguan	1952	May 9, 2016	Beijing	
洪侶明	Hong Lüming (Lucy)	1946	October 17, 2015	Shanghai	
			December 3, 2015	Shanghai	
			December 7, 2015	Shanghai	
			March 20, 2016	Shanghai	
			March 27, 2016	Shanghai	
			April 1, 2016	Shanghai	
			April 18, 2016	Shanghai	Group interview with Lannie Zhang
			October 22, 2016	Shanghai	Group interview with Cao Shengjie
			July 3, 2017	Shanghai	
賈韻儀	Jia Yunyi	1951	December 9, 2014	Shanghai	

APPENDIX

Chinese Name	English Name/Pinyin	Left School[1]	Interview Date	Location	Notes
淩又融	Ling Yourong (Meimi)	1949	November 7, 2016	San Mateo	
劉澤墀	Liu Zechi	1947	November 24, 2016	Beijing	
宋寶蓮	Song Baolian (Paulina Soong)	1947	November 4, 2017	San Mateo	
陶霞芳	Tao Xiafang	1956	March 9, 2016 August 2, 2018	Shanghai Shanghai	
王義芳	Wang Yifang	1947	November 10, 2016	San Mateo	
巫漪雲	Wu Yiyun	1951	December 5, 2016	Shanghai	
席與時	Xi Yushi (Edith)	1947	November 9, 2016	Palo Alto	
肖嘉珣	Xiao Jiaxun	1952	March 17, 2016	Shanghai	Group interview with Xu Meizhen
			April 15, 2016	Shanghai	Group interview with Xu Meizhen
徐美貞	Xu Meizhen	1946	March 17, 2016	Shanghai	Group interview with Xiao Jiaxun
			April 15, 2016	Shanghai	Group interview with Xiao Jiaxun
薛徽音	XueHuiyin (Georgiana)	1945	November 9, 2016	Palo Alto	
楊燠華	Yang Yuhua	1956	April 8, 2016	Shanghai	
張瓏	Zhang Long	1947	July 6, 2016	Shanghai	
張羅羅	Zhang Luoluo	1947	November 8, 2016	San Mateo	
			November 12, 2016	San Mateo	Group interview with Zhu Yalan and Jiang Weiliang
			November 6, 2017	San Mateo	
			November 7, 2017	San Mateo	Group interview with Pearl Chen
張蔭生	Zhang Yinsheng	1952	March 22, 2016	Shanghai	
朱麗中	Zhu Lizhong	1950	November 11, 2016	Los Altos	
鄒思敏	Zou Simin	1947	November 4, 2017	San Mateo	
朱素非	Zhu Sufei (Sophie)	1941	November 7, 2016	San Francisco	
朱永琳	Zhu Yonglin	1951	December 13, 2016	Shanghai	

Chinese Name	English Name/Pinyin	Left School[1]	Interview Date	Location	Notes
甬江女中	**Riverside**				
範愛侍	Fan Aishi	Remembering Margaret Fan, 範博理, 1925	November 27, 2015	Ningbo	Brother of Margaret Fan
			December 2, 2016	Ningbo	
			December 19, 2016	Ningbo	
範美玲	Fan Meiling	1960	November 28, 2015	Ningbo	Group interview with Xu Zhenzhu
葛萄娥	Ge Tao'e	1954	October 16, 2015	Ningbo	
			December 1, 2016	Ningbo	
何愛盈	He Aiying	1958	November 26, 2015	Ningbo	
賀莉清	He Liqing	1954	December 2, 2015	Shanghai	
王家瑜	Wang Jiayu	Remembering Wang Yunqin, 王韻琴, 1926	December 1, 2015	Hangzhou	Nephew of Wang Yunqin
徐珍珠	Xu Zhenzhu	1950	November 28, 2015	Ningbo	Group interview with Fan Meiling
姚惠娟	Yao Huijuan	1951	December 1, 2016	Ningbo	
聖約翰中學	**St. John's Middle School**				
蔣維良	Jiang Weiliang	1947	November 12, 2016	San Mateo	Group Interview with Zhang Luoluo and Yalan Zhu
陶樹玉	Tao Shuyu	1953	August 2, 2018	Shanghai	
Other					
	Janny Ye	N/A	August 20, 2022	London	

1. Some alumnae left school before they were due to graduate. This is the date at which students left the school or graduated.

Notes

Abbreviations

ABHS   American Baptist Historical Society
CMS   Church Missionary Society
HCA   Hangzhou City Archives
MAHC   Methodist Archives and History Center
MMS   Methodist Missionary Society
NCA   Ningbo City Archives
PHS   Presbyterian Historical Society
SMA   Shanghai Municipal Archives
SOAS   School of Oriental and African Studies
YDS   Yale Divinity School
ZPL   Zhejiang Provincial Library

Introduction

1. In 1952 McTyeire was merged with American Episcopal St. Mary's Hall (founded 1881) to form the Shanghai Number Three Girls' School.
2. Interview with Rosalyn Koo, November 5, 2016, San Mateo.
3. Interview with Rosalyn Koo, November 5, 2016, San Mateo.
4. Interview with Rosalyn Koo, November 5, 2016, San Mateo.
5. *Qipao* was a one-piece woman's dress which became popular in China during the 1920s.
6. Ida Kahn, *An Amazon in Cathay* (Boston: Women's Foreign Missionary Society, 1912). For more on Ida Kahn, see Hu Ying, "Naming the First New Woman," *Nan Nü: Men, Women, and Gender in Early and Imperial China* 3, no. 2 (January 2001): 196–231; Connie Shemo, "How Better to Serve Her Country? Cultural Translators, US Women's History and Kang Cheng's 'An Amazon in Cathay,'" *Journal of Women's History* 21, no. 4 (Winter 2009): 111–133; Zeng Baosun, *Zeng Baosun huiyilu* Hong Kong: Christian Literature Council, 1970). Thomas Kennedy has also translated Zeng's memoir into English: Zeng Baosun, *Confucian Feminist: Memoirs of Zeng Baosun, 1893–1978*, trans. Thomas L. Kennedy (Philadelphia: American Philosophical Society, 2002); Christiana Tsai, *Queen of the Dark Chamber: The Story of Christiana Tsai as Told to Ellen L. Drummond* (Chicago: Moody Press, 1953), Buwei Yang Chao, *Autobiography of a Chinese Woman* (New York: John Day Company, 1947).

7. Pui-Lan, Kwok, "Chinese Women and Protestant Christianity at the Turn of the Century," in *Christianity in China: From the Eighteenth Century to the Present*, ed. Daniel H. Bays (Stanford: Stanford University Press, 1996), 12.
8. Wang Zheng, *Women in the Chinese Enlightenment: Oral and Textual Histories* (Berkeley: University of California Press, 1999), 145–187 and 259–287.
9. Xiang Jingyu, "Zhongguo zuijin funü yundong," in *Zhongguo funü yundong wenxian ziliao huibian: Vol. 1: 1918-1949*, ed. Zhongguo funü guanli ganbu xueyuan (Beijing: Zhongguo funü chubanshe, 1988), 92–100.
10. Paul A. Cohen, *Discovering History in China: American Historical Writing on the Recent Chinese Past* (New York: Columbia University Press, 1984), 9–57.
11. Robert Culp, *Articulating Citizenship: Civic Education and Student Politics in South-Eastern China, 1912–1940* (Cambridge, MA: Harvard University Press, 2007).
12. See Ryan Dunch, *Fuzhou Protestants and the Making of Modern China, 1857-1927* (New Haven, CT: Yale University Press, 2001); Lian Xi, *Redeemed by Fire: The Rise of Popular Christianity in Modern China* (New Haven, CT: Yale University Press, 2010); Daryl L. Ireland, *John Song: Modern Chinese Christianity and the Making of a New Man* (Waco, TX: Baylor University Press, 2020).
13. Connie Shemo, *The Chinese Medical Ministries of Kang Cheng and Shi Meiyu, 1872-1937: On a Cross-Cultural Frontier of Gender, Race, and Nation* (Bethlehem, PA: Lehigh University Press, 2011).
14. See M. Cristina Zaccarini, "Chinese Nationalism and Chinese Womanhood in Early Twentieth-Century China: The Story of Mary Gao (Gao Meiyu)," in *Pioneer Chinese Christian Women: Gender, Christianity, and Social Mobility*, ed. Jessie G. Lutz (Bethlehem, PA: Lehigh University Press, 2010), 351–370; Dong Wang, "The Advance to Higher Learning: Power, Modernization, and the Beginnings of Women's Education at Canton Christian College," in *Pioneer Chinese Christian Women*, ed. Jessie G. Lutz, 371–386; Jennifer Bond, "'The One for the Many': Zeng Baosun, Louise Hester Barnes and the Yifang School for Girls at Changsha, 1893–1918," *Studies in Church History* 55 (2019): 441–462; Xia Shi, *At Home in the World: Women and Charity in Late Qing and Early Republican China* (New York: Columbia University Press, 2018); Aihua Zhang, *The Beijing Young Women's Christian Association, 1927–1937: Materializing a Gendered Modernity* (Lanham, MD: Lexington, 2021).
15. Dunch, *Fuzhou Protestants*, 178–201.
16. For more on how Chinese women's homemaking role became professionalized during the Republican era, see Helen Schneider, *Keeping the Nation's House: Domestic Management and the Making of Modern China* (Toronto: UBC Press, 2011).
17. Wai Ching Angela Wong and Patricia P. K. Chu (eds.), *Christian Women in Chinese Society: The Anglican Story* (Hong Kong: Hong Kong University Press, 2018). Kwok Pui-Lan, *Chinese Women and Christianity, 1860–1927* (Atlanta: Scholars Press, 1992).
18. Hyaeweol Choi, *Gender Politics at Home and Abroad: Protestant Modernity in Colonial-Era Korea* (Cambridge: Cambridge University Press, 2020).
19. Choi, *Gender Politics at Home and Abroad*, 15.
20. Chen Nan-hua (Chen Hengzhe), *Autobiography of a Young Chinese Girl* (Beijing, 1935), 187.

21. See, for example, Leo Ou-fan Lee, *Shanghai Modern: The Flowering of a New Urban Culture in China, 1930–1945* (Cambridge, MA: Harvard University Press, 1999).
22. Hanchao Lu, *Beyond the Neon Lights, Everyday Shanghai in the Early Twentieth Century* (Berkeley: University of California Press: 1999), 121; and Isabella Jackson, *Shaping Modern Shanghai: Colonialism in China's Global City* (Cambridge: Cambridge University Press, 2017), 33–34.
23. For more on the many native place networks which constituted modern Shanghai see Bryna Goodman, *Nation Place, City, and Nation: Regional Networks and Identities in Shanghai, 1853–1937* (Berkeley: University of California Press, 1995).
24. Nara Dillon and Jean C. Oi (eds.), *At the Crossroads of Empires: Middlemen, Social Networks and State-Building in Republican Shanghai* (Stanford: Stanford University Press, 2008).
25. Jeffrey N. Wasserstrom, "Cosmopolitan Connections and Transnational Networks," in *At the Crossroads of Empires: Middlemen, Social Networks and State-Building in Republican Shanghai*, ed. Nara Dillon and Jean C. Oi (Stanford: Stanford University Press, 2008), 215–216.
26. For example, in 1915 eighty-two students left McTyeire in protest at the expulsion of two students who had criticized Principal Helen Richardson for slapping the hand of a classmate for talking during the study hour. See "Telling Women's Lives: In Search of McTyeire, 1892–1992," ed. McTyeire Alumnae Association (unpublished oral history collection, 1992).
27. Ryan Dunch, "Beyond Cultural Imperialism: Cultural Theory, Christian Missions and Global Modernity," *History and Theory* 41, no. 3 (October, 2002), 301–325; Henrietta Harrison, *The Missionary's Curse and Other Tales from a Chinese Catholic Village* (Berkeley: University of California Press, 2013).
28. Dunch, "Beyond Cultural Imperialism," 325.
29. Xia Shi, *At Home in the World: Women and Charity in Late Qing and Early Republican China* (Columbia: Columbia University Press, 2018), 12.
30. Jennifer Bond, "'The One for the Many': Zeng Baosun, Louise Hester Barnes and the Yifang School for Girls at Changsha, 1893–1918," *Studies in Church History* 55 (2019): 441–462.
31. Jesse Gregory Lutz, *China and the Christian Colleges, 1850–1950* (Ithaca: Cornell University Press, 1971); Daniel H. Bays and Ellen Widmer (eds.), *China's Christian Colleges: Cross-Cultural Connections* (Stanford: Stanford University Press, 2009); Stephen Uhalley and Xiaoxin Wu (eds.), *China and Christianity: Burdened Past Hopeful Future* (Armonk, NY: M. E. Sharpe, 2001). Few studies of missionary middle schools for girls exist. These include: Heidi A. Ross, "'Cradle for Female Talent': The McTyeire Home and School for Girls: 1892–1937," in *Christianity in China from the Eighteenth Century to the Present*, ed. Daniel D. Bays (Stanford: Stanford University Press, 1996), 209–227; Judith Liu and Donald Kelly, "An Oasis in a Heathen Land': St. Hilda's School for Girls Wuchang, 1928–1936," in *Christianity in China from the Eighteenth Century to the Present*, ed. Daniel D. Bays (Stanford: Stanford University Press, 1996), 228–242; Judith Liu, *Foreign Exchange: Counterculture Behind the Walls of S. Hilda's School for Girls, 1929–1937* (Bethlehem, PA: Lehigh

University Press, 2011). A recent history of the Shanghai Number Three Girls' School also provides many details of the changes to St. Mary's and McTyeire from their foundation: Liu Xiaoyan, *The Changing Face of Women's Education in China: A Critical History of St. Mary's Hall, McTyeire School and Shanghai No. 3. Girls' Middle School* (Zürich: Lit Verlag, 2017).

32. An exception to the trend toward co-education was Ginling College in Nanjing, which staunchly defended its autonomy from the overtures of male missionary educators at Ginling University who wanted to merge the colleges. Jin Feng, *The Making of a Family Saga: Ginling College* (Albany, NY: SUNY Press, 2009), 142–152.

33. Earl Herbert Cressy and C. C. Chih, *Middle School Standards, Second Study*, East China Studies in Education 5 (Shanghai: East China Christian Educational Association, 1929), 8.

34. For more on the making of the Chinese Bourgeoisie during China's rapid industrialization to meet growing demand from Europe during the First World War see Marie-Claire Bergere, *The Golden Age of the Chinese Bourgeoisie, 1911–1937* (Cambridge: Cambridge University Press, 1986).

35. These include: Riverside Academy's *Riverside Echo* (*Yongjiang sheng* 甬江聲), Hangzhou Union Girls' School's *Hongdao* 弘道, St. Mary's *The Phoenix* (*Fengzao*, 鳳藻), McTyeire's *The McTyeirean* (*Moti* 墨梯), and Laura Haygood's *Laura Haygood Star* (*Jinghai xing* 景海星).

36. "Forward," *The McTyeirean* (1917), 1. As Siao-chen Hu has shown, the editors of women's magazines in this period conceived of these publications as a pedagogical space where female students and educators could hone their literary talents and exchange opinions, forming a network of educated women. Siao-chen Hu, "Voices of Female Educators in Early Twentieth Century Women's Magazines," in *Women and the Periodical Press in China's Long Twentieth Century: A Space of Their Own?* ed. Michel Hockx, Joan Judge, and Barbara Mittler (Cambridge: Cambridge University Press: 2018), 180.

37. Catherine Sloan, '"Periodicals of an Objectionable Character': Peers and Periodicals and Croydon Friend's School, 1826–1875," *Victorian Periodicals Review* 50, no. 4 (Winter, 2017): 769–786.

38. Renee Kwang Ming Nieh, in "Telling Women's Lives: In Search of McTyeire, 1892–1992," ed. McTyeire Alumnae Association (unpublished oral history collection, 1992).

39. Weili Ye, *Seeking Modernity in China's name: Chinese Students in the United States, 1900–1927* (Stanford: Stanford University Press, 2002), 139.

40. Interview with Chen Tianmi, May 17, 2016, Beijing.

41. Aaron William Moore, "Growing Up in Nationalist China: Self-Representation in the Personal Documents of Children and Youth 1927–1949," *Modern China* 42, no. 1 (January 2016): 78.

42. Interview with Rosalyn Koo, November 5, 2016, San Mateo.

43. "Telling Women's Lives."

44. For McTyeire these three volumes of the school history include: Chen Jinyu (ed.), *Zhongxi nüzhong, 1892–1952* (Shanghai: Tongji daxue chubanshe, 2016); Zhang Long (ed.), *Huiyi Zhongxi nüzhong, 1900–1948* (Shanghai: Tongji daxue chubanshe, 2016);

Chen Jinyu and McTyeire School History Group (eds.), *Huiyi Zhongxi nüzhong, 1949–1952* (Shanghai: Tongji daxue chubanshe, 2016). For St. Mary's there are also three volumes of the school history: Xu Yongchu and Chen Jinyu (eds.), *Shengmaliya nüxiao, 1881–1952* (Shanghai: Tongji daxue chubanshe, 2014); Xu Yongchu and Chen Jinyu (eds.), *Zhuiyi Shengmaliya nüxiao* (Shanghai: Tongji daxue chubanshe, 2014); and Xu Yongchu and Chen Jingu (eds.), *Zhuixun Shengmaliya xiaoyou zuji* (Shanghai: Tongji daxue chubanshe, 2014).

45. Gail Hershatter, *The Gender of Memory: Rural Women and China's Collective Past* (Berkeley: University of California Press, 2011), 20.
46. Interview with Rosalyn Koo, November 5, 2016, San Mateo.
47. Interview with Zhang Luoluo, November 8, 2016, San Mateo.
48. Antoinette Burton, *Burdens of History: British Feminists, Indian Women and Imperial Culture* (Chapel Hill: University of North Carolina Press, 1994), 212.
49. Hershatter, *The Gender of Memory*, 23.

Chapter 1

1. PHS RG8-23-2, Esther M. Gauss to Dr. Scott, August 18, 1922.
2. NCA 旧 10-1-310. For more on Republican-era missionary school architecture, see Jeffrey W. Cody, "American Geometrics and the Architecture of Christian Campuses in China," in *China's Christian Colleges: Cross-Cultural Connections 1900–1950*, ed. Daniel H. Bays and Ellen Widmer (Stanford: Stanford University Press, 2009), 27–56.
3. PHS RG82-23-2, Esther M. Gauss to Dr. Scott, August 18, 1922.
4. Aldersey was an independent missionary to China. See E. Aldersey White, *A Woman Pioneer in China: The Life of Mary Ann Aldersey* (London: Livingston Press, 1932).
5. PHS RG82-23-2, Esther M. Gauss to Dr. Scott, August 18, 1922.
6. PHS RG82-23-2, Esther M. Gauss to Dr. Scott, August 18, 1922.
7. SOAS MMS -1326, Women's Work Ningbo—1946–1950, Doris Coombs to Hilda, March 31, 1949.
8. PHS RG82, Esther M. Gauss, Personal Report, 1937–1938.
9. PHS RG82-23-2, Esther M. Gauss to Dr. Scott, August 18, 1922.
10. PHS MS-Sm65ln, Mable C. Smith, Circular letter, February 23, 1950.
11. Kenneth Scott Latourette, *A History of Christian Missions in China* (London: The Macmillan Company, 1929), 479.
12. CMS CCH 056/1, Laurence to Mr. Wright, May 17, 1878.
13. CMS CCH 056/1, Laurence to Mr. Wright, May 17, 1878.
14. At this conference, the Educational Association of China was established by a group of missionary educators to co-ordinate the production of textbooks for mission schools and a triennial meeting of the association was established. See: M. T. Yates (ed.), *Records of the General Conference of the Protestant Missionaries of China, Held at Shanghai, May 10–14, 1877* (Shanghai: American Presbyterian Mission Press, 1878); W. J. Lewis, W. T. A. Barber, and J. R. Hykes (eds.), *Records of the General Conference of the Protestant Missionaries of China Held at Shanghai, May 7–20,*

1890 (Shanghai: American Presbyterian Mission Press, 1890); Chinese Educational Commission (ed.), *Christian Education in China: A Study Made by an Educational Commission Representing the Mission Boards and Societies Conducting Work in China* (New York: Committee of Reference and Counsel of the Foreign Missions Conference of North America, 1922), 317.

15. Dana L. Roberts (ed.), *Gospel Bearers, Gender Barriers: Missionary Women in the Twentieth Century* (New York: Orbis Books, 2002), 5.
16. Latourette, *A History of Christian Missions in China*, 408.
17. Irwin Hyatt, *Our Ordered Lives Confess: Three Nineteenth Century American Missionaries in Eastern Shantung* (Cambridge, MA: Harvard University Press, 1976), 70.
18. Hyatt, *Our Ordered Lives Confess*, 92.
19. CMS CCH O 56/12, Annual letter from Laurence to Mr. Fenn, December 21, 1875.
20. CMS CCH O 56/12, Annual letter from Laurence to Mr. Fenn, December 21, 1875.
21. M. Laurence, "Female Boarding Schools," in *Records of the General Conference of the Protestant Missionaries of China Held at Shanghai, May 10–17, 1877*, ed. M. T. Yates (Shanghai: American Presbyterian Mission Press, 1878); 469.
22. Chinese Educational Commission (ed.), *Christian Education in China*, 256.
23. Margaret Burton, *The Education of Women in China* (New York: Fleming H. Revell, 1911), 35.
24. Aldersey, *A Woman Pioneer in China*, 38.
25. Susan Mann, "The Education of Daughters in the Mid-Ch'ing Period," in *Education and Society in Late Imperial China, 1600–1900*, ed. Alexander Woodside and Benjamin A. Elman (Berkeley: University of California Press, 1994), 19–49; Dorothy Ko, "Pursuing Talent and Virtue: Education and Women's Culture in Seventeenth and Eighteenth Century China," *Late Imperial China* 13, no. 1 (June 1992): 9–39; Ellen Widmer (ed.), *Writing Women in Late Imperial China* (Stanford: Stanford University Press, 1997).
26. CMS G1 CH/O 1883/164, Laurence to Mr. Fenn, May 30, 1883; CMS G1 CH2/O 1886/39, Laurence to Mr. Fenn, February 9, 1886.
27. Liang Qichao, cited by Paul John Bailey in *Gender and Education in China: Gender Discourses and Women's Schooling in the Early Twentieth Century* (New York: Routledge, 2007), 21.
28. Douglas Reynolds, *China 1898–1912: The Xinzheng Revolution and Japan* (Cambridge, MA: Harvard University Press, 1993).
29. Bailey, *Gender and Education*, 32.
30. Joan Judge, *The Precious Raft of History: The Past, The West and The Woman Question in China* (Stanford: Stanford University Press), 113.
31. Judge, *The Precious Raft of History*, 114.
32. *Nü xuebao*, originally entitled *Nü bao*, was published in Shanghai from 1899. See Nanxiu Qian, "The Mother Nü xuebao Versus the Daughter Nü xuebao: Generational Differences between 1898 and 1902 Women Reformers," in *Different Worlds of Discourse: Transformations of Gender and Genre in Late Qing and Early Republican*

China, ed. Nanxiu Qian, Grace S. Fong, and Richard J. Smith (Oxford: Oxford University Press, 2016), 257.
33. Baily, *Gender and Education*, 25.
34. Baily, *Gender and Education*, 26.
35. "Xiao Shi" [School history], in *Shanghai shili Wuben nüzi zhongxue gaikuang* (Shanghai, 1934), 1.
36. Joan Judge, *Republican Lens: Gender, Visuality and Experience in the Early Chinese Periodical Press* (Oakland: University of California Press, 2015), 151.
37. Huixing nüzi zhongxue, "Ben xiao zhi lüe shi," in *Zhejiang Hangzhou shi sili Huixing nüzi chuji zhongxue yilan* (Hangzhou, 1937), 1.
38. "Appendix I: Table 1: Christian Elementary and Secondary Schools," in *Christian Education in China: The Report of the Educational Commission of 1921–1922*, ed. Chinese Educational Commission (Shanghai: Commercial Press, 1922), 317.
39. Dana Lee Robert, *American Women in Mission: A Social History of Their Thought and Practice* (Atlanta: Mercer University Press, 1996), 5.
40. "The Anglo-Chinese School for Girls," *The North China Daily News*, March 18, 1892, 247.
41. CMS/G1/CH2/O/1909/177, Louise Barnes to Mr. Baring-Gould, August 23, 1909.
42. CMS/G1/CH2/O/1909/175, Louise Barnes to Mr. Baring-Gould, August 19, 1909.
43. Interview with Zhang Long, July 6, 2016, Yan'an Hotel, Shanghai.
44. Wang Zheng, *Women in the Chinese Enlightenment*; Susan Glosser, *Chinese Visions of Family and State, 1915–1953* (Berkeley: University of California Press, 2003).
45. Xu Yongchu and Chen Jinyu (eds.), *Shengmaliya nüxiao, 1881–1952* (Shanghai: Tongji daxue chubanshe, 2014), 56.
46. Mae Yih in "Telling Women's Lives."
47. Chindon Yiu Tang, "Women's Education in China," in *Bulletins on Chinese Education Issued by the Chinese National Association for the Advancement of Education*, Vol. 2, Bulletin 9 (Shanghai: Commercial Press, 1923), 4.
48. Tang, "Women's Education in China," 5.
49. Co-education at the lower primary level was sanctioned by the government as early as 1907, and the majority of missionary schools were co-educational at the primary level. Tang, "Women's Education in China," 23.
50. Jin Feng, *The Making of a Family Saga: Ginling College* (New York: SUNY Press, 2009), 142–152.
51. Interview with Lucy Hong, December 7, 2015, Shanghai.
52. CMS G1/CH2/O/1908/198, Louise Barnes to Mr. Baring-Gould, November, 30, 1908.
53. CMS G1 AL 1917-34 WJ- 2, Wolfe to CMS Secretary, November 22, 1918. For more on Annie Wolfe, see Frances Slater, "The Wolfe Sisters of Foochow, China: Born to Evangelize," published by Frances Slater and John Fitzgerald (2016).
54. John Cleverly, *The Schooling of China* (Sydney: George Allen & Unwin, 1985), 21.
55. Earl Herbert Cressy, "Christian Middle Schools Fourth Annual Statistics, 1935–1936," *China Christian Educational Association, Bulletin no. 39* (Shanghai: China Christian Educational Association, 1936), 7.

56. The new Riverside Academy building was completed in 1923. St. Mary's also moved to a new site on Brenan Road in Shanghai in 1923, Caroline A. Fullerton, "St. Mary's Hall," in *St. Mary's Hall Shanghai 50th Anniversary volume, 1881–1931* (Shanghai, 1931), 2–6; McTyeire moved to a new site in 1916, constructing a new dormitory and gymnasium in 1922 and 1929, respectively, YDS A236.08, Jean Craig, "A Brief History of McTyeire School for Girls, Shanghai, China" (1982), 16; Hangzhou Union Girls' School also moved to a larger campus on Xueshi road in 1915 and constructed a new gymnasium and dormitory in 1922–23. HCA 旧 36-1-12, "Ben xiao shi lüe," *Hongdao ershi zhou jinian kan* (1932), 101–102.

57. Milton T. Stauffer (ed.), *The Christian Occupation of China: A General Survey of the Numerical Strength and Geographical Distribution of the Christian Forces in China, Made by the Special Committee on Survey and Occupation, China Continuation Committee, 1918–1921* (Shanghai: China Continuation Committee, 1922), iii and xx.

58. Xiaoping Cong, *Teachers' Schools and the Making of Modern China* (Vancouver: UBC Press 2007), 91.

59. HCA 旧 36-1-12. "Biyesheng zhuangkuang tongji," *Hongdao ershi zhou jinian kan* (1932), 509.

60. Missionary schools tended to include informal teacher training in their middle schools through the Sunday School work with poor children in the local vicinity that pupils carried out. Missionary school pupils would thus learn how to teach by being "thrown in." An exception to this trend was the Laura Haygood Normal School run by the American Methodist Mission in Suzhou, which had a dedicated primary and kindergarten teacher training program. Stauffer (ed.), *The Christian Occupation of China*, 411.

61. Stauffer, *The Christian Occupation of China*, 411.

62. Stauffer, *The Christian Occupation of China*, 303, 305, 402.

63. Tang, "Women's Education in China," 16.

64. In 1909 Zeng Baosun, the great granddaughter of Zeng Guofan transferred to the CMS Mary Vaughan middle school in Hangzhou to prepare herself academically for higher education overseas. Kennedy, *Confucian Feminist*, 30.

65. Cong, *Teachers' Schools*, 93.

66. Chen Nan-hua (Chen Hengzhe), *Autobiography of a Young Chinese Girl* (Beijing, 1935), 187.

67. Peter Zarrow, *Educating China, Knowledge, Society and Textbooks in a Modernizing World, 1902–1937* (Cambridge: Cambridge University Press, 2015), 25; and Kumiko Fujimura-Fanselow, "Women's Participation in Higher Education in Japan," *Comparative Education Review* 29, no. 4 (November 1985): 473.

68. PHS RG82-32-10, F. R. Millican, "Data and Reflections on the Situation in Chekiang Provinces re the Future of Mission Schools," July 27, 1927.

69. PHS RG82-32-10, Esther Gauss to Mission Board, January 21, 1927.

70. Liu Xiaoyan, *The Changing Face of Women's Education in China: A Critical History of St. Mary's Hall, McTyeire School and Shanghai No. 3. Girls' Middle School* (Zürich: Lit Verlag, 2017), 66.

71. St. Mary's group interview, May 11, 2016, Beijing.

72. Xu and Chen, *Shengmaliya nüxiao*, 56.
73. NCA 旧 10-1-307, Principal's Report, April 16, 1932.
74. ABHS 262-3-8, Florence Webster to McVeigh and friends of the Board, January 29, 1926.
75. MAHC 1459-4-1-24, Annie Elouise Bradshaw, Circular Letter, 1948; HCA旧 36-1-12, "Our Principals," in *Hongdao ershi zhou jinian kan* (1932), 2–4.
76. NCA 旧 10-1-307, Principal's Report, May 9, 1935.
77. NCA 旧 10-1-307, Principal's Report, May 9, 1935.
78. NCA 旧 10-1-307, Principal's Report 1933–34.
79. Laura Haygood Principal Jiang Guiyun rejoiced that they "had the privilege of giving Christian training to the future teachers of these widely scattered schools." MAHC 1459-4-1-24, Kwe Yuin Kiang, "Annual Report—1946," Laura Haygood Normal School Suzhou, China.
80. HCA 旧 36-1-12, "Zai xiao xuesheng jiazhang zhiye tongji," in *Hongdao ershi zhou jinian kan* (1923), 505; NCA 旧 10-1-307, "Distribution of Occupations of the Students' Parents," Principal's Report, April 16, 1932; "Xiao Shi," "Quan xiao xuesheng jiashu zhiye bijiao tu," in *Shanghai shili Wuben nüzi zhongxue gaikuang* (1934), 7; Ding Wanzhen, "Benxiao xuesheng jiazu zhiye yilan," *Shengmaliya nüxiao wushi zhou jinian tekan* (1931).
81. Robert Culp, *Articulating Citizenship: Civic Education and Student Politics in South-Eastern China, 1912–1940* (Cambridge, MA: Harvard University Press, 2007), 26; Earl Herbert Cressy and C. C. Chih., "Middle School Standards, Second Study," *East China Studies in Education*, No. 5 (Shanghai: East China Christian Educational Association, 1929), 50.
82. Culp, *Articulating Citizenship*, 26.
83. Tang, "Women's Education in China," 16.
84. "The Alumnae Scholarship," *The Phoenix* (1932), 92.
85. Cressy and Chih, "Middle School Standards, Second Study," 50.
86. Interview with Dai Lizhen, April 12, 2019, Shanghai.
87. "The Anglo-Chinese School for Girls," 247.
88. HCA 旧 36-1-12, "Ershi nian du zai xiao xuesheng jiguan tongji," *Hongdao ershi zhou jinian kan* (1932), 503; "Zai xiao xuesheng jiguan bijiao biao," *Shanghai xianli Wuben nüzi zhong xuexiao ershiwu zhou jinian ce*, ed. Wuben nüzi zhong xuexiao chuban bu (Shanghai: Shanghai zheyitang yinshuasuo, 1926), front matter.
89. ZPL 377-309-2676, "Xuesheng jiguan tongji biao," *Huixing sili nüzi chuji zhongxue zuijin gaikuang* (1934), 6.
90. Cressy and Chih, "Middle School Standards, Second Study," 40.
91. According to Cressy, the use of Chinese as the main medium for instruction increased for missionary girls' schools in the years 1923–1926. However, girls in more senior years were more likely to be taught in English for subjects such as Social Problems, Algebra, Psychology, History, Music, and typewriting. See C. C. Chih and Earl Herbert Cressy, "Middle School Standards," *East China Studies in Education*, No. 2 (Shanghai: China Christian Educational Association, 1926), 58–59; Cressy and Chih, "Middle School Standards, Second Study," 42.

92. "The Anglo-Chinese School for Girls," 247.
93. Interview with Gwendolin Jie, October 17, 2015, Shanghai.
94. Zhu Wenqing, St. Mary's Group Interview, May 11, 2016, Beijing.
95. Interview with Zhao Fengfeng, June 14, 2016, Beijing.
96. Interview with Ling Yourong, November 7, 2016, San Mateo. Ling Yourong attended McTyeire from 1947–1949, at which point her family fled to Hong Kong, so she did not graduate from McTyeire.
97. Interview with Zhu Yonglin, November 13, 2016, Shanghai.
98. Ruth Lea Tsai in "Telling Women's Lives."
99. Joint recollections, the class of 1947 at their fiftieth anniversary of entering McTyeire, in "Telling Women's Lives."
100. Kuan Yu Chen in "Telling Women's Lives."
101. "The Chinese Music Club," *The Laura Haygood Star* (Suzhou, 1922); Mo Sih Tsung, "The Influence of Music in the Future Homes of China," *The McTyeirean* (Shanghai, 1919): 29.
102. "Music," *The Phoenix* (1922): 53.
103. Interview with Gwendolyn Jie, October 17, 2015, Shanghai.
104. Interview with Xu Meizhen, March 17, 2016, Shanghai.
105. For a discussion of the ways in which missionary educators responded to changing civics curricula in higher education, see Susan Rigdon, "National Salvation: Teaching Civic Duty in China's Christian Colleges," in *China's Christian Colleges: Cross Cultural Connections, 1900–1950*, eds. Daniel H. Bays and Ellen Widmer (Stanford: Stanford University Press, 2009), 193–217.
106. The Three People's Principles was a political philosophy formulated by Sun Yat-sen, founder of the Nationalist Party. They can be translated as "Nationalism," "Democracy," and "The People's Livelihood." After Sun's death in 1925 they were enshrined as part of the official political doctrine of the Nationalist Party and became an important part of the civics curriculum in the 1930s. For more see Culp, *Articulating Citizenship*, 39.
107. ABHS 262-3-8, Florence Webster to McVeigh and Friends of the Board, January 29, 1926.
108. Interview with Zhang Long, July 6, 2016, Shanghai.
109. Interview with Zhang Long, July 6, 2016, Shanghai.
110. Interview with Theresa Chen, November 10, 2016, San Mateo.
111. Interview with Dong Yue, November 26, 2016, Beijing.
112. Interview with Zhang Luoluo, November 8, 2016, San Mateo.
113. Lian Shu Tsao in "Telling Women's Lives."
114. Interview with Zhang Luoluo, November 8, 2016, San Mateo.
115. Culp, *Articulating Citizenship*, 106.
116. Tsao Zok Tung, "The Student Council," *The McTyeirean* (1918): 39.
117. Helen Lefkowitz Horowitz, *Alma Mater: Design and Experience in the Women's Colleges from Their Nineteenth-Century Beginnings to the 1930s* (New York: Knopf, 1984), 145.
118. *The Phoenix* (1920).

119. Henrietta Harrison, *The Making of the Republican Citizen, Political Ceremonies and Symbols in China, 1911-1929* (Oxford: Oxford University Press, 2000), 4; Ryan Dunch, *Fuzhou Protestants and the Making of Modern China, 1857-1927* (New Haven, CT: Yale University Press, 2001), 317; Culp, *Articulating Citizenship*, 212.
120. Culp, *Articulating Citizenship*, 112.
121. Tsao, "Wu Pen Girls Fight against Blue Jacket 'Cultural Control,'" in *China Forum* 3, no. 2 (November 30, 1933): 9. Wuben Girls' School became government run in 1912. See "Xiao Shi," *Shanghai shili Wuben nüzi zhongxue gaikuang* (1934), 1-2.
122. Culp, *Articulating Citizenship*, 178-183.
123. Qu Mingming, "Zhongxi nüzhong aiguo xuesheng yundong de huigu," in *Bainian nüzhong—xian gei yibaiyishi zhounian xiao qing*, ed. He Yanan (Shanghai: Shanghai shi di san nüzi zhongxue, 2002) 121-127; Cao Baozhen, "Sanshi niandai de Zhongxi nüzhong," in *Bainian nüzhong—xian gei yibaiyishi zhounian xiao qing*, ed. He Yanan (Shanghai: Shanghai shi di san nüzi zhongxue, 2002), 66-68.
124. Lefkowitz Horowitz, *Alma Mater*, 173-174.
125. Li Mei, "Shengmaliya nüxiao de jiemei ban," in *Zhuixun Shengmaliya xiaoyou zuji*, ed. Xu Yongchu and Chen Jinyu (Shanghai: Tongji daxue chubanshe, 2014), 182.
126. Interview with Gong Zhengguan, May 9, 2016, Beijing.
127. PHS RG82-32-19, "Constitution of the Board of Directors of the Riverside Girls Academy," Article 2- Aim.

Chapter 2

1. Margaret Van, "Church Activities in China," *Riverside Echo* (1925): 5.
2. Margaret Van, "A Meeting at the Factory," *Riverside Echo* (1925): 6-7.
3. Van, "A Meeting at the Factory," 6-7.
4. Interview with Pastor Fan Aisi, November 27, 2015, Ningbo; "Ningbo riren chuoshang huaren an xuwen," *Shenbao*, June 26, 1925.
5. Milton T. Stauffer (ed.), *The Christian Occupation of China: A General Survey of the Numerical Strength and Geographical Distribution of the Christian Forces in China, Made by the Special Committee on Survey and Occupation, China Continuation Committee, 1918-1921* (Shanghai: China Continuation Committee, 1922).
6. For more on the anti-Christian Movement, see Jessie Gregory Lutz, *Chinese Politics and Christian Missions: The Anti-Christian Movements of 1920-1928* (Notre Dame, IN: Cross Cultural Publications, 1988); Ka-Che Yip, *Religion, Nationalism, and Chinese Students: The Anti-Christian Movement of 1922-1927* (Bellingham: Western Washington University, 1980); Han Shu, "Shouhui jiaoyuquan yundong zai shen guan—cong shengyuehan daxue dao guanghua daxue" [A deeper look at the movement to recover educational rights—from St. John's University to Guanghua University], in *Jidujiao yu jindai zhongguo jiaoyu*, ed. Li Ling and Xiao Qinghe (Shanghai: Shanghai yiwen chubanshe, 2018), 94-120.
7. See, for example, Ryan Dunch, *Fuzhou Protestants and the Making of Modern China, 1857-1927* (New Haven, CT: Yale University Press, 2001); Lian Xi, *Redeemed*

by Fire: The Rise of Popular Christianity in Modern China (New Haven, CT: Yale University Press, 2010); and Daryl L. Ireland, John Song: Modern Chinese Christianity and the Making of a New Man (Waco, TX: Baylor University Press, 2020).
8. Dunch, Fuzhou Protestants, 137.
9. Chu I Shiu, "China's Rip Van Winkle," The McTyeirean (1921): 101.
10. On the May Fourth Movement, see: Chow Ts'e-tsung, The May Fourth Movement: Intellectual Revolution in Modern China (Cambridge, MA: Harvard University Press, 1960); Vera Swartz, The Chinese Enlightenment: Intellectuals and the Legacy of the May Fourth Movement of 1919 (Berkeley: University of California Press, 1986); and Elizabeth Forster, 1919—The Year that Changed China: A New History of the New Culture Movement (Berlin: De Gruyter, 2018).
11. Eleanor MacNeil, "The Situation in Shanghai," in Supplement to the Green Year: Concerning the Events on and Since May 30 in Shanghai, July 1, 1925: 4.
12. Rana Mitter, A Bitter Revolution: China's Struggle with the Modern World (Oxford: Oxford University Press, 2005), 4.
13. Wong We-Kyoen, "St. Mary's and the Student Movement," The Phoenix (1920): 53.
14. Tsang Kyi-ying, "A Long Trip to Longhua," The Phoenix (1920): 62.
15. Wong, "St. Mary's and the Student Movement," 53.
16. For more on women's public political participation in the 1911 revolution and the May Fourth period, respectively, see Louise Edwards, Gender, Politics and Democracy: Women's Suffrage in China (Stanford: Stanford University Press, 2008); and Wang Zheng, Women in the Chinese Enlightenment: Oral and Textual Histories (Berkeley: University of California Press, 1999).
17. Tsang Kyi-ying, "A Memorial Meeting," The Phoenix (1920): 59.
18. Symbols of nationalism were vital ingredients in the identity formation of Chinese citizens in the early Republic. Henrietta Harrison, The Making of the Republican Citizen: Political Ceremonies and Symbols in China, 1911–1929 (Oxford: Oxford University Press, 2000), 4.
19. Wong, "St. Mary's and the Student Movement," 54.
20. Eur Yang-Sih, "October 10 of 1919" The Phoenix (1920): 58.
21. David Strand, An Unfinished Republic: Leading by Word and Deed in Modern China (Berkeley: University of California Press, 2011), 82–120.
22. Strand, An Unfinished Republic, 108.
23. Yen Wei Tsing, "Chinese Women," The McTyeirean (1919): 46.
24. Tsu Tsung Kyung, "Present situation of Popular Democracy in China," The McTyeirean (1922): 68.
25. Kyung Ming-ge, "The Student Meeting in Shasi," The Phoenix (1920): 65.
26. Kyung, "The Student Meeting in Shasi," 65.
27. Tsiang Ku Yin, "How Earnest Found His Kingdom," The McTyeirean (1919): 23–24.
28. Tsao Ming Zok, "The Call for Women Leaders," The McTyeirean (1922): 34.
29. Tsu Tsung Kyung, "What Christ Means to Me," The McTyeirean (1921): 72.
30. For more on craze for mass education, see Kate Merkel-Hess, The Rural Modern: Reconstructing Self and State in Republican China (Chicago: University of Chicago Press, 2016).

31. Georgina Brewis, *A Social History of Student Volunteering: Britain and Beyond, 1880-1980* (New York: Palgrave McMillian, 2014), 43.
32. For more on James Yen's work, see Charles Hayford, *To the People: James Yen and Village China* (New York: Columbia University Press, 1990).
33. Hayford, *To the People*, 38.
34. Hoo Lu Tuh, "A Letter Relating to Village Work," *The McTyeirean* (1922): 46.
35. Li Rongmei, "Qingnian hui," *Yongjiang sheng* (1931): 188.
36. Zhang Hanchu, "Suzhou pingmin jiaoyu," *Jinghai xing* (1924): 3–5.
37. Zhang, "Suzhou pingming jiaoyu," 3–5.
38. SMA U121-0-30-1, National Committee, Young Women's Christian Association of China (ed.), *Student Handbook: Constitution and Organisation of a Student Y.W.C.A.* (Shanghai, 1924), 27.
39. Xia Shi, *At Home in the World: Women and Charity in Late Qing and Early Republican China* (Columbia: Columbia University Press, 2018), 146.
40. Tu Fengyun, "Ben xiao de xuesheng hui," *Yongjiang sheng* (1931): 178.
41. Chang E. Tsung, "A Study of the Village Life around McTyeire High School," *The McTyeirean* (Shanghai): 115.
42. Tsung, "A Study," 114.
43. Tsung, "A Study," 113.
44. Helen Schneider, *Keeping the Nation's House: Domestic Management and the Making of Modern China* (Vancouver: UBC Press, 2011), 20–56; Susan L. Glosser, "'The Truths I Have Learned': Nationalism, Family Reform and Male Identity in China's New Culture Movement, 1915–1923," in *Chinese Femininities, Chinese Masculinities: A Reader*, ed. Susan Brownell and Jeffrey N. Wasserstrom (Berkeley: University of California Press, 2002), 120–144.
45. Tsung, "A Study," 112.
46. Tsu Tsung Ling and Wong Yoeh Wo, "Is the Village School Worthwhile?" *The McTyeirean* (Shanghai): 56–57.
47. Helen Schneider, "Raising the Standards of Family Life: Ginling Women's College and Christian Social Service in Republican China," in *Divine Domesticities: Christian Paradoxes in Asia and the Pacific*, ed. Hyaeweol Choi and Margaret Jolly (Canberra: ANU Press, 2014), 139.
48. Merkel-Hess, *The Rural Modern*, 72.
49. Tsong Tuh Wei, "The Two Wills," *The McTyeirean* (1930): 185.
50. Jane Hunter, *The Gospel of Gentility: American Women Missionaries in Turn-of-the-Century China* (New Haven, CT: Yale University Press, 1984), 35–40.
51. Helen Schneider, *Keeping the Nation's House*.
52. The NARC was a cross-party organization that grew out of new cooperation between New Life Movement's Women's Advisory Council headed by Song Meiling, the Women's National Salvation Association, and prominent female CCP members in Wuhan during the wartime. Vivienne Xiangwei Guo, *Women and Politics in Wartime China: Networking across Geopolitical Boundaries* (London: Routledge, 2019), 42–44.
53. T'sao Ai Fang, "The Adoption of Christianity as the State Religion of China," *The Laura Haygood Star* (1921): 23.

54. Mo Sih Tsung, "The Influence of Music in the Future Homes of China," *The McTyeirean* (1919): 29.
55. Isabella Jackson, *Shaping Modern Shanghai: Colonialism in China's Global City* (Cambridge: Cambridge University Press, 2017), 144.
56. The newspaper was established in June 1920 in the aftermath of the May Fourth movement by Jin Runxiang 金潤庠, a native of Ningbo and a leader of the group for National Salvation in Zhejiang (Jiuguo shi ren tuan 救國十人團). The newspaper thus had a left-leaning political orientation from its foundation, and its editors were strongly influenced by May Fourth ideology. Indeed, its founder, Jin Runxiang, had been expelled from Presbyterian Feidi middle school (Feidi zhongxue 斐迪中學) for a rebellion against his foreign missionary teachers. The newspaper had a wide readership among the commercial classes in Ningbo, with a daily print run of 15,000 copies by 1940. Wu Weinong, "Jin Runxiang yu Shishi gongbao," in *Ningbo wenshi ziliao*, vol. 3, ed. Zhongguo renmin zhengzhi xie shang huiyi, Ningbo shi weiyuanhui wenshi ziliao yanjiu weiyuan (Ningbo, 1985), 182–192.
57. Zhang Chuanshen, "Jidu zhenli he zai?" *Shishi gongbao*, August 8, 1925.
58. Lin Wentian, "Jidutu duiyu shiju de ganxiang he taidu," *Shishi gongbao*, September 4, 1925.
59. Lin, "Jidutu duiyu shiju de ganxiang he taidu."
60. The slogan "Restore Education Rights" was first coined by Yu Chia-Chu in his article "The Question of Religious Education," published in the journal *Chinese Education Review* in 1923. The intellectuals who launched the campaign were those who had participated in the anti-Christian movement of 1922, and they often drew on similar texts and debates in their new attack. The first protests occurred within missionary schools themselves when, in the summer of 1924, students at Trinity College in Guangzhou called for the restoration of China's educational rights, and the movement was quickly given support and publicity by the left-leaning Guangzhou Student Union. Attempts by the school to stop the movement by expelling its ringleaders added fuel to the flames, and the movement quickly spread across China, sparking student protests in missionary schools in Nanjing, Suzhou, Fuzhou, and Shanghai. Lingnan College in Canton, Yali in Changsha, Huazhong in Wuchang, and Ginling College in Nanjing all suffered disruption from protests within and outside the school in this period. See Gregory Lutz, *China and the Christian Colleges, 1850–1950* (Ithaca, NY: Cornell University Press, 1971), 236; and "Guangdong xueshenghui shouhui jiaoyu quanli yundong weiyuanhui xuanxin" [Selected letters from the Guangdong student union committee for the recovery of educational rights], in *Diguozhuyi qin hua jiaoyu shi ziliao—jiaohui xuexiao*, ed. Li Chucai (Beijing: Jiaoyu kexue chubanshe, 1987), 583–585.
61. Wang Qixian, "Wo he jiaohui xuexiao xuesheng de fuxiong tan hua" [A conversation with the fathers and elder brothers of missionary school students], *Shishi gongbao*, August 1, 1925.
62. Fu Lüe, "Jiaohui xuexiao yu jingji qinlüe" [Mission Schools and Economic encroachment], *Shishi gongbao*, August 7, 1925.
63. Interview with Zhang Ruiyun, May 10, 2016, Beijing.

64. Lin Shiguang, "Tuoli jiaohui xuexiao de ji zhong yuanyin" [A few reasons to leave missionary schools], *Shishi gongbao*, September 14, 1925.
65. Gan Mengxiong, "Fenggao na hai liu bu li jiaohui xuexiao de tongxue ji juhua," *Shishi gongbao*, August 6, 1925.
66. Gan, "Fenggao na hai liu bu li jiaohui xuexiao de tongxue ji juhua."
67. Elizabeth J. Perry, "Managing Student Protest in Republican China: Yenching and St. John's Compared," *Frontiers of History in China* 8, no. 1 (2013): 8.
68. Literally meaning "Glorify China." Perry, "Managing Student Protest," 14.
69. Yeh, Wen-hsin, *The Alienated Academy: Culture and Politics in Republican China, 1919–1937* (Cambridge, MA: Harvard University Press, 1990), 84.
70. "Ben xiao sanshi nian lai renshu bijiao biao" [Table showing the number of students in this school over the past thirty years], in *Shengmaliya nüxiao wushi zhou jinian tekan* (1931), front matter.
71. Gan, "Fenggao na hai liu bu li jiaohui xuexiao de tongxue ji juhua."
72. ABHS BMI Pre WW2- G1-75-9, Florence Webster to Mabel Rae McVeigh, July 12, 1925.
73. ABHS MF 262-3-8, Florence Webster to McVeigh, January 29, 1926.
74. ABHS MF 262-3-8, Florence Webster to McVeigh, January 29, 1926.
75. Rev. Harris E. Kirk of Baltimore, "New Mission Philosophy," an extract from an address at Washington Missionary Convention, in *Supplement to The Green Year: Concerning the Events on and since May 30 in Shanghai* (1925), 18.
76. ABHS BMI Pre WW2- G1-75-9, Florence Webster to Miss McVeigh, July 12, 1925.
77. ABHS MF 262-3-8, Florence Webster to Miss McVeigh, January 29, 1926.
78. The Chinese members of the administrative and teaching staffs of the Suzhou University College of Arts and Sciences, and Suzhou University Middle School No. 1, "Our Message to the Missionaries in China," in *Supplement to The Green Year: Concerning the Events on and since May 30 in Shanghai* (1925), 13.
79. B. S. Siao, "An Appeal to All Concerned," in *Supplement to The Green Year: Concerning the Events on and since May 30 in Shanghai* (1925), 12.
80. ABHS BMI Pre WW2- G1-75-9, Florence Webster to Mabel Rae McVeigh, July 12, 1925.
81. Julia C. Strauss, *Strong Institutions in Weak Polities: State Building in Republican China, 1927–1940* (Oxford: Oxford University Press, 1998).
82. Lutz, *Chinese Politics*, 214.
83. As Jin Feng notes, accounts differed over who was responsible for the Nanjing incident. Nationalist officers blamed northern warlord troops dressed in the uniforms of Nationalist soldiers, while foreign diplomats in the city as well as Chiang's supporters blamed Communists within the GMD-CCP coalition. Jin Feng, *The Making of a Family Saga: Ginling College* (New York: SUNY Press, 2009), 114.
84. NCA 旧10-1-307/308, Riverside Board of Director's Minute Meetings and Principal's Reports, 11.
85. The Presbyterian mission annual report of 1926–27 includes a group photo of the students and teachers who "stuck by the school, absolutely loyal and brave." PHS MR7-PA-ZCAS Central China Mission, Presbyterian Church in the U.S.A, annual report, 1926–1927, 15.

86. NCA 旧10-1-307/308, Riverside Board of Director's Minute Meetings and Principal's Reports, 11.
87. "Yongjiang nüzhong shuqing xuban" [Yongjiang female middle school requests to be allowed to continue to operate], *Shishi gongbao*, August 24, 1927.
88. "Shouhui jiaoyu quan jijin hui wei yongjiang zhao sheng gao min ju" [An announcement that the committee for the quick taking back of educational rights is enrolling students at Yongjiang], *Shishi gongbao*, August 24, 1927.
89. PHS RG82-32-10, F. R Millican, "Data and Reflections on the Situation in Chekiang Provinces re the Future of Mission Schools," July 27, 1927.
90. The Nationalists defeated the armies of Warlord Sun Chuanfang in March 1927, Hans Van de Ven, *War and Nationalism in China, 1925–1945* (London: Routledge, 2003), 109.
91. According to Riverside missionary teacher Esther Gauss, it was the "left-wing" within the United Front forces in Ningbo who were vehemently anti-Christian. PHS RG82-32-10, Esther E. Gauss, Circular Letter, January 21, 1927.
92. Van de Ven, *War and Nationalism in China*, 109.
93. PHS RG82-32-10, Ester E. Gauss, Circular Letter, May 9, 1927.
94. PHS RG82-32-10, F. R. Millican, "Data and Reflections on the Situation in Chekiang Provinces re the Future of Mission Schools," July 27, 1927; PHS MR7-PA-ZCAS, Central China Mission, Presbyterian Church in the U.S.A, annual report, 1926–1927, 15.
95. Front matter, *Riverside Echo* (1931).
96. PHS MR7-PA-ZCAS, Central China Mission, Presbyterian Church in the U.S.A, annual report, 1926–1927, 14–15.
97. Interview with Pastor Fan Aisi, November 27, 2015, Ningbo.
98. According to her brother, Margaret was expelled from school when her name appeared in the newspaper, listing her as an attendee of a patriotic student rally. Although Margaret denied that she had attended the rally, she was not prepared to write to the newspaper to correct the information and was consequently expelled by Principal Zimmerman. Interview with Pastor Fan Aisi, November 27, 2015, Ningbo. According to the Shanghai *Shenbao* newspaper, a student rally took place in Ningbo on June 26, 1925, after the stabbing of five Chinese citizens by a Japanese living in the city. Margaret's name is listed as one of twenty Riverside students who declared their intention of leaving their school and never returning. They were aggrieved that their school was not letting them take part in the patriotic student movement. We do not know if this was the rally for which Margaret was expelled, or if she had already been excluded and then wanted to publicly declare her intention of leaving Riverside. "Ningbo riren chuoshang huaren an xuwen," *Shenbao*, June 26, 1925.
99. Interview with Pastor Fan Aisi, November 27, 2015, Ningbo.
100. "Funü jiezhihui jiang chu fei gai zhuanhao" [The Chinese Women's Christian Temperance Union plan to publish a special issue on how to eliminate beggars], *Shenbao*, December 18, 1925.
101. "Minzhong weilao guomin jun" [The people comfort the National Revolutionary Army], *Shenbao*, March 26, 1927.

NOTES TO PAGES 78–85   233

102. Interview with Pastor Fan Aisi, November 27, 2015, Ningbo.
103. Louise Edwards, *Woman Warriors and Wartime Spies of China* (Cambridge: Cambridge University Press, 2016), 66–90. Sources do not tell us whether Margaret formally joined the army in this period, although her brother believed she did. Interview with Pastor Fan Aisi, November 27, 2015, Ningbo.
104. PHS – MR7-PA-ZCAS, Central China Mission, Presbyterian Church in the U.S.A., annual report, 1926–1927, 15.
105. Yang Yinsui, "Ben xiao bei [shouhui jiaoyu quan jijin hui] zhanju shi de huiyi" [Remembering the time when our school was occupied by the Committee for the quick taking back of educational rights], in *Yinxian sili Yongjiang nüzi zhongxue nianwu zhounian jinian kan* (1948), 1–2.
106. Sun Yat-sen, known as the "Father of the Nation" in mainland China, was the figurehead of the 1911 revolution which ended the Qing dynasty and founder of China's Nationalist Party, the Guomindang, in 1912. Sun's nationalist thinking was most famously developed in his Three People's Principles (Sanmin zhuyi 三民主義) of "Nationalism" (Minzu zhuyi 民族主義), "Democracy" (Minquan zhuyi 民權主義), and "People's Livelihood" (Minsheng zhuyi 民生主義). These principles became principal tenets of the Republic after the Guomindang victory in 1927 and became a compulsory subject of study in civics classes in schools in the 1930s. For more on Sun Yat-sen see Marie-Claire Bergère, *Sun Yat-sen* (Stanford: Stanford University Press, 1998).
107. PHS RG82-32-10, Esther E. Gauss, Letter to friends from Shanghai, May 9, 1927.
108. "Yongjiang nüzhong shuqing xuban," *Shishi gongbao*, August 24, 1927.
109. Chen Aizhen, "Jiaohui nüxiao duiyu xiandai zhongguo zui shao xiandu de gongxian" [The smallest contribution of missionary schools for girls to modern China], *Yongjiang sheng* (1931): 42.
110. Chen, "Jiaohui nüxiao," 43.
111. Chen, "Jiaohui nüxiao," 43.
112. Chen, "Jiaohui nüxiao," 43.
113. Gan Mengxiong, "Fenggao na hai liu bu li jiaohui xuexiao de tongxue ji juhua," in *Shishi gongbao*, August 8, 1925.

Chapter 3

1. Deu Miao Kung, "Class Prophesy," *The McTyeirean* (1923): 14–17.
2. Deu, "Class Prophesy," 14–17.
3. Vivian W. Yen in "Telling Women's Lives: In Search of McTyeire, 1892–1992," ed. McTyeire Alumnae Association (unpublished Oral History Collection, 1992).
4. Joan Judge, "Citizens or Mothers of Citizens? Gender and the Meaning of Modern Citizenship in China," in *Changing Meanings of Citizenship in Modern China*, ed. Merle Goldman and Elizabeth J. Perry (Cambridge, MA: Harvard University Press, 2002), 25.

5. Peter Zarrow, "He Zhen and Anarcho-Feminism in China," *Journal of Asian Studies* 47, no. 4 (November 1988): 796–813.
6. Paul Bailey, "'Unharnessed Fillies': Discourse on the 'Modern' Female Student in Early Twentieth-Century China," in *Women and Culture in Modern China 1600–1950*, ed. Luo Liurong and Lü Miao-fen (Taipei: Academia Sinica, 2003), 327–357.
7. Joan Judge, *Republican Lens: Gender, Visuality and Experience in the Early Chinese Periodical Press* (Oakland: University of California Press, 2015), 151.
8. Wang Zheng, *Women in the Chinese Enlightenment: Oral and Textual Histories* (Berkeley: University of California Press, 1999), 72.
9. Hsiao-pei Yen, "Body Politics, Modernity and National Salvation: The Modern Girl and the New Life Movement," *Asian Studies Review* 29, no. 2 (June 2005): 165–186.
10. Helen Schneider, "The Professionalization of Chinese Domesticity: Ava B. Milan and Home Economics at Yenching University," in *China's Christian Colleges: Cross Cultural Connections, 1900–1950*, ed. Daniel H. Bays and Ellen Widmer (Stanford: Sanford University Press, 2009), 145.
11. Laurence, "Female Boarding Schools," in *Records of the General Conference of the Protestant Missionaries of China Held at Shanghai, May 10–17, 1877*, ed. M. T. Yates (Shanghai: American Presbyterian Mission Press, 1878), 469.
12. CMS CCH 056/14, Laurence annual letter to Mr. Fenn, December 1877.
13. Chinese Educational Commission, *Christian Education in China: A Study Made by an Educational Commission Representing the Mission Boards and Societies Conducting Work in China* (New York: Committee of Reference and Counsel of the Foreign Missions Conference of North America, 1922), 258.
14. Susan Mann, "The Education of Daughters in the Mid-Ch'ing Period," in *Education and Society in Late Imperial China, 1600–1900*, ed. Alexander Woodside and Benjamin A. Elman (Berkeley: University of California Press, 1994), 22.
15. NCA 旧 10-1-307, Minutes of the Board of Directors, April 17, 1923; and NCA 旧 10-1-307, Principal's Report May 9, 1931.
16. PHS RG82-18-17, Esther M. Gauss to Mr. Speer, February 26, 1920.
17. NCA 旧 10-1-307, "Faculty 1935 Fall," in Principal's Report, March 27, 1936.
18. Federica Ferlanti, "The New Life Movement in Jiangxi Province, 1934–1938," *Modern Asian Studies* 44, no. 5 (September 2010): 961–1000.
19. Ferlanti, "The New Life Movement," 963.
20. Ferlanti, "The New Life Movement," 978. See also Arif Dirlik, "The Ideological Foundations of the New Life Movement: A Study in Counterrevolution," *Journal of Asian Studies* 34, no. 4 (August 1975): 954–980.
21. Liu Wang Liming, "Sishi nian lai zhongguo funü jiezhi yundong," *Zhonghua funü jiezhi xiehui nian kan* (1934): 2; Feng Ling, "Xin shenghuo yundong de zumu," *Zhonghua funü jiezhi xiehui nian kan* (1934): 7.
22. Ferlanti, "The New Life Movement," 974.
23. Chiang Kai-shek, "Essentials of the New Life Movement" (Speech, 1934), in *Sources of Chinese Tradition: From 1600 through the Twentieth Century*, 2nd ed., Vol. 2., ed. Wm. Theodore de Bary and Richard Lufrano (New York: Columbia University Press, 2000), 337–343.

24. PHS – MR7-PA-ZCAS, Central China Mission, Presbyterian Church in the U.S.A, Annual report, 1926–1927, 15.
25. NCA 旧 10-1-307, Principal's Report, 1933–1934.
26. NCA 旧 10-1-307, Principal's Report, 1932–1933.
27. Robert Culp, *Articulating Citizenship: Civic Education and Student Politics in Southeastern China, 1912–1940* (Cambridge, MA: Harvard University Press, 2007), 202.
28. NCA 旧 10-1-307, Principal's Report, June 7, 1930.
29. Zhou Yuyin, "Shenghuo zai Yongjiang," *Yinxian sili Yongjiang nüzi zhongxue nianwu zhounian jinian kan* (1948): 15.
30. NCA 旧 10-1-307, Principal's Report, April 16, 1932.
31. Jane Hunter, *The Gospel of Gentility: American Women Missionaries in Turn-of-the-Century China* (New Haven, CT: Yale University Press, 1984), 188.
32. NCA 旧 10-1-307, Principal's Report, May 9, 1935.
33. Zhou Yuyin, "Shenghuo zai Yongjiang," 15.
34. NCA旧 10-1-307, Principal's Report, June 7, 1930, and May 9,1933.
35. Zhou Yuyin, "Shenghuo zai Yongjiang," 15.
36. NCA 旧 10-1-307, Principal's Report, 1933–1934.
37. Ke Hailun, "Funü yu guonan," *Yongjiang sheng* (1933): 45.
38. Tu Fengyun, "Ben xiao de xueshenghui," *Yongjiang sheng* (1931): 178.
39. Lin Mixuan, "Wuli zhunbei yu shenti xunlian," *Yongjiang sheng* (1933): 48.
40. Ruth Rogaski, *Hygienic Modernity: Meanings of Health and Disease in Treaty-Port China* (Berkeley: University of California Pres, 2004), 252.
41. Weili Ye, "Nü Liuxuesheng; The Story of American Educated Chinese Women 1880–1920s," *Modern China* 20, no. 3 (July 1994): 315–346.
42. Hu Ying, "Naming the First New Woman," *Nan Nü: Men, Women, and Gender in Early and Imperial China* 3, no. 2 (January 2001): 196–231; Connie Shemo, *The Chinese Medical Ministries of Kang Cheng and Shi Meiyu, 1872–1937* (Bethlehem: Lehigh University Press, 2011).
43. Mei-ying Ding, "What a Chinese Girl Should Know before Going for Study Abroad," *The McTyeirean* (1918): 24.
44. For example, when Zeng Baosun 曾寶蓀 (1893–1978), a great-granddaughter of Zeng Guofan 曾國藩 (1811–1872), accompanied CMS missionary Louise Barnes to England during her furlough in 1911 to enroll in Westfield Women's College, she became aware of Barnes' rather "ordinary" background. Louise Barnes' father, Peter Frederick Barnes', was a bricklayer by trade (see Kew, TNA, WO 97/559, Royal Hospital Chelsea: Soldiers' Service Documents). Zeng hints in her memoirs that she was aware of Barnes' very "ordinary" background: "I discovered that she was not extremely learned and articulate, simply an ordinary person"; see *Confucian Feminist: Memoirs of Zeng Baosun, 1893–1978*, trans. Thomas L. Kennedy (Philadelphia: American Philosophical Society, 2002), 29.
45. Jeffrey N. Wasserstrom, "Questioning the Modernity of the Model Settlement: Citizenship and Exclusion in Old Shanghai," in *Changing Meanings of Citizenship in Modern China*, ed. Merle Goldman and Elizabeth Perry (Cambridge, MA: Harvard University Press, 2002), 117.

46. Interview with Wu Qihui, June 15, 2016, Beijing.
47. Interview with Yang Zhiling, July 20, 2016, Beijing.
48. Kuan Yu Chen in "Telling Women's Lives."
49. Zung Seu Ling, "The Science of Homemaking," *The McTyeirean* (1918): 46.
50. Interview with Yang Zhiling, July 20, 2016, Beijing.
51. Cover image, *Linglong*, no. 21, August 1931.
52. Tsih Zoen Shang, "Changing Styles," *The McTyeirean* (1923): 65.
53. Tsih, "Changing Styles," 65.
54. Madeleine Y. Dong, "Who Is Afraid of the Chinese Modern Girl?" in *The Modern Girl around the World: Consumption, Modernity, and Globalization*, ed. The Modern Girl around the World Research Group et al. (Durham, NC: Duke University Press, 2008), 194–219.
55. Yen, "Body Politics," 165–186.
56. Louise Edwards, "The Shanghai Modern Woman's American Dreams: Imagining America's Depravity to Produce China's 'Moderate Modernity,'" *Pacific Historical Review* 81, no. 4 (November 2012): 567–601.
57. Hoo Loo Ming, "She Made Her Bed," *The McTyeirean* (1930): 195–202; Tsih Zoen Shang, "The Old-Fashioned Mother and Her New-Fashioned Daughter," *The McTyeirean* (1922): 98–99.
58. Soong Jung-wo, "My Great-Grandmother," *The Phoenix* (1923): 6.
59. Interview with Rosalyn Koo, November 5, 2016, San Mateo.
60. Interview with Zhang Long, July 6, 2016, Shanghai.
61. Interview with Zhang Long, July 6, 2016, Shanghai.
62. Focus group with St. Mary's alumnae, May 11, 2016, Beijing; Interview with Zhang Long, July 6, 2016, Shanghai.
63. Paratha Chatterjee, "The Nationalist Resolution of the Woman Question," in *Recasting Women: Essays in Colonial History*, ed. Kumkum Sangari and Sudesh Vaid (New Brunswick: Rutgers University Press, 2006), 233–253.
64. Karl Gerth, *China Made: Consumer Culture and the Creation of the Nation* (Cambridge, MA: Harvard University Press, 2003), 285.
65. Tu, "Ben xiao de xueshenghui," 178.
66. Chen Aizhen, "Zai qiuxue lichang shang shuo ji juhua," *Yongjiang sheng* (1931): 22–27.
67. Ke, "Funü yu guonan," 46.
68. Chen Xingying, "Jiaoyu geming de husheng," *Yongjiang sheng* (1931): 20–21.
69. Ding, "What a Chinese Girl Should Know," 23–24.
70. In March 1943, Song Meiling was featured on the front cover of *Time* magazine.
71. Interview with Rosalyn Koo, November 5, 2016, San Mateo.
72. Tseng Pao-sun, "The Chinese Woman Past and Present," in *Chinese Women through Chinese Eyes*, ed. Li Yu-ning (New York: Routledge, 1992), 86.
73. This irony has been highlighted by Jane Hunter in *The Gospel of Gentility*, 35. This was not the first example of women escaping marriage in Chinese history, as Robert Entenmann has shown in his study of Catholic virgins in nineteenth-century Sichuan. Robert Entenmann, "Christian Virgins in Eighteenth Century Sichuan," in *Christianity in China from the Eighteenth Century to the Present*, ed. Daniel D. Bays

(Stanford: Stanford University Press, 1996), 8–23. Marjory Topley has also shown that a small number of women did resist marriage in rural Guangdong by forming all-female communities which supported themselves via sericulture from the early nineteenth century. Marjorie Topley, "Marriage Resistance in Rural Kwangtung," in *Women in Chinese Society*, ed. Margery Wolf and Roxanne Witke (Stanford: Stanford University Press, 1975), 67–88.

74. Interview with Ding Yuming, November 9, 2016, San Mateo.
75. Interview with Ding Yuming, November 9, 2016, San Mateo.
76. Tseu Mei Yuin, "The Broken Engagement," *The McTyeirean* (1921): 77–81.
77. Rosalyn Koo (1947) in "Telling Women's Lives."
78. Jean Koo Lea (1929) in "Telling Women's Lives."
79. Cecilia Zung (1920) in "Telling Women's Lives."
80. Amy Siao Yen (1928) in "Telling Women's Lives."
81. Jin Feng, *The Making of a Family Saga: Ginling College* (Albany, NY: SUNY Press, 2009), 8.
82. Jannette Elwood and Caroline Gipps, *Review of Recent Research on the Achievement of Girls in Single-Sex Schools* (London: University of London Institute of Education, 1999), 37–40.
83. Kuan Yu Chen (1936) in "Telling Women's Lives."
84. Anita Li Chun (1943) in "Telling Women's Lives."
85. Rosita Li Wang (1946) in "Telling Women's Lives."
86. Mae Yih (1946) in "Telling Women's Lives."
87. Zhang Luoluo (1947) in "Telling Women's Lives."
88. Rosalyn Koo (1947) in "Telling Women's Lives."
89. Interview with Rosalyn Koo, November 6, 2011, San Mateo.
90. Rosalyn Koo (1947) in "Telling Women's Lives."
91. Xue Zheng in "Telling Women's Lives."
92. A rather tongue-in-cheek article appeared in the Shanghai tabloid periodical *Haijing* 海晶 in 1946 which described the historical play by Guo Moruo, *The Peacock's Gallbladder*, put on by seniors at McTyeire as a chance for male visitors to see inside this "aristocratic school for girls," which was usually barred to them. "Zhongxi nüxiao biaoyan kongque dan quwen," *Haijing*, no. 20 (1946): 7.
93. Interview with Dong Yue, November 26, 2016, Beijing.
94. Mae Yih (1946) in "Telling Women's Lives."
95. Jiang Jin, *Women Playing Men: Yue Opera and Social Change in Twentieth-Century Shanghai* (Seattle: University of Washington Press, 2009), 81, 255.
96. Interview with Xu Meizhen, March 17, 2016, Shanghai.
97. Helen Lefkowitz Horowitz, *Alma Mater: Design and Experience in the Women's Colleges from Their Nineteenth-Century Beginnings to the 1930s* (New York: Knopf, 1984), 163.
98. Republican writer Xie Bingying 謝冰瑩 (1906–2000), also styling herself a "tomboy," recalled how she and a classmate who had an unrequited love for her were teased by their dormitory mates by being forced to share a dormitory bed for the night. Xie Bingying, *Autobiography of a Chinese Girl: A Genuine Autobiography by Hsieh Ping-Ying*, trans. Tsui Chi (London: Allen and Unwin, 1943), 76.

99. Tze-lan D. Sang, *The Emerging Lesbian: Female Same-Sex Desire in Modern China* (Chicago: University of Chicago Press, 2003), 121.
100. Interview with Theresa Chen, November 10, 2016, San Mateo.
101. Interview with Rosalyn Koo, November 5, 2016, San Mateo.
102. Gillian Avery, *The Best Type of Girl: A History of Girls' Independent Schools* (London: Deutsch, 1991), 304.
103. Lefkowitz Horowitz, *Alma Mater*, 106.
104. Lefkowitz Horowitz, *Alma Mater*, 68.
105. Lefkowitz Horowitz, *Alma Mater*, 190.
106. Hunter, *The Gospel of Gentility*, 62–70.
107. "Answers to Probable Proposals," *The McTyeirean* (1921): 11.
108. Sang, *The Emerging Lesbian*, 136.
109. Tuh Wei Tsong, "The Two Wills," *The McTyeirean* (1930): 184.
110. Tsong, "The Two Wills," 185–186.
111. Barbara Solomon, *In the Company of Educated Women: A History of Women and Higher Education in America* (New Haven, CT: Yale University Press, 1985), 115.
112. Ling Van Chang Tang in "Telling Women's Lives."
113. Chang Liu, "Searching for a New Lifestyle: Single Women in Shanghai, 1915–1949" (PhD Diss., King's College London), 2018.
114. Interview with Rosalyn Koo, November 6, 2011, San Mateo.
115. Lu Xun, "What Happens after Nora Leaves Home?" Originally given as a talk at Beijing Women's Normal College on December 26, 1923, in *Women in Republican China: A Sourcebook*, ed. Hua Lan and Vanessa Fong (New York: M. E. Sharpe, 1999), 176–181.
116. "Alumnae Directory," *The McTyeirean* (1930): 167.
117. Kuan Yu Chen in "Telling Women's Lives."
118. Dou Xueqian, "Zhongguo funü de diwei jiaoyu yu zhiye," cited in Zhao Ma, *Runaway Wives: Urban Crimes and Survival Tactics in Wartime Beijing, 1937–1949* (Cambridge, MA: Harvard University Press, 2015), 52.
119. Joseph Esherick, "War and Revolution: Chinese Society during the 1940s," *Twentieth Century China* 27, no. 1 (November, 2001): 22.

Chapter 4

1. Tsang Sieu-ai, "The Centre of a Tornado," *The Phoenix* (1938): unpaginated.
2. Diana Lary, "War and Remembering: Memories of China at War," in *Beyond Suffering: Recounting War in Modern China*, ed. James Flath and Norman Smith (Vancouver: UBC Press, 2011), 282.
3. Susan Glosser, "Women's Culture of Resistance: An Ordinary Response to Extraordinary Circumstances," in *In the Shadow of the Rising Sun: Shanghai under Japanese Occupation*, ed. Christian Henriot and Wen-Hsin Yeh (Cambridge: Cambridge University Press, 2004), 303. See also Harriet Zurndorfer, "Wartime Refuge Relief in Chinese Cities and Women's Political Activism," in

New Narratives of Urban Space in Republican Chinese Cities, ed. B. So and M. Zelin (Leiden: Brill, 2013), 65–91; Danke Li, *Echoes of Chongqing: Women in Wartime China* (Urbana: University of Illinois Press, 2010); and Chen Yan, *Xingbie yu zhanzheng, Shanghai 1932–1945* (Beijing: Shehui kexue wenxian chubanshe, 2014).

4. Harriet Zurndorfer, "War and the Silent Women: the Retrieval of Chinese and European Jewish Women's Narratives of World War II," *Research on Women in Chinese History*, 17 (December, 2009): 107–115.
5. Jessie G. Lutz, "Comments," in *Nationalist China During the Sino-Japanese War, 1937–1945*, ed. Paul K. T. Sih (New York: Exposition Press, 1977), 130. For studies of relocated higher education institutions, see John Israel, *Lianda: A Chinese University in War and Revolution* (Stanford: Stanford University Press, 1998). On students in occupied North and East China, see Keith Schoppa, *In a Sea of Bitterness: Refugees during the Sino-Japanese War* (Cambridge, MA: Harvard University Press, 2011), 189–213; and Marjorie Dryburgh, "Re-Centring Education in Manshūkoku (1931–1945): School and Family in Chinese Oral History," *Japan Forum* 34, no. 2 (November 2019): 248–272.
6. Jennifer Liu, "Defiant Retreat: The Relocation of Middle Schools to China's Interior, 1937–1945," *Frontiers of History in China* 8, no. 4 (December 2013): 560.
7. Jesse Gregory Lutz, *China and the Christian Colleges, 1850–1950* (Ithaca, NY: Cornell University Press, 1971), 363.
8. Hongdao nüzhong xiaoyouhui bianjizu (ed.), *Hongdao nüzhong jinian kan* (Hangzhou, 2008), 4.
9. Hongdao nüzhong xiaoyouhui bianjizu, *Hongdao nüzhong jinian kan*, 4.
10. PHS RG 82-5811, Esther M. Gauss, Personal Report, 1938–1939.
11. PHS RG 82-59-13, Esther M. Gauss, Personal Report, 1939–1940.
12. Li, *Echoes of Chongqing*.
13. Schoppa, *In a Sea of Bitterness*, 189–213.
14. PHS RG 82-58-11, Esther M. Gauss, Personal Report, 1938–1939.
15. Schoppa, *In a Sea of Bitterness*, 213.
16. PHS RG 82-58-11, Esther M. Gauss, Personal Report, 1938–1939.
17. SOAS MMS – FBN7 – Women's Work – Correspondence – China – 1933–1945, Doris Coombs to MMS secretary, May 12, 1939.
18. PHS RG 82-59-13, Esther M. Gauss, Personal Report, 1939–1940.
19. Li, *Echoes of Chongqing*, 18; Helena Lopes, "Wartime Education at the Crossroads of Empires: The Relocation of Schools to Macau during the Second World War, 1937–1945," *Twentieth Century China* 46, no. 2 (April, 2021): 130–152.
20. Later known as the Cishu Building 慈淑大樓 and today as the Donghai Building 東海大樓 on 353 Nanjing Road. See Xu Yongchu and Chen Jinyu (eds.), *Shengmaliya nüxiao* [St. Mary's School for Girls, 1881–1952] (Shanghai: Tongji daxue chubanshe, 2014), 47.
21. Xu and Chen, *Shengmaliya nüxiao*, 47.
22. Today Huashan Road 華山路. This school had been formerly occupied by the Japanese to conduct a primary school, but with the intervention of Xue Zheng, the primary school agreed to move out to make way for McTyeire. See Chen Jinyu (ed.), *Zhongxi nüzhong, 1892–1952* (Shanghai: Tongji daxue chubanshe, 2016), 48.

23. Yau Ding-Vi, "Disappointments," *The Phoenix* (1938)..
24. Interview with Xu Meizhen, March 17, 2016, Shanghai.
25. To avoid being labeled a collaborator, Xue Zheng was at pains to highlight in her memoir how she was only persuaded to attend an educational advisory board when invited by the collaborationist government when she realized that food supply for teachers would be discussed. See Xue Zheng, "Wo suo zhidao de Zhongxi nüzhong," in *Jiefang qian Shanghai de xuexiao, Shanghai wenshi ziliao xuanji di wushijiu ji*, bian. Wenshi ziliao gongzuo weiyuanhui (Shanghai: Shanghai renmin chubanshe, 1988), 321.
26. Kuan Yu Chen in "Telling Women's Lives."
27. Voices of McTyeire at War, Recovery, and Transformation, 1937–1949, in "Telling Women's Lives."
28. For more on Pan-Asianism and the Co-Prosperity Sphere, see Erri Hotta, *Pan-Asianism and Japan's War 1931–1945* (New York: Palgrave Macmillan, 2007), 205.
29. Chen, *Zhongxi nüzhong*, 49.
30. Xiaoyan Liu, *The Changing Face of Women's Education in China: A Critical History of St. Mary's Hall, McTyeire School and Shanghai No. 3. Girls' Middle School* (Zürich: Lit Verlag, 2017), 113.
31. Interview with Hong Lüming, April 1, 2016, Shanghai.
32. Joint recollections at the fiftieth anniversary reunion of the class of 1947, in "Telling Women's Lives."
33. Interview with Xu Meizhen, March 17, 2016, Shanghai.
34. Interview with Xu Meizhen, March 17, 2016, Shanghai.
35. Interview with Xu Meizhen, March 17, 2016, Shanghai.
36. Rosalyn Koo in "Telling Women's Lives."
37. Interview with Rosalyn Koo, November 5, 2016, San Mateo.
38. Interview with Yang Zhiling, July 20, 2016, Beijing.
39. Glosser, "Women's Culture of Resistance," 311.
40. Fredrick Wakeman, Jr., "Shanghai Smuggling," in *In the Shadow of the Rising Sun, Shanghai under Japanese Occupation*, ed., Christian Henriot and Wen-Hsin Yeh (Cambridge: Cambridge University Press, 2004), 123.
41. Interview with Yu Huigeng, June 16, 2016, Beijing.
42. Tsu Foh-Pau, "Difficult Conditions," *The Phoenix* (1941).
43. Interview with Xiao Jiaxun, March 16, 2016, Shanghai.
44. Li, *Echoes of Chongqing*.
45. Isabella Jackson, *Shaping Modern Shanghai: Colonialism in China's Global City* (Cambridge: Cambridge University Press, 2017), 1.
46. Tsang Vung-Chung, "A Dangerous Outing," *The Phoenix* (1938).
47. There are some inconsistencies in her story, which starts with the author and her brother setting off to buy food but ends with both of their "dresses" getting wet through, which would suggest a female companion. This may, however, be due to the student's level of English.
48. Interview with Theresa Chen, November 10, 2016, San Mateo.
49. Interview with Rosalyn Koo, November 5, 2016, San Mateo.

50. Interview with Lucy Hong and Cao Shengjie, October 22, 2016, Shanghai.
51. Interview with Zhu Lizhong, November 11, 2016, Los Altos.
52. Personal email from Zhu Lizhong to Jennifer Bond, May 21, 2018.
53. Interview with Yang Zhiling, July 20, 2016, Beijing.
54. Interview with Ying Manrong, July 2, 2016, Beijing.
55. Iris Chang, *The Rape of Nanking: The Forgotten Holocaust of WWII* (New York: Basic Books, 1997); Timothy Brook, *Documents on the Rape of Nanking* (Ann Abor: University of Michigan Press, 1999); Joshua A. Fogel (ed.), *The Nanjing Massacre in History and Historiography* (Berkeley: University of California Press, 2000). For literature on comfort women, see Yoshimi Yokshiaki, *Comfort Women: Sexual Slavery in the Japanese Military during World War Two* (London: Routledge, 2000); George Hicks, *The Comfort Women: Sex Slaves of the Japanese Imperial Forces* (London: Allen and Unwin, 1995); and Qiu Peipei, *Chinese Comfort Women: Testimonies from Imperial Japan's Sex-Slaves* (Vancouver: UBC Press, 2013).
56. Julia Tsai Li in "Telling Women's Lives."
57. Wakeman, "Shanghai Smuggling," 116.
58. Sung Sing Ling, "Oh! The Bus! Oh! The tram!" *The Phoenix* (1938).
59. Zia Ung-sing, "Why I Like Day School," *The Phoenix* (1938).
60. Diana Lary, *The Chinese People at War: Human Suffering and Social Transformation, 1937-1945* (Cambridge: Cambridge University Press, 2010).
61. Hans Van de Ven, *China at War: Triumph and Tragedy in the Emergence of the New China* (London: Profile Books, 2017), 107.
62. According to Diana Lary, 800,000 people were killed outright and four million people became refugees as a result of the flood. Diana Lary, "Drowned Earth: The Strategic Breaching of the Yellow River Dyke, 1938," *War in History* 8, no. 2 (April 2001): 191–207.
63. Lopes, "Wartime Education at the Crossroads of Empires."
64. Li Me-Chung, "The Piteous Sight I Witnessed," *The Phoenix* (1938).
65. Tseu We-Kyoen, "Out in the Rain," *The Phoenix* (1938).
66. Louise Edwards, *Woman Warriors and Wartime Spies of China* (Cambridge: Cambridge University Press, 2016), 66–90.
67. Helen Schneider, "Mobilising Women: The Women's Advisory Council, Resistance, and Reconstruction during China's War with Japan," *European Journal of East Asian Studies* 11, no. 2 (December 2012): 218.
68. Li, *Echoes of Chongqing*, 42–43.
69. Number Two Historical Archives, Nanjing, 668-12, "Jinling nüzi wenli xueyuan renshou xiangcun fuwuchu gongzuo jihua ji huodong xiangxi qingxing baogaoshu" (1941.1–1943.9).
70. Helen Schneider, *Keeping the Nation's House: Domestic Management and the Making of Modern China* (Vancouver: UBC Press, 2011), 148–168.
71. Vivienne Guo, "Forging a Women's United Front: Chinese Elite Women's Networks for National Salvation and Resistance, 1932–1938," *Modern Asian Studies* 53, no. 2 (March 2019).

72. Number Two Historical Archives, Nanjing, 668-12, "Jinling nüzi wenli xueyuan renshou xiangcun fuwuchu gongzuo jihua ji huodong xiangxi qingxing baogaoshu" (1941.1–1943.9).
73. Loh Oen-vung, "What We Did for the Refugees," *The Phoenix* (1939): 39–40.
74. Loo Kyuan-Faung, "A Day's Work in the Red Cross Society," *The Phoenix* (1938).
75. Loh Oen-vung, "Correspondence," *The Phoenix* (1940): 106.
76. Jin Feng, *The Making of a Family Saga*, 215.
77. SOAS CBMS-385, Winifred Galbraith to National Committee of the Y.W.C.A. of China, March 1, 1945.
78. Number 2 Historical Archives, Nanjing, 668-117, "Jinling nüzi wenli xueyuan sushe qingkuang baogao" (1939).
79. Jean F. Craig in "Telling Women's Lives."
80. Toby Lincoln, "The Rural and Urban at War: Invasion and Reconstruction in China during the Anti-Japanese War of Resistance," *Journal of Urban History* 38, no. 1 (January 2012): 115.
81. Wu Vong Ching, "Beware! Are You Properly Groomed?" *The McTyeirean* (1940): 27; Chen Ping Tsung, "Types of People that Bore Me," *The McTyeirean* (1940): 14–15; Kiang Ye, "My Lady's Wardrobe," *The McTyeirean* (1940): 23–24.
82. Aaron William Moore, "Growing Up in Nationalist China: Self-Representation in the Personal Documents of Children and Youth 1927–1949," *Modern China* 42, no. 1 (January 2016): 95.
83. Nying Hsueh, "Class History 1945," *The McTyeirean 1942–1946* (1946).
84. Chang Ching Yu, "Class History," *The McTyeirean 1942–1946* (1946).
85. After the Japanese entered into the international settlement and requisitioned their school, McTyeire ceased publication of its yearbook from 1942 to 1945. In 1946 a retrospective volume was published to cover these years. St. Mary's also halted the publication of its yearbook after 1941.
86. Kuan Yu Chen in "Telling Women's Lives."
87. Kuan Yu Chen in "Telling Women's Lives."
88. Ling Kuo-fen, "A Helping Hand," *The Phoenix* (1939): 37–38.
89. Emily Honig, "Christianity, Feminism and Communism: The Life and Times of Deng Yuzhi," in *Christianity in China from the Eighteenth Century to the Present*, ed. Daniel D. Bays (Stanford: Stanford University Press, 1996), 243–262.
90. Interview with Lucy Hong and Cao Shengjie, October 22, 2016, Shanghai.
91. From 1937 to 1940, CCP membership grew from 40,000 to 800,000, many of whom were urban youths. Van de Ven, *China at War*, 146–149.
92. Interview with Ellen Cao, Beijing, November 25, 2016.
93. Interview with Ellen Cao, Beijing, November 25, 2016.
94. Interview with Ellen Cao, Beijing, November 25, 2016.
95. Interview with Ellen Cao, Beijing, November 25, 2016.
96. *The McTyeirean* (1939).
97. Interview with Ellen Cao, Beijing, November 25, 2016.
98. Lucien Bianco, *Origins of the Chinese Revolution, 1915–1949* (Stanford: Stanford University Press, 1971).

99. Interview with Rosalyn Koo, November 5, 2016, San Mateo.

Chapter 5

1. Interview with Ying Manrong, July 2, 2016, Beijing.
2. Jessie Gregory Lutz, "The Chinese Student Movement of 1945–1949," *Journal of Asian Studies* 31, no. 1 (November 1971): 96–97.
3. "Some Co.eds' Views," *The China Press*, January 5, 1947, 11.
4. "St. John's Co.eds' Scorned," *The China Press*, January 7, 1947, 11.
5. Scholars including Gail Hershatter have shown how traditional tropes of female virtue persisted well into the 1950s, often perpetuated by female cadres themselves, profoundly affecting the life choices of women. Gail Hershatter, *The Gender of Memory: Rural Women and China's Collective Past* (Berkeley: University of California Press, 2011), 120.
6. Chen Jinyu, *Zhongxi nüzhong* [McTyeire School 1892–1952] (Shanghai: Tongji daxue chubanshe, 2016), 52.
7. Chen Jinyu, *Zhongxi nüzhong*, 52.
8. Chu Yee-yun, "Class History," *The McTyeirean* (1947).
9. Jeffrey N. Wasserstrom, *Student Protests in Twentieth-Century China: The View from Shanghai* (Stanford, CA: Stanford University Press, 1991).
10. Interview with Zhu Lizhong, November 11, 2016, Los Altos.
11. Interview with Ying Manrong, July 2, 2016, Beijing.
12. Louise Edwards, *Woman Warriors and Wartime Spies of China* (Cambridge: Cambridge University Press, 2016), 137–157; Stephanie Hemelryk Donald, "Tang Wei: Sex, the City and the Scapegoat in Lust, Caution," *Theory, Culture and Society* 27, no. 4 (August 2010): 46–68.
13. Qiu Peipei, *Chinese Comfort Women: Testimonies from Imperial Japan's Sex-Slaves* (Vancouver: UBC Press, 2013), 130.
14. Hans Van de Ven, *China at War: Triumph and Tragedy in the Emergence of the New China* (London: Profile Books, 2017), 166.
15. Catherine R. Schenk, "Another Asian Financial Crisis: Monetary Links between Hong Kong and China 1945–50," *Modern Asian Studies* 34, no. 3 (July 2000): 746–747.
16. Wang Shaolan, "Xiangyata li de liang shan chuang," in *Huiyi Zhongxi nüzhong 1949–1952*, ed. Chen Jinyu (Shanghai: Tongji daxue chubanshe, 2016), 22.
17. Wu Li-chun, "My McTyeire Years 70 Years Ago," Speech delivered at McTyeire Alumnae Association Reunion, San Mateo, November 4, 2017.
18. Interview with Rosalyn Koo, November 5, 2017, San Mateo.
19. Qu Mingming, "Zhongxi nüzhong shi wo nanwang de jia," in *Huiyi Zhongxi nüzhong 1949–1952*, ed. Chen Jinyu (Shanghai: Tongji daxue chubanshe, 2016), 39.
20. Chen Jinyu, *Zhongxi nüzhong*, 60.
21. Qu Mingming, "Zhongxi nüzhong shi wo nanwang de jia," 39.

22. See Emily Honig, "Christianity, Feminism and Communism: The Life and Times of Deng Yuzhi," in *Christianity in China from the Eighteenth Century to the Present*, ed. Daniel D. Bays, 243–262 (Stanford: Stanford University Press, 1996).
23. This was also the way in which the Three-Self Patriotic Movement (Sanzi aiguo yundong 三自愛國運動) made Christianity and Communism ideologically compatible and indeed mutually constructive after 1949, and again post-cultural revolution. See Cao Shengjie, "Huigu wo guo jidujiao funü shi gong chuantong," in *Jingyu zhong de sicao—Cao Shengjie wenji*, ed. Chen Yilin (Shanghai: Zhongguo jidujiao xiehui, 2006), 190–196.
24. Interview with Chen Tianmi, May 17, 2016, Beijing.
25. Qu Mingming, "Zhongxi nüzhong aiguo xuesheng yundong de huigu," in *Bainian nüzhong—xian gei yibaiyishi zhounian xiao qing*, ed. He Yanan (Shanghai: Shanghai shi di san nüzi zhongxue, 2002), 122.
26. Qu Mingming, "Zhongxi nüzhong aiguo xuesheng yundong de huigu," 122.
27. Voices of McTyeire at War, Recovery and Transformation, 1937–1949, in "Telling Women's Lives."
28. Interview with Chen Tianmi, May 17, 2016, Beijing.
29. Chen, *Zhongxi nüzhong*, 59.
30. Interview with Chen Tianmi, May 17, 2016, Beijing, 2:36:50–2:39:00. "Flowers in May" (Wuyue de xianhua 五月的鮮花) was originally a poem by Guan Weiran 光未然 commemorating the sacrifices of the May Fourth Student movement published in 1935. The composer Yan Shushi 閻述詩 was moved by the poem and set it to music. The song became popular among students during the Second Sino-Japanese War and Civil War.
31. Kuan Yu Chen in "Telling Women's Lives."
32. After 1949 Rosalyn decided to stay in the United States. Her rebellious activities did not come to an end, however. She dropped out of Mills after two years and married a man she knew her parents would object to in the United States without informing them. She later pursued a successful career at an architecture firm. Interview with Rosalyn Koo, November 5, 2016, San Mateo.
33. Rosalyn Koo in "Telling Women's Lives."
34. Qu, "Zhongxi nüzhong shi wo nanwang de jia," 40.
35. Interview with Dong Yue, November 21, 2016.
36. Ruth Harris in *Journeys that Opened Up the World: Women, Student Christian Movements and Social Justice, 1955–1975*, ed. Sara M. Evans (New Brunswick, NJ: Rutgers University Press, 2003), 23.
37. Qu, "Zhongxi nüzhong shi wo nanwang de jia," 40–41.
38. Interview with Tao Xiafang, August 2, 2018, Shanghai.
39. Jean Craig in "Telling Women's Lives."
40. Jean Craig in "Telling Women's Lives."
41. SOAS MMS – 1218 – Special Series – Notes and Transcripts, NT56-56, Doris Coombs, "Recollections of Ningpo under the Communists (1949–1950)."
42. Ruth Harris in Evans (ed.), *Journeys that Opened Up the World*, 24.
43. Interview with McTyeire alumna, December 2016, Shanghai.
44. SOAS MMS – 1326 – Women's Work Ningbo, 1946–1951, Doris Coombs to Mrs. Ladlay, May 25, 1950.

45. SOAS MMS – 1218 – Special Series – Notes and Transcripts. NT56-56, Doris Coombs, "Recollections of Ningpo under the Communists (1949–1950)."
46. Ruth Harris in Evans (ed.), *Journeys that Opened Up the World*, 24.
47. Chen, *Zhongxi nüzhong*, 64.
48. Sherman Cochran, "Capitalists Choosing Communist China: The Liu Family of Shanghai," in *The Dilemmas of Victory: The Early Years of the People's Republic of China*, ed. Jeremy Brown and Paul G. Pickowitz (Cambridge, MA: Harvard University Press, 2007), 359–385.
49. For more on the decisions made by individuals on whether to stay in or leave Communist China in 1949, see Joseph Esherick, "The Ye Family in New China," in *The Dilemmas of Victory: The Early Years of the People's Republic of China*, ed. Jeremy Brown and Paul G. Pickowitz (Cambridge, MA: Harvard University Press, 2007), 311–336.
50. NCA, 旧 10-1-50, *Yongjiang nüzhong guanyu Shen Yixiang jiaoyu sixiang de pipan daimei aiguo dahui jilu deng wenjian*, May 27, 1952.
51. Yu Huigeng, cited in Xu and Chen (eds.), *Shengmaliya nüxiao 1881–1952*, 59.
52. St. Mary's Reunion, June 16, 2016, Beijing.
53. Interview with Yu Huigeng, June 16, 2016, Beijing.
54. Jeremy Brown and Paul G. Pickowitz, "The Early Years of the People's Republic of China: An Introduction," in *The Dilemmas of Victory: The Early Years of the People's Republic of China*, ed. Jeremy Brown and Paul G. Pickowitz (Cambridge, MA: Harvard University Press, 2007), 10.
55. Cochran, "Capitalists Choosing Communist China," 359–385.
56. Interview with Tao Shuyu, August 2, 2018, Shanghai.
57. Although a National Christian Council had been formed as early as 1922, it was not until 1930 that several missions joined together to form the Church of Christ in China. Despite these precursors of an ecumenical Chinese-led Church, the influence of denominations remained strong throughout the Republican period and they continued to receive funding and staff from foreign missions. Winifred Galbraith, *New Life in China: The Growth of the Church in the Wartime* (London: Edinburgh House Press, 1941), 7.
58. Interview with Cao Shengjie, December 12, 2016, Shanghai.
59. Honig, "Christianity, Feminism, Communism," 257.
60. SOAS MMS – 1218 – Special Series – Notes and Transcripts. NT56-56, Doris Coombs, "Recollections of Ningpo under the Communists (1949–1950)."
61. Harris in Evans (ed.), *Journeys That Opened Up the World*, 25.
62. Harris in Evans (ed.), *Journeys That Opened Up the World*, 25.
63. SOAS MMS – 1326 – Woman's Work Ningbo – 1946–1950, Doris Coombs to Mrs. Ladlay, March 15, 1950.
64. Lucy Hong, who worked for the YWCA before and after the Cultural Revolution, thought that the CCP borrowed from the organizational structures of the YWCA. Interview with Lucy Hong, December 3, 2015, Shanghai.
65. Chen, *Zhongxi nüzhong*, 69.
66. Interview with Zhang Luoluo, November 8, 2016, San Mateo.
67. SOAS MMS – 1218 – Special Series – Notes and Transcripts. NT56-56, Doris Coombs, "Recollections of Ningpo under the Communists (1949–1950)."

68. Interview with St. Mary's alumna, November 2016, Beijing.
69. Interview with Chen Tianmi, May 17, 2016, Beijing.
70. Xue Zheng in "Telling Women's Lives."
71. SOAS MMS – 1218 – Special Series – Notes and Transcripts. NT56-56, Doris Coombs, "Recollections of Ningpo under the Communists (1949–1950)."
72. SOAS MMS – 1218 – Special Series – Notes and Transcripts. NT56-56, Doris Coombs, "Recollections of Ningpo under the Communists (1949–1950)."
73. For more on the influence of music in modern Chinese political history, see Laikwan Pang, Paul Clark, and Tsan-Huang Tsai (eds.), *Listening to China's Cultural Revolution: Music, Politics, and Cultural Continuities* (Basingstoke: Palgrave, 2016). See also Andrew Jones, *Like a Knife: Ideology and Genre in Contemporary Chinese Popular Music* (Ithaca: Cornell University Press, 1992).
74. SOAS MMS – 1326 –Women's work Ningbo – 1946-1950, Doris Coombs to Mrs. Ladlay, August 30, 1949.
75. Kuan Yu Chen in "Telling Women's Lives."
76. Chen, *Zhongxi nüzhong*, 67.
77. Kuan Yu Chen in "Telling Women's Lives."
78. Joint recollections at the fiftieth anniversary reunion of the class of 1947, in "Telling Women's Lives."
79. Chen, *Zhongxi nüzhong*, 67.
80. Interview with McTyeire alumna, May 2016, Beijing.
81. Louise Edwards, *Woman Warriors*, 12–14.
82. On December 29, 1950, the People's Government issued an order regarding the "Resolution on the policy of how to deal with cultural education organisations and religious groups which are subsidised by America," cited in Cheng, *Zhongxi nüzhong*, 70.
83. Ruth Harris in Evans (ed.), *Journeys That Opened Up the World*, 26.
84. SOAS MMS – 1218 – Special Series – Notes and Transcripts. NT56-56, Doris Coombs, "Recollections of Ningpo under the Communists (1949–1950)."
85. Interview with McTyeire alumna, December 2016, Shanghai.
86. Chen, *Zhongxi nüzhong*, 70.

Chapter 6

1. Chen Jinyu, *Zhongxi nüzhong* 中西女中 [McTyeire School 1892–1952] (Shanghai: Tongji daxue chubanshe, 2016), 70.
2. Interview with Zhang Luoluo, November 6, 2017, San Mateo. By then Zhang Luoluo had changed her name to Zhang Chuanling 張傳玲.
3. Indeed, the classes of 1951 and 1952 were so keen to retain their identities as McTyeire students, that they retrospectively published their own yearbooks to celebrate the achievements of their classmates and keep in touch with each other.
4. Interview with Rosalyn Koo, November 5, 2016, San Mateo.
5. Interview with Rosalyn Koo, November 5, 2017, San Mateo.

6. NCA 旧10-1-50, *Yongjiang nüzhong guanyu Shen Yixiang jiaoyu sixiang de pipan daimei aiguo dahui jilu deng wenjian* [National Assembly records and documents regarding the criticism of the pro-American educational thinking of Yongjiang Female Middle School's Shen Yixiang], May 27, 1952.
7. Jean Craig in "Telling Women's Lives."
8. Focus group with St. Mary's alumnae, May 11, 2016, Beijing.
9. Interview with Cao Shengjie, October 22, 2016, Shanghai.
10. Interview with Ying Manrong, July 2, 2016, Beijing.
11. Wu Yiyun, "Yi ben cidian beihou de gushi—caifang Shengmaliya nüzhong 1945 jie xiaoyou Ying Manrong" [The story behind a dictionary—An interview with St. Mary's alumnae from the class of 1945, Ying Manrong], in *Zhuixun Shengmaliya xiaoyou zuji*, ed. Chen Jinyu and Xu Yongchu (Shanghai: Tongji daxue chubanshe), 93–96.
12. Today this institute has become the Comparative and International Education Research Institute at Beijing Normal University (Guoji yu bijiao jiaoyu yanjiuyuan 国际与比较教育研究院).
13. Yang Zhiling "Shengmaliya nüxiao, wo xin zhong de fengbei" [St. Mary's School for Girls, a monument in my heart], in *Huiyi Shengmaliya nüxiao*, ed. Xu Yongchun and Chen Jinyu (Shanghai: Tongji daxue chubanshe 2014), 137.
14. Interview with Yang Zhiling, July 20, 2016, Beijing.
15. Interview with Zhao Fengfeng, June 14, 2016, Beijing.
16. Zhao Fengfeng, "In Memory of the American Woman Writer, Anna Louise Strong," *Women of China* 2 (1980): 36–38.
17. Interview with Wu Qihui, June 15, 2016, Beijing.
18. Interview with Yang Zhiling, July 20, 2016, Beijing.
19. Yao Nianyuan 姚念媛, who worked for the British petroleum company Shell, was imprisoned for seven years during the Cultural Revolution. In her autobiography, *Life and Death in Shanghai*, she remembers that the idea of a divine creator helped her to mentally endure her ordeal, which involved physical torture. Nien Cheng, *Life and Death in Shanghai* (London: Flamingo, 1987), 131
20. Interview with Theresa Chen, November 10, 2016, San Mateo, California, USA.
21. Shen Yifan, *Jiangtai shifeng—Shen Yifan zhujiao wenji*, Vol. 1 (Shanghai: Zhongguo jidujiao liang hui chuban, 2015).
22. Interview with Lucy Hong, December 7, 2015, Shanghai.
23. Luo Weihong, *Cao Shengjie koushu lishi* (Shanghai: Shanghai shudian chubanshe, 2017).
24. Interview with Cao Shengjie, October 22, 2016, Shanghai.
25. Interview with Rosalyn Koo, November 5, 2017, San Mateo.
26. The project sponsored by Rosalyn in Shaanxi ran from 2010–2019, sponsoring 1000 girls through elementary and middle school, 275 of whom went on to high school and 200 to vocational schools. 170 students went on to university and colleges in China. See https://www.1990institute.com/spring-bud. Rosalyn's philanthropic contributions were widely recognized and celebrated. Upon her death in January 2021, her obituary, which appeared in the *New York Times* on March 4, 2021, was syndicated around the world.

27. Interview with Rosalyn Koo, November 5, 2017, San Mateo.
28. Interview with Zhang Luoluo, November 8, 2016, San Mateo.
29. PHS – RG82-70-7, Edith G. Traver, *Five Women of China* (New York, 1942); HCA 旧36-1-12, "Our Principals," in *Hongdao ershi zhou jinian kan* (1932), 2–4; Chen Jinyu, *Zhongxi nüzhong*, 155.
30. In 1948-50 Xue Zheng went to study for her PhD in Education at Columbia University, where she had previously earned her MA degree. Chen Jinyu, *Zhongxi nüzhong*, 155. In 1935–1937, Shen Yixiang was sponsored by the Baptist Mission to pursue MA studies at the Crozer Theological Seminary and University of Pennsylvania, where she took advanced courses in Education. Transcript, Shen I-Hsing, University of Pennsylvania, Graduate School; *University of Pennsylvania One Hundred and Eighty-First Commencement for the Conferring of Degrees*, Municipal Auditorium, Wednesday, June 9, 1937, at 10 o'clock, 19.
31. The first YWCA in China was established in 1890 within an American Southern Presbyterian missionary school for girls in Hangzhou, which later became the Hangzhou Union School for Girls. The foundation of the YWCA followed the visit of an American traveler who spoke about the work of the YWCA in the United States. Burke Library, Union Theological Seminary, Columbia University, MRL12-3-2-7, Tsai Kuei and Lily K. Haass, "A Study of the Young Women's Christian Association of China: 1890–1930." (Shanghai: National Young Women's Christian Association of China, 1930), 23.
32. "What Our Graduates Are Doing," *The McTyeirean* (1925), 119–126.
33. Aihua Zhang, "Chinese Women's New Practicality. Social Service, and Broad Cooperation: A Case Study of YWCA Women in the 1920s and 1930s," in *Christianity and the Modern Woman in East Asia*, ed. Garrett L. Washington (Leiden: Brill, 2018), 44.
34. Interview with Rosalyn Koo, November 5, 2017, San Mateo.
35. Li Tsing Lian, "Our Responsibility," *The McTyeirean* (1921): 121–123.
36. YDS A236.08, Jean Craig, "A Brief History of McTyeire School for Girls, Shanghai, China" (1982), 8.
37. "The Alumnae Scholarship," *The Phoenix* (1932): 92; Chu Yee-yun, "Class History," *The McTyeirean* (1947); MAHC 1459-4-1-24 - Kwe Yuin Kiang, "Annual Report – 1946," Laura Haygood Normal School Suzhou, China.
38. Interview with Sally Chen, November 7, 2017, San Mateo.
39. Jin Xie, *Zuihou de guizu* (Shanghai dianying zhipianchang, 1989).
40. Wang Zheng, *Finding Women in the State: A Socialist Feminist Revolution in the People's Republic of China, 1949–1964* (Berkeley: University of California Press, 2017).
41. Gail Hershatter, *The Gender of Memory: Rural Women and China's Collective Past*. Berkeley: University of California Press, 2011); Wang Zheng, *Finding Women in the State*; Harriet Evans, "Sexed Bodies, Sexualized Identities and the Limits of Gender," *China Information* 22, no. 2 (July 2008): 361–386.
42. Emily Honig, "Socialist Sex: The Cultural Revolution Revisited," *Modern China* 29, no. 2 (April 2003): 153–175; Louise Edwards, *Women Warriors and Wartime Spies of China* (Cambridge: Cambridge University Press, 2016), 205).
43. For more on the "new socialist housewife" and "prettification campaign" toward the end of China's first five-year plan, see Delia Davin, *Woman-Work: Women and the*

Party in Revolutionary China (Oxford: Oxford University Press, 1979), 108–110. For more on the re-entrenchment of domestic roles for women as the reform and opening policies led to urban unemployment in some areas, see Julia F. Andrews and Shen, Kuiyi, "The New Chinese Woman and Lifestyle Magazines in the Late 1990s," in *Popular China: Unofficial Culture in a Globalizing Society*, eds. Perry Link, Richard P. Madsen, and Paul G. Pickowicz (Lanham, MD: Roman and Littlefield, 2002); Wang Zheng, *Finding Women in the State*, 242–264.

44. Interview with Lucy Hong and Cao Shengjie, October 22, 2016, Shanghai.
45. Interview with Lucy Hong and Cao Shengjie, October 22, 2016, Shanghai.
46. Interview with Rosalyn Koo, November 5, 2016, San Mateo.
47. For more on the performance of elite gender identities in contemporary China, see Kailing Xie, *Embodying Middle Class Gender Aspirations: Perspectives from China's Privileged Young Women* (London: Palgrave Macmillan, 2021).
48. In 2021 the Chinese government launched the "double reduction" policy (Shuangjian zhengce 雙減政策), which aims to reduce the amount of homework and tutoring Chinese children are expected to undertake outside of school hours.
49. The exhibition was held at Hoxton Books in London from August 15–21, 2022. It was co-curated by Janny Ye and Carwyn Morris. I interviewed Janny Ye on August 20, 2022, at Hoxton Books, London.
50. The exhibition curators interviewed other overseas Chinese students in London, producing a magazine, *Pomelo*, inspired by *Linglong* in format. The magazine includes excerpts from these interviews alongside images of Janny's clothes juxtaposed with the images from *Linglong* which inspired them. See https://fruitpressed.com/.
51. Mengwei Tu and Kailing Xie, "Privileged Daughters? Gendered Mobility among Highly Educated Chinese Female Migrants in the UK," *Social Inclusion* 8, no. 2 (2020): 68–76.
52. Interview with Janny Ye, August 20, 2022, London.
53. Interview with Rosalyn Koo, November 5, 2016, San Mateo.
54. Shanghai shi di san nüzi chuji zhongxue, Shanghai guanchi wenhua chuanbo youxian gongsi, Chang Lin gongzuoshi lianhe shezhi, "Shanghai shi di san nüzi zhongxue," posted on YouTube, September 28, 2016, accessed July 21, 2020, https://www.youtube.com/watch?v=ZQtBhr6bhyE.
55. The official logo has recently been updated.
56. Zui mei hechangtuan xiangmu zu [Most Beautiful Choir Programme Group], "Zuimei hechangtuan wanwan mei xiangdao! Zhe xie zhiming nüxing dou laizi zheli" [Most Beautiful Choir did not expect that all these famous women were coming!] February 12, 2019, 10:45:50, accessed July 21, 2020, http://www.kankanews.com/a/2019-02-01/0038742347.shtml.
57. Vanessa L. Fong, "China's One Child Policy and the Empowerment of Urban Daughters," *American Anthropologist* 104, no. 4 (December 2002): 1098–1109.
58. Zuimei hechangtuan xiangmu zu, "Zuimei hechangtuan wanwan mei xiangdao! Zhe xie zhiming nüxing dou laizi zheli."
59. NCA 旧 10-1-310.
60. The inscription reads: "Ningbo School for Girls, the predecessor of Yongjiang Girls' High School, founded in 1844, was the first girls' school in China. The building, erected in 1922 and then burned in the wars twice, was rebuilt in 1951. Designated as

a Ningbo cultural relic protection site in 2003, it was renewed with an investment of RMB 15 million yuan in as Ningbo Museum of Education 2013. The tablet was established by Ningbo People's Government in May 2015." "Tablet Inscription for Ningbo Museum of Education" (Ningbo shi jiaoyu bowuguan beiji, 寧波市教育博物碑記), erected by the Ningbo City Government (Ningbo shi renmin zhengfu li 寧波市人民政府立), May 2015.

61. See, for example, Sinan Mansions 思南公館 on South Chongqing Road, Shanghai. This luxury residence of thirty-nine mansions, close to the former residence of Song Qingling, all imitate the Western style of this Republican-era mansion, originally built in the 1920s.
62. Arif Dirlik, "Architectures of Global Modernity, Colonialism and Places," *Modern Chinese Literature and Culture* 17, no. 1 (Spring 2005): 38.
63. Dirlik, "Architectures of Global Modernity," 46.
64. As Lu Pan has explored, widespread use of Western architectural styles in Shanghai's urban redevelopment can also be seen as a continuance of a historic artistic competition between Shanghai (*haipai*) and Beijing (*jingpai*) and a nostalgia on the part of local government and city planners for an era when Shanghai was the epicenter of China's economic, cultural, and literary production. Lu Pan, "Nostalgia as Resistance: Memory, Space and the Competing Modernities in Berlin and Shanghai," *European Journal of East Asian Studies* 12, no. 1 (2013): 135–160; Sizheng K. Fan, "Culture for Sale: Western Classical Architecture in China's Recent Building Boom," *Journal of Architectural Education (1984-)* 63, no. 1 (October, 2009): 64–74.
65. Raffles City, Changning (Changning Laifushi Guangchang 長寧來福士廣場) located on 1191 Changning Road, Changning district, Shanghai.
66. "Slumber and Dream: Pott Hall," sign located at former St. Mary's School site, today: Raffles City, Changning (Changning Laifushi Guangchang 長寧來福士廣場) located on 1191 Changning Road, Changning district, Shanghai.
67. Email from George Wu to St. Mary's Alumnae, August 7, 2019.
68. For more on the nationalization of colonial-era architecture in East Asia see Clark Sorensen and Andrea Gevurtz Arai (eds.), *Spaces of Possibility: In, Between, and Beyond Korea and Japan* (Seattle, WA: University of Washington Press, 2016).
69. Interview with Fan Meiling and Xu Zhenzhu, November 28, 2015, Ningbo; Interview with Xu Meizhen and Xiao Jiaxun, April 15, 2016, Shanghai.
70. Email from George Wu to St. Mary's Alumnae, August 7, 2019.

Bibliography

Archival Collections

American Baptist Historical Society (ABHS) Archives, Mercier University, Atlanta, USA:
253-3-4. Ellen J. Peterson to Miss McVeigh, November 13, 1925.
262-3-8; 306-1-3; 306-1-4; 352-1-3. Correspondence of Florence Webster (Microfilm).
264-5-6 and 307-3-6. Correspondence of Dora Zimmerman (Microfilm).
BMI – Pre WW2- G1-75-9. Florence Webster to Mabel Rae McVeigh, Mokanshan, July 12, 1925.

Burke Theological Seminary Archives, New York, USA:
MRL12-3-2-7. Tsai Kuei and Lily K. Haass, *A Study of the Young Women's Christian Association of China, 1890–1930* (National Young Women's Christian Association of China: Shanghai, 1930).

Church Missionary Society (CMS) Archives, Cadbury Research Library, University of Birmingham, UK:
CMS CCH 056/12. Laurence to Mr. Fenn, December 21, 1875.
CMS CCH 056/14. Laurence to Mr. Fenn, December 1877.
CMS CCH 056/1. Laurence to Mr. Wright, May 17, 1878.
CMS G1 AL 1917-34 WJ- 2. Wolfe to CMS Secretary, November 22, 1918.
CMS G1 CH/O 1883/ 164. Laurence to Mr. Fenn, May 30, 1883.
CMS G1 CH2/O 1886/ 39. Laurence to Mr. Fenn, February 9, 1886.
CMS G1/CH2 /O /1908/198. Barnes to Mr. Baring-Gould, November 30, 1908.

Crozner Theological Seminary Archives, The University of Pennsylvania, USA:
UPB 4.6: Graduate School of Education Student Transcripts, box 36, folder 7.

Hangzhou City Archives (HCA), Hangzhou, China:
旧36-1-12. *Hongdao ershi zhou jinian kan* 弘道二十週紀念刊 [Hangzhou Union Girls' School Twentieth Anniversary publication] (1932).

Methodist Archives and History Centre (MAHC), General Commission on Archives and History for the United Methodist Church, Drew University, Madison, New Jersey, USA:
1131 - Correspondence of Laura Haygood (Microfilm).
1265-5-1-24; 2193-3-7-101; 2599-4-1-16 - Correspondence of Sallie Lou MacKinnon.
1459-4-1-24, Kwe Yuin Kiang "Annual Report – 1946," Laura Haygood Normal School, Suzhou, China.

School of Oriental and African Studies (SOAS) Archives, University of London, UK:

CBMS-385, Winifred Galbraith to National Committee of the Y.W.C.A. of China, March 1, 1945.
MMS - 1218 - Special Series Notes and Transcripts.
MMS - 1326 - Women's Work Ningbo, 1946–1950.
MMS - FBN7 - Women's work – correspondence – China – 1933–1945.

Ningbo City Archives (NCA), Ningbo, China:

旧10-1-50. *Yongjiang nüzhong guanyu Shen Yixiang jiaoyu sixiang de pipan daimei aiguo dahui jilu deng wenjian* 甬江女中關於沈貽薌教育思想的批判歹美愛國大會記錄等文件 [National Assembly records and documents regarding the criticism of the Pro-American educational thinking of Yongjiang Female Middle School's Shen Yixiang]. May 27, 1952.
旧10-1-207. *Yongjiang sheng* 甬江聲 [Riverside Echo] (1933).
旧10-1-307/308. *Yongjiang nüzi zhongxue xiaodong hui jilu huiji* 甬江女子中學校董會記錄匯集 [Yongjiang Board of Director's Minute Meetings and Principals' Reports].
旧10- 1-401. *Yongjiang xiao kan* 甬江校刊 [Yongjiang School Magazine], 1948.
X.1.1 -1. *Yongjiang sheng* 甬江聲 [Riverside Echo] (1931).

Number Two Historical Archives, Nanjing, China:

668– 12. "Jinling nüzi wenli xueyuan renshou xiangcun fuwuchu gongzuo jihua ji huodong xiangxi qingxing baogao shu" 金陵女子文理學院仁壽鄉村服務處工作計劃及活動詳細情形報告書 [Ginling College work plan and detailed report for rural service work at Renshou village]. January 1941 – September 1943.
668– 117. "Jinling nüzi wenli xueyuan sushe qingkuang baogao" 金陵女子文理學院宿舍情況報告 [Report on the situation in the dormitories at Ginling College] (1939).

Presbyterian Historical Society (PHS) Archives, The National Archives of the Presbyterian Church, Philadelphia, USA:

RG82-4-10. Hangzhou Union Girls' School - Juniata Ricketts, "A Suicide or a Heroine?"
RG82-18-17. Esther M. Gauss to Mr. Speer, February 26, 1920.
RG82-32-10. Esther M. Gauss, letter to friends from Shanghai, May 9, 1927.
RG82-32-10. Esther Gauss to Mission Board, Ningpo, January 21, 1927.
RG82-32-10. F. R. Millican, "Data and Reflections on the Situation in Chekiang Province: Re the Future of Mission Schools," July 27, 1927.
RG82-32-10. F. R. Millican, "Further Reflections on the Educational Situation," August 3, 1927.
RG82-56-19. Esther M. Gauss, personal letter, 1937–1938.
RG82-58-11. Esther M. Gauss, personal report, 1938–1939.
RG82-59-13. Esther M. Gauss, personal report, 1939–1940.
RG82-70-7. Edith G. Traver, *Five Women of China* (New York, 1942).
RG82-360-32-8. Esther Mary Gauss, personnel file.
RG431-2-8. "Hangzhou Christian College: Information and Illustrations," 1918.
RG431-2-13. Hangzhou Union Girls' School principal's report. Sarah Chow, annual report.
MR7-PA-ZCAS. Central China Mission, Presbyterian Church in the U.S.A., annual report, 1926–1927.

NT6.3H793MC. Hangchow Union Girls' School, Hangchow, China, 1912.
NT6-3HI93UP. Hangchow Union Girls' High School, Hangchow, China, principal's report, 1921–1922.
NT6-3HI93UP. Hangchow Union Girls' High School, Hangchow, China, principal's report, May 21, 1924.
NT6.3H193ag. Hangzhou Union Girls' School, announcement, 1925–1926.

Shanghai Municipal Archives (SMA), Shanghai, China:

U121-0-30-1. National Committee, Young Women's Christian Association of China, *Student Handbook: Constitution and Organisation of a Student Y.W.C.A.* (Shanghai, 1924).
U121-0-18. The National Committee, Young Women's Christian Association of China. *The YWCA of China 1933–1947* (Shanghai, 1947).

Shanghai Number Three Girls' School, Shanghai, China:

Box 7. Xueji ka 學籍卡 [student record cards].
Box 7. *St. Mary's Hall Shanghai 50th Anniversary Volume, 1881–1931* (Shanghai, 1931).

Yale Divinity School (YDS) Archives, Yale University, New Haven, Connecticut, USA:

A236.08. Jean Craig, "A Brief History of McTyeire School for Girls, Shanghai, China" (1982).

Speeches

Wu Li-chun, "My McTyeire Years 70 Years Ago." Speech delivered at McTyeire Alumnae Association reunion, San Mateo, California, November 4, 2017.

Email Correspondence

Zhu Lizhong to Jennifer Bond, May 21, 2018.
George Wu to St. Mary's Alumnae, August 7, 2019.

Films and Television Programs

Xie Jin 谢晋. *Zuihou de guizu* 最后的贵族 [The last aristocrats]. Shanghai dianying zhipianchang 上海电影制片厂 [Shanghai Film Studio] (1989).

Books and Articles

Aldersey White, E. *A Woman Pioneer in China: The Life of Mary Ann Aldersey.* London: Livingston Press, 1932.
"Alumnae Directory." *The McTyeirean* (1930): 161–179.
"The Alumnae Scholarship." *The Phoenix* (1932): 92.

Andrews, Julia F., and Shen, Kuiyi. "The New Chinese Woman and Lifestyle Magazines in the Late 1990s." In *Popular China: Unofficial Culture in a Globalizing Society*, ed. Perry Link, Richard P. Madsen, and Paul G. Pickowicz, 242–264. Lanham, MD: Rowman and Littlefield, 2002.

"The Anglo-Chinese School for Girls." *The North China Daily News*, March 18, 1892.

"Answers to Probable Proposals." *The McTyeirean* (1921): 11.

"Appendix I: Table 1: Christian Elementary and Secondary Schools." In *Christian Education in China: The Report of the Educational Commission of 1921–1922*, ed. Chinese Educational Commission, 317. Shanghai: Commercial Press, 1922.

Avery, Gillian. *The Best Type of Girl: A History of Girls' Independent Schools*. London: Deutsch, 1991.

Bailey, Paul John. *Gender and Education in China: Gender Discourses and Women's Schooling in the Early Twentieth Century*. New York: Routledge, 2007.

Bailey, Paul. "'Unharnessed Fillies': Discourse on the 'Modern' Female Student in Early Twentieth-Century China." In *Women and Culture in Modern China 1600–1950*, ed. Luo Liurong and Lü Miao-fen, 327–357. Taipei: Academia Sinica, 2003.

Bays, Daniel H., and Ellen Widmer (eds.). *China's Christian Colleges: Cross Cultural Connections*. Stanford: Stanford University Press, 2009.

"Ben xiao sanshi nian lai renshu bijiao biao" 本校三十年來人數比較表 [Table showing the number of students in this school over the past thirty years]. In *Shengmaliya nüxiao wushi zhounian tekan* 聖瑪利亞女校五十週年特刊 [St. Mary's Girls' School Fiftieth Anniversary Volume] (1931), front matter.

"Ben xiao shi lüe" 本校史略 [A brief history of our school]. *Hongdao ershi zhou jinian kan* 弘道二十週紀念刊 [Twentieth Anniversary Publication, Union Girls' School, Hangzhou] (1932), 101–102.

"Ben xiao xuesheng jiazu zhiye yilan" 本校學生家族職業一覽 [A look at the employment of students' families]. In *Shengmaliya nüxiao wushi zhou jinian tekan* 聖瑪利亞女校五十週紀念特刊 [St. Mary's fiftieth anniversary volume] (1931).

"Ben xiao zhi lüe shi" 本校之略事 [A brief history of our school]. In *Zhejiang Hangzhou shi sili Huixing nüzi chuji zhongxue yilan* 浙江杭州市私立惠興女子初級中學一覽 [Catalogue of the Private Huixing Girls' Junior Middle School in Hangzhou], ed. Huixing nüzi zhongxue 惠興女子中學 [Huixing Female Middle School], 1–2. Hangzhou, 1937.

Bergère, Marie-Claire. *The Golden Age of the Chinese Bourgeoisie, 1911–1937*. Cambridge: Cambridge University Press, 1986.

Bergère, Marie-Claire. *Sun Yat-sen*. Stanford: Stanford University Press, 1998.

Bianco, Lucien. *Origins of the Chinese Revolution, 1915–1949*. Stanford: Stanford University Press, 1971.

"Biyesheng zhuangkuang tongji" 畢業生狀況統計 [Statistics about our graduating students]. *Hongdao ershi zhou jinian kan* 弘道二十週紀念刊 [Twentieth Anniversary Publication, Union Girls' School, Hangzhou] (1932), 509.

Bond, Jennifer. "'The One for the Many': Zeng Baosun, Louise Hester Barnes and the Yifang School for Girls at Changsha, 1893–1918." *Studies in Church History* 55 (2019): 441–462.

Brewis, Georgina. *A Social History of Student Volunteering: Britain and Beyond, 1880–1980*. New York: Palgrave McMillian, 2014.

Brook, Timothy. *Documents on the Rape of Nanking*. Ann Abor: University of Michigan Press, 1999.

Brown, Jeremy, and Paul G. Pickowitz. "The Early Years of the People's Republic of China: An Introduction." In *The Dilemmas of Victory: The Early Years of the People's Republic of China*, ed. Jeremy Brown and Paul G. Pickowitz, 1–18. Cambridge, MA: Harvard University Press, 2007.

Burton, Antoinette. *Burdens of History: British Feminists, Indian Women and Imperial Culture*. Chapel Hill: University of North Carolina Press, 1994.

Burton, Margaret. *The Education of Women in China*. New York: Fleming H. Revell, 1911.

Cao Baozhen 曹宝贞. "Sanshi niandai de Zhongxi nüzhong" 三十年代的中西女中 [McTyeire in the 1930s]. In *Bainian nüzhong—xian gei yibaiyishi zhounian xiao qing* 百年女中——献给一百一十周年校庆 [One hundred years of girls' middle school—Presented in celebration of the 110th school anniversary], ed. He Yanan 何亚男, 66–68. Shanghai: Shanghai shi di san nüzi zhongxue, 2002.

Cao Shengjie 曹圣洁. "Huigu wo guo jidujiao funü shi gong chuantong" 回顾我国基督教妇女事工传统 [Remembering the traditional work of Chinese Christian women]. In *Jingyu zhong de sikao, Cao Shengjie wenji* 境遇中的思考—曹圣洁文集 [Thoughts on the situation—Collected works of Cao Shengjie], ed. Chen Yilin 陈以琳, 190–196. Shanghai: Zhongguo jidujiao xiehui, 2006.

Chang Ching Yu. "Class History." *The McTyeirean 1942–1946* (1946): unpaginated.

Chang E. Tsung. "A Study of the Village Life around McTyeire High School." *The McTyeirean* (1921), 111–116.

Chang, Iris. *The Rape of Nanking: The Forgotten Holocaust of WWII*. New York: Basic Books, 1997.

Chatterjee, Paratha. "The Nationalist Resolution of the Woman Question." In *Recasting Women: Essays in Colonial History*, ed. Kumkum Sangari and Sudesh Vaid, 233–253. New Brunswick, NJ: Rutgers University Press, 2006.

Chen Aizhen 陳愛貞. "Jiaohui nüxiao duiyu xiandai zhongguo zui shao xiandu de gongxian" 教會女校對於現代中國最少限度的貢獻 [The smallest contribution of missionary schools for girls to modern China]. *Yongjiang sheng* 甬江聲 [Riverside Echo] (1931): 42–45.

Chen Aizhen 陳愛貞. "Zai qiuxue lichang shang shuo ji juhua" 在求學立場上說幾句話 [A few words on the prospective of studying]. *Yongjiang sheng* 甬江聲 [Riverside Echo] (1931): 22–27.

Chen Jinyu 陈瑾瑜 (ed.). *Huiyi Zhongxi nüzhong* 回忆中西女中 [Remembering McTyeire School 1949–1952]. Shanghai: Tongji daxue chubanshe, 2016.

Chen Jinyu 陈瑾瑜 (ed.). *Zhongxi nüzhong* 中西女中 [McTyeire School 1892–1952]. Shanghai: Tongji daxue chubanshe, 2016.

Chen Nan-hua (Chen Hengzhe). *Autobiography of a Young Chinese Girl*. Beijing, 1935.

Chen Ping Tsung. "Types of People That Bore Me." *The McTyeirean* (1940): 14–15.

Chen Xingying 陳杏英. "Jiaoyu geming de husheng" 教育革命的呼聲 [The demand for revolutionary education]. *Yongjiang sheng* 甬江聲 [Riverside Echo] (1931): 19–21.

Chen Yan 陈雁. *Xingbie yu zhanzheng: Shanghai 1932–1945* 性别与战争:上海 1932–1945 [Gender and War: Shanghai, 1932–1945]. Beijing: Shehui kexue wenxian chubanshe, 2014.

Chiang Kai-shek, "Essentials of the New Life Movement" (speech, 1934). In *Sources of Chinese Tradition: From 1600 through the Twentieth Century*, 2nd ed., Vol. 2, ed. Wm. Theodore de Bary and Richard Lufrano, 337–343. New York: Columbia University Press, 2000.

Chih, C. C., and Earl Herbert Cressy. "Middle School Standards." In *East China Studies in Education*, No. 2. Shanghai: China Christian Educational Association, 1926.

Chinese Educational Commission (ed.). *Christian Education in China: A Study Made by an Educational Commission Representing the Mission Boards and Societies Conducting Work in China*. New York: Committee of Reference and Counsel of the Foreign Missions Conference of North America, 1922.

The Chinese Members of the Administrative and Teaching Staffs of the Suzhou University College of Arts and Sciences, and Suzhou University Middle School No. 1. "Our Message to the Missionaries in China." In *Supplement to The Green Year: Concerning the Events on and since May 30 in Shanghai* (1925), 13.

Choi, Hyaeweol. *Gender Politics at Home and Abroad: Protestant Modernity in Colonial-Era Korea*. Cambridge: Cambridge University Press, 2020.

Chow, Ts'e-tsung. *The May Fourth Movement: Intellectual Revolution in Modern China*. Cambridge, MA: Harvard University Press, 1960.

Chu I Shiu. "China's Rip Van Winkle." *The McTyeirean* (1921): 100–101.

Chu Yee-yun. "Class History." *The McTyeirean* (1947): unpaginated.

Cleverly, John. *The Schooling of China*. Sydney: George Allen & Unwin, 1985.

Cochran, Sherman. "Capitalists Choosing Communist China: The Liu Family of Shanghai." In *The Dilemmas of Victory: The Early Years of the People's Republic of China*, ed. Jeremy Brown and Paul G. Pickowitz, 359–385. Cambridge, MA: Harvard University Press, 2007.

Cody, Jeffrey W. "American Geometrics and the Architecture of Christian Campuses in China." In *China's Christian Colleges: Cross-Cultural Connections 1900–1950*, ed. Daniel H. Bays and Ellen Widmer, 27–56. Stanford: Stanford University Press, 2009.

Cohen, Paul A. *Discovering History in China: American Historical Writing on the Recent Chinese Past*. New York: Columbia University Press, 1984,

Cong, Xiaoping. *Teachers' Schools and the Making of Modern China*. Vancouver: UBC Press 2007.

Cressy, Earl Herbert, and C. C. Chih, "Middle School Standards, Second Study." In *East China Studies in Education*, No. 5. Shanghai: China Christian Educational Association, 1929.

Cressy, Earl Herbert. "Christian Middle Schools Fourth Annual Statistics, 1935–1936." In *China Christian Educational Association Bulletin*, no. 39. Shanghai: China Christian Educational Association, 1936.

Culp, Robert. *Articulating Citizenship: Civic Education and Student Politics in South-Eastern China, 1912–1940*. Cambridge, MA: Harvard University Press, 2007.

Davin, Delia. *Woman-Work: Women and the Party in Revolutionary China*. Oxford: Oxford University Press, 1979.

Deu Miao Kung. "Class Prophesy." *The McTyeirean* (1923): 14–17.

Dillon, Nara, and Jean C. Oi (eds.). *At the Crossroads of Empires: Middlemen, Social Networks and State-Building in Republican Shanghai*. Stanford: Stanford University Press, 2008.

Ding Mei-ying. "What a Chinese Girl Should Know Before Going for Study Abroad." *The McTyeirean* (1918): 19–24.

Dirlik, Arif. "Architectures of Global Modernity, Colonialism and Places," *Modern Chinese Literature and Culture* 17, no. 1 (Spring 2005): 33–61.

Dirlik, Arif. "The Ideological Foundations of the New Life Movement: A Study in Counterrevolution." *Journal of Asian Studies* 34, no. 4 (August 1975): 954–980.

Dong, Madeleine Y. "Who Is Afraid of the Chinese Modern Girl?" In *The Modern Girl around the World: Consumption, Modernity, and Globalization*, ed. The Modern Girl around the World Research Group et al., 194–219. Durham, NC: Duke University Press, 2008.

Dryburgh, Marjorie. "Re-centring Education in Manshūkoku (1931–1945): School and Family in Chinese Oral History." *Japan Forum* 34, no. 2 (November 2019): 248–272.

Dunch, Ryan. "Beyond Cultural Imperialism: Cultural Theory, Christian Missions and Global Modernity." *History and Theory* 41, no. 3 (October, 2002): 301–325.

Dunch, Ryan. *Fuzhou Protestants and the Making of Modern China, 1857–1927*. New Haven, CT: Yale University Press, 2001.

Edwards, Louise. "The Shanghai Modern Woman's American Dreams: Imagining America's Depravity to Produce China's 'Moderate Modernity.'" *Pacific Historical Review* 81, no. 4 (November 2012): 567–601.

Edwards, Louise. *Woman Warriors and Wartime Spies of China*. Cambridge: Cambridge University Press, 2016).

Elwood, Jannette, and Caroline Gipps. *Review of Recent Research on the Achievement of Girls in Single-Sex Schools*. London: University of London Institute of Education, 1999.

Entenmann, Robert. "Christian Virgins in Eighteenth Century Sichuan." In *Christianity in China from the Eighteenth Century to the Present*, ed. Daniel D. Bays, 8–23. Stanford: Stanford University Press, 1996.

"Ershi nian du zai xiao xuesheng jiguan tongji" 二十年度在校學生籍貫統計 [Statistics on the native place of our students over the past twenty years]. *Hongdao ershi zhou jinian kan* 弘道二十週紀念刊 [Twentieth Anniversary Publication, Union Girls' School, Hangzhou] (1932): 503.

Esherick, Joseph. "The Ye Family in New China." In *The Dilemmas of Victory: The Early Years of the People's Republic of China*, ed. Jeremy Brown and Paul G. Pickowitz, 311–336. Cambridge, MA: Harvard University Press, 2007.

Esherick, Joseph. "War and Revolution, Chinese Society during the 1940s." *Twentieth Century China* 27, no. 1 (November, 2001): 1–37.

Eur Yang-Sih. "October 10 of 1919." *The Phoenix* (1920): 57–58.

Evans, Harriet. "Sexed Bodies, Sexualized Identities and the Limits of Gender." *China Information* 22, no. 2 (July 2008): 361–386.

Evans, Sara M. (ed.). *Journeys That Opened Up the World: Women, Student Christian Movements and Social Justice, 1955–1975*. New Brunswick, NJ: Rutgers University Press, 2003.

Fan, Sizheng K. "Culture for Sale: Western Classical Architecture in China's Recent Building Boom." *Journal of Architectural Education (1984–)* 63, no. 1 (October, 2009): 64–74.

Fang T'sao Ai. "The Adoption of Christianity as the State Religion of China." *The Laura Haygood Star* (1921): 21–23.

Feng, Jin. *The Making of a Family Saga: Ginling College*. Albany, NY: SUNY Press, 2009.

Feng Ling 鳳令. "Xin shenghuo yundong de zumu" 新生活運動的祖母 [The Grandmother of the New Life Movement]. *Zhonghua funü jiezhi xiehui nian kan* 中華婦女節制協會年刊 [Temperance] (1934): 7–9

Ferlanti, Federica. "The New Life Movement in Jiangxi Province, 1934–1938." *Modern Asian Studies* 44, no. 5 (September 2010): 961–1000.

Fogel, Joshua A. (ed.). *The Nanjing Massacre in History and Historiography*. Berkeley: University of California Press, 2000.

Fong, Vanessa L. "China's One Child Policy and the Empowerment of Urban Daughters." *American Anthropologist* 104, no. 4 (December 2002): 1098–1109.

Forster, Elizabeth. *1919—The Year That Changed China: A New History of the New Culture Movement*. Berlin: De Gruyter, 2018.

"Forward." *The McTyeirean* (1917).

Fu Lüe 傅掠, "Jiaohui xuexiao yu jingji qinlüe" 教會學校与經濟侵略 [Mission schools and economic encroachment]. *Shishi gongbao* 時事公報, July 8, 1925.

Fujimura-Fanselow, Kumiko. "Women's Participation in Higher Education in Japan." *Comparative Education Review* 29, no. 4 (November 1985): 471–489.

Fullerton, Caroline A. "St. Mary's Hall." In *St. Mary's Hall Shanghai 50th Anniversary volume, 1881–1931* (1931): 2–6.

"Funü jiezhihui jiang chu fei gai zhuanhao" 婦女節制會將出廢丐專號 [The Chinese Women's Christian Temperance Union plan to publish a special issue on how to eliminate beggars]. *Shenbao* 申報, December 18, 1925.

Galbraith, Winifred. *New Life in China: The Growth of the Church in the Wartime*. London: Edinburgh House Press, 1941.

Gan Mengxiong 幹孟雄. "Fenggao na [hai liu bu li jiaohui xuexiao de tongxue] ji ju hua" 奉告那[還留不離教會學校的同學] 幾句話 [A few words addressed to those classmates who have not yet left missionary schools]. *Shishi gongbao* 時事公報, August 7, 1925.

Gan Mengxiong 幹孟雄. "Fenggao na [hai liu bu li jiaohui xuexiao de tongxue] ji ju hua" 奉告那[還留不離教會學校的同學] 幾句話 [A few words addressed to those classmates who have not yet left missionary schools]. *Shishi gongbao* 時事公報, August 8, 1925.

Gerth, Karl. *China Made: Consumer Culture and the Creation of the Nation*. Cambridge, MA: Harvard University Press, 2003.

Glosser, Susan L. "'The Truths I Have Learned': Nationalism, Family Reform and Male Identity in China's New Culture Movement, 1915–1923." In *Chinese Femininities, Chinese Masculinities: A Reader*, ed. Susan Brownell and Jeffrey N. Wasserstrom, 120–144. Berkeley: University of California Press, 2002.

Glosser, Susan. *Chinese Visions of Family and State, 1915–1953*. Berkeley: University of California Press, 2003.

Glosser, Susan. "Women's Culture of Resistance: An Ordinary Response to Extraordinary Circumstances." In *In the Shadow of the Rising Sun: Shanghai under Japanese Occupation*, ed. Christian Henriot and Wen-Hsin Yeh, 302–320. Cambridge: Cambridge University Press, 2004.

Goodman, Bryna. *Nation Place, City, and Nation: Regional Networks and Identities in Shanghai, 1853–1937*. Berkeley: University of California Press, 1995.

"Guangdong xueshenghui shouhui jiaoyu quanli yundong weiyuanhui xuanxi" 广东学生会收回教育权利运动委员会选信 [Selected letters from the Guangdong student union committee for the recovery of educational rights] (1924). In *Diguo zhuyi qinhua jiaoyu shi ziliao: jiahui xuexiao* 帝国主义侵华教育史资料：教会学校 [Historical materials on the imperialist invasion of China: Missionary schools], ed. Li Chucai 李楚材, 583–585. Beijing: Jiaoyu kexue chubanshe, 1987.

Guo, Vivienne. "Forging a Women's United Front: Chinese Elite Women's Networks for National Salvation and Resistance, 1932–1938." *Modern Asian Studies* 53, no. 2 (March 2019): 483–511.

Guo, Vivienne Xiangwei. *Women and Politics in Wartime China: Networking across Geopolitical Boundaries*. London: Routledge, 2019.
Han Shu 翰戍. "Shouhui jiaoyu quan yundong zai shen guan—cong shengyuehan daxue dao guanghua daxue" 收回教育权运动再深观—从圣约翰大学到光华大学 [A deeper look at the movement to recover educational rights—from St. John's University to Guanghua University]. In *Jidujiao yu jindai zhongguo jiaoyu* 基督教与近代中国教育 [Christianity and education in modern China], ed. Li Ling 李灵 and Xiao Qinghe 肖清和, 94–120. Shanghai: Shanghai yiwen chubanshe, 2018.
Harrison, Henrietta. *The Making of the Republican Citizen: Political Ceremonies and Symbols in China, 1911–1929*. Oxford: Oxford University Press, 2000.
Harrison, Henrietta. *The Missionary's Curse and Other Tales from a Chinese Catholic Village*. Berkeley: University of California Press, 2013.
Hayford, Charles. *To the People: James Yen and Village China*. New York: Columbia University Press, 1990.
Hemelryk Donald, Stephanie. "Tang Wei: Sex, the City and the Scapegoat in Lust, Caution." *Theory, Culture and Society* 27, no. 4 (August 2010): 46–68.
Hershatter, Gail. *The Gender of Memory: Rural Women and China's Collective Past*. Berkeley: University of California Press, 2011.
Hicks, George. *The Comfort Women: Sex Slaves of the Japanese Imperial Forces*. London: Allen and Unwin, 1995.
Hongdao nüzhong xiaoyouhui bianjizu 弘道女中校友会编辑组 [Hongdao Girls' School Alumnae Association] (ed.). *Hongdao nüzhong jinian kan* 弘道女中纪念刊 [In Memory of The Hongdao Girls' Middle School]. 2008.
Honig, Emily. "Christianity, Feminism and Communism: The Life and Times of Deng Yuzhi." In *Christianity in China from the Eighteenth Century to the Present*, ed. Daniel D. Bays, 243–262. Stanford: Stanford University Press, 1996.
Honig, Emily. "Socialist Sex: The Cultural Revolution Revisited." *Modern China* 29, no. 2 (April 2003): 153–175.
Hoo Loo Ming. "She Made Her Bed." *The McTyeirean* 1930: 195–202.
Hoo Lu Tuh. "A Letter Relating to Village Work." *The McTyeirean* (1922): 46–48.
Horowitz, Helen Lefkowitz. *Alma Mater: Design and Experience in the Women's Colleges from Their Nineteenth-Century Beginnings to the 1930s*. New York: Knopf, 1984.
Hotta, Erri. *Pan-Asianism and Japan's War 1931–1945*. New York: Palgrave Macmillan, 2007.
Hsueh Nying. "Class History 1945." *The McTyeirean 1942–1946* (1946): unpaginated.
Hu, Siao-Chen. "Voices of Female Educators in Early Twentieth-Century Women's Magazines." In *Women and the Periodical Press in China's Long Twentieth Century: A Space of Their Own?*, ed. Michel Hockx, Joan Judge, and Barbara Mittler, 176–191. Cambridge: Cambridge University Press, 2018.
Hu, Ying. "Naming the First New Woman." *Nan Nü: Men, Women, and Gender in Early and Imperial China* 3, no. 2 (January 2001): 196–231.
Hunter, Jane. *The Gospel of Gentility: American Women Missionaries in Turn-of-the-Century China*. New Haven, CT: Yale University Press, 1984.
Hyatt, Irwin T., Jr. *Our Ordered Lives Confess: Three Nineteenth-Century American Missionaries in East Shantung*. Cambridge, MA: Harvard University Press, 1976.
Ireland, Daryl L. *John Song: Modern Chinese Christianity and the Making of a New Man*. Waco, TX: Baylor University Press, 2020.

Israel, John. *Lianda: A Chinese University in War and Revolution*. Stanford: Stanford University Press, 1998.
Jackson, Isabella. *Shaping Modern Shanghai: Colonialism in China's Global City*. Cambridge: Cambridge University Press, 2017.
Jiang, Jin. *Women Playing Men: Yue Opera and Social Change in Twentieth-Century Shanghai*. Seattle: University of Washington Press, 2009.
Jones, Andrew. *Like a Knife: Ideology and Genre in Contemporary Chinese Popular Music*. Ithaca, NY: Cornell University Press, 1992.
Judge, Joan. "Citizens or Mothers of Citizens? Gender and the Meaning of Modern Citizenship in China." In *Changing Meanings of Citizenship in Modern China*, ed. Merle Goldman and Elizabeth J. Perry, 23–43. Cambridge, MA: Harvard University Press, 2002.
Judge, Joan. *The Precious Raft of History: The Past, the West and the Woman Question in China*. Stanford: Stanford University Press, 2008.
Judge, Joan. *Republican Lens: Gender, Visuality and Experience in the Early Chinese Periodical Press*. Oakland: University of California Press, 2015.
Kahn, Ida. *An Amazon in Cathay*. Boston: Women's Foreign Missionary Society, 1912.
Ke Hailun 可海倫. "Funü yu guonan" 婦女與國難 [Women and the national crisis]. *Yongjiang sheng* 甬江聲 [Riverside Echo] (1933): 44–46.
Kiang Ye. "My Lady's Wardrobe." *The McTyeirean* (1940): 23–24.
Kirk, Harris E. "New Mission Philosophy: An Extract from an Address at Washington Missionary Convention." In *Supplement to The Green Year: Concerning the Events on and since May 30 in Shanghai*, 18 (Shanghai, 1925).
Ko, Dorothy. "Pursuing Talent and Virtue: Education and Women's Culture in Seventeenth- and Eighteenth-Century China." *Late Imperial China* 13, no. 1 (June 1992): 9–39.
Kwok, Pui-Lan. *Chinese Women and Christianity, 1860–1927*. Atlanta: Scholars Press, 1992.
Kwok, Pui-Lan. "Chinese Women and Protestant Christianity at the Turn of the Century." In *Christianity in China: From the Eighteenth Century to the Present*, ed. Daniel H. Bays, 194–208. Stanford: Stanford University Press, 1996.
Kyung Ming-ge. "The Student Meeting in Shasi." *The Phoenix* (1920): 63–65.
Lary, Diana. *The Chinese People at War: Human Suffering and Social Transformation, 1937–1945*. Cambridge: Cambridge University Press, 2010.
Lary, Diana. "Drowned Earth: The Strategic Breaching of the Yellow River Dyke, 1938." *War in History* 8, no. 2 (April 2001): 191–207.
Lary, Diana. "War and Remembering: Memories of China at War." In *Beyond Suffering: Recounting War in Modern China*, ed. James Flath and Norman Smith, 262–287. Vancouver: UBC Press, 2011.
Latourette, Kenneth Scott. *A History of Christian Missions in China*. London: The Macmillan Company, 1929.
Laurence, M. "Female Boarding Schools." In *Records of the General Conference of the Protestant Missionaries of China Held at Shanghai, May 10–17, 1877*, ed. M. T. Yates, 467–470. Shanghai: American Presbyterian Mission Press, 1878.
Lee, Leo Ou-fan. *Shanghai Modern: The Flowering of a New Urban Culture in China, 1930–1945*. Cambridge MA: Harvard University Press, 1999.
Lefkowitz Horowitz, Helen. *Alma Mater: Design and Experience in the Women's Colleges from Their Nineteenth-Century Beginnings to the 1930s*. New York: Knopf, 1984.

Lewis, W. J., W. T. A. Barber, and J. R. Hykes (eds.), *Records of the General Conference of the Protestant Missionaries of China Held at Shanghai, May 7–20, 1890*. Shanghai: American Presbyterian Mission Press, 1890.

Li, Danke. *Echoes of Chongqing: Women in Wartime China*. Urbana: University of Illinois Press, 2010.

Li Me-Chung. "The Piteous Sight I Witnessed." *The Phoenix* (1938): unpaginated.

Li Mei 李玫. "Shengmaliya nüxiao de jiemei ban" 圣玛利亚女校的姐妹班 [The big sister-little sister classes in St. Mary's Girls' School]. In *Zhuiyi Shengmaliya nüxiao* 追忆圣玛利亚女校 [Remembering St. Mary's Girls School], ed. XuYongchu 徐永初 and Chen Jinyu 陈瑾瑜, 180–185. Shanghai: Tongji daxue chubanshe, 2014.

Li Rongmei 李榮美. "Qingnian hui" 青年會 [The YWCA]. *Yongjiang sheng* 甬江聲 [Riverside Echo] (1931): 184–188.

Li Tsing Lian. "Our Responsibility." *The McTyeirean* (1921): 121–123.

Lin Mixuan 林米軒. "Wuli zhunbei yu shenti xunlian" 武力準備與身體訓練 [Military preparation and drilling the body]. *Yongjiang sheng* 甬江聲 [Riverside Echo] (1933): 47–48.

Lin Shiguang, 林時光. "Tuoli jiaohui xuexiao de ji zhong yuanyin" 脫離教會學校的幾種原因 [A few reasons to leave missionary schools]. *Shishi gongbao* 時事公報, September 14, 1925.

Lin Wentian 林聞天. "Jidutu duiyu shiju de ganxiang he taidu" 基督徒對於時局的感想和態度 [The feelings and attitudes of Christians toward the current political situation]. *Shishi gongbao* 時事公報, September 4, 1925.

Lincoln, Toby. "The Rural and Urban at War: Invasion and Reconstruction in China during the Anti-Japanese War of Resistance." *Journal of Urban History* 38, no. 1 (January 2012): 114–132.

Ling Kuo-fen. "A Helping Hand." *The Phoenix* (1939): 37–38.

Liu, Chang. "Searching for a New Lifestyle: Single Women in Shanghai, 1915–1949." (PhD Diss., King's College London), 2018.

Liu, Jennifer. "Defiant Retreat: The Relocation of Middle Schools to China's Interior, 1937–1945," *Frontiers of History in China* 8, no. 4 (December 2013): 558–584.

Liu, Judith. *Foreign Exchange: Counterculture behind the Walls of S. Hilda's School for Girls, 1929–1937*. Bethlehem, PA: Lehigh University Press, 2011.

Liu, Judith, and Donald Kelly. "'An Oasis in a Heathen Land': St. Hilda's School for Girls Wuchang, 1928–1936." In *Christianity in China from the Eighteenth Century to the Present*, ed. Daniel D. Bays, 228–242. Stanford: Stanford University Press, 1996.

Liu, Xiaoyan. *The Changing Face of Women's Education in China: A Critical History of St. Mary's Hall, McTyeire School and Shanghai No. 3. Girls' Middle School*. Zürich: Lit Verlag, 2017.

Liu Wang Liming 劉王立明. "Sishi nian lai zhongguo funü jiezhi yundong" 四十年來中國婦女節制運動 [Forty years of Chinese CWTU]. *Zhonghua funü jiezhi xiehui nian kan* 中華婦女節制協會年刊 [Temperance]. (1934): 2–3.

Loh Oen-vung. "Correspondence." *The Phoenix* (1940): 106.

Loh Oen-vung. "What We Did for the Refugees." *The Phoenix* (1939): 39–40.

Loo Kyuan-Faung. "A Day's Work in the Red Cross Society." *The Phoenix* (1938): unpaginated.

Lopes, Helena. "Wartime Education at the Crossroads of Empires: The Relocation of Schools to Macau during the Second World War, 1937–1945." *Twentieth Century China* 46, no. 2 (April 2021): 130–152.

Lu, Hanchao. *Beyond the Neon Lights: Everyday Shanghai in the Early Twentieth Century*. Berkeley: University of California Press, 1999.

Lu Xun. "What Happens after Nora Leaves Home?" Originally given as a talk at Beijing Women's Normal College on December 26, 1923. In *Women in Republican China: A Sourcebook*, ed. Hua Lan and Vanessa Fong, 176–181. New York: M. E. Sharpe, 1999.

Luo Weihong 罗伟虹. *Cao Shengjie koushu lishi* 曹圣洁口述历史 [Cao Shengjie: An oral history]. Shanghai: Shanghai shudian chubanshe, 2017.

Lutz, Jessie G. "Comments." In *Nationalist China during the Sino-Japanese War, 1937–1945*, ed. Paul K. T. Sih, 124–130. New York: Exposition Press, 1977.

Lutz, Jesse Gregory. *China and the Christian Colleges, 1850–1950*. Ithaca, NY: Cornell University Press, 1971.

Lutz, Jessie Gregory. *Chinese Politics and Christian Missions: The Anti-Christian Movements of 1920–1928*. Notre Dame, IN: Cross Cultural Publications, 1988.

Lutz, Jessie Gregory. "The Chinese Student Movement of 1945–1949." *Journal of Asian Studies* 31, no. 1 (November 1971): 89–110.

Ma, Zhao. *Runaway Wives, Urban Crimes and Survival Tactics in Wartime Beijing 1937–1949*. Cambridge, MA: Harvard University Press, 2015.

MacNeil, Eleanor. "The Situation in Shanghai." *Supplement to the Green Year: Concerning the Events on and since May 30 in Shanghai*, July 1, 1925.

Mann, Susan. "The Education of Daughters in the Mid-Ch'ing Period." In *Education and Society in Late Imperial China, 1600–1900*, ed. Alexander Woodside and Benjamin A. Elman, 19–49. Berkeley: University of California Press, 1994.

McTyeire Alumnae Association (eds.). "Telling Women's Lives: In Search of McTyeire, 1892–1992." Unpublished Oral History Collection, 1992.

Merkel-Hess, Kate. *The Rural Modern: Reconstructing Self and State in Republican China*. Chicago: University of Chicago Press, 2016.

"Minzhong weilao guomin jun" 民眾慰勞國民軍 [The people comfort the National Revolutionary Army]. *Shenbao* 申報, March 26, 1927.

Mitter, Rana. *A Bitter Revolution: China's Struggle with the Modern World*. Oxford: Oxford University Press, 2005.

Mo Sih Tsung. "The Influence of Music in the Future Homes of China." *The McTyeirean* (1919): 27–29.

Moore, Aaron William. "Growing Up in Nationalist China: Self-Representation in the Personal Documents of Children and Youth 1927–1949." *Modern China* 42, no. 1 (January 2016): 73–110.

"Music." *The Phoenix* (1922): 53.

National Committee, Young Women's Christian Association of China (ed.). *Student Handbook: Constitution and Organisation of a Student Y.W.C.A.* Shanghai, 1924.

Nien Cheng. *Life and Death in Shanghai*. London: Flamingo, 1987.

"Ningbo riren chuoshang huaren an xuwen" 寧波日人戳傷華人案續聞 [Continued news on the case of the stabbing of a Chinese by a Japanese in Ningbo]. *Shenbao* 申報, June 26, 1925.

"Our Principals." In *Hongdao ershi zhou jinian kan* 弘道二十週紀念刊 [Twentieth Anniversary Publication, Union Girls' School, Hangzhou]. (1932), 2–4.

Pan, Lu. "Nostalgia as Resistance: Memory, Space and the Competing Modernities in Berlin and Shanghai." *European Journal of East Asian Studies* 12, no. 1 (2013): 135–160.

Pang, Laikwan, Paul Clark, and Tsan-Huang Tsai, (eds.). *Listening to China's Cultural Revolution: Music, Politics, and Cultural Continuities*. Basingstoke: Palgrave, 2016.

Perry, Elizabeth J. "Managing Student Protest in Republican China: Yenching and St. John's Compared." *Frontiers of History in China* 8, no. 1 (2013): 3–31.

Qian, Nanxiu. "The Mother Nü Xuebao versus the Daughter Nü Xuebao: Generational Differences between 1898 and 1902 Women Reformers." In *Different Worlds of Discourse: Transformations of Gender and Genre in Late Qing and Early Republican China*, ed. Nanxiu Qian, Grace S. Fong, and Richard J. Smith, 257–292. Oxford: Oxford University Press, 2016.

Qiu Peipei, Su Zhiliang, and Chen Lifei. *Chinese Comfort Women: Testimonies from Imperial Japan's Sex-Slaves*. Vancouver: UBC Press, 2013.

Qu Mingming 瞿明明. "Zhongxi nüzhong aiguo xuesheng yundong de huigu" 中西女中爱国学生运动的回顾 [A look back at the patriotic student movement at McTyeire]. In *Bainian nüzhong—xian gei yibaiyishi zhounian xiao qing* 百年女中—献给一百一十周年校庆 [One hundred years of girls' middle school—Presented in celebration of the 110th School Anniversary], ed. He Yanan 何亚男, 121–127. Shanghai: Shanghai shi di san nüzi zhongxue, 2002.

Qu Mingming 瞿明明. "Zhongxi nüzhong shi wo nanwang de jia" 中西女中是我难忘的家 [McTyeire was my unforgettable home]. In *Huiyi Zhongxi nüzhong* 回忆中西女中 [Remembering McTyeire School 1949–1952], ed. Chen Jinyu 陳瑾瑜, 39–41. Shanghai: Tongji daxue chubanshe, 2016.

"Quan xiao xuesheng jiashu zhiye bijiao biao" 全校學生家屬職業比較表 [Statistics on the occupation of students' families]. In *Shanghai shili Wuben nüzi zhongxue gaikuang* 上海市立務本女子中學概況 [Overview of Shanghai City Wuben Girls' Middle School], 7. Shanghai, 1934.

Reynolds, Douglas. *China 1898–1912: The Xinzheng Revolution and Japan*. Cambridge, MA: Harvard University Press, 1993.

Rigdon, Susan. "National Salvation: Teaching Civic Duty in China's Christian Colleges." In *China's Christian Colleges: Cross Cultural Connections, 1900–1950*, ed. Daniel H. Bays and Ellen Widmer, 193–217. Stanford: Stanford University Press, 2009.

Robert, Dana L. *American Women in Mission: A Social History of Their Thought and Practice*. Atlanta: Mercer University Press, 1996.

Robert, Dana L. (ed.). *Gospel Bearers, Gender Barriers: Missionary Women in the Twentieth Century*. New York: Orbis Books, 2002.

Rogaski, Ruth. *Hygienic Modernity: Meanings of Health and Disease in Treaty-Port China*. Berkeley: University of California Press, 2004.

Ross, Heidi A. "'Cradle for Female Talent': The McTyeire Home and School for Girls: 1892–1937." In *Christianity in China from the Eighteenth Century to the Present*, ed. Daniel D. Bays, 209–227. Stanford: Stanford University Press, 1996.

Sang, Tze-Ian D. *The Emerging Lesbian: Female Same-Sex Desire in Modern China*. Chicago: University of Chicago Press, 2003.

Schenk, Catherine R. "Another Asian Financial Crisis: Monetary Links between Hong Kong and China 1945–50." *Modern Asian Studies* 34, no. 3 (July 2000): 739–764.

Schneider, Helen. *Keeping the Nation's House: Domestic Management and the Making of Modern China*. Vancouver: UBC Press, 2011.

Schneider, Helen. "Mobilising Women: The Women's Advisory Council, Resistance, and Reconstruction during China's War with Japan." *European Journal of East Asian Studies* 11, no. 2 (December 2012): 213–236.

Schneider, Helen. "The Professionalization of Chinese Domesticity: Ava B. Milan and Home Economics at Yenching University." In *China's Christian Colleges: Cross

Cultural Connections, 1900–1950, ed. Daniel H. Bays and Ellen Widmer, 125–146. Stanford: Sanford University Press, 2009.

Schneider, Helen. "Raising the Standards of Family Life: Ginling Women's College and Christian Social Service in Republican China." In *Divine Domesticities: Christian Paradoxes in Asia and the Pacific*, ed. Hyaeweol Choi and Margaret Jolly, 113–142. Canberra: ANU Press, 2014.

Schoppa, Keith. *In a Sea of Bitterness: Refugees during the Sino-Japanese War*. Cambridge, MA: Harvard University Press, 2011.

Shemo, Connie. "How Better to Serve Her Country? Cultural Translators, US Women's History and Kang Cheng's 'An Amazon in Cathay.'" *Journal of Women's History* 21, no. 4 (Winter 2009): 111–133.

Shen Yifan 沈以藩. *Jiangtai shifeng—Shen Yifan zhujiao wenji (shang)* 讲台侍奉—沈以藩主教文集（上） [Serving on the altar—Bishop Shen Yifan's collected works] Vol. 1. Shanghai: Zhongguo jidujiao liang hui chuban, 2015.

Shi, Xia. *At Home in the World: Women and Charity in Late Qing and Early Republican China*. New York: Columbia University Press, 2018.

"Shouhui jiaoyu quan jijin hui wei yongjiang zhao sheng gao min ju" 收回教育權急進會為甬江招生告居民 [An announcement that the committee for the quick taking back of educational rights is enrolling students at Yongjiang]. *Shishi gongbao* 时事公报, August 24, 1927.

Siao, B. S. "An Appeal to All Concerned." In *Supplement to The Green Year: Concerning the Events on and since May 30 in Shanghai* (1925): 12.

Slater, Frances. "The Wolfe Sisters of Foochow, China: Born to Evangelise." Published by Frances Slater and John Fitzgerald (2016).

Sloan, Catherine. "'Periodicals of an Objectionable Character': Peers and Periodicals and Croydon Friends' School, 1826–1875." *Victorian Periodicals Review* 50, no. 4 (Winter, 2017): 769–786.

Solomon, Barbara. *In the Company of Educated Women: A History of Women and Higher Education in America*. New Haven, CT: Yale University Press, 1985.

"Some Co.eds' Views." *The China Press*, January 5, 1947: 11.

Soong Jung-wo. "My Great-Grandmother." *The Phoenix* (1923): 6–7.

Sorensen, Clark, and Andrea Gevurtz Arai (eds.). *Spaces of Possibility: In, Between, and Beyond Korea and Japan*. Seattle: University of Washington Press, 2016.

"St. John's Co.eds' Scorned." *The China Press*, January 7, 1947: 11.

Stauffer, Milton T. (ed.). *The Christian Occupation of China: A General Survey of the Numerical Strength and Geographical Distribution of the Christian Forces in China, Made by the Special Committee on Survey and Occupation, China Continuation Committee, 1918–1921*. Shanghai: China Continuation Committee, 1922.

Strand, David. *An Unfinished Republic, Leading by Word and Deed in Modern China*. Berkeley: University of California Press, 2011.

Strauss, Julia C. *Strong Institutions in Weak Polities: State Building in Republican China, 1927–1940*. Oxford: Oxford University Press, 1998.

Sung Sing Ling. "Oh! The Bus! Oh! The Tram!" *The Phoenix* (1938): unpaginated.

Swartz, Vera. *The Chinese Enlightenment: Intellectuals and the Legacy of the May Fourth Movement of 1919*. Berkeley: University of California Press, 1986.

Tang, Chindon Yiu. "Women's Education in China." In *Bulletins on Chinese Education Issued by the Chinese National Association for the Advancement of Education*, Vol. 2.

Bulletin 9, ed. Chinese National Association for the Advancement of Education, 1–36. Shanghai: The Commercial Press, 1923.

Topley, Marjorie. "Marriage Resistance in Rural Kwangtung." In *Women in Chinese Society*, ed. Margery Wolf and Roxanne Witke, 67–88. Stanford: Stanford University Press, 1975.

Tsai, Christiana. *Queen of the Dark Chamber: The Story of Christiana Tsai as Told to Ellen L. Drummond*. Chicago: Moody Press, 1953.

Tsai Kuei, and Lily K. Haass. *A Study of the Young Women's Christian Association of China: 1890–1930*. Shanghai: National Young Women's Christian Association of China, 1930.

Tsang Kyi-ying. "A Memorial Meeting," *The Phoenix* (1920): 59.

Tsang Kyi-ying. "A Long Trip to Longhua." *The Phoenix* (1920): 61–62.

Tsang Sieu-ai. "The Centre of a Tornado." *The Phoenix* (1938): unpaginated.

Tsang Vung-Chung. "A Dangerous Outing." *The Phoenix* (1938): unpaginated.

Tsao. "Wu Pen Girls Fight against Blue Jacket 'Cultural Control.'" *China Forum* 3, no. 2 (November 30, 1933): 9.

Tsao Ming Zok. "The Call for Women Leaders." *The McTyeirean* (1922): 34–35.

Tseng Pao-sun. "The Chinese Woman Past and Present." In *Chinese Women through Chinese Eyes*, ed. Li Yu-ning, 72–86. New York: Routledge, 1992.

Tseu Mei Yuin. "The Broken Engagement." *The McTyeirean* (1921): 77–81.

Tseu We-Kyoen. "Out in the Rain." *The Phoenix* (1938): unpaginated.

Tsiang Ku Yin. "How Earnest Found His Kingdom." *The McTyeirean* (1919): 23–24.

Tsih Zoen Shang. "Changing Styles." *The McTyeirean* (1923): 63–70.

Tsih Zoen Shang. "The Old-Fashioned Mother and Her New-Fashioned Daughter." *The McTyeirean* (1922): 98–99.

Tsong Tuh Wei. "The Two Wills." *The McTyeirean* (1930): 183–190.

Tsu Foh-Pau. "Difficult Conditions." *The Phoenix* (1941): unpaginated.

Tsu Tsung Kyung. "Present Situation of Popular Democracy in China." *The McTyeirean* (1922): 68–70.

Tsu Tsung Kyung. "What Christ Means to Me." *The McTyeirean* (1921): 72.

Tsu Tsung Ling, and Wong Yoeh Wo. "Is the Village School Worthwhile?" *The McTyeirean* (Shanghai): 56–57.

Tu Fengyun 屠鳳韻. "Ben xiao de xueshenghui" 本校的學生會 [Our school student union]. *Yongjiang sheng* 甬江聲 [Riverside Echo]. (1931): 175–178.

Tung Tsao Zok. "The Student Council." *The McTyeirean* (1918): 39.

Uhalley, Stephen, and Xiaoxin Wu (eds.). *China and Christianity: Burdened Past Hopeful Future*. Armonk, NY: M. E. Sharpe, 2001.

Van, Margaret. "Church Activities in China." *Riverside Echo* (1925): 5.

Van, Margaret. "A Meeting at the Factory." *Riverside Echo* (1925): 6–7.

Van de Ven, Hans. *China at War: Triumph and Tragedy in the Emergence of the New China*. London: Profile Books, 2017.

Van de Ven, Hans. *War and Nationalism in China, 1925–1945*. London: Routledge, 2003.

Wakeman, Frederic, Jr. "Shanghai Smuggling." In *In the Shadow of the Rising Sun: Shanghai under Japanese Occupation*, ed. Christian Henriot and Wen-Hsin Yeh, 116–156. Cambridge: Cambridge University Press, 2004.

Wang Shaolan 汪绍兰. "Xiangyata li de liangshan 'chuang'" 象牙塔里的两扇"窗" [Two "windows" in an ivory tower]. In *Huiyi Zhongxi nüzhong* 回忆中西女中 [Remembering

McTyeire School 1949–1952], ed. Chen Jinyu 陈瑾瑜, 22–23. Shanghai: Tongji daxue chubanshe, 2016.

Wang Zheng. *Finding Women in the State: A Socialist Feminist Revolution in the People's Republic of China, 1949–1964*. Berkeley: University of California Press, 2017.

Wang Zheng. *Women in the Chinese Enlightenment: Oral and Textual Histories*. Berkeley: University of California Press, 1999.

Wang Qixian 王啟賢. "Wo he jiaohui xuexiao xuesheng de fuxiong tan hua" 我和教會學校學生的父兄談話 [A conversation with the fathers and elder brothers of missionary school students]. *Shishi gongbao* 时事公报, August 1, 1925.

Wasserstrom, Jeffrey N. "Cosmopolitan Connections and Transnational Networks." In *At the Crossroads of Empires: Middlemen, Social Networks and State-Building in Republican Shanghai*, ed. Nara Dillon and Jean C. Oi, 215–216. Stanford: Stanford University Press, 2008.

Wasserstrom, Jeffrey N. "Questioning the Modernity of the Model Settlement: Citizenship and Exclusion in Old Shanghai." In *Changing Meanings of Citizenship in Modern China*, ed. Merle Goldman and Elizabeth Perry, 110–132. Cambridge, MA: Harvard University Press, 2002.

Wasserstrom, Jeffrey N. *Student Protests in Twentieth-Century China: The View from Shanghai*. Stanford: Stanford University Press, 1991.

"What Our Graduates Are Doing." *The McTyeirean* (1925): 119–126.

Widmer, Ellen (ed.). *Writing Women in Late Imperial China*. Stanford: Stanford University Press, 1997.

Wong, Wai Ching Angela, and Patricia P. K. Chu (eds.). *Christian Women in Chinese Society: The Anglican Story*. Hong Kong: Hong Kong University Press, 2018.

Wong We-Kyoen. "St. Mary's and the Student Movement." *The Phoenix* (1920):53–54.

Wu Vong Ching. "Beware! Are You Properly Groomed?" *The McTyeirean* (1940): 27.

Wu Weinong. "Jin Zhenxiang yu Shishi gongbao" 金振祥与时事公报 [Jin Zhenxiang and the Shishi gongbao]. In *Ningbo wenshi ziliao* 宁波文史资料 [Historical sources on Ningbo]. Vol. 3, ed. Zhongguo renmin zhengzhi xie shang huiyi, Ningbo shi weiyuanhui wenshi ziliao yanjiu weiyuan, 182–192 (Ningbo, 1985).

Wu Yiyun 巫漪云. "Yi ben cidian beihou de gushi—caifang Shengmaliya nüzhong 1945 jie xiaoyou Ying Manrong" 一本词典背后的故事—采访圣玛利亚女中1945届校友应曼蓉 [The story behind a dictionary—An interview with St. Mary's alumna from the class of 1945, Ying Manrong]. In *Zhuixun Shengmaliya xiaoyou zuji* 追寻圣玛利亚校友足迹 [Following the footprints of St. Mary's Alumnae], ed. Xu Yongchu 徐永初 and Chen Jinyu 陳瑾瑜, 93–96. Shanghai: Tongji daxue chubanshe, 2014.

Xi, Lian. *Blood Letters: The Untold Story of Lin Zhao, a Martyr in Mao's China*. New York: Basic Books, 2018.

Xi, Lian. *Redeemed by Fire: The Rise of Popular Christianity in Modern China*. New Haven, CT: Yale University Press, 2010.

Xiang Jingyu 向警予. "Zhongguo zuijin funü yundong" 中国最近妇女运动 [The most recent women's movement in China]. In *Zhongguo funü yundong wenxian ziliao huibian* 中国妇女运动文献资料汇编 [Historical materials on the Chinese Women's Movement]. Vol. 1: 1918–1949, ed. Zhongguo funü guanli ganbu xueyuan 中国妇女管理干部学院 [College for Chinese Women Cadres], 92–100. Beijing: Zhongguo funü chubanshe, 1988.

"Xiao shi" 校史 [School History]. In *Shanghai shili Wuben nüzi zhongxue gaikuang* 上海市立務本女子中學概況 [Overview of Shanghai City Wuben Girls' Middle School], 1–2. Shanghai, 1934.

Xie Bingying. *Autobiography of a Chinese Girl: A Genuine Autobiography by Hsieh Ping-Ying*, trans. Tsui Chi. London: Allen and Unwin, 1943.

Xie, Kailing. *Embodying Middle Class Gender Aspirations: Perspectives from China's Privileged Young Women*. London: Palgrave Macmillan, 2021.

Xu Yongchu 徐永初, and Chen Jinyu 陳瑾瑜 (eds.). *Shengmaliya nüxiao* 圣玛利亚女校 [St. Mary's School for Girls, 1881–1952]. Shanghai: Tongji daxue chubanshe, 2014.

Xu Yongchu 徐永初, and Chen Jinyu 陳瑾瑜 (eds.). *Zhuixun Shengmaliya xiaoyou zuji* 追寻圣玛利亚校友足迹 [Following the footprints of St. Mary's Alumnae]. Shanghai: Tongji daxue chubanshe, 2014.

Xu Yongchu 徐永初, and Chen Jinyu 陳瑾瑜 (eds.). *Zhuiyi Shengmaliya nüxiao* 追忆圣玛利亚女校 [Remembering St. Mary's School for Girls]. Shanghai: Tongji daxue chubanshe, 2014.

Xue Zheng 薛正. "Wo suo zhidao de Zhongxi nüzhong" 我所知道的中西女中 [Everything I know about McTyeire School]. In *Jiefang qian Shanghai de xuexiao, Shanghai wenshi ziliao xuanji di wushijiu ji* 解放前上海的学校,上海文史资料选辑,第五十九辑 [Schools in pre-liberation Shanghai, Selected Historical Materials]. Vol. 59], ed. Wenshi ziliao gongzuo weiyuanhui 文史资料工作委员会 [Historical materials working team], 293–326. Shanghai: Shanghai renmin chubanshe, 1988.

"Xuesheng jiguan tongji biao" 學生籍貫統計表 [Statistics on students' native places]. In *Huixing sili nüzi chuji zhongxue zuijin gaikuang* 惠興私立女子初級中學最近概況 [Overview of the private Huixing Girls' Junior Middle School]. (1934): 6.

Yang Chao, Buwei. *Autobiography of a Chinese Woman*. New York: John Day Company, 1947.

Yang Yinsui 楊音綏. "Ben xiao bei [shouhui jiaoyu quan jijin hui] zhanju shi de huiyi" 本校被[收回教權急進會]佔據時的回憶 [Remembering the time when our school was occupied by the Committee for the quick taking back of educational rights]. In *Yinxian sili Yongjiang nüzi zhongxue nianwu zhounian jinian kan* 鄞縣私立甬江女子中學廿五週年紀念刊 [Yonjiang private middle school for girls in Yin county twenty-fifth anniversary magazine] (1948): 1–2.

Yang Zhiling 杨之岭. "Shengmaliya nüxiao, wo xin zhong de fengbei" 圣玛利亚女校,我心中的丰碑 [St. Mary's School for Girls, a monument in my heart]. In *Zhuiyi Shengmaliya nüxiao* 追忆圣玛利亚女校 [Remembering St. Mary's School for Girls], ed. Xu Yongchu 徐永初 and Chen Jinyu 陳瑾瑜, 137–143. Shanghai: Tongji daxue chubanshe, 2014.

Yates, M. T. (ed.). *Records of the General Conference of the Protestant Missionaries of China, Held at Shanghai, May 10–14, 1877*. Shanghai: American Presbyterian Mission Press, 1878.

Yau Ding-Vi. "Disappointments." *The Phoenix* (1938): unpaginated.

Ye, Weili. "Nü Liuxuesheng: The Story of American Educated Chinese Women 1880–1920s." *Modern China* 20, no. 3 (July 1994): 315–346.

Ye, Weili. *Seeking Modernity in China's Name: Chinese Students in the United States, 1900–1927*. Stanford: Stanford University Press, 2002.

Yeh, Wen-hsin. *The Alienated Academy: Culture and Politics in Republican China, 1919–1937*. Cambridge, MA: Harvard University Press, 1990, 84.

Yen, Hsiao-pei. "Body Politics, Modernity and National Salvation: The Modern Girl and the New Life Movement." *Asian Studies Review* 29, no. 2 (June 2005): 165–186.

Yen Wei Tsing. "Chinese Women." *The McTyeirean* (1919): 45–46.

Ying, Hu. "Naming the First New Woman." *Nan Nu: Men, Women, and Gender in Early and Imperial China* 3, no. 2 (January 2001): 196–231.

Yip, Ka-Che. Religion, Nationalism, and Chinese Students: The Anti-Christian Movement of 1922–1927. Bellingham: Western Washington University, 1980.

Yokshiaki, Yoshimi. *Comfort Women: Sexual Slavery in the Japanese Military during World War Two.* London: Routledge, 2000.

"Yongjiang nüzhong shuqing xuban" 甬江女中書請續辦 [Yongjiang Female Middle School requests to be allowed to continue to operate]. *Shishi gongbao* 時事公報, August 24, 1927.

"Zai xiao xuesheng jiazhang zhiye tongji" 在校學生家長職業統計 [Statistics on the occupations of students' parents]. In *Hongdao ershi zhou jinian kan* 弘道二十週紀念刊 [Twentieth Anniversary Publication, Union Girls' School, Hangzhou], 505 (1932).

"Zai xiao xuesheng jiguan bijiao biao" 在校學生籍貫比較表 [A comparison of students' native places]. In *Shanghai xianli Wuben nüzi zhong xuexiao ershiwu zhou jinian ce* 上海縣立務本女子中學校二十五周紀念冊 [Shanghai Wuben girls' public middle school Twenty-fifth Anniversary Publication], ed. Wuben nüzi zhong xuexiao chuban bu 務本女子中學校出版部, front matter. Shanghai: Shanghai zheyitang yinshuasuo, 1926.

Zarrow, Peter. *Educating China: Knowledge, Society and Textbooks in a Modernizing World, 1902–1937.* Cambridge: Cambridge University Press, 2015.

Zarrow, Peter. "He Zhen and Anarcho-Feminism in China." *Journal of Asian Studies* 47, no. 4 (November 1988): 796–813.

Zeng Baosun. *Confucian Feminist: Memoirs of Zeng Baosun, 1893–1978,* trans. Thomas L. Kennedy. Philadelphia: American Philosophical Society, 2002.

Zeng Baosun. *Zeng Baosun huiyilu.* Hong Kong: Christian Literature Council, 1970.

Zhang Aihua. "Chinese Women's New Practicality, Social Service, and Broad Cooperation: A Case Study of YWCA Women in the 1920s and 1930s." In *Christianity and the Modern Woman in East Asia,* ed. Garrett L. Washington, 38–61. Leiden: Brill, 2018.

Zhang Chuanshen 張傳申. "Jidu zhenli he zai" 基督真理何在 [Where is the truth of Jesus Christ?]. *Shishi gongbao* 時事公報, August 8, 1925.

Zhang Hanchu 張菡初. "Suzhou pingmin jiaoyu" 蘇州平民教育 [Mass education in Suzhou]. *Jinghai xing* 景海星 [Laura Haygood Star] (1924): 3–5.

Zhang Long 张珑 (ed.). *Huiyi Zhongxi nüzhong* 回忆中西女中 [Remembering McTyeire, 1900–1948]. Shanghai: Tongji daxue chubanshe, 2016.

Zhao Fengfeng. "In Memory of the American Woman Writer, Anna Louise Strong." *Women of China* 2 (1980): 36–38.

"Zhongxi nüxiao biaoyan kongque dan quwen" 中西女校表演孔雀膽趣聞 [Interesting news about McTyeire School's performance of the play "Peacock's Gallbladder"] *Haijing* 海晶 no. 20 (1946): 7.

Zhou Yuyin 周裕蔭. "Shenghuo zai Yongjiang" 生活在甬江 [Life at Yongjang]. *Yinxian sili Yongjiang nüzi zhongxue nianwu zhounian jinian kan* 鄞縣私立甬江女子中學廿五週年紀念刊 [Yongjiang private middle school for girls in Yin county twenty-fifth anniversary magazine] (1948): 15–16.

Zia Ung-sing. "Why I Like Day School." *The Phoenix* (1938): unpaginated.

Zung Seu Ling. "The Science of Homemaking." *The McTyeirean* (1918): 45–46.

Zurndorfer, Harriet. "War and the Silent Women: The Retrieval of Chinese and European Jewish Women's Narratives of World War II." *Research on Women in Chinese History* 17 (December, 2009): 107–115.

Zurndorfer, Harriet. "Wartime Refuge Relief in Chinese Cities and Women's Political Activism." In *New Narratives of Urban Space in Republican Chinese Cities*, ed. B. So and M. Zelin, 65–91. Leiden: Brill, 2013.

World Wide Web Sources

"Image Spokesman in Promotion Video of Shanghai No. 3 Girls' Middle School." Filmed June 2016. Accessed September 18, 2022. https://www.youtube.com/watch?v=ZQtBhr6bhyE.

"Pomelo." Accessed September 18, 2022. https://fruitpressed.com/

"Spring Bud Girls' Education." (Accessed November 6, 2016). https://www.1990institute.com/spring-bud

Xinhua News Agency. "'Spring Bud' Program Helps 1.15 Million Girl Dropouts." Last modified June 1, 2002. Accessed November 6, 2016. https://www.wikigender.org/wiki/spring-bud-project/.

Zui mei hechangtuan xiangmu zu 最美合唱团项目组 [Most Beautiful Choir Programme Group]. "Zui mei hechangtuan wanwan mei xiang dao! Zhe xie zhiming nüxing dou lai zi zheli." 最美合唱团|万万没想到!这些知名女性都来自这里 [Most Beautiful Choir did not expect that all these famous women were coming!] Last modified February 12, 2019, 10:45:50. Accessed July 21, 2020. http://www.kankanews.com/a/2019-02-01/0038742347.shtml.

THE OXFORD ORAL HISTORY SERIES

Erin Jessee (University of Glasgow)
Nicholas Ng-A-Fook (University of Ottawa)
Annie Valk (CUNY Graduate Center)
Series Editors

Donald A. Ritchie (Historian Emeritus, US Senate)
Senior Advisor

Rethinking Oral History and Tradition: An Indigenous Perspective   *Nepia Mahuika*
Sisterhood and After: An Oral History of the UK Women's Liberation Movement, 1968–present   *Margaretta Jolly*
Narrating South Asian Partition: Oral History, Literature, Cinema   *Anindya Raychaudhuri*
Voices of Guinness: An Oral History of the Park Royal Brewery   *Tim Strangleman*
Fly Until You Die: An Oral History of Hmong Pilots in the Vietnam War   *Chia Youyee Vang*
Edward M. Kennedy: An Oral History   *Barbara A. Perry*
The Land Speaks: New Voices at the Intersection of Oral and Environmental History   *Edited by Debbie Lee and Kathryn Newfont*
The Voice of the Past: Oral History, Fourth Edition   *Paul Thompson with Joanna Bornat*
When Sonia Met Boris: An Oral History of Jewish Life under Stalin   *Anna Shternshis*
Inside the Clinton White House: An Oral History   *Russell L. Riley*
Escape to Miami: An Oral History of the Cuban Rafter Crisis   *Elizabeth Campisi*
Velvet Revolutions: An Oral History of Czech Society   *Miroslav Vaněk and Pavel Mücke*
Pioneers and Partisans: An Oral History of Nazi Genocide in Belorussia   *Anika Walke*
Doing Oral History, Third Edition   *Donald A. Ritchie*
A Guide to Oral History and the Law, Second Edition   *John A. Neuenschwander*
Chinese Comfort Women: Testimonies from Imperial Japan's Sex Slaves   *Peipei Qiu, with Su Zhiliang and Chen Lifei*
Listening on the Edge: Oral History in the Aftermath of Crisis   *Edited by Mark Cave and Stephen M. Sloan*
Dedicated to God: An Oral History of Cloistered Nuns   *Abbie Reese*
Lady Bird Johnson: An Oral History   *Michael L. Gillette*
Bodies of Evidence: The Practice of Queer Oral History   *Edited by Nan Alamilla Boyd and Horacio N. Roque Ramírez*
Soviet Baby Boomers: An Oral History of Russia's Cold War Generation   *Donald J. Raleigh*
Freedom Flyers: The Tuskegee Airmen of World War II   *J. Todd Moye*
Habits of Change: An Oral History of American Nuns   *Carole Garibaldi Rogers*

They Say in Harlan County: An Oral History *Alessandro Portelli*
The Wonder of Their Voices: The 1946 Holocaust Interviews of David Boder *Alan Rosen*
Launching the War on Poverty: An Oral History, Second Edition *Michael L. Gillette*
The Firm: The Inside Story of the Stasi *Gary Bruce*
Singing Out: An Oral History of America's Folk Music Revivals *David K. Dunaway and Molly Beer*
Approaching an Auschwitz Survivor: Holocaust Testimony and Its Transformations *Edited by Jürgen Matthäus*
The Oxford Handbook of Oral History *Edited by Donald A. Ritchie*

Index

For the benefit of digital users, indexed terms that span two pages (e.g., 52–53) may, on occasion, appear on only one of those pages.

Tables and figures are indicated by *t* and *f* following the page number

Aldersey, Mary Ann, 20–21, 25–26
Allen, Young John, 37
American military presence in China, 153, 156–57
anti-Christian sentiment, 13, 52–54, 68–69, 75–79, 81–82, 181
anti-foreign sentiment, 13, 26, 52–53, 68–69, 70–71, 72, 75, 78–79, 80–82
Ashcroft, Deaconess, 92, 175–76
Association for Protesting against American Atrocities, 153
Aurora Women's College, 11

ballroom dancing, 41–42, 103
baptism and conversion of students, 44–45
Barnes, Louise, 28–29, 235n.44
Beijing Women's Normal University, 33
Black Saturday bombing (1937), 132
"Blue Jacket" secret police, 46–47
Boxer Indemnity scholarships, 33
Boxer Rebellion (1901), 26–27, 28

Cai Sujuan (Tsai, Christiana), 5–6
Campaign to Resist America and Aid Korea, 178–79
Cao Aifang (Fang, T'sao Ai), 67–68
Cao, Ellen, 3–4, 147–51, 159, 174
Cao Shengjie, 171–72, 188–89, 193, 198–99
Cao Rulin, 56
catchment, 36–37
CCP. *See* Chinese Communist Party
Chen Aizhen, 77, 78–80
Chen Guanyu (Chen Kuan Yu), 40, 97, 116, 145, 146, 177–78

Cheng Xiuling (Zung, Cecilia S. L), 93, 100, 116
Chen Hengzhe, 8–9
Chen Jinming (Koo, Rosalyn), 1–3, 17, 18–19, 97–98, 100, 102–3, 109–10, 115, 130–31, 134, 158–59, 163–64, 193–94, 195, 196, 200
Chen Lifu, 121
Chen Tianmi, 160, 161–62, 163, 176
Chen Xingying, 97
Chen Yongshen, 6
Chen Zongci (Chen, Theresa), 43, 107–9, 133, 191–92
Chiang Kai-shek, 46–47, 75, 76–77, 87–88
China Dream, 206–7
Chinese Christian Women's Temperance Union (CWTU), 78, 88
Chinese Communist Party (CCP)
  appeal of, 154, 163–64
  Communist Youth League, 165–66
  GMD purge of, 75
  growth in support for, 157–58
  negotiating Christian identities and, 154, 155–56, 159–60
  recruitment and infiltration efforts of, 147–48, 154, 155–56, 159–60
  underground members of, 161–63, 169–70
  use of student patriotism during war by, 148
  YWCA infiltrated by, 147–48, 159
Chinese School for Girls, 27–28
Chinese womanhood, modern, 84, 91–98, 196–97

Christianity. *See also* Young Women's Christian Association (YWCA)
  backlash to, 13, 52–54, 68–69, 75–77, 78–79, 81–82, 181
  gendered notion of citizenship and, 6–8
  harnessing for purposes of Nationalism of, 54–62
  independent conception of, 10
  negotiating and defending Christian identities, 68–75
  Sinicization of, 6–7
  war years and, 143–47
  Christian values, 43–45, 191
Chun, Anita Li, 101–2
citizenship, gendered notion of, 6–8, 50–51, 53, 87–88
civics education, 42
Cixi, Empress Dowager, 26–27
co-educational changes, 11–12, 30
comfort women, 136, 157
Coombs, Doris, 124, 166–68, 172, 173–75, 176–77, 181
Craig, Jean, 166–67, 187–88, 196
Cultural Revolution, 14–15, 17–18, 42, 93, 96, 187, 189–90, 191–93, 198–200, 202, 203–4, 207–8
curriculum and academic standards, 127–30, 166–67

Dai Lizhen (Dai, Mary Jean), 36–37
Datong Middle School, 30
Deng Xiaoping, 186–87
Deng Yuzhi (Deng, Cora), 147–48, 159–60, 171–72, 174
Ding Maoying (Ting Mei-Ying), 91, 98–100
Ding Yuming, 98–99
Dong Rujing, 161
Dong Yue, 165
Dou Miaogen (Deu Miao Kung), 83–84
Dou Xueqian, 116
drama and theater, 101–13
dress and fashion, 93–96

East China Association of Christian Schools, 121–22
educational reforms, 26–28, 30.
  See also May Fourth Period

elite status, 1–6, 7–9, 12–13, 16–18, 21, 23–24, 28–29, 36, 37, 48–49, 50–51
English language instruction, 127–30

family, rhetoric of, 66, 67–68, 101, 180–81, 186
Fan Aisi, 77–78
Fan Boli (Fan, Margaret), 52, 77–79
fashion and dress, 93–96
fees, 36–37
femininity, 111*f*, 120, 180–81, 197
Fitch, Robert, 20
friendships, 194–97

Gan Mengxiong, 71
Gauss, Esther, 21–22, 76, 86–87, 123*f*, 124, 168, 174
gender. *See also* New Woman
  elite conceptions of, 200–3
  identity experiments with, 117–18
  inverting binaries of, 101–13
GI girls, 153, 156–57
Ginling College, 30, 33, 66, 101, 141, 143
GMD. *See* Guomindang (GMD)
Gong Zhengguan, 48*f*, 49*f*, 50
good wife and worthy mother ideal, 27–28
Green Year (magazine), 55–56
Guanghua University, 71–72
Guomindang (GMD)
  anger toward, 155–58
  disillusionment with, 155–58
  government school use of patriotism and, 46–47
  inflation challenges of, 157–58
  lack of control over content of missionary schools of, 42
  monitoring of student-led activities by, 46–48
  purge of communists by, 75, 76
  registration requirement of schools with, 6, 33–35
  resistance to Japanese by, 120
  scorched-earth tactics of, 139–40
  student clubs and organizations recruitment by, 46–47
  Taiwan retreat of, 1–3, 165
  university students killed by, 162
  wartime tactics of, 130–31, 139–40

Guo Qingguang, 56–57, 57f
Gu Xiuzhen, 77–78

Hangzhou Union Girls' School
  catchment of, 37
  establishment of, 11
  May Thirtieth protests at, 74
  outcomes of students from, 31–32
  overview of, 11
  registration with GMD of, 34
  relocation of, 121–22
  student unrest at, 72–73, 74
  tuition cost of, 36
Harris, Ruth, 143–44, 165, 166–67, 169, 172, 174, 181
Hattori Shigeko, 27
Haygood, Laura, 28–29
He Zhen, 85
Home Economics, 38, 39, 67, 85–87, 93, 103, 158
homemaking, 5, 7, 65, 67, 81, 84, 85–88, 90–91, 196–97
Hong Deying, 3–4, 134
Hong Lüming (Hong, Lucy), 3–4, 30, 128–29, 134, 147–48, 192–93, 198–99
Howe, Gertrude, 91
Huanan College, 33
Huang Yuehua (Wong Yoeh Wo), 65–66
Hu Binxia, 13–14
Hui Xing, 28
Hundred Days' Reform, 26–27

identities of schools, 46–50
indigenization of the church, 34, 80–81

Japan. *See also* Second Sino-Japanese War
  language instruction in Japanese, 127–30
  Meiji period in, 27
  occupation of China by, 119–20, 121–22, 130, 146, 156–57
  soldiers from Japan, 120, 135–37, 153
Jiang Menglin, 76
Jiang Ruying (Tsiang Ku Ying), 60–61
Jiangsu Normal College, 183–84
Jin Mingqi (Kyung Ming-Ge), 59–60
Jin Runxiang, 230n.56

Kang Cheng (Ida, Khan), 5–7, 91
Kawahara Misiko, 27
Ke Hailun, 89–90
Kirk, Harris E., 73
Koo, Rosalyn (Chen Jinming), 1–3, 17, 18–19, 97–98, 100, 102–3, 109–10, 115, 130–31, 134, 158–59, 163–64, 193–94, 195, 196, 200
Korean War, 174–84, 182f

Laboratory, missionary school as, 117–18
Laura Haygood Normal School, 11, 28–29, 36–37, 63, 183–84, 196
Laura Haygood Star, The (magazine), 41
Laurence, Matilda, 24, 25
Lea, Jean Koo, 100
leadership skill development, 101–13
Liang Qichao, 26–27, 29
liberation, 165–71
life in wartime Shanghai, 130–33
Li Kui (Jie, Gwendolin), 41–42
Ling Guofang (Ling Kuo-fen), 146–47
Linglong (magazine), 95f, 200–1
Ling Yourong, 39
Lin Mixuan, 89–90
Lin Shiguang, 71
Lin Wentian, 69–70
Li Rongmei, 63
Liu Zechi, 190–91
Lu Anwen (Loh Oen-vung), 142–43
Lu Jianfang (Loo Kyan-Faung), 142
Lu Lihua, 6
Luo Mingfeng, 162
Lu Xun, 115

MacNeil, Eleanor, 55–56
Mae Yih, 29, 102
magazines and yearbooks, 13–15, 15f, 50, 83–84, 85–87
manners, 9, 18–19, 29, 87, 91–98, 117, 189–90
Mao's China, 1–3, 4–5, 16–17, 22, 197–200
Marco Polo Bridge incident (1937), 121
marriage, 25–26, 98–101
Mary Vaughan High School, 28–29, 30–31
Mass Education Movement, 62–63
matchmaking role, 25–26, 107–9
Ma Xuezhen (Mo Sih Tsung), 68

May Fourth Period
  anti-foreign hostility during, 68–69
  education as prerequisite for suffrage and, 58–59
  envisioning a gendered Christian republic and, 54–62, 65, 68–69, 81–82
  harnessing Christianity to Nationalism in, 54–62
  marriage during, 99–100
  New Woman and, 99–100
  reaction to reforms of, 58
  role of missionary education in, 59–61
  Treaty of Versailles and, 56
  as turning point in women's public political participation, 56–57
May Thirtieth Incident (1925), 68–75
McTyeire
  big-sister/little-sister pairings at, 49–50
  catchment of, 37
  centennial anniversary of, 1, 2f
  Chinese teachers of English hired at, 127–28
  communist victory celebrated at, 165
  Communist Youth League at, 165–66
  curriculum at, 166–67
  damage suffered in war by, 155
  disruption following liberation at, 167
  distinctive features of alumnae of, 18–19
  domestic education at, 87
  English instruction at, 38–40, 181–82
  founding of, 1, 11, 28–29, 37
  Japanese instruction at, 128–30
  Korean War and, 178–81, 182f
  Lambuth-Clopton Hall at, 2f
  left-wing literature at, 161–62
  manners taught by, 92, 94–96
  merger with St. Mary's of, 183–84, 186
  modern girl image critiqued at, 97
  New Woman and, 83–84
  overview of, 1–3, 11
  patriotic resistance at, 128–29
  photographs of, 2f, 48f, 49f, 182f
  piano playing at, 41–42, 41f
  as refuge, 194
  relocation during war years of, 125, 146
  restoration of, 3, 155, 186–87
  same-sex relationships at, 107–9
  school identity of, 47f, 49f
  senior play at, 104
  social service at, 64
  spiritual revival at, 172–73
  student societies at, 46
  successful alumnae of, 29
  tensions between students at, 176
  tuition fees of, 36–37
  underground CCP members at, 161–63
  yearbooks and magazines of, 13–14, 83–84
  YWCA and, 195
McTyeirean, The (magazine), 13–15, 41, 65–66, 112f
McTyeire New Democracy Youth, 162
McTyeire Student Union New Democracy Association, 165
Mencius, 63–64
Millican, Frank, 76
missionary schools. See also Hangzhou Union Girls' School; Laura Haygood Normal School; McTyeire; Riverside Academy; St. Mary's Hall
  backlash to, 1–3, 13
  catchment of, 36–37
  curriculum at, 127–30, 166–67
  disbanding of, 22–23, 121, 155, 183–84
  distinctive features of, 7, 11–12
  establishment of, 11, 20–51
  fees of, 36–37
  foreign perception of, 6
  as lab, 117–18
  merger of, 11–12, 20, 183–84, 186
  networks and, 8–10, 194–97
  oral and archival sources for, 13–19
  as refuge, 98–101
  registration with GMD of, 6, 11–12
  shift in composition and governance of, 6–7
  Sinicization of Christianity and, 6–7
  successful alumnae of, 3–4
  yearbooks and magazines of, 13–15
modern Chinese womanhood, 84, 91–98, 196–97. See also New Woman
modern girl image, 84, 94–97
modernity, 7–10, 12–13, 64–65, 88
motherhood, 114–16
  of citizens approach, 27–28
Movement to Restore Educational Rights, 52–53, 70

Nanjing Massacre (1937), 136
Nanjing University, 30, 148
Nationalist Party. *See* Guomindang (GMD)
National Products Movement, 96–97
networks, 8–10, 194–97
"Never forget the National Humiliation," 155–65, 156*f*
New Culture Movement, 55–56
New Democracy period, 162, 165, 171
New Life Movement
  aims of, 7, 87–88
  building a healthy body and, 87–91
  domestic science in, 196–97
  as example of Christian-influenced form of modernity, 88
New Woman
  building a healthy body and, 87–91
  conducting gendered experiments and, 117–18
  contradictions within, 98
  Cultural Revolution and, 96
  domestic education and, 85–87
  fashion and, 93–96
  inverting gender binaries and, 101–13
  leadership skill development and, 101–13
  making Christian homes for China and, 85–87
  manners and, 91–98
  marriage and, 98–101
  May Fourth Period and, 99–100
  modern girl image contrasted with, 84, 94–97
  New Life Movement and, 87–91
  playing men's roles and, 101–13
  purpose of education and, 84, 85
  same-sex relationships and, 107–13
  school as lab and, 117–18
  school as refuge and, 98–101
Nie Guangming (Kwang Ming Nieh, Renee), 13–14
North China Union Women's College, 33
Northern Expedition, 52–53, 75–82
nostalgia, 203–9
Number Three Girls' School, 1, 3, 186, 202–3

Ouyang Xue (Eur Yang-Sih), 58

Pan Guangdan, 107–9
Pan Lu, 250n.64
Party, The. *See* Chinese Communist Party (CCP)
Patriotic Girls' School, 27–28
patriotism, 46–47, 58–61, 68–69, 74, 77–79, 148, 155–56
Pearl Harbor bombing (1941), 121–22, 125, 127–28, 136–37
Peking University, 33, 56–57, 152, 154
People's Liberation Army (PLA), 165
People's Republic of China (PRC), 11–12, 16–17, 22–23, 155, 165–66, 189, 197
Phoenix (magazine), 14–15, 111*f*, 119, 125–27, 132, 142–43, 146
piano playing, 40–42, 97, 127
political education meetings, 168
post-war period, 155–65
Pott, Francis Lister Hawks, 71–72
principals, 34–35, 77, 169, 194–95
Provincial Educational Associations, 30

Qu Mingming, 159, 161, 162, 165–66

reforms, educational, 26–28, 30. *See also* May Fourth Period
refugees, 121, 124–25, 130–31, 139–41, 142, 146–47, 157–58
registration requirement for missionary schools, 6, 33–35
relief activities during war years, 141–47
religious education, 38, 42–45, 192, 200
relocation of missionary schools, 121–27, 130–31
Richardson, Helen, 98–99
Riverside Academy
  bombing of, 22–23, 122
  curriculum at, 166–67
  domestic education facilities at, 86–87
  establishment of, 11, 20
  financial problems of, 35
  liberation at, 167–68
  New Life Movement at, 88–90
  Northern Expedition and, 76, 77–78
  occupation of, 76–77
  overview of, 11, 20–21

Riverside Academy (*cont.*)
  photographs of, 90*f*
  political education meetings at, 168
  registration with Guomindang government and, 34
  re-laying ceremony at, 20–23, 23*f*
  relocation of, 122–24
  social service at, 63–64
  student societies at, 89–90
  tensions between students at, 176–77
  volleyball team at, 90*f*
Rural Reconstruction Movement, 62–63

same-sex relationships, 107–13, 117, 200–1
school identities, 46–50
schools, missionary. *See* Hangzhou Union Girls' School; Laura Haygood Normal School; McTyeire; missionary schools; Riverside Academy; St. Mary's Hall
Schoppa, Kennith, 123–24
Second Sino-Japanese War
  academics and, 127–30
  Black Saturday bombing during, 132
  CCP recruitment during, 147–48
  children's writing during, 145
  Christianity and, 143–47
  commuting to school during, 134–47
  danger during years of, 134–47
  English and Japanese instruction during, 127–30
  lack of source materials on, 120
  life in wartime Shanghai during, 130–33
  lonely island of neutrality and, 124–25
  political awakenings during, 147–50
  pupils criticizing others for not doing enough during, 146–47
  rationing during, 131–32
  refugees during, 139–41
  relocation of missionary schools during, 121–27
  sexual threat posed by soldiers during, 135–36
  Shanghai invaded during, 125
  trauma of relocation during, 130–31
  victim trope during, 120
  warrior trope during, 120
  wartime relief activities and, 141–47
  "women soldiers" and, 141–42
Second World War. *See* Second Sino-Japanese War
secularization, 16–17, 24, 34–35, 43, 50–51
self-Orientalizing, 65
Shanghai, life during war years in, 125, 130–33
Shanghai Missionary conference of 1877, 24–25
Shanghai Municipal Council, 8–9, 11, 92
Shen Chong, 152–54, 156–57, 163
Shen Shuqin (Sung Sing-Ling), 137–38
Shen Yixiang (Esther Sing), 35, 76–77, 88–89, 122, 174–75, 187, 196
Shen Zaichen, 21
Shi Meiyu (Mary Stone), 6–7, 91
Shimoda Utako, 27
Shishi Gongbao (newspaper), 69, 70
Shu Lian (Lian Shu Tsao), 44–45
Siao, B. S., 74
Sing, Esther (Shen Yixiang). *See* Shen Yixiang (Esther Sing)
social gospel, 52, 62–63, 65, 77–78, 147–48, 154
social service, 62–68
Song Meiling, 9–10, 76–77, 88, 97–98, 141, 188
spiritual revival, 171–74
St. John's University, 15–16, 37, 71–72, 125
St. Mary's Hall
  American military presence and, 156–57
  big-sister/little-sister pairing at, 49–50
  catchment of, 37
  Chinese teachers of English hired at, 127–28
  choir at, 126*f*
  closure during war years of, 125
  communist victory celebrated at, 165
  dance training at, 41–42
  alumnae of, 18–19
  English instruction at, 38
  founding of, 11
  Korean War and, 178–79
  manners taught by, 92–93
  May Fourth Period and, 56–60, 57*f*
  merger with McTyeire of, 183–84, 186

moral training at, 191
nurse training program at, 142
overview of, 11
photographs of, 57f, 126f, 138f, 206f
redevelopment of, 205–6
registration with Guomindang government and, 34
relocation of, 125, 135, 138f
same-sex relationships at, 107–9
scholarships offered by, 36
student societies at, 46
tuition fees of, 36
underground CCP members at, 169–70
yearbooks and magazines of, 13–14, 15f, 83–84
student fees, 36–37
student societies, 23–24, 46–50
suffrage, 55, 58–59
Sun Yat-sen, 42, 78–79

Taiping Rebellion, 28–29
Tang Qunying, 58–59
Tan Ying, 183–84
Tao Shuyu, 171
Tao Xiafang, 166
Tao Xinde, 171
theater and drama, 101–13
Three People's Principles, 42, 78–79
tomboys, 3–4, 102–4, 111f, 194
Treaty of Versailles, 55–56
Tsai, Ruth Lea, 39–40
Tsai Li, Julia, 136–37
Tu Fengyun, 63–64, 96–97
Twenty-One Demands (1915), 55

university preparation, 32–33

Wang, Rosita Li, 101–2
Wang Shaolan, 157–58, 162
Ward, Ralph Ansel, 181
war years. See Second Sino-Japanese War
Webster, Florence, 34–35, 72–75
White Terror, 76
Williams, John, 75
Wolfe, Annie, 30–31
womanhood, modern Chinese, 84, 91–98, 196–97. See also New Woman
Women's Advisory Council (WAC), 141

Women's Association for National Salvation, 141–42
"women soldiers," 141–42
"women's work," 25, 67
World Student Christian Federation, 52–53
World War II. See Second Sino-Japanese War
Wu, George, 206–8
Wuben Girls' School, 28, 46–47
Wu Huaijiu, 28
Wu Qihui, 92, 190–91
Wu Xiurong, 158–59
Wu Yifang, 9–10
Wu Yiyun, 178–79

Xiang Jingyu, 6
Xie Bingying, 78, 141
Xing Fengbao (Tsu Foh-Pau), 131
Xinzheng reform period (1901–1911), 26–27
Xue Yin (Hsueh Nying), 145
Xue Zheng, 1, 104, 106–7, 127, 155, 174–75, 176, 177–78, 187, 194–95
Xu Meizhen, 41–42, 104–7, 107f, 108f, 127, 129
Xu Ren, 206–7

Yang Buwei, 5–6, 9–10
Yang Yinsui, 77, 78–79
Yang Zhiling, 92, 93, 130–31, 135, 189–90, 191–92
Yan Shunzhen, 116
Yan Wanqing (Yen Wei Tsing), 58–59
Yan Yangchu (Yen, James), 62–63
Yao Meidi (Yau Ding-Vi Yao), 125–27
yearbooks and magazines, 13–15, 15f, 50, 83–84
Ying Manrong, 135–36, 152–54, 156–57, 189
Young Women's Christian Association (YWCA)
  CCP recruitment in, 147–48, 159
  network provided by, 10, 195
  New Life Movement and, 88
  social service at, 63–64
  student counseling during war years at, 143
  student handbook of, 63–64
  wartime recruitment efforts of, 143–44, 147–48

Yuan Weitong, 159–60
Yu Chia-Chu, 230n.60
Yu Huigeng, 169–71, 188
YWCA. *See* Young Women's Christian Association (YWCA)

Zeng Baosun, 5–6, 10, 28–29, 98, 235n.44
Zeng Guofan, 28–29, 235n.44
Zhang Aizhen (Chang E. Tsung), 67
Zhang Baixi, 64–65, 85
Zhang Chuanshen, 69
Zhang Dewei (Tsong Tuh Wei), 67, 113–14
Zhang Hanchu, 63
Zhang Jiying (Tsang Kyi-ying), 56–57
Zhang Lingfan (Ling Van Chang Tang), 114–15
Zhang Long, 29, 42–43, 94–96
Zhang Luoluo, 18–19, 44, 45, 102, 105f, 186
Zhang Ruiyun, 70–71
Zhang Xiaoru, 159–60
Zhang Xiuai (Tsang Sieu-ai), 119
Zhang Yuanji, 29
Zhang Zhaohan, 58–59
Zhang Zhidong, 85
Zhao Fengfeng, 39, 190
Zhao Minshu (Tsao Ming Zok), 61
Zhao Shen, 39
Zheng Peide, 161
Zhou Huijuan (Tseu We-kyoen), 140
Zhou Meiyun (Tseu Mei Yuin), 99–100
Zhu Chunjing (Tsu Tsung Kyung), 59, 62
Zhu Lizhong, 134–35, 155–56, 156f, 158
Zhu Wenqian (Zhu, Lydia), 38–39
Zhu Yixuan (Chu I Shiu), 54
Zhu Yonglin, 39
Zhu Zengling (Tsu Tsung Ling), 65–66
Zimmerman, Dora, 77–78